# MURDERED AT AGE 2:

Mother convicted of "should have known"

by Jody Ortiz

MURDERED AT AGE 2

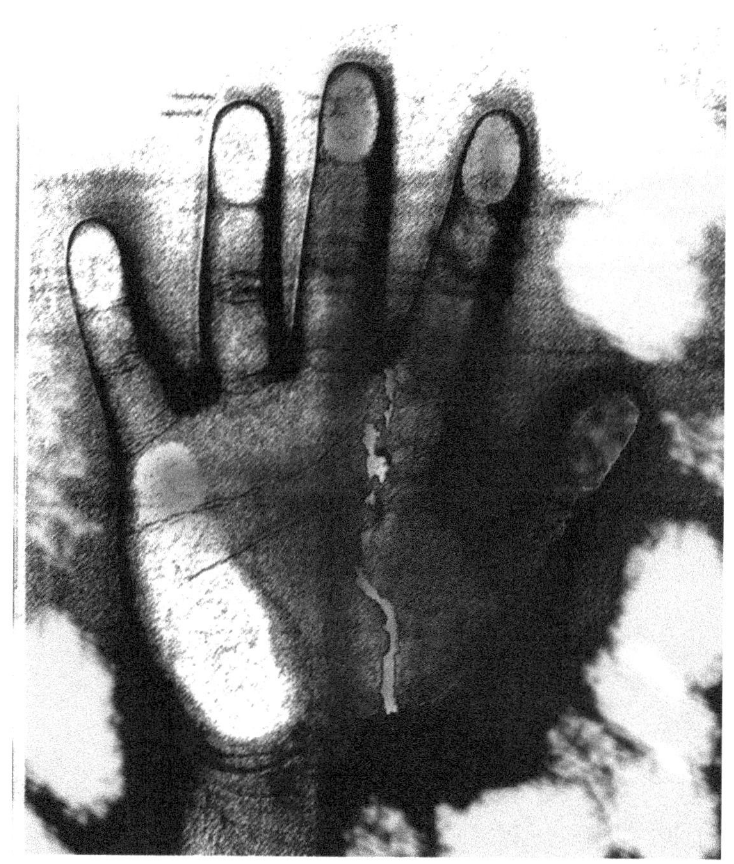

# MURDERED AT AGE 2



Grateful acknowledgement is made to the following for permission to reprint previously published material:

Regnery Publishing Inc., Washington, D.C. *The Murder Business* by Mark Fuhrman. Copyright©2009. ISBN 978-1-59698-584-1

Craig Key, *A Deadly Game of Tug of War: The Kelsey Smith Briggs Story* published by Morgan James Publishing, LLC. ISBN 978-1-60037-312-1

*US Observer* article: *"***Kelsey Smith-Briggs - Murder & Exploitation:** Prosecutor Smothermon pushes false charges?" www.usobserverok.com

ISBN is 978-1-962490-03-0

Cover/Interior Design by:
Morbid Panther Designs

Edited by:
Julie Jones
and Julie Rea Harper

# Table of Contents

**Dedication** VIII

**Prologue** XIII

**Special Note** XIV

**Introduction** XVI

**1 Already in too Deep** 1

**2 The Dark Side of the Web** 5

**3 The Judge** 9

**4 Kelsey's Mom** 16

**5 Downward Spiral** 24

**6 Media Persecution** 28

**7 The Trial** 41

**8 Kelsey, a Person – Not a Purpose** 43

**9 The Briggs Pamphlet** 45

**10 We All Got Sucked In…** 71

**11 A Ray of Light- Someone Speaks the Truth** 85

**12 Day One - Trial Media Coverage** 113

**13 Day Two – Trial Media Coverage** 125

**14 Day Three - Trial Media Coverage** 135

**15 Day Four – Who Knows Who?** 147

16 Day Five - Trial Media Coverage 153

17 Day Six - Trial Media Coverage 157

18 Charged! 161

19 Day Seven - Trial Media Coverage 165

20 It All Comes Down to Money 167

21 Motion for a New Trial 177

22 The Witnesses 233

23 The Jurors 266

24 The Blog 272

25 Seeking the Truth about Kelsey 290

26 A Bright Idea 300

27 The Bullies 312

28 First Signs of Hate 316

29 Justice for Mike Porter? 322

30 The Plot 375

31 Civil Lawsuits 403

32 The "Bash Boards" 411

33 Man in the Hole 427

**34 YouTube and Erin Brockovich** **435**

**35 "Kathie, I forgive you."** **441**

**36 Oklahoma State Bureau of Investigation** **449**

**37 Rally for Hope** **453**

**38 Freedom March** **471**

**39 Putting a "Price Tag on" Kelsey** **475**

**40 The Bully is Revealed** **491**

**41 Stalker Blog and Book** **509**

**42 Raye's Supporters** **513**

Conclusion 539

Appendix A 543

Appendix B 545

# *Dedication*

This book is dedicated to everyone who stood beside me as I dove into the madness of fighting for the truth.

To my daughter, who always had good advice and told me to ignore what others think of me. I love you. You are my miracle child and my world.

To my husband, who didn't want me to get involved, but had my back during the times I thought somebody was going to kill me. I love you. Thank you for putting up with me.

To my parents, who never once doubted my passion for the truth and didn't attempt to talk me out of supporting those who are hated. I love you and thank you for being my parents.

To my grandma, whom I have neglected over the past two years, I love you and I'm sorry for not visiting.

To Judge Craig Key and his family, you are all wonderful people and I am blessed to have known you.

To Gayla and the Smith/Winter family, I love all of you. You took me into your fold and accepted me as I am. You are the epitome of graciousness and love and Kelsey was blessed to have been a part of your family.

To the moderators and the members of the Free Kelsey's Mom forum, thank you for rescuing me. You have all been a blessing in my life.

Special thanks to Charity, Faith, Hope, Prudence, Temperance, Justice, Fortitude, and last but certainly not least, Sherri for encouraging me to tell my story and for your endless support and love. I love you so much! Sherri, I don't know how I would have made it this far without our lunchtime chats. Your shoulders must be made of steel because you were a strong shoulder to Raye and Gayla, and now me. I thank God for you.

A special thanks to all of the contributors to this book; to those who went the extra mile to ensure it became the best it could be, and to Alexis A. Moore, the Founder and President of Survivors in Action. I am excited and thrilled to be a part of your mission of "no victim left behind."

An extra special thanks to my close friends who read through the book and pointed out mistakes and gave me advice, and also thanks to my wonderful editors, Julie J. and Julie H. Your grammar and content editing have made such a difference in my work. I don't know what I would have done without your help! You've been amazing and Julie J., Kelsey was blessed to have you in her life. Thank you!

To Raye, your continued strength and faith that things will someday be made right and that your daughter will at last rest in peace have inspired me. Keep your head up. You know the truth and so do Kelsey and God. That's all that matters.

And finally, Kelsey, your story has touched me more than any other and I'm deeply pained that you suffered for even a minute of your life. You were a pawn in the deadly game, and you're still being used as a pawn to this day. I will continue to pray that your true story is finally told by the person who knows the truth. May you rest in peace, child, and my prayers are that people will finally stop using you and exploiting your memory to serve their own purposes.

Jody Ortiz

# *Prologue*

Jody Ortiz is a cyberstalking victim that has one of the most compelling and tragic stories of cyberstalk that I have had on my desk in the past five years. Cyberstalk victims reach out for help to law enforcement, the courts, crime victim organizations, and to public officials and find that there is no real help! Cyberstalk victims continue to feel isolated and alone while enduring what can only be described as "the living hell of the 21$^{st}$ century."

Ortiz has done nothing more than speak candidly in a free society and has been terrorized for doing so by relentless predators using technology to stalk, hence creating another victim of what is known today as "cyberstalking." What separates her case from others is that her stalkers have acted with a gang mentality with multiple people attacking at once. Due to the number of people involved and the current laws in her state and around the country, Ortiz is left to fend for herself against her attackers. In turn, her life has been a living hell since 2007, prompting her to speak out once again in her own defense and in an effort to silence the attacks.

As evidenced in Ortiz's case, tragically, our world has arrived at the day when a person can no longer speak freely and candidly without fear of a new kind of retaliation - reprisal known as cyberstalking.

It is my hope that *Murdered at age 2* will be the catalyst for crime victim resource reform and improve awareness and understanding so that "no victim is left behind."

By: Alexis A. Moore, Founder and President of Survivors in Action (www.SurvivorsinAction.com), a nationwide non-profit advocacy group that supports victims of crimes including domestic violence, identity theft, elder abuse, cyberstalking, stalking, child abuse, rape, and sexual assault.

## *Special Note*

This is a true story, but some of the names have been changed, in part, to protect those who are referenced as distant supporters and are not central players in the story.

Also, all captured statements and posts are presented in their original format. Any grammatical errors, misspellings, or typos are attributed to the original author and not the book author.

Trigger warning: This is a true story of a two-year-old child who died while home alone with her stepfather. Topics of rape, murder, stalking, harassment, and death threats, etc are discussed.

Jody Ortiz

# *Introduction*

"If God only used perfect people, nothing would ever get done."
~ Rick Warren

The presentation and structure of how media share an event lead us to believe they are telling every known detail and the truth. In reality, some members of the media portray merely what they want the public to believe, and it's rarely a version decided by facts alone. They necessarily report in a way that will best sell their story by only relaying what's on the surface. Few journalists dig deep to ensure what they're communicating is based on solid evidence, and they seldom explain situations that lead up to the event. Fact-based stories are not as exciting or scandalous as the initial, hearsay-version media obtain from witnesses. Scandal, drama, and heroes sell, and media outlets are in business, not public service. What sells is what makes the news. Period.

Unfortunately, this often leads to a public perception that is distorted and one-sided. This is what happened in a certain case in the State of Oklahoma that has unfolded over a five-year span of intense media coverage. Despite multiple gag orders, one side blatantly found a way to express their opinions and sealed documents were leaked to the press, while the other side followed the rules and remained silent.

Oklahomans got an earful of the off-balance story and they were hooked. As time passed without any public argument against the story that had been created, the details surrounding the case became contorted, as a seething hate caused pitchforks to be raised against one person, and then another, and so on. The witch-hunt claimed multiple victims who sat defenseless against the growing mob that hid their true agenda and actions from the general public.

As the campaign stage for a conviction was being played out under Oklahoma media's spotlight, behind the curtain and in secret shadows the tale of true hate was acted out; a hate so strong that it's still claiming victims to this day.

Due to the ongoing hostility, this book was written to convey the "behind the case" documentation of communication and the real emotions that propelled the hate. Though the characters in the drama realized their ultimate goal, thus far the animosity continues five years later with multiple targets, including myself. Hence, I now reveal ways in which the public has been misled to believe the lies that have been dominant in much of the media's and courts' presentations of the story as well as the truth that has not been publicly revealed. Moreover, I offer proof of the malicious intentions that fueled the lies from the start.

In order to understand the story and my involvement, one must first understand the case. Therefore, following is a brief case summary taken from witness accounts, medical reports, legal documents, and a book about the case:[1]

### *AN OVERVIEW*

Kelsey Shelton Smith was born into a broken home on December 28, 2002. Kelsey's mom, Raye Dawn Smith, divorced Kelsey's dad Raymond Lance (Robinson) Briggs, before Kelsey was born. Raymond, who goes by "Lance," was born and raised with the surname of Robinson, but he changed his name to his stepfather's surname—Briggs—just before marrying Raye and without a legal adoption.

Raye had allegedly suffered physical and emotional abuse at the hands of Lance during their two year marriage.

Raye stated about the relationship: "I married Raymond Lance Briggs July of 2000. I lost my first child that month at three months due to a blow to the stomach by the fist of Lance. Other than that time he had hit on me several times leaving black eyes, a bruised rib, my hair pulled out, and a lot of my stuff throughout the house that all meant something to me he would break. He even threw my Pomeranian dog against the wall at one time. He busted my nose at the river in front of all of our friends one summer.[2] I finally got enough of all of that and left. I went to live back with my

---

[1] Important aspects of the case will be expanded upon throughout the book. The book about the case is *A Deadly Game of Tug-of-War: The Kelsey Smith-Briggs Story* by Craig Key.

[2] See Appendix B – Exhibit 12

parents. Lance a few weeks later broke into the house we lived in while we were married and broke a bathroom mirror, threw groceries all over the kitchen, threw stuff in the pond, in the creek, and plus stole some school albums..."

In early 2002, Raye and Lance separated and she began dating another man before the divorce was final. When Raye discovered she was pregnant, she prayed that the baby did not belong to Lance, but a paternity test proved he was the father. The parties went to court and a hyphen was added to Kelsey's last name. She would be known as Kelsey Shelton Smith-Briggs, taking the name of Lance's stepfather along with her maternal family's name. (Kelsey was a suggestion from Raye's grandmother, Mildred, and Shelton was Raye's father's middle name.) Kelsey's new legal name and double birth announcements (one for baby girl Smith and one for baby girl Briggs) would be telling of the battle for Kelsey that would create an explosive atmosphere that would allow an unforeseen tragedy to end her life just months before her third birthday.

Kelsey lived a fairly normal life for the first two years with no allegations of abuse from either family. Things changed when Raye started dating a man named Mike Porter in the fall of 2004 at the same time that Kathie Briggs, Kelsey's paternal grandmother, was awarded grandparent visitation. Bruises were noticed on Kelsey by her daycare worker after she returned from her visits with Kathie. Raye describes seeing bruises on Kelsey's legs that looked like "finger marks" and a bruise on her ear. Raye states that she assumed they were from Kathie or Lance or that Kelsey had a medical problem and bruised easily—a test determined the latter was not the issue. Kathie states that she assumed Raye was to blame. Because of the tension that was a powder keg ready to explode if one side dared to withhold Kelsey during a scheduled time for her to be with the other family, the families did not get along well, nor did they communicate on Kelsey's behalf. The situation grew far worse when a former friend of Kelsey's maternal grandmother told her to "get ready" because Lance and Kathie were going to "seek custody of Kelsey." This warning was later echoed in court when Kathie stated on the stand that Lance's new wife told her that she didn't want to have children of her own, "she'd just keep Kelsey." Statements such as these that were based on hearsay only added to the tension.

In January of 2005 Kelsey broke her clavicle (the most commonly broken bone in children) reportedly after a fall from her crib. At the end of January, bruises and scratches on her bottom that were discovered approximately four hours after Kathie and Lance had Kelsey at their respective homes were termed "abuse" by her paternal family when she was taken to the emergency room. Kelsey was then taken from Raye.

Four months passed with Kelsey in Kathie's care and Raye seeing Kelsey during supervised and then unsupervised visits after Raye fully cooperated with the state's

Department of Human Services (DHS). Reports show that she completed every course and every evaluation she needed to accomplish in order to regain custody of Kelsey.

Hearings were held in Judge Key's courtroom, with one person missing from each and every hearing, Kelsey's father.

Abuse allegations continued to be made against Raye that were unfounded, "screened out," and termed "normal childhood injuries" by child welfare workers. Kathie stated in court that she undressed Kelsey and took pictures of her and that she had three to four witnesses view Kelsey's entire body each time she would arrive at her home and each time she left. Witnesses state that Kelsey began counting her bruises and self-mutilating by biting and scratching herself and picking at her fingernails and toenails—one toenail she had completely picked off on the day that she died.

Judge Craig Key described Kelsey's strange behavior in his book about the case. He stated, *"Although she was in protective custody, it was apparent that Kelsey wasn't adjusting to being in the Briggs home. A red flag was raised for me, as a judge, when DHS told me Kelsey's hair began falling out in clumps while in the care of Kathie Briggs. Kelsey's hair was falling out to the point that she had a bald spot on the back of her head the size of a baseball. She began self-mutilating by biting her arms, and as clearly stated in Kelsey's obituary submitted by the Briggs, she was apparently biting the Briggs family as well. Kelsey's behavior and hair loss during this time were all documented by DHS...Why Kelsey acted differently while in the custody of Kathie Briggs is unclear. Why Kelsey was timid, lethargic, and asleep during almost every DHS visit is also unclear. But what's clear is the tug-of-war was starting to get to the child both mentally and physically."*[3]

In April of 2005, Raye married Mike Porter. Her father had lost his battle with cancer the previous year and with everything Raye was facing in fighting for her daughter, she needed someone to be a knight in shining armor for her. Mike Porter fit the description. He had custody of his eight-year-old daughter and regular visitation with his son who was slightly younger than Kelsey. Mike Porter claimed that he was a college graduate (untrue) and he inherited the family business after both of his parents died. He seemed to be just what Raye and Kelsey needed in their lives.

Just days before the marriage ceremony, Kelsey sprained her ankle while at the zoo with her maternal aunt and she was returned to Kathie's home with a doctor's note. Four days later when Raye picked Kelsey up from Kathie's home, Kelsey refused to walk. Kathie claimed she took a couple of steps and then crawled for the rest of the week. Kathie didn't think anything about it. She had taken Kelsey to the emergency room for a bump on her nose, but

---

[3] Key, Craig. *A Deadly Game of Tug of War: The Kelsey Smith-Briggs Story*. Garden City, NY: Morgan James Publishing, 2007. p. 51-52.

she didn't see a need for a second opinion when Kelsey couldn't walk.

Raye took Kelsey to a doctor when her legs became progressively worse and the doctor stated that the first fracture was consistent with Kelsey's fall at the zoo and that her other leg had been injured more recently and was from overcompensation. Kelsey then went through two sets of casts. Raye and Gayla Smith, Raye's mom, had the casts put on, and Kathie had the first set removed after only six days. After Kelsey's legs were determined to be broken from abuse by a doctor Kathie had found and reportedly told that Raye was abusing Kelsey, Kelsey was removed from Kathie's home and placed with her maternal grandmother, Gayla.[4]

According to records and witnesses, Kelsey lost weight and hair while with Kathie. A bald spot the size of a baseball was discovered. Once removed from Kathie's home, Kelsey reportedly improved.

After DHS viewed Kelsey's interactions with both Kathie and Raye during separate, supervised visits at the DHS office and reported their findings at a hearing in June in Judge Key's courtroom, Kelsey was returned to Raye's custody with three child welfare services assigned by the Judge to

[4] The issue with Kelsey's broken legs is explained in more detail later in the book.

watch over Kelsey and visit her home on an almost daily basis.

A total of five agencies were involved in Kelsey's life at this point, and they were: Court Appointed Special Advocates (CASA), Comprehensive Home Based Services (CHBS), Department of Human Services (DHS - Oklahoma's child protective service), the District Attorney's office, and a Guardian ad litem. None of the services in Kelsey's home ever brought to Raye's attention that there was anything unusual going on in her home. The "experts" didn't suspect abuse, and neither did Raye.

Once Kelsey went home with Raye, Kathie quit visiting Kelsey. It was reported that she did not want to be supervised because she did not like what was said about her in court.

In August of 2005, Kelsey, Raye Dawn, and Mike Porter were in a hit-and-run accident. The man who hit the truck was pulled over a few blocks from the accident and was charged with drunk driving and leaving the scene of an accident. He caused over $14,000 in damage, bending the frame of Mike Porter's truck and shattering the back glass where Kelsey was sitting.[5] Against the rules, Kathie attended a visit with Kelsey and her stepmother shortly after the accident. Kathie took video and pictures of Kelsey's injuries from the accident to later use to gain custody of Kelsey, but they have since been used to show "abuse."

---

[5] See AppendixB – Exhibit 1

Kelsey lost her appetite and started to deteriorate after the accident, so Raye took Kelsey to specialists and signed her up for play therapy in an effort to determine what was happening to her daughter.

On October 11, 2005, Raye and Kelsey were napping together in the master bedroom. Raye only had two pull-ups left and Kelsey was in the process of potty training. She had an accident just before their nap, so Kelsey went to sleep wearing only a long, black t-shirt and no underwear or diaper.

Mike Porter arrived home from work between 2:30 and 2:45 PM. Raye awoke to Mike Porter standing above her and she left Kelsey in her bed sleeping while she drove the forty- to fifty-minute round trip to pick up Mike Porter's eight-year-old daughter from school in a nearby town.

When Raye returned home, Kelsey was in the arms of a first responder, and was being passed to an EMT. Raye screamed and ran to the ambulance. She noticed that Kelsey was wearing a pull-up. Mike Porter later stated that he had put it on her because he didn't want anyone "thinking anything" about her not wearing pants. He told Raye that he found a pull-up on the bar, but Raye states the pull-ups were in a bathroom closet.

On that day, Mike Porter described Kelsey's episode as a seizure, and nobody in the family questioned it since Kelsey had been reportedly having seizures for a while.

Kathie called the sheriff's office on the night of Kelsey's death and stated that it was murder and that her ex-daughter-in-law, Raye, had done it. She had already begun a quest to put Raye in prison for murder. Later, it became clear she was willing to take down anyone who got in the way of her stated mission.

Autopsy results showed that Kelsey had suffered from a possible sexual assault and that her death was from "blunt force trauma to the abdomen," which meant she had been murdered. (A second autopsy confirmed the sexual assault.) Shortly after Kelsey's death Mike Porter was charged with first degree murder. The charge of sexual assault was added in April of 2006 after the second autopsy confirmed "signs of repeated, forcible sexual assault."

Five years later, the focus is still on Raye. Many question why Kathie hates Raye so much that the hate spills over to Raye's family and supporters. Is it because she's jealous of Raye's close family? Was it due to her inability to get Kelsey to love her, when she clearly preferred to be with her own mother, instead, even though Kathie tried so hard to take her away from Raye? Is it because Raye jilted her son and exposed him as a man who beats women? I am one among many who have researched this case and I don't understand why the focus has always been on Raye, the devoted mom who wasn't home at the time of her daughter's alleged rape and murder and not on the man charged with sexual assault and murder.

These are the questions that have come to my mind as well as the minds of others who have attempted to piece together the puzzle that surrounds Kelsey's short life and her tragic death. In asking these questions, I have become the next target in the campaign of hate.

The rational mind simply doesn't comprehend such a situation except to suggest, in this author's opinion, that Kathie Briggs isn't really focused on finding justice for her granddaughter so much as she has an unhealthy but passionate rage toward her ex-daughter-in-law. And the reason for that? Alas, hate is never a rational thing.

# 1 Already in too Deep

"Hate is too great a burden to bear. It injures the hater more than it injures the hated." ~ Coretta Scott King

"I can't find the movie." Mom's voice was a mixture of irritation at me for not assisting in the search and disappointment that the store seemed to have at least one copy of everything except the movie she most wanted to buy.

Mom has always been a movie fanatic. My teenage years were spent watching movies on VHS. One of Mom's favorites was *National Lampoon's Vacation*. I watched it so many times that I could recite lines from the movie in a heartbeat. I also learned every verse of the "Marty Moose" song and I can still sing it without missing a word twenty-five years later. Since my mom's health has gone downhill over the past decade, movies have become her escape. On every holiday or special occasion, I ask her what she wants me to buy for her and she gives me a list of movies. So, on that day, while she was desperately searching for her movie, I was struggling to make sense of the turn of events I never anticipated. . .

"Did you check with the cashier?" I asked half paying attention. I was preoccupied with the vibrations on my leg. My blackberry had been in constant motion since Mom, my daughter, Mia, and I had left the house. As I read the petition signatures from Raye's family members and friends, my hidden smile quickly turned dark and a look of disgust took its place. The signatures took on a new tone, one filled with hate.

"HAHAHAHA!!!! SHE GOT WHAT SHE DESERVED!!!! HOPE SHE ROTTS IN PRISON!!!!!!!!!!!!!!"

"eveything that happens to her,she deserves."

"[She] deserves anything but but to have her ass beat to helll sorry low life bitch"

"OK Hell no I do not support this at all, I can't even believe you have the gaul to have a petition!!!!!"

"go to hell"

"i think she is giong to hell"

"i wish when [she] is in the jail sells someone abuses [her]"

"This site needs to be shut down, she got what she deserved. I hope someone kills her in prison, but slow so she'll suffer."

"May she burn in hell, starting the day before she's due to be released from prison."

The hate-filled messages appeared on my screen, one after another. *This can't be right*, I thought to myself while rolling the track wheel through the text and wondering how they learned of the Web site so soon. I hadn't even finished designing it.

As Mom and Mia continued their search for Mom's movie, I stared at my blackberry in disbelief. The messages poured in as I fought to keep hold of my composure. I didn't want my secret life exposed to my family, not yet, and certainly not in the middle of Vintage Stock.

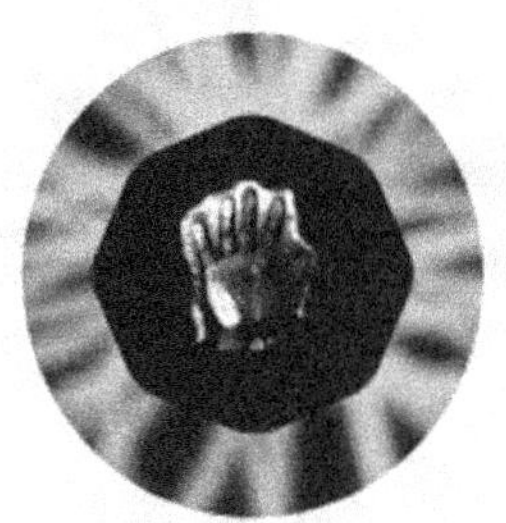

# 2 The Dark Side of the Web

"A single event can awaken a stranger totally unknown to us. To live is to be slowly born." ~ Antoine de Saint-Exupery

In March of 2007, I received a phone call that would forever change my life. A potential client was interested in hiring me to edit his book. The call was different from those I normally received. He was local.

During the four years I had been working as an editor and ghost writer, I worked with hundreds of clients from around the globe, and it kept my job exciting. With each new client came exhilaration and fascination as I heard colorful details in the life stories that most people never get the opportunity to hear, and I learned how to work with people on a professional level, even through language and cultural barriers. However, even though I'd worked with a worldwide clientele, no one knew my name in Oklahoma. The previous year I was surprised when a local reporter searched me out and wanted to interview me about my business. My initial answer to her request was an emphatic "NO!" I liked my privacy. But after discussing the offer with friends and family, I decided it might give my business a boost, so I agreed to do the interview and realized that being on camera wasn't as nerve-wracking as anticipated.

Not long after, a local man contacted me about an editing job. The intriguing caller was Craig Key, a former Judge, who seemed like a well educated but down-to-earth man. He questioned me about my knowledge of the Kelsey Smith-Briggs case, a high-profile story in Oklahoma in which a two-year-old blonde-haired and blue-eyed precious little girl was murdered, and a case that I had noticed only in passing.

At the time of the call, my business was successful and thriving. Besides the ghostwriting, editing, and transcription that were at the heart of my company, there was also the editorial work I did for a New York based publisher who provided me with numerous well-known names and celebrities. Among my clients were best-selling authors, famous entrepreneurs, and a country music artist who had been nominated for County Music Artist of the Year. In short, I was on a first-name basis with important people.

Since my life was consumed by my business, which has always been a labor of love, I had no time to watch television. Consequently, the case that was on the minds and lips of most Oklahomans had escaped my attention. This left me clueless about the identity of the man who was interested in my editing services, and a perfect candidate for the job.

After hanging up the phone with the Judge, curiosity took over and I Googled his name. It was during this search that I first encountered the all-consuming hate that surrounds Kelsey's case. I had never experienced anything like it in my life. Within just a few minutes, I saw where this man, this former Judge, was ridiculed, scorned, and called harsh things such as a "baby killer" due to his decision to return Kelsey to her home months before she was allegedly sexually assaulted and murdered. His decision was based on evidence and arguments that had been presented in his courtroom. As a Judge, that's all he can use to come to a decision. But I saw posts that stated he should have researched further or investigated.

My mind logically responded to these arguments that a judge's role is to listen to and disseminate evidence presented. They don't research. It seemed that most of the comments were coming from a place of ignorance of judicial procedures. I found it sad that people would make such harsh judgments based on ignorance.

It was a surreal moment as I realized there was more to the Internet than what it was to me—my tool for business contacts, research, and support groups for home schooling and writing. I didn't belong to any forums. I didn't use any instant messaging services. The Internet was not a place to socialize, play games, or have fun, and it certainly wasn't a place to spread hate or scorn. Until then, I had lived in a protected bubble, unaware of the dark side of the Web.

# 3 The Judge

"We acquire the strength we have overcome."
~ Ralph Waldo Emerson

After a brief meeting with Judge Key – a tall, light-haired man with a bigger than life personality and a heart for children and his wife, one of the most warm and gracious women I've ever met – we began working on the book he was in the process of writing about Kelsey's case. He knew the recorded facts of the case as well as anyone since he had presided over the hearings, while, according to witnesses, abuse allegations were made from Kelsey's paternal family in an effort to gain custody of her.

At the time, the only exposure I had to the case was a brief news clip of Mike Porter, Kelsey's stepfather, being led into a building in handcuffs while the reporter spoke of him filing for divorce against Raye. In the clip, Mike Porter looked like a clean-cut, dark-haired man. In comparison to the officers leading him onto the small porch, he looked tall and overweight, but there was nothing sinister that stood out about him. I didn't see any tattoos; he wasn't wearing a wife-beater with a beer gut hanging out, and he appeared to have all of his teeth. His appearance was clean and well-kept and I didn't have any feelings toward him one way or the other. I vaguely recall making the assumption that Raye must have been the one who murdered Kelsey. But I don't recall seeing a picture of her, so I didn't pass any judgment on her appearance either. I guess it just seemed logical that she must have been the one to have been responsible for the murder because Mike Porter was requesting the divorce, which came with a list of demands. To me, the report and the way things were worded made him look like the victim who had been framed by Raye. However, it was only a passing thought in my mind, one in which you acknowledge a situation, but it doesn't involve you, so you don't devote any energy to it or dwell on it.

From March to June of 2007, the Judge and I worked nonstop on the book. During this time, I became slightly depressed. I put on weight and didn't sleep well. Eventually, my immune system crashed. I was working on several other books and various projects at the same time, but they didn't leave me with the sadness the Judge's book seemed to instill. The content and the story of a child being murdered affected me deeply. I was going through some issues with a drawn-out adoption and was still mourning the loss of two of my babies: one stillborn, the other miscarried. At the age of twenty-three, a necessary string of surgeries ended my chances of ever giving birth to another child. Barren and dealing with my own issues of loss, my heart broke for everyone involved, especially the Key family that had become like my own.

In May of 2007, my forty-five minute trips to Chandler, Judge Key's hometown, became increasingly frequent as we worked out the editing details of the final chapters in his book. At the time, my lack of sleep and the depressing subject of his book had played havoc on my health, and chronic bronchitis soon turned to pneumonia. My illness didn't stop me, as my desire to help the Judge tell the true story of what happened to Kelsey outweighed any concern for my health. My eyes blurred and my mind was in a fog, but I kept going. Upon reading the book some time later, I discovered several editing mistakes, but by that time, it was too late. The book had gone to print. The perfectionist in me was devastated and ashamed that the book had flaws. This shame would later come back to haunt me as the Judge's critics tore the book apart and made fun of me for being sick. This was my first taste of how mean-spirited people can be...something I didn't realize existed before 2007.

To announce the release of the book, Judge Key called a press conference. I was nervous for him because I knew how important it was to him and his family that the public be made aware of the truth about his role in the case.

On the day of the press conference, my pneumonia was at its peak. Despite my fever and blurred vision, I threw together a Web site as a temporary Web presence for people to pre-order his book. Copies were not to be delivered until the conclusion of Raye's trial just a few weeks later. However, after word of his book was somehow leaked, he was eager to publicly announce its existence and to set the record straight on the lies that had been told in the case. The press conference was scheduled within days of the book's completion.

As the press conference was taking place, I uploaded his Web site from bed while I prayed that the Judge would be treated with respect and not have a repeat of the town parade during which, according to witnesses, Lance Briggs, Kelsey's biological father, stood in front of the local car wash and yelled, "Judge Key fucking sucks!" as the Judge drove by with his wife and children as his passengers. When the story was relayed to me, I knew little of the characters in the case. I had never seen a picture of Lance or any other members of Kelsey's family. The witness who told me about the day of the parade described Lance to me as a short, small-framed "punk."

Lance's mother, Kathie Briggs, is described in the Judge's book, *A Deadly Game of Tug of War: The Kelsey Smith-Briggs Story* and that description became an issue at the press conference. A day or two before the press conference, Judge Key asked me to send a chapter of his book to a reporter with our local NBC affiliate. Somehow, Kathie's reporter/friend, Ms. Ballard, got her hands on the pages that were from a chapter on the June 2005 hearing that took place in the Judge's courtroom. In this chapter, Judge Key described the events of the hearing and the evidence that had been misrepresented to the media and the public by Kathie and her family. Instead of arguing or questioning the evidence that had never been revealed before the release of the Judge's book, Ms. Ballard, who presents herself as an unbiased, "investigative journalist" complained about the way the Judge had described Kathie.

The Judge stated, "Kathie always seemed to dress in plain clothing. On this day, she wore a beige dress..."[6] Ms. Ballard read this description during the press conference and asked something similar to, "What was that about?" If she truly was an unbiased, "investigative journalist," what difference does it make how someone's attire is described? I remember seeing the clip and being bothered by her obvious dismay over the way the Judge described Kathie. These were the kinds of thoughts I was having about the verbal messages that those who would play large roles in the story were sending about what was important to them on this day. In my mind, these stand out as examples of who I came to know them to be – how they would continue to act, the kinds of things they would focus on, and what mattered to them.

Worry about the overall response to the book turned to relief for me as the press conference came to a close and the report was good. Judge Key was able to say what he wanted, and the press's attitude toward him seemed to shift as he presented the facts that had never before been told due to his position in public office and his expressed feelings that it was inappropriate to comment on a case while he held that position. The only reporter who left in a huff was Kathie Briggs's friend in the media, Ms. Ballard. Ms. Follett, Kathie's other reporter/friend who is with the local Fox station, was not present. To me, this was fascinating to watch unfold because I had always been one to believe what I saw on the news. Now I was on the other side of the story and

---

[6] Key, Craig. *A Deadly Game of Tug of War: The Kelsey Smith-Briggs Story*. Garden City, NY: Morgan James Publishing, 2007. p. 60.

getting an up-close and personal account of what happens to those whose lives are publicly ripped apart by members of the media who allow their biased opinions to seep through to their broadcasts. This is a lesson that my entire family has now learned as well. It has come at a very high price and over several painful years. At the time this took place, they were as gullible as everyone else.

After getting to know Judge Key and his family, I mentioned to my mom that the Judge had hired me to be his book editor. She looked at me with a straight face and matter-of-factly stated, "That Judge needs to be hung."

"What?" I responded, shocked to hear those words coming out of my mother's mouth.

She stuttered for a moment and said, "I saw a billboard when going to Grandma's, and what Judge Key did was terrible."

"Where?" I asked. "Where did you see a billboard?"

"In Meeker, Kelsey's hometown," she responded.

"Oh!" I exclaimed, and I educated her about what she had seen in the media and on the billboard and what was being hidden from the public. I explained that Judge Key had been the target of a hate campaign. Apparently, everyone in both my immediate and extended family believed Judge Key to be at fault, and they didn't know anyone involved. Their opinions had been derived from the media storm that had surrounded the case. I was quickly becoming aware of the reason Judge Key chose to work with me—I was too busy to watch television and, as such, I had not been brainwashed like the rest of Oklahoma. My mind was still open to reason, to logic, and to fact.

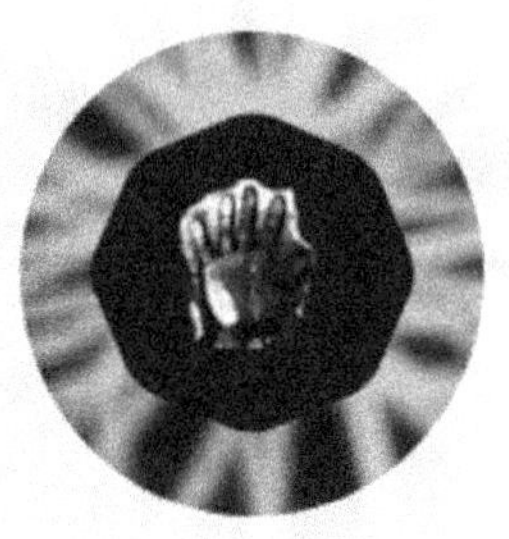

# 4 Kelsey's Mom

"Take the first step in faith. You don't have to see the whole staircase. Just take the first step."
~ Dr. Martin Luther King, Jr.

Eventually, my thoughts about Raye changed. Once the realization set in of how unfairly Judge Key was treated in the Oklahoma media, and subsequently, in the public's opinion, I wanted to meet Raye Dawn for myself as well. While working on Judge Key's book, I noted that in the list of Kelsey's injuries, most occurred while she was with her mom. At the time, I didn't know that the list was from Raye's reporting to child protective services about each and every scrape and bump a two-year-old could have while working through her treatment plan to regain custody of her daughter, or that Kelsey sustained injuries while with her paternal grandmother that were never reported so they weren't added to the list. Therefore, the list presents a pattern of injuries that states, "with the mother," "with the mother," "with the mother," and doesn't clarify these injuries were "screened out" or that all but two of them were deemed "normal childhood injuries" and not abuse. That information was shared neither with me nor with the public, and it made Raye seem to be either abusive or careless.

After working on the Judge's book, I had learned the facts and wanted to know more, sensing that possibly the truth wasn't as simplistic as a first glance at the report had made things appear.

I made contact with Raye shortly before her trial. I told my family, "I'm going to meet a murderer," and gave them the address where we were meeting. I had never met a criminal, and I was terrified. But as a mom, I had to know.

Raye's mom, Gayla, joined us at the meeting. Gayla is very small in both her frame and stature with hair that is almost white in color and is always in place. She has beautifully made-up, crystal, blue eyes and dainty features. She dressed in what I've since come to know as her style, which shows her impeccable taste, in a pair of capri pants, a button-front shirt, and fashionable sandals. Gayla always looks like she's going somewhere important.

When I asked a question about Kelsey, Gayla watched me intently as if her entire soul were open and she wanted to make sure she fully understood what I was asking. I could tell from Gayla's words and actions that she loved and missed Kelsey and that she had been very close to her. Kelsey was her grandbaby and she was a proud grandma. She choked back tears as she stated, "Kelsey was so much fun" and she went into details about how Kelsey changed after she went to live with Kathie into a lethargic, non-thriving child who seemed to only want to sleep instead of the energetic, happy, little girl her maternal family members had known. Gayla described moments with Kelsey as if they were moving pictures that would forever be in her heart. Her love for her grandchild was evident and her sorrow was overwhelming, but it didn't affect me as much as Raye's. It was as if her world had been taken from her and she had nothing left.

Like her mom, Raye was tiny, fragile-looking, and petite. Raye's style mimicked her mom's in her crisp-looking blue jeans and casual, slip-on shirt. Raye's shoulder-length, lightly-colored hair seemed effortlessly in place and it framed her stunning features for which women spend thousands of dollars to obtain. To say that Raye is a beautiful woman would be an understatement. Her sorrow only seemed to add to her natural beauty with her eyes moist from tears that had been there for a long time and they were obviously going to stay.

The diminutive women shared a love seat that only added to their seemingly fragile state as they sank into the cushions. I positioned myself across from them in a mission style chair with a glass table between us. The office was small and dark with the only light coming from the fluorescent bulbs above our heads, but it was private. It was Saturday, and we met in an office building across town; a place that was deserted for the weekend.

When Raye and Gayla first arrived, I instantly knew it was them. Gayla's small, black car featured a large sticker that covered most of the back window with a picture of Raye and Kelsey in matching blue jeans and white shirts with bare feet. Kelsey was positioned on her mom's back and as a friend described Kelsey in that picture, "She absolutely beamed her excitement and joy."

Their frozen smiles seemed to capture a moment in time when mother and daughter were truly happy.

On the day I first met Kelsey's mom, and to this day, the smile that was so radiant in the picture with Kelsey would forever be hidden.

At first, both Raye and Gayla seemed to be on their guard as I asked questions about the content of Judge Key's book. It was all I had to go on about the case, and there were issues that were concerning to me. I wanted to know if Raye really cared about Kelsey, or if it was just about herself, as I had originally assumed. Looking back, they had nothing to prove to me. I was nobody in their world.

But for some reason, they trusted me, and since then, I've learned that it's not my place to judge.

All of my questions were forgotten as Raye flipped through the pages of the baby book she had lovingly prepared for her daughter. Her face was a mixture of pride and grief. Tears spilled from her troubled, blue eyes. It was almost a form of torture watching the young mother's pain as she showed me the lock of Kelsey's hair. It was half brown, half blonde and thoughtfully placed in this book of a proud mother's memories along with the first flower Kelsey had picked for her mommy and an extended list of Kelsey's firsts that were handwritten to the bottom of the page.

Kelsey's baby book made me feel like a bad mom. Mia was a miracle child, and the only baby I will ever have, and I didn't spend a fraction of the amount of time on her baby book as Raye had spent on Kelsey's.

Kelsey's baby book was kept in a manila envelope filled with cards from Kelsey's birth as well as a list of possible names for Kelsey. At the bottom of the envelope, I discovered a simple, gold wedding band that was too big for Raye's tiny fingers. I assumed it must have belonged to a man. When asked why the man's ring was mixed in with treasured memories of Kelsey's birth, Raye explained that the band belonged to Lance. It had been his wedding ring. She stated, "I kept it so that some day when Kelsey was old enough to understand, I could give her the ring to show her that her parents really did love each other."

I left the meeting with a new realization that Raye did love her child. She was clearly in mourning and confused about what had happened. She thought possibly Kelsey's death was the result of the drunk driving accident they had been the victims of in August, 2005, and a trip to a local amusement park during which Kelsey had ridden many of the rides with a bar across her stomach, and finally whatever Mike Porter had done to Kelsey while Raye was away from home for forty to fifty minutes on that fateful day while picking up Mike Porter's daughter from school.

For the first time, I saw the tragedy from Raye's point-of-view. I felt a new, almost maternal feeling toward Raye. She wasn't young enough to be my daughter. But she was tiny, like a teenager, and she seemed so vulnerable and filled with pain, and I empathized with her on a deep level, from one grieving mother to another.

After arriving home from the meeting, I went straight to bed and mourned along with Raye and Gayla. My eyes were fully opened to the media's distorted portrayal of the case. I suddenly wanted to help Raye, and at that time, I offered to help her write her story. I was finished editing Judge Key's book, so there would be no conflict of interest if I worked with Raye. Since I offered to work pro-bono, it wouldn't be a burden on her family. However, I didn't realize the depth of her grief and how much she needed another shoulder to cry on. She had not been allowed to go to counseling. She had few supporters outside of her family and closest friends.

During some of our late night phone calls, Raye would speak of Kelsey as if she were still with her. It broke my heart and I unknowingly fell deeper into depression as I grew closer to Raye and Gayla and I took on their grief as well as the pain felt by Judge Key and his family. I didn't realize that their loss was being compounded by the hate that was in the media and on the Internet. I had not yet started working with Raye on her book; we were waiting for the conclusion of her trial. I continued with my business and struggled to hold things together as I felt myself slipping from the once cheerful work-a-holic into a dispirited shell.

# 5 Downward Spiral

"A human life is a story told by God."
~ Hans Christian Anderson

In the summer of 2007, during the time of Raye's trial, I was busy with my business and had been hired to work on a book for a country music artist. It was an exciting opportunity for me. I had worked with celebrities in the past, but none of the caliber of my new client. He wanted the book finished within a month, so we signed an exclusive agreement. Other than overseeing my contract labor, I did little else but honor my obligation. Trouble started to brew, however, as my mind continually drifted to Raye's trial. I wanted to be there to show my support, and I wanted first-hand knowledge of the evidence as it was presented. The book was an uplifting, motivational book, but my mind and heart just weren't in it.

Always the professional, I trudged forward and did the best I could for my client. Ultimately, I missed the deadline to finish the book, so I lost the job. The loss of that book was the beginning of the downward spiral of my career as my heart took the lead and I searched for ways to "help Raye."

## *A WHOLE NEW WORLD*

It was as if I woke up and found myself in the movie, *The Matrix,* and I had decided to take the red pill. I couldn't live without accepting the truth now that I knew what it was. It was at this point that I became completely lost in an effort to secure Raye's innocence. It has since taken over a portion of my life. I believe the fight for her freedom is the fight for justice in this case and in this county. And it has grown into a cause beyond that which I could have anticipated.

As a result, the rest of my story focuses on how my world began to revolve around trying to understand what was happening and how it could happen in a country where justice is supposed to be done, and where we are supposed to have a right to free speech.

My struggles to see these freedoms exercised, I submit to the public for judgment. During the past three years I have writhed in anguish while trying to understand what seems to be a lack of freedom, and I even became someone I would rather not be for a time while I struggled with the reality I found. Ultimately, you will see me come to the point of completing this story in the only way I can – as an unfinished work in progress. It is a plea for help. Accept it as an invitation to not only hear Raye's cry, but mine as well. I cannot leave my post without some others to continue the fight. For when some have been lost or offered as sacrifices unjustly, we must all refuse to abide this or our society will be no better than those which have burned so-called witches at the stake. Raye is no more a murderess or an abuser than she is a witch. Of this I am sure. As such, her innocence has become my story, necessarily. So now my story will shift to Raye as I provide details that prove her innocence and wrongful prosecution and conviction—the reasons I became involved in her explosive case.

The manner in which I will reveal many of those facts I liken to how one would take apart one of my grandma's patchwork quilts. I will peel away the blocks which form the quilt top that hides and controls the "fluff" that was fed to the public. Then, in turn, this will expose the bottom layer, the facts. After the blocks of decorative cover-up and the fluff are removed, you will clearly see why there was no possibility of fair treatment for Raye or of justice in Kelsey's case, and why the exposure of the true motives and actions of certain people unleashed a firestorm of hate and revenge targeted at me.

# 6 Media Persecution

"The media want a case to drag on as long as humanly possible, and do all they can to extricate every last bit of drama, drop by bloody drop, in order to hold the attention of the millions of viewers who have gotten hooked."

~ Mark Fuhrman[7]

Although Mike Porter had been charged with sexual assault and murder after Kelsey's death, he wasn't the person that Kelsey's paternal family seemed to want "brought to justice." Shortly after his arrest, his $1 million bond was reduced to $250,000 so that he could bond out and await his trial. No time was wasted before he opened up the lines of communication between himself, Kathie Briggs, and two of her daughters.

---

[7] From the book *The Murder Business* by Mark Fuhrman. Copyright©2009. Published by Regnery Publishing, Inc. All rights reserved. Reprinted by special permission of Regnery Publishing Inc., Washington, D.C.

Mike Porter joined Kathie's Web site entitled, "Kelsey's Purpose" that was created just weeks after Kelsey's death and he posted on "bash boards" that had been created with the approval of the Briggs family where the focus was always on Raye.[8] He also communicated with these same parties in private e-mails that were captured and collected by the Briggs and later turned over to the district attorney for evidence. In these e-mails, plots and connections were made with a common goal: Raye would be charged with Kelsey's murder instead of Mike Porter. Protests were also planned to ensure as their signs proclaimed: "No plea for the blonde bombshell," and Mike Porter was given a plea of thirty years for the culpability he would admit to in Kelsey's case: enabling child abuse. He is currently in an out-of-state prison and hidden "for his protection." In a public statement, the district attorney commented that he wanted to take Mike Porter to trial, but that he would not due to the plea bargain that the Briggs family "desired" for Mike Porter. A member of the Briggs family publicly stated, "Lance couldn't sit through a trial." The Smiths were not consulted, though several of Kelsey's maternal family members were packed into the district attorney's office when he stated that he didn't believe that Raye had any part in Kelsey's death. This was a belief that the district attorney expressed to other witnesses as well.

Raye recently brought up a valid point to members of her family. She stated, "There was not one police officer or

[8] See Appendix B – Exhibit 2

investigator who was against me. Not one testified against me at my trial, which is usually the State's main witness."

Yet, in stark contrast to Mike Porter's treatment, the Briggs and their supporters pushed for a murder charges against Raye. They picketed, protested, harassed, and threatened the district attorney to press charges. It has been stated that the district attorney has an entire box of communications from the Briggs and their supporters that he received during the time he was being pressured. It is my belief, that as a result of their efforts, Raye was charged with enabling child abuse and child neglect in early 2006. The charges were later changed to either enabling child abuse or child abuse. Her trial was held in July of 2007, but the media reports started before the attorneys had their turn at jury selection.

From Kelsey's death on October 11, 2005 to May of 2007 (nineteen months), there had been 910 reports on Kelsey's case in the Oklahoma City and Tulsa markets (not including print). This averages out to be one and a half reports per day over the nineteen-month period.

In fact, Kelsey's case has become the most highly publicized case in the State of Oklahoma, even shockingly more so than that of the conspirators in the Oklahoma City bombing of 1995, in which the Alfred P. Murrah Federal Building was bombed by a United States citizen. In that bombing, 168 innocent lives were taken, including those of my co-worker and her two small grandchildren. It was a senseless crime that most Oklahomans remember with strong feelings of sadness, confusion, and loss. However, the media machine that Kathie Briggs created had thundered through Oklahoma much louder than that of the hundreds of families mourning loved ones lost in the bombing. As one witness stated, "Kathie has created an unstoppable media machine."

With the media storm on this case, it wasn't surprising that on the night before her trial was to begin there were nine news clips revolving around Raye and her upcoming trial in the Oklahoma City and Tulsa markets. After a request for a change of venue, Raye's trial had been moved just one county over from where the crime took place, in the Tulsa viewing audience.

One such story was on at 5:50 PM on KOTV in Tulsa, Oklahoma. They reported, "Jury selection begins tomorrow for the trial of Raye Dawn Smith, Kelsey Smith-Briggs's mom… Kelsey died from blunt force trauma to the stomach in the fall of 2005…News 9's legal analyst believes the public has already heard much of what will be presented in the trial for Kelsey's mother, Raye Dawn." The legal analyst stated: "…In this case, we have a timeline that is disputed. We have two people involved. One already plead guilty. It's going to be an interesting case. I wouldn't be surprised at any verdict in this case. Even if Raye Dawn is convicted and sentenced, the impact of this case will be felt for some time…I don't think this case is going to put to rest who actually caused the death of Kelsey." The reporter added, "… If convicted and sentenced, our legal expert says Raye Dawn could face life in prison."

Meanwhile, Oklahoma's statewide newspaper, *The Oklahoman*, continued its media attack against Raye ahead of the news stations with an article dated July 3, 2007 entitled "Witness to Describe Kelsey's Treatment" that spoke of a witness who had allegedly seen Raye yell at and spank

Kelsey and then throw her over the front seat of her "red car." What wasn't reported was a fact that I've since learned regarding this witness. Raye's family members state that he was a former employee of Raye's father. According to family members, this witness had been fired for reportedly stealing from the company. Also, the car the witness described that Raye had been driving was a car that had been owned by Raye's father, but records show that it had been sold well before the date of the reported incident. According to Raye's family, there wasn't a red car she would have been driving during that time.

Another witness listed was a former co-worker of Raye's. She told authorities that Raye called Kelsey "Little Miss Attitude" and that in January of 2005, Raye had admitted to her that she spanked Kelsey with a hair brush through her diaper. This testimony was a change from her original statement to authorities. She stated that one day Raye was mad because Kathie was accusing her of using a hairbrush on Kelsey, not that she had done it. In later chapters, you'll discover that this witness had been contacted by Kathie Briggs before the trial and the witness's daughter-in-law was an active member in Kathie's group with a single mission: "Justice for Kelsey" that focused solely on convicting Raye and her family.

This co-worker also stated that the conversation started with a comment about the engagement ring that Raye was wearing. Evidence and witness accounts prove that Raye never had an engagement ring. Mike Porter purchased Raye's wedding ring on the day the couple married. Evidence contrary to her testimony creates doubt about the rest of her statements, and Raye denies ever spanking Kelsey with a brush or telling anyone that she did.

Further information given in the news article included Kelsey's injuries, but no information was provided as to the details of the injuries. The article closed with information about an alleged bruise that had been found in a picture of Kelsey from 2003. In the photograph, Kelsey wore a shirt that was tied at the bottom so it was short in the front, showing her stomach.

(This picture shows Kelsey with a shadow on her stomach.) The tie from her shirt had cast what appears to be a shadow onto her stomach, but Mike Porter called it a "bruise" and brought it to the Briggs' attention after "blunt force trauma to the abdomen" was determined to be the cause of Kelsey's death in hopes that the picture would also cast a shadow of doubt about his guilt in the prosecutor's mind.

In Raye's preliminary hearing, the store manager of the photo studio who was said to be the one who took the picture was questioned about the possibility that the alleged "bruise" was just a shadow. It was determined that not only was Kathie a former manager of the same store and long-time friend to the current manager, but through recent evidence and questioning, the determination was made that the manager did not take the picture. In addition, it was brought out at the preliminary hearing that the store manager had a sticker on her car that was in support of Kathie's Web site and her campaign for "Justice for Kelsey."[9] Also, the shadow was never investigated as or confirmed to be abuse. Many "others" claim it is proof of abuse before Raye met Mike Porter, and they claim the plea for Raye was pulled by the DA, and that the picture was the cause. This is not true. There was never a plea deal revoked by the district attorney. Two plea deals were offered to Raye. The first was for five years in prison and five years of probation, and the second was a blind plea. The prerequisite to both pleas included Raye admitting that she spanked Kelsey with a hair brush, something she adamantly denied doing. This accusation came from Raye's former co-worker after Kathie spoke with her. Raye stated, "I didn't do it. I won't take it." and instead, she took her chance in court with the consequence of a possible life sentence if found guilty, but with the emotional promise that the truth would set her free.

The pre-trial media coverage was merely a glimpse of what was to come. Throughout Raye's trial, the media didn't back down from their one-sided attack against Raye. Some reports made it sound as if Kelsey was found with multiple bruises, broken bones, and various other injuries on the day that she died. This wasn't the case. It seemed that most of

---

[9] Clay, Nolan. "Witness to Describe Kelsey's Treatment." *NewsOK.com*. July 18, 2010. < http://www.newsok.com/article/3075428?searched=raye%20dawn%20smith%20trial&custom_click=search>

Oklahoma's media were confused about the facts, and the confusion spilled over onto the viewing audience. With the constant media coverage and inaccuracies in reporting the story, I knew that Raye's defense would fall on deaf ears, and it did.

## *IGNORANCE BREEDS HATE*

The media did not investigate the claims made by the Briggs and they passed on the misinformation to the public. Consequently, less than a month after Kelsey's death, although Mike Porter was the only one charged with murder, hatred and anger toward Raye grew to such a degree that Raye received an anonymous, handwritten letter from an Oklahoma City address as follows:

*"Raye Dawn*

*I don't know if you will get this letter or if you will even finish it after you read the first line, but I feel compelled, on the behalf of your sweet, sweet baby, Kelsey. To tell you a little about myself, I am a 35 year old woman with 2 little kids, a 9 year old boy and a 3 year old daughter. Like Kelsey, I grew up in an abusive home. Even though I have never met you or your family, never met Kelsey, or know anything about that sweet baby, I feel extremely close to her. I have cried more in the last 2 weeks (since the story came out) than I have in years. I am overtaken with grief over the pure hell and torture this baby went through. I sit and cry as I write this. Being a mother and growing up the way I did, I have to wonder How a mother could allow a bastard like Mike Porter, to do the horrible things he did to Your baby. Those babies have a sweet innocence to them and they look especially to their mothers for protection. You did not give Kelsey that. You chose the devil himself over your baby. How, how could you bring a man into your life, around Kelsey, that was already labeled a child abuser? Yes, I have looked up his criminal record, and its there. Clear as day.*

[Mike Porter had no previous criminal record. This person was sadly mistaken.]

*Why after the first incident did you not get rid of that bastard? You could have given Kelsey to the Britts [sic], if you truly wanted to stay with that monster. But you kept her there, left her to be abused over and over. Stating 'I have no idea where the bruises were coming from.' What the HELL? Children don't get bruises or injuries like Kelsey's simply from playing. That baby went through hell for over two years and you did NOTHing to protect her. She was taken from you for a reason only to be Stupidly put back. There were so many people that could have helped that baby and failed.*

*I read the reports that said she quit eating properly, was sad all the time, and had a glazed look. HOW can you live with yourself looking at your sweet baby going through this? She was horrifically afraid of that monster and you, the one person who she depended on to take care of her and protect her, left her again and again to be abused. The DHS worker reported that she didn't want to get away from you. She was Scared to death. She went through more pain in her short life than most adults do their entire life. I have had horrible nightmares about those last few minutes of her life. I Bet she woke up, looking and crying for you, and he was there. He started kicking her over and over again in her butt, vagina and stomach. Can you only imagine the fear she had and the horrible pain she was in? This big man towering over her, beating her literally to a pulp. She wanted her mommy, but once again she was no where to be found.*

*Finally, when her little body could no longer take it anymore she passed to be with Jesus. I truly hope you hear her cries and screams over and over again, just as I do. See her little terrified face. Feel the pain she must have been in. I truly am overwhelmed with grief. Your worthless excuse of a mother ASS should be locked up with that monster, and both of you should suffer the same death your baby did! But no, your out free, living day to day, And the icing on the cake is your having another child you don't deserve or need. You and your stupid family can sit around pretending no one knew anything was wrong, but you all knew and let this baby suffer a hellish life, just to have a sorry man. All I can hope for you is that you take care of this little baby in a way you never did Kelsey and I also hope that this haunts you the rest of your life. You deserve NO happiness and that little girl's memory should never leave your mind. I am leaving you no contact information because you deserve no right to say anything. Everything has been spelled out in black and white – there is nothing to say except bless that little girl's soul. I know she sits up in Heaven as Jesus' Princess. That baby did not deserve any of the brutalness she was dealt. You should feel torn up inside that you allowed this to happen. I hope you hear her scream everyday. I also hope you burn in hell when judgement day comes. I hope when its cold outside, you think about your poor baby, laying in the ground, cold & frozen instead of in her warm bed or in your warm arms where she should be."*

How could this amount of anger be directed at a grieving mother less than a month after her child's death when she had not been charged nor convicted of any crime?

# 7 The Trial

"All trials are trials for one's life, just as all sentences are sentences of death." ~ Oscar Wilde

It was July 9, 2007, a characteristically hot summer day in Oklahoma when jury selection commenced. While it would normally take attorneys more than a day for a high-profile trial such as Raye's, the district attorney and Raye's defense attorney had selected the members of this jury before lunch-time. Raye's attorney explained in a sworn statement that the trial judge put restrictions on the process and controlled it in a way in which the jury pool couldn't be questioned to the extent that he would have preferred. Raye's motion for a new trial explains that the restrictions included the fact that only the trial judge was allowed to question the jury in regards to the media and only three questions were asked: 1) Do you have any prior knowledge of this case? 2) If so, where did you obtain your knowledge? 3) Will your prior knowledge keep you from making a fair and impartial verdict? Raye's defense attorney was not allowed to further the questioning, even after some of the jury members admitted to prior knowledge. The restrictions made the jury selection process swift—too swift! This is unusual in a case of this magnitude because of the constant media coverage, as well as the hundreds of stories on the Internet about the case. And it constitutes a serious issue related to fairness and had a critical role in the outcome which shows up time and time again as one looks back on how the trial went.

In an effort to try to minimize possible jury pool tainting before the trial, Raye's defense attorney requested a change of venue, which was granted. However, the trial was only moved as far as Creek County, the Bristow division, a straight shot up Interstate 44 and a 34-minute drive from the location of the original courthouse in Chandler, which is in Lincoln County. So his effort—while appreciated—ended up being somewhat ineffectual.

Kathie and her gang of supporters left no stone unturned as they blanketed Oklahoma with pamphlets telling their version of Kelsey's story and Creek County was on their list of target areas. The match was ignited in Raye's home county and those who held the torches caused a brushfire throughout the state. Some say the intent was clear—jury tainting.

Someone we'll call "Blue" posted a message on January 30, 2007 regarding the April, 2007 "Kelsey Saturday." They were targeting key cities/towns in counties all over Oklahoma in an effort to ensure they reached the one where Raye's trial would be held. Several cities were listed that were the seats of many Oklahoma courthouses.

**"32 people have joined the Kelsey Saturday project. Groups are organizing in the following locations:**

**Norman** ***[location of Cleveland County courthouse]***

**OKC/metro area** ***[location of Oklahoma County courthouse]***

**Guthrie** ***[location of Logan County courthouse]***

**Stillwater** ***[location of Payne County courthouse]***

**Sapulpa** ***[location of Creek County courthouse. Trial was ultimately held in a Creek County District Court in Bristow, just 20 miles away.]***

**Pawnee** ***[location of Pawnee County courthouse]***

**Cleveland** ***[located in Pawnee County]***

**Weatherford** ***[located in Custer County and about 20 minutes from the Custer County courthouse in Arapaho (Weatherford is a bigger town than Arapaho and is just off I-40, the main highway)]***

**Elk City** ***[located in Beckham County and about 15 miles from the Beckham County courthouse in Sayre (Elk City is a bigger town than Sayre)]***

**Woodward** ***[location of Woodward County courthouse]***

**Lawton** ***[location of Comanche County courthouse]***

**Tulsa** ***[location of Tulsa County courthouse]...***"

The following post was also made by "Blue" one week later, on February 5, 2007:

**"*****Drum Roll Please***** Kelsey Saturday is growing rapidly. This year I have incorporated delegation. With that said......Now Announcing the 2007 Kelsey Saturday Area Directors!!"**

A list of areas across Oklahoma was provided along with the counties that each "director" represented. It seemed only the Southeast portion of Oklahoma wasn't covered. This was verified with the ending statement, **"Southeastern Oklahoma — Available! Contact me!"**

The following map provides a visual of their efforts to blanket Oklahoma with their version of Kelsey's story. The stars indicate Lincoln County, the county where Kelsey was murdered, and Creek County, the location of Raye's trial. The checkmarks indicate counties that were covered with "Kelsey Day" events and their pamphlets and stickers. The dots indicate counties in which volunteers had already agreed to cover at the time of the post. As you can see by this map, this group worked hard to cover all bases once they learned that Raye's trial could be moved out of her home county.[10]

On "Kelsey Saturday," pamphlets are handed out that tell Kelsey's paternal family's version of her story and donations are requested to support "Kelsey's Purpose."

---

[10] *US Census Bureau.* July 18, 2010. <http://quickfacts.census.gov/qfd/maps/oklahoma_map.html>.

# 8 Kelsey, a Person – Not a Purpose

"[Kelsey] was a very busy baby, but a very good baby. Did I mention well mannered and very independent? She would tell you 'God bless you' if you sneezed. If she was trying to get past someone and it was a tight squeeze she would say, 'Cuse (Excuse) me' and if anyone tried to help her do something she would say, 'No, I do it.' Everything Kelsey did was an event to me." ~ Raye Dawn Smith describing her daughter, Kelsey Smith-Briggs

"Kelsey's Purpose" is Kathie Briggs's Web site. It was established with the stated goal of turning Kelsey into a poster child for abuse with the claim that it was "Kelsey's purpose to die so that other children can live." It has also been used to garner media attention and public support for this purpose. This was played out in so many ways throughout the entire case. It was exemplified in a variety of ways in the entire story of Kelsey's life and during the custody battle and now in Raye's fight for freedom. But it can be seen even as we continue to look at how the Briggs continued to blanket the potential jury pool by tainting it with the philosophy that Kelsey was nothing more than a sacrifice to make her mother a monster that Kathie Briggs was going to see convicted.

Stickers were distributed within the mapped areas of the "Kelsey day" sites that were pink-colored, heart-shaped stickers that display a picture of Kelsey with the Web address to the Kelsey's Purpose Web site and they state "Justice for Kelsey Briggs."

*Something I still fail to understand is why demand "Justice for Kelsey" when the man charged with her murder and sexual assault was given a plea deal? This is one of the many questions that have plagued me throughout the time I have followed this case. The argument that they seek "Justice for Kelsey," which is what makes up the content of their pamphlets that still promote things as fact which have since been disproven in a court of law, remains their cry. It is time their specious arguments be challenged.*

# 9 The Briggs Pamphlet

***"The fact that a great many people believe something is no guarantee of its truth." ~ W. Somerset Maugham***

Instead of challenging the facts presented in Kelsey's case, and then determining the truth based on findings, it seems that most of the general public, as well as Oklahoma media, blindly trusted the story that was promoted through the Briggs' pamphlet. It was their basic story of what had happened and it was seriously inaccurate.

The pamphlet has evolved through the years, but their current "story" is similar to the one they passed out in 2007, just before Raye's trial.[11]

"Who was Kelsey?

[11] See Appendix B – Exhibit 4

> Kelsey... was a vibrant two-year-old toddler... who died as a direct result of child abuse. She had been under the watchful eyes of the Oklahoma Department of Human Services with nine months of documented abuse when she died. Injuries ranged from scrapes and bruises to a broken collar bone, retinal hemorrhaging and two broken legs. Kelsey's father was serving in Iraq during this time and in his absence, his family continually contacted everyone they could in an effort to find help for Kelsey. Their cries for help went unanswered. Despite the evidence presented to the court, Kelsey was placed back in her mother's home where she later died from blunt force trauma to her abdomen."

## *THE FACTS*

Inconsistencies in their story include the following facts:

1. It has not been proven that Lance was in Iraq during the allegations of abuse.

2. Lance's four to five month stint in Iraq or Kuwait (May 3, 2005 to August or early September of 2005) was during a time when there were no findings of abuse toward Kelsey. As such, there

was clearly no evident “crisis” with Kelsey during the short timeframe that Lance would have been in Iraq or Kuwait.

3. Contrary to what Kathie presents, Kelsey had been taken from Kathie’s home by DHS after the realization that Kelsey’s legs could most likely have been broken while in Kathie’s care. Kathie and Lance were both added to the Deprived Child Petition at this point.

4. Once Kelsey was removed and placed with her maternal grandmother, Gayla Smith, reports state that she was gaining back both the weight she had lost while with Kathie and the hair from the bald spot on the back of her head.

5. There is no evidence that Kelsey was experiencing abuse while at the home of Raye and Mike Porter for any particular amount of time during which the paternal family make their claims she was abused; and certainly not for nine months prior to her tragic assault and resulting death.

6. To the contrary, there is ample evidence that Raye worked hard to watch over her daughter’s health to make sure she was being well-cared for in all the ways she could; and that Raye and her family members thought Kelsey may have been

suffering abuse at the hands of her paternal family during that time.

7. Kelsey's injuries had been reported to Oklahoma's Department of Human Services, or DHS, by Raye immediately after each incident, once DHS became involved in the child's life. This was presented in court, and the state did not prove there were nine months of "documented abuse" as the Briggs claim.

8. Kelsey had two injuries that were confirmed abuse besides the day she was allegedly sexually assaulted and murdered. Timelines and their own statements tell us that Kathie, Raye, and Lance had been with Kelsey at the time of the first incident (the bruises and scratches on her bottom in January) and Kelsey had been with Kathie at the time of the second incident (her second leg injury that was said to occur after the sprained ankle from the zoo). At the time of the January injury, DHS pointed the finger where Kathie was pointing, at Raye. This later changed when Ka-thie and Lance were added to the list of possible abusers.

### *The Timeline and Witness and Medical Accounts*

I realize that it's not fair to present facts and not back them up with the documentation and statements that have caused me to draw conclusions about the facts I am presenting. Therefore, allow me to present a breakdown of the evidence which has enabled me to make these statements with certainty.

***Fact Number One***: It has not been proven that Lance was in Iraq during the allegations of abuse.

***Fact Number Two:*** Kelsey was not in a "crisis" during the time that Lance would have been in Iraq or Kuwait.

***My Findings***:

- Kathie Briggs stated in an e-mail as follows: "Since the mother had pointed her finger to me they had to investigate and put Kelsey into DHS custody. This is also the day my son landed in Kuwait to begin his service in Operation Iraqi Freedom. Kelsey was placed with the maternal Grandmother." This date was May 3, 2005.
- Judge Craig Key questions Lance's whereabouts during the time period of the abuse allegations in his book, *A Deadly Game of Tug of War: The Kelsey Smith-Briggs Story* with this statement: *"It was at the February, 2005 hearing that I began to question Lance's military obligation. I was told Lance was in Meeker until the morning of the guardianship hearing, and then he left to return to Fort Leonard Wood, Missouri. However, he returned to Oklahoma that same night. In all of my judicial dealings with the military, any time a service member's child is being abused, the Red Cross can typically arrange for emergency leave to allow a soldier to attend to his family situation.*

*I was never presented with a viable explanation for Lance's absence during this hearing. What continued to raise red flags was how Lance was in Oklahoma randomly throughout March and April, including returning for his birthday. It was as if he could control his military obligation to be at home whenever he pleased, but why did he always miss Kelsey's court hearings? During Kathie's DHS supervised visits in May, 2005, it was odd to me that Lance called during many of her two hour visits, yet when Kathie was continually asked by DHS for Lance's contact information, she always had an excuse as to why she could not provide the information requested...Finally, on September 23, 2005, Lance contacted DHS. He informed DHS that he was injured while driving a truck in Iraq. He stated his orders were sitting on someone's desk and he should be home in the next two weeks...Lance called DHS again on October 6, 2005, and apologized for having lied about what happened to him and his location. He admitted that he had been in Fort Benning, Georgia since at least September, 2005, and not Iraq."*[12]

- On August 11, 2009 Lance Briggs was deposed for a settlement hearing he had against DHS.[13] He was asked by Raye's attorney, "How long were you in Iraq?" His answer, "Five

[12] Key, Craig. *A Deadly Game of Tug of War: The Kelsey Smith-Briggs Story*. Garden City, NY: Morgan James Publishing, 2007. p. 85.
[13] The deposition can be found at www.RayeDawnSmith.com

months...May, June, July, August, and September of 2005."

- In the same deposition, he was asked, "Why were you not at...any of those court proceedings? He answered, "Because I was not in the state." He was asked, "Did you ever request a leave of the military to come home for any of those court proceedings?" He answered, "They told me as long as somebody was here to take care of it that I didn't need to be here." Raye's attorney questioned, "Are you aware they can take measures to bring you home if there's a proceeding involving your child?" Lance answered, "No."
- In regards to when Lance was home during the abuse allegations, in the same deposition he stated that he was home for "about a week" at Christmastime and into the New Year of January, 2005. Raye's attorney brought to Lance's attention that he told the investigators at the time of Kelsey's death that he had been home for seventeen days at Christmas. Lance admitted that he did state that he was home for that amount of time and he further stated that the seventeen-day time period was not three weeks but "closer to two." Raye's attorney asked why he was home again on January 8, 2005 and he stated probably because "it was a weekend." He stated that he was home again on January 14, 2005, "because it was the weekend." Raye's attorney asked why Lance was

still at home on January 17, 2005 because he returned Kelsey to Raye. He answered, "I stayed longer because of her injury." Raye's attorney asked, "The military allowed that?" Lance replied, "Yes, they did." Raye's attorney questioned, "But they did not allow you to come back for any court proceeding involving her [Kelsey]?" Lance stated, "No." Lance did not recall where he was in February at the time of the hearing that he did not attend, though court testimony proved that Kelsey had spent the night with him the night before, and he was said to have been in town the same evening of the hearing. Lance then admitted to being home on April 8, 2005 for his birthday and taking Kelsey to the zoo that day. Raye's attorney then stated, "You know that she [Kelsey] was monitored by DHS from January, 2005 to October, 2005." Lance stated, "Correct." Raye's attorney asked, "Were you in Iraq during that entire time period?" Lance stated, "No."

- As further proof, the following is from an instant message conversation written by Lance's "best friend" and reportedly his girlfriend at the time of the trial. [Lance's girlfriend]: *"he Lance told me a little one day. he said that everything was fine between him and [April—his second wife and Kelsey's stepmom] and they spoke on the phone often. one day he asked her about some money that he had in a savings account before he left. it was quite a bit of money and he found out it was almost gone. she told him, she would call the next day and tell him what was going on....the next day [April] called and told him that she was filing for divorce. she didnt say why. Lance said he was distraught. in so many words, he told me he was suicidal. he said that because of that he was no longer allowed to carry a gun. you cant be in iraq right now and NOT carry a gun. so, they had to put him in a sick ward and process him out of iraq. that's how he ended up in georgia and thats where he was when Kelsey died." This statement was also verified in an e-mail from Lance's sister.*

- The first allegation of abuse was received by DHS on January 14, 2005 and allegations or the "crisis" period for Kelsey lasted until May 3, 2005, after which Kelsey was placed with Gayla Smith. By September 8, 2005, Kelsey was reportedly doing so well that the DA's office wanted to remove all services from her home. Judge Craig Key denied the request and kept the services in Kelsey's home watching over her. If she had been in crisis at that point, the DA's office would have not asked to have the services removed. Therefore, Lance was not in Iraq or Kuwait as reported during the abuse investigations.

***Fact Number Three:*** Contrary to what Kathie presents, Kelsey had been taken from her home by DHS after the realization that her legs could have possibly been broken while in Kathie's care. Kathie and Lance were both added to the Deprived Child Petition at this point, which named Raye, Kathie, and Lance as possible perpetrators of Kelsey's abuse. Mike Porter's name was not on that petition. Therefore, he was not a suspect.

***My Findings:***

- The following is from Judge Key's timeline: "April 14, 2005 – Kelsey suffers a sprained ankle while at the zoo with Raye Dawn Smith's sister-in-law... Raye Dawn and [her sister-in-law] take Kelsey to the emergency room where her ankle is X-rayed and she is diagnosed with a sprained ankle. (Allegedly, Kathie later stated that [Raye's sister-in-law] should be charged with child abuse because Kelsey was in [her] care when she fell at the zoo.)"
- The following is from Kathie Briggs's timeline: "4-14-2005--sprained ankle-bite mark that Kelsey said she put on herself on her lower arm, another bruise on arm, bruise on right thigh April 14—Kelsey sprains ankle while with maternal aunt. She is returned to me at 6:30pm for a birthday party and Raye is to pick her up again that night at 9:00pm. We called the DHS hotline to report the injury as instructed by [DHS worker]. They said keep her over night and she needed to be taken to the DHS office the next morning."
- The following is from the Oklahoma Commission on Children and Youth (OCCY) timeline:

> "On the evening of Thursday April 14, 2005, the DHS was contacted regarding a sprained ankle and bruising on the child. Referral 977194 was initiated, alleging that Kelsey had a sprained ankle, and bruising on her arms and lower back. The caller also reported a 'yellowish bruising' on Kelsey's middle back. The on-call child welfare worker...contacted [April], Kelsey's stepmother, and Raye Dawn Smith and interviewed the child welfare investigator...and the child welfare supervisor... According to the referral the supervisor reported: . . . that there is a bruise on the child's left arm about the size of a half-dollar below the elbow; Kelsey said that she bit herself but can't tell for sure if there are teeth marks. There is another bruise on her right arm about the size of a pencil width, not an inch long, and is black. There is a bruise smaller than a dime on the left side of lower back, one on the spine that is yellowish. The child has a sprained ankle which she got at the zoo and was taken to Unity North. This referral was screened out. In the findings narrative, the worker documented, 'There is a current ongoing investigation addressing the same allegations.'"

The following statements are from the timelines of Judge Key, Kathie Briggs, and OCCY that describe the events that lead up to Kelsey being removed from the Briggs home:

OCCY - On Monday April 14, 2005, Raye Dawn Smith reported to DHS she had taken Kelsey to see Dr. [K]. The doctor drew Kelsey's blood but did not give indication she knew what could be causing the hair loss.

Kathie Briggs - 4-15-2005--two bruises on left thigh and one on same leg straight across on inside of leg. April 15—Raye and [her sister-in-law] picked Kelsey up at 9:15 to take her to the DHS office. I asked Raye to call me on Monday morning and let me know how Kelsey's foot was so I could cancel her Gymnastics class. –[The DHS worker] scolded me for calling the hotline.

Judge Key- April 18, 2005 – Raye Dawn Smith marries Michael Porter.

Kathie Briggs - April 18—Raye did not call to give me an update on Kelsey's foot so [April] called and spoke with Gymnastics instructor and they advised waiting a week since the injury was so fresh and eliminate any further damage. Raye returned Kelsey at 5:00pm and stated she did not want to walk on her foot yet. She and Mike Porter had married earlier that day.

Kathie Briggs - April 19—My daughter and I took Kelsey to Wal-Mart. She wanted to walk so I put her down and she tried four steps and was done.

Judge Key - April 19 – 21, 2005 – Kelsey is in the home of Kathie Briggs. Raye Dawn takes Kelsey to DHS to report that Kelsey is not walking. Some time later, when questioned about the injury, Kathie tells DHS that Kelsey took four steps on April 19, 2005, but never walked again while in her care. Kathie never contacted anyone or took Kelsey to a doctor after she quit walking. Why?

Kathie Briggs - April 21—My Aunt...came by for a visit around noon. She played with Kelsey and we visited. Around 2:15 she left, Kelsey and I then went to the Elementary School to pick up the other Grandchildren. We sat outside for a few minutes waiting for my daughter. Kelsey tried to take around five steps. We then went into the office and sat and visited with other school personnel. We arrived home around 3:30 and Raye picked Kelsey up at 4:00. Kelsey had stood some during the previous days next to the furniture, but did not try to walk. I did ask the PE Teacher at the school how long I should expect this sprain to last. She stated it depended on the sprain.

Kathie Briggs - April 22—Saw Raye at her apartment in Meeker loading stuff for a garage sale.

Kathie Briggs - April 23—Raye had a garage sale.

Judge Key - April 25, 2005 – Kelsey is in the care of Raye Dawn, who notices the leg Kelsey did not injure is swollen and hot to the touch. She takes Kelsey to the DHS office in Lincoln County and is advised by workers and DHS's nurse to immediately take Kelsey to the emergency room. Dr. [B], an orthopedic specialist in Shawnee, diagnoses Kelsey with two broken legs.

Kathie Briggs - April 25—[A DHS worker] called and questioned me about Kelsey's swollen legs. I was not aware of any swelling. She stated both legs were swollen and had fever in them. She instructed Raye to take her to the Doctor. [The DHS worker] called back that afternoon and stated Kelsey had 2 broken legs. She had given Raye permission to keep her overnight and take her for casts the next day. [The DHS worker] called again around 4:00 and advised me to go to the appointment to listen to care instructions by the Doctor.

OCCY - On Monday April 25, 2005 Raye Dawn Porter and Kelsey's maternal grandmother, Gayla Smith, visited the DHS office with Kelsey. The child presented with pain, swelling and fever, apparently associated with injuries to her legs. The DHS advised the mother to take Kelsey to the emergency room immediately. Following the examination by a Shawnee medical Center Clinic physician, Dr. [K], the DHS was notified that Kelsey had bi-lateral factures on her right and left tibias. Referral number 979294 was initiated. The referral was assigned as a Priority One.

OCCY - In a Shawnee Medical Center Clinic medical record, dated April 26, 2005, Dr[K] reported: X-rays of her tibia show a non-displaced long spiral fracture on both tibia... Consult was obtained from Dr. [B] who evaluated these and felt like the right tibia fracture was consistent with the injury of walking on the flip-flops and twisting her ankle approximately one and a half to two weeks ago and that dated appropriate with the site of the fracture as well as the age of the fracture. Dr. [B] felt like the fracture on the left tibia was actually more recent than that, but felt like this could have been due to compensating from the right fracture and felt like there did not necessarily have to be any secondary severe injury to cause this. The doctor reported that the hair loss was probably due to the child's stress over the custody dispute. She recommended to the mother Kelsey take a multivitamin and drink "Pediasure" to help with her nutritional needs. Dr. [K] recommended that Kelsey submit to a bone density test at Children's hospital. Kelsey's legs were scheduled to be placed in casts the following day...[A] child welfare worker, contacted Kathie Briggs on Monday April 25, 2005 and explained that Kelsey had two broken legs. On the following day, [the worker] contacted Kathie Briggs to inquire of contact information for the father, Lance Briggs. Kathie Briggs reported that Lance Briggs was scheduled to leave for Kuwait on Tuesday and she did not want him upset with the news. [The worker] documented that Kathie Briggs reported contact with the father was not possible.

Judge Key- April 26, 2005 – Dr. [B] places casts on both of Kelsey's legs.

Kathie Briggs - April 26—Got a call from my daughter stating Raye's appointment was earlier than the original time. Dr. [B's] nurse stated she had changed the time and did not know she was to notify me. Raye calls from her Grandmothers around 12:00pm and asked when I wanted Kelsey home. I told her to finish her visit and bring her to me.

Judge Key - April 27, 2005 – Kelsey suffers a bruise to her nose and eyebrow from her step-sister elbowing her in bed while in the care of Raye Dawn Smith and Michael Porter.

Kathie Briggs - April 28—Met Raye at noon to get Kelsey back. She had a knot on her nose. Raye stated to my daughter and myself that her seven-year-old stepdaughter had elbowed her. I also told Raye that it had been recommended to me to get a second opinion on Kelsey's legs. I asked her if she would like to take her and she did. That afternoon Kelsey was crying dramatically for her Mommy. She had never done this before so we contacted Raye to come take her for a ride or to just visit. Before Raye got to my home she had stopped crying and was playing. When Raye tried to pick her up, she would only say "I want Grandma". While Raye was here we asked her more about Kelsey's legs and she stated that they had swollen up on Thursday night and had fever in them. She stated she thought it was because she had not been using them and was making her walk all weekend

OCCY - Referral 979997 was received by the DHS on Friday April 29, 2005. The referral was assigned as a Priority One. A caller reported injuries to the bridge of Kelsey's nose. Reportedly her nose was purple up to her eyebrows and she had a knot the size of a quarter by her right eye. Allegedly, Kelsey was sleeping in bed with her stepsister when the stepsister elbowed her in the nose. The reporter also stated that there were little bruises on Kelsey's cheeks, as if someone had grabbed her by the face with their fingers...

Kathie Briggs - April 28--April 29—[The DHS supervisor] called and stated someone had seen Kelsey's nose and reported it. He wanted me to bring Kelsey to Chandler. I had a play at the Elementary to attend and asked him to come to my house. He and [a DHS worker] came over about 3:45...[The DHS supervisor] took pictures of Kelsey's nose. It had already gone down over night and looked fine. [April] had taken some pictures the night before to put in our file...

Kathie Briggs - April 30—Raye called to see if I could reschedule appointment [with foot specialist] due to a family funeral. I told her I would try, but if it was going to be several days away that I would take her myself. She asked to have Kelsey during our weekend if there were any family gatherings due to the passing of her Great Grandmother. I agreed.

Kathie Briggs - May 2—I called the OU Physicians Clinic to reschedule appointment. The next opening was more than a week away so I kept the one for that same day. Raye came and picked Kelsey up at 11:45 that day for a dinner before the funeral. I met them at the Church at 12:45 to take Kelsey to the doctor. Raye

Dawn was disappointed that the appointment was not re-scheduled. My Aunt... went with me. Dr. [S] told me of his suspicion and suggested I call my caseworker.

OCCY - On May 2, 2005, the OSJO received a complaint alleging DHS allowed a child, Kelsey Smith-Briggs, visitation with an abusive parent.

Judge Key - May 2, 2005 – Kathie takes Kelsey to OU Medical Center in Oklahoma City for a second opinion on Kelsey's broken legs. Dr. [S], an orthopedic specialist, determines Kelsey's legs may have been broken by non-accidental trauma.

OCCY - Kelsey was seen by Dr. [S], a pediatric orthopedist, at Children's Hospital on Monday May 2, 2005, regarding her legs. In an affidavit filed in Lincoln Co. on Tuesday May 3, 2005 DHS recommended emergency protective custody of Kelsey into DHS custody and documented the following reasons:

1. It was alleged that on April 14, 2005 the child sprained her right ankle while visiting the zoo with her aunt. On April [25], 2005 the mother brought the child to DHS office and the child was observed not to walk and wanting to be carried. The worker instructed the mother to take the child to the doctor. On April [25], 2005 the child was taken to a physician in Shawnee for examination. The physician reported to the worker that the child had two bi-lateral fractures of the tibia. The physician reported that she felt it was over-compensation from the right sprained ankle which was a fracture instead of a sprain. The physician recommended bone genetics testing. The physician [stated] that a blood test was completed and the blood work came back normal.

2. On April 29, 2005, the worker received allegations that Kelsey's nose was purple up to her eyebrows and that she had a knot the size of a quarter by her right eye. The worker observed the bruise on Kelsey's nose the same day, and pictures were taken. It was Alleged that Kelsey got the bruise from being elbowed by another child while sleeping on the night of April 27, 2005.

3. On May 3, 2005 the worker received information from an orthopedic surgeon at OU Medical Center in Oklahoma City. The orthopedist saw the child on May 2, 2005. The physician

indicated that Kelsey was brought to him for a second opinion and not physician referred. He reported that Kelsey's injuries (the bilateral fracture of each tibia) were caused from abuse. He reported that a great amount of force was required to cause a fracture to the tibia. In the "Report of Suspected Child Abuse and/or Neglect" from OU Medical Center, dated Monday May 2, 2005 Dr. [S] reported: Child has bilateral tibia fractures probably at different stages of healing. Mechanism of injury is twist to the leg. Stress fractures do not occur at this age. I have never seen bilateral toddler fractures of tibia. My diagnosis is bilateral fractures of tibias secondary to abuse.

[Another] MD, reviewed the x-rays of Kelsey's legs on May 3, 2005. The Diagnostic Radiology Consultation Report...stated: There are fractures of the bilateral tibiae[tibia]. Fracture on the right is a spiral fracture of the upper tibiae{tibia] involving the metadiaphyseal region, and the fracture of the left tibia also involves the letadiaphyseal region but is more linear. These fractures appear to be differing ages with periosteal reaction present on the right but not on the left. While these findings can be seen as toddler's fractures, consideration should be made for the possibility of non-accidental trauma. This should be correlated closely clinically.

On Tuesday May 3, 2005, the Lincoln County Court placed Kelsey in the emergency protective custody of DHS. A 'show cause' hearing was ordered for Thursday May 5, 2005. Documentation does not indicate that the court appointed an attorney to represent the child. DHS placed the child with the maternal grandmother. According to DHS documentation [a worker], contacted the paternal grandmother, Kathie Briggs, regarding the new placement. During the conversation, Kathie Briggs placed [the worker] on hold to receive a call from the father, Lance Briggs. [The worker] requested Kathie Briggs to inform Lance Briggs of the placement of Kelsey into DHS custody. Kathie Briggs refused, reportedly because Lance Briggs was "heading off to fight for his country". Reportedly, Kathie Briggs also stated that she did not have a telephone number or an address for Lance Briggs. [The

DHS worker] documented a first interview with Kelsey regarding her legs on Tuesday May 3, 2005. [The worker] wrote: Worker asked Kelsey has anyone hurt you and she nodded "Yes". Worker asked her who hurt you and she wouldn't answer. Worker asked her if she knew what hurt means and she nodded "yes" and pointed to her cast. .. Worker observed Kelsey to pucker up her lips and get a sad look on her face when she was asked who hurt her legs.

On Wednesday May 4, 2005, DHS received a medical report of suspected child abuse. Referral 981030 was initiated. Reportedly, the injuries to Kelsey's legs were inconsistent with the explanation given by the family. The DHS reported that this referral was regarding the same allegations as referral 979294 and combined referral 981030.

On Wednesday May 4, 2005 [a] Pottawatomie County child welfare worker contacted the Porters and requested an interview with Raye Dawn Porter, Mike Porter(step-father), and Mike Porter's daughter... [Mike Porter's daughter] was still in school and [the worker] was able to interview her there. The worker asked about the incident regarding bruising to Kelsey's nose. [Mike Porter's daughter] reported that her father came to wake her up that morning. He asked her if she remembered hitting Kelsey during the night with her elbow. [Mike Porter's daughter] told Mike Porter she did not. According to [his daughter], Mike Porter told her he thought she did.

Following [Mike Porter's daughter's] interview, [the worker], visited the home of Mike Porter and Raye Dawn Porter. DHS documentation indicated that Mike Porter reported Raye Dawn Porter picked Kelsey up from Kathie Briggs at noon on Wednesday April 27, 2005. Raye Dawn Porter's sister visited the home that evening. Mike Porter stated that the sister could verify that Kelsey did not have any bruising at that time. That evening Kelsey requested to sleep with [Mike Porter's daughter] because she did not like to sleep alone. The following morning Mike Porter noticed the bump on the left side of Kelsey's nose and eye.

When [the DHS worker] asked about Kelsey's broken legs, step-father Mike Porter stated that Raye Dawn Porter's sister [in-law] had taken Kelsey to the zoo. He went with Raye Dawn Porter to pick up Kelsey that evening after dark. Raye Dawn Porter asked him to carry Kelsey to the car. When the car door shut, she woke up and stated "Dad, my foot hurts." Mike Porter told the DHS worker that Raye Dawn Porter took Kelsey to Dr. [K] first, and then upon referral to Dr. [B]. Then Kelsey went back to stay with Kathie Briggs for a week and a half. Mike Porter referred to the ankle as a "twist fracture." Reportedly, Dr. [B] dated the break to the fall at the zoo. He then stated that the break on the other leg was more recent, but ***Raye Dawn Porter did not have Kelsey at that time.***

Raye Dawn Porter was also interviewed by [the DHS worker] that evening, May 4. [The DHS worker] inquired about Kelsey's legs. The following is a summary of [the DHS worker's] interview with Raye Dawn Porter: [Raye's sister-in-law], took Kelsey to the zoo on Thursday April 14, 2005. [Raye's sister-in-law] called her at work and told her that Kelsey had twisted her ankle wearing platform flip-flops shoes and Kelsey was refusing to walk. [Raye's sister-in-law] accompanied Raye Dawn Porter to the hospital. X-rays were taken and Kelsey was diagnosed with a sprained ankle. After leaving the hospital, they dropped Kelsey off at the baseball park in the care of the paternal grandmother, Kathie Briggs. Raye Dawn Porter returned to Kathie Briggs home that evening for Kelsey. According to Raye Dawn Porter, a girl that was not a family member met her outside of the residence and informed her that Kelsey would not be given back to her...DHS advised Kathie Briggs to keep her overnight. The following day Raye Dawn Porter was allowed to pick Kelsey up and take her to the DHS office to meet with [the DHS supervisor and a DHS worker]. Kelsey was limping at the time.

Kelsey went to a sleep over at the maternal aunt's home on Saturday April 16, 2005. Kelsey stayed up until 1:30 am playing with her cousins. Raye Dawn Porter returned Kelsey to Kathie Briggs on Monday April 18, 2005. According to Raye Dawn Porter Kelsey was crawling when she picked her up on Thursday April

21, 2005. Kathie Briggs informed Raye Dawn Porter that Kelsey had taken four steps and had fallen.

On Monday April 25, 2005 Raye Dawn Porter and Gayla Smith took Kelsey to the DHS office to let the worker see how Kelsey was acting. Raye Dawn Porter stated she left the DHS office and proceeded with Kelsey to Dr. [K's] office. According to Raye Dawn Porter, Dr. [K] and Dr. [B] stated that the right leg was consistent with the zoo injury and the left fracture was about a week old. Raye Dawn Porter stated that she did not have Kelsey when the left leg was injured. The interview was then concluded with Raye Dawn Porter.

Kathie Briggs - May 3—I called [The DHS supervisor] to report the Doctors opinion. He stated it was possible he would be taking Kelsey into custody. At 4:00 [a DHS worker] called and asked me to bring Kelsey to Chandler to be placed in a foster home.

Judge Key- May 3, 2005 – The District Attorney's office, at the request of DHS asks that I place Kelsey in protective custody when they determine that both Kathie Briggs and Raye Dawn Smith are suspects to the alleged abuse. Kelsey is placed in the care of Gayla Smith, her maternal grandmother, by DHS.

Kathie Briggs - May 4—We find out Gayla Smith has Kelsey.

Judge Key - May 5, 2005 – Raye Dawn's attorney files an application to terminate the Briggs' guardianship. I conduct a "show cause" hearing and leave legal custody of Kelsey with DHS. Both Raye Dawn and the Briggs are granted four hours of visitation per week, with visitation to occur at and be supervised by DHS. The next hearing is set for June 6, 2005.

OCCY - On Thursday May 5, 2005 Mike Porter was interviewed at the DHS office by [a DHS worker]. He reported to [the worker] that the bruising to Kelsey's rib cage and thighs occurred at a friend's house when Kelsey leaned on a screen door causing it to open. The same day... the mother's attorney, filed application to terminate guardianship previously awarded to the paternal grandmother. The application stated that the mother had completed her "guardianship plan". A show cause hearing occurred on May 5, 2005. [Kelsey's guardian ad litem] was the third guardian ad litem appointed to represent Kelsey's interest. The Assistant District Attorney…made a recommendation to "retain or leave custody with DHS for the time being". Legal counsel for the mother…concurred. Legal counsel on behalf of the guardians…entered an objection to placement with the maternal grandmother (Gayla Smith). The guardian ad litem entered an objection to "The department of human services entering this matter to begin with". The guardian ad litem recommended placement with the maternal grandmother with liberal visitation with regards to the paternal grandparents. Legal counsel on behalf of the mother recommended placement with the maternal grandmother, and to remove the restrictions on visitation by Michael Porter. Legal counsel on behalf of the guardians recommended that the restriction to visitation by the step father be maintained. The Assistant District Attorney recommended that visitation be supervised at the DHS office. The guardian ad litem recommended unsupervised visitation. Legal counsel on behalf of the mother recommended that the mother be allowed visitation without DHS supervision. Legal counsel on behalf of the guardians recommended equal supervision for both parties. … a DHS supervisor, recommended supervised visitation at the DHS offices.

After considering testimony the Court Determined:

- The deprived petition is stale (filed on February 23, 2005)
- Amended petition must be filed by May 11, 2005 [Names listed were: Raye, Kathie, and Lance]
- The child shall remain in the custody of DHS
- Placement to be determined by DHS [child remained in the home of the maternal grandmother]
- Each party to be allowed visitation until the next court date
- Visitation to be four hours a week for the natural mother and the legal guardians
- Visit to occur at the DHS

  - Hearing set for June 6, 2005

- The combined timelines along with testimony given at Raye's trial provide evidence that Kelsey was not with Raye when either leg was injured. [See more in Raye's motion for a new trial, chapter 21]
- The following is from the Attorney General in answer to Raye's appeal: "…unlike other injuries, the leg fractures were less directly linked to the defendant [Raye] and there was no link to Michael Porter."[14]

***Fact Number Four:*** Once Kelsey was removed and placed with her maternal grandmother, Gayla Smith, reports state that she was gaining back the weight she had lost while with Kathie and the bald spot from her hair loss was improving.

***My Findings:***

- The following is from the OCCY report: "On Wednesday and Thursday June 15 and 16, 2005 District Court of Lincoln County considered the matter of Kelsey S. Smith-Briggs, deprived child as defined by the laws of the State of Oklahoma, case no JD-05-10, and in the matter of the guardianship of Kelsey S. Smith-Briggs, minor child case no. PG-05-03. During the proceedings, CASA worker… recommended that the child be placed back with her mother. [A] child welfare treatment worker, recommended that the child remain in her present placement with the maternal grandmother, Gayla Smith, with continued

[14] See Appendix B – Exhibit 5

visitation as previously ordered and "phase-in" placement with the mother following services provided by CHBS. When asked if the child may be returned to Kathie Briggs' home, the treatment worker responded "Not through our recommendation, NO." The Court directed a question to the treatment worker: "If there was an adjudication, are there any additional requirements that you would have of Ms. Porter, Raye Dawn Smith Porter?" She replied, "No your Honor, there's not."

- Witnesses state that Kelsey improved after her placement with her maternal grandmother, Gayla Smith

***Facts Number Five, Seven, and Eight:*** There is no evidence that Kelsey was experiencing abuse while at the home of Raye and Mike Porter for any particular amount of time during which the paternal family make their claims she was abused, and certainly not for nine months prior to her tragic assault and resulting death.

***My Findings:***

I present as evidence Proposition Five from Raye's Reply Brief of Appellant dated January 22, 2009:

"**Proposition 5 – There was insufficient evidence to support the verdict reached by the jury** – Raye Dawn did not permit any abuse. She was not home when Michael Porter murdered Kelsey, nor could she predict Mr. Porter's homicidal tendencies. The collarbone was not abuse. The leg fractures happened either under Mrs. Briggs' care or at the zoo while Raye Dawn was at work. Moreover, children are going to have bumps and bruises. That goes with the territory of being a child…"

- To clarify the timeline of abuse that Kelsey reportedly suffered, DHS confirmed two instances of abuse to Kelsey other than the day she died. They were the January finding of scratches and bruises on Kelsey's bottom and Kelsey's broken legs in April. The abuser was ultimately ruled an "unknown perpetrator."
- Two instances of abuse in a four-month period does not equal nine months of "documented abuse" in this author's opinion.

***Fact Number Six:*** There is ample evidence that Raye worked hard to watch over her daughter's health to make sure she was being well-cared for in all the ways she could, and that Raye and her family members thought Kelsey may have been suffering abuse at the hands of her paternal family during that time.

***My Findings:***

Judge Craig Key stated in *A Deadly Game of Tug of War: The Kelsey Smith Briggs Story*, "After Kelsey returned home to her mother, Raye Dawn, DHS kept a close eye on Kelsey, and along with other agencies, visited her on a regular basis monitoring for signs of abuse. Between June 16, 2005 and October 11, 2005 someone from one of the various agencies charged with overseeing Kelsey's welfare visited Kelsey in her home on 33 separate occasions. At the request of Raye Dawn, someone from one of these agencies went with Kelsey and Raye Dawn to almost every one of Kelsey's doctor visits. Apparently, during the course of these contacts, nothing was seen to warrant removing Kelsey from the home."[15]

These are the facts, but the paternal family and their supporters have continued to ignore the actual facts in their Web sites and videos.

[15] Key, Craig. *A Deadly Game of Tug of War: The Kelsey Smith-Briggs Story*. Garden City, NY: Morgan James Publishing, 2007. p. 81.

# 10 We All Got Sucked in . . .

"Chaos in the world brings uneasiness, but it also allows the opportunity for creativity and growth." ~ Tom Barrett

Reality television shows such as *Trading Spouses* and *Wife Swap* (with a show premise of blending two families with no common values or beliefs such as a conservative Christian, home schooling family with a liberal family in which the children make their own rules) give the general public insight into the turmoil that occurs when two families with different belief systems and backgrounds are suddenly thrown into the unfamiliar world of a daily life that is different than the norm and seems strange. This mixture makes good television because it begins with drama and chaos. Episodes typically end as they began once families are reunited and the familiar is reintroduced. Acceptance, at times, is only fleeting. Only the mature, grounded families hold onto the acceptance and make the best of the situation.

With this insight, imagine what life was like for Raye once she found herself in a family dynamic that was unlike her own. Raye went from a family that shared a close bond with three generations of women who spoke on a daily basis, often several times per day, into a family that Raye describes as detached whose members go weeks, even months without speaking. Imagine the turmoil that Raye faced as she tried to find her place in the new environment she entered when she married Lance, and the continued disturbance she experienced while trying to make life peaceful for her daughter…a peace that would never be realized. Chaos was a constant in Raye's world. It seems that Raye and Lance were like oil and water from the start, but one questions why acceptance was never reached between Raye and her daughter's paternal family...for no other reason than out of respect for Raye carrying, loving, and nurturing Kelsey, a child the Briggs loved.

Facts available at this juncture would perhaps begin to provide substance for a darker motive behind the Briggs's aggressive campaign against Raye when they knew factually that she had been a caring mother to Kelsey should one wish to explore such a hypothesis.

After my research, I have removed any doubt from my mind that they know she both loved and watched over Kelsey with tender loving care. The reports from the supervised visits at DHS showed this as well. On the contrary, Kathie's visits were discontinued by Kathie herself after criticism of Kelsey's reactions to her paternal grandmother. Reportedly,

Kathie was publicly ashamed and defensive. Pitiful as it may be, perhaps these are some of the reasons for her rage.[16]

## *RAGE WENT ROVING ON THE WEB*

It is evident in the various forms of media presentation about the case—which were on the Internet both during and previous to the trial—that the misconceptions detailed above were predominant in those versions of the story which had been put forth about Kelsey's experience. At the time of Raye's trial, I counted sixty-three videos on YouTube with the paternal family's version of Kelsey's story. There wasn't a single video that accurately portrayed the facts of Kelsey's lived experience nor was there a Web site that was presented from the perspective of Raye's family.

The reasons for this are numerous. It is not as simple as the fact that her family didn't have a desire to voice their pain, grief, and complete devastation at what had occurred.

Something that few people understand is that before Raye's trial, her public support base was minimal. The reasons for this include the fact that vicious things started going on behind the scenes that were both bizarre and quickly became traumatic for herself and her family—as though they needed one more horrific thing to occur amidst the nightmare they were already living! And, others began to find themselves intimidated. If they voiced support for Raye, they

[16] See Appendix B – Exhibit 3

quickly became the target of intimidation and a focus of assault as well.

I am but one among many who have experienced this onslaught of hate and violence against my right to free speech when I simply wished to ask a few questions and sought the truth in a situation that was available for public purview. As such, threats and fear kept many people from talking about what they knew.

In an effort to change the tide of hate, Raye's younger sister, Rachelle, finally began an online petition, and a family friend created a small Web site that included articles about Lance's issues with domestic violence, along with a few pictures of Kelsey, among other things that I can't recall. But, because the signatures on the petition were made public, the petition was soon used by those against Raye Dawn as a resource to find people to harass. It was, however, one small effort against unending statements of hate. Though, admittedly, it was almost lost among dozens, if not hundreds, of Web sites that promoted hate against Raye. Stories written by Kathie were unavoidable all over the Internet in response to any search for the names Kelsey, Raye Dawn, or other key tags that had anything to do with the case. It seemed that every media outlet and Web site promoted their same story. To outsiders, it appeared to be the truth. But it was far from it.

### *BLAMING EVERYBODY*

Some people live by the motto "spread the love." I've always tried to follow this practice because it seems to work well for me. Others, I have been sad to learn, seem to live by an opposite composite of this idea. They seem to spread the hate.

Kathie wasn't satisfied to just blame a few people whom she said committed the acts. She started right away to blame the agencies that had tried to help. She even blamed them for the things she'd failed to do—for not keeping Kelsey at a healthy weight and without any hair loss while in her care.

Following is text copied from one such Web site, which was posted in 2005, shortly after Kelsey's death:[i]

> "Below is the tragic story of how DHS has failed yet ANOTEHR child. Failed to protect her, failed to keep her safe and failed to keep her alive. This story is told by [Kelsey's paternal] Grandmother. My deepest thanks go out to her and to also to Kelsey's Aunt who brought this story to my attention. There is no way that I could tell you what happened to this innocent little girl any better than by allowing her Grandmother to let us all know what happened."

This introduction was followed by Kathie's version of Kelsey's story.

> "The last time we saw her she wasn't a normal little girl anymore. She had lost a lot of weight, her eyes looked glazed, she didn't have the light in her eyes she had. She was sad. She was a sad little girl and before that, she never had any reason to be sad. It was like she wasn't even in there. I am the [paternal] Grandmother of Kelsey. After nine months of documented abuse we lost our precious Kelsey at the age of two years, nine months, and thirteen days. Her cause of death was blunt force trauma to the abdomen. Her stepfather,

Mike Porter, sits in the Lincoln County jail on the charge of first-degree murder. Kelsey's death could have and should have been prevented.

When my son was called to active duty, he left behind a happy, healthy little girl. She was living with her mother and while he was gone we had received his visitation. The abuse began in January with a broken clavicle, twenty-nine bruises and multiple abrasions. The ER documented this as possible abuse and contacted our...police department. After their investigation, they concluded it was a toddler accident and returned Kelsey to her mother.

This was the beginning of many moments of outrage towards someone who could have and should have helped. We hired an attorney and received legal guardianship on January 24th. It was never our intention to keep Kelsey from her mother indefinitely, but to take whatever steps necessary to keep her safe. We were told by the DHS caseworker that our job was to work with the mother and to work towards reunification. Kelsey's mother received weekend visits, supervised by her mother for one month. After the next court hearing she received unsupervised visits each weekend and one day during the week. She was ordered to attend Parenting Classes, Anger Management, and Alcohol Assessment.

We were also concerned with the new boyfriend and asked that he not be present during these visits. Kelsey was returned to me several times with bruises. DHS was contacted and documentation was always kept. One worker felt supervised visits were still needed, but did not take steps towards making this happen. That same worker later told me to stop calling unless I knew for sure it was abuse.

In March I took Kelsey to the ER after she was returned to me with a swollen and blue nose. The following morning when I called the same worker, once again I was scolded, for not calling the night before. On April 4th, my son returned home for his last visit before deploying over seas. He stayed until the morning of April 11th, this was the last time he saw Kelsey. He left behind a little girl who adored her father, who knew he was a soldier and that her Daddy was in the Army. Kelsey's mother was upset that her visit was interrupted with Lance's leave and wanted the time made up. I contacted DHS for advice, but did not receive a definite answer. I had not received a copy of the court order and my attorney was out of the office, so trying to work with the mother I chose to let her make up her missed visit. A decision that later came back to haunt me.

On April 14th, Kelsey was returned with a sprained ankle. Her explanation once again was plausible and collaborated; however, given the history of our situation DHS was once again called and this time I was scolded for calling. On April 18th, the mother and boyfriend married. The mother and I decided together that going back and forth every two days was too much for Kelsey and we switched one day. That was the weekend when Kelsey's legs were broken. The mother took Kelsey to the DHS five days after receiving her from me to say I had hurt Kelsey. They instructed her to take Kelsey to the doctor. The doctor Kelsey had been seeing during this time was later discovered to be the sister of the attorney retained by Kelsey's mother. She and her colleague concluded the sprained ankle was misdiagnosed and was actually broken and the other leg was a stress fracture due to over compensation. No abuse was suspected and I did not think other wise. Kelsey was put in full casts, which she referred to as her socks.

It was pointed out to me that a second opinion should be sought to check for abnormal growth plates. An appointment was made at the OU Physicians Clinic for May 2nd. I was shocked and horrified when the Doctor diagnosed the broken legs as abuse.

[*According to testimony from Kathie's aunt who went with her to the appointment, Kathie told the doctor that Raye was abusing Kelsey. This was also stated in the doctor's testimony at Raye's trial.*]

I called DHS with his report. Since the mother had pointed her finger to me they had to investigate and put Kelsey into DHS custody. This is also the day my son landed in Kuwait to begin his service in Operation Iraqi Freedom. Kelsey was placed with the maternal Grandmother. Calls were made on our behalf to many officials for help. BACA, (Bikers Against Child Abuse) was called. They stated DHS was correct in keeping her away from our home, all without talking to us. We thought this organization was there to help and they let us down and ultimately let Kelsey down.

The Governor was also contacted. I knew he would help after all he and Kelsey were members of the same family. We were referred to the state director of DHS. He referred us to other workers. Our pleas were ignored and we became very untrusting of the people who should have and could have helped. At the next court hearing the mother, my husband and myself were given four hours supervised visitation each week at the Lincoln County Office. We left court that day for our first visit and immediately the stepfather was allowed in. We questioned this, but they allowed it anyway.

These visits went on for one month until a court hearing on June 14th. At that time witnesses were called in one by one to testify. The Court Appointed Special Advocate, known as CASA testified as well. She stated she had interviewed her own sister who worked with this mother. When questioned as to whether or not she interviewed anyone from our family she stated she only dealt with parents and that Lance was allegedly in the Army and she could not locate him. She recommended Kelsey be returned to the mother and that we get one hour supervised visitation per month and that Lance should get the same when he returned.

At the end of the hearings, the Judge ruled that he could not determine who hurt Kelsey and she should be returned to the mother with no visitation with our family. We could not believe his decision. As hard as it would have been we would rather have seen Kelsey go to foster care than to be returned to her mother's care. The day of court we received a copy of the DHS report and found our son listed as an alleged perpetrator. How could he be, he was not even in the state? I set out once again to contact any and everyone. No one listened when I was only talking about abuse of a small child, but maybe if they know a soldier fighting for our country has been falsely accused they would help. So I sat at my computer night after night writing my story over and over again. I went to our Oklahoma State web site and wrote a letter to every State Representative, every Congressman, the Attorney General, the Lt. Governor, our Senators and many more. I received replies from Kris Steele and Gus Blackwell. Kris Steele, from Shawnee, gave us the number for OCCY. They contacted us on several occasions, but could not offer a different solution. I began writing the media and once again no one was interested in this story. Time went on with out visits with Kelsey.

Finally in August my daughter-in-law, [April], was contacted by DHS to tell her she could have a two hour supervised visit with Kelsey in their office. She was excited to finally have some contact with her. After two visits another court hearing was set. It was determined [April] could receive a five hour unsupervised visit every other Saturday. They also requested she participate in a service plan. This was great news to our family. The morning of the visit [April] was called by the DHS worker and informed that Kelsey had been in a car accident and the visit was cancelled. The accident was minor; Kelsey was taken to the ER at the request of the DHS worker for precautionary measures, but because the wait was to long the mother left. We were told her stomach was sore due to the car seat, but Kelsey was otherwise fine. The visit was rescheduled for the following Saturday, August 27th. We were once again excited and anxious to see Miss Kelsey. I planned on taking video to send to her Daddy and I wanted to take a picture of all seven of my Grandchildren together.

When we arrived we could not believe what we saw. Kelsey had lost weight, there was bruising on the side of her face and down her left arm, she had retinal hemorrhaging, and appeared heavily medicated. I called my daughter and told her not to bring the other children, for fear it might be too much for her. I took video, but did not want my son to see how bad she looked while so far away. She remembered us, but she was not the Kelsey we had known. We watched her swing, something that had always made her happy. This time she had lost the spark that had once been there. We knew something was wrong, but did not know what.

When we left her that day we did not know it would be our last visit with this precious child. We started making calls that night, looking for answers. I contacted the DHS county director on Monday asking what was wrong with Kelsey. I stated her condition was declining and if someone did not do something she may not be here when her father returned. I was told they noticed the changes. My Aunt went to the Pott. County office on August 29th and asked them to open a new investigation. They did not act on her concerns. It was determined the bruises and retinal hemorrhaging could have been caused by the accident eight days before. We were told she was having seizures and needed tests. After this visit the pediatrician, in Shawnee wrote the Judge and recommended that the visits be stopped.

I remind you once again she is the sister of the attorney representing the mother. She felt only the mother in case of a seizure should monitor Kelsey. An emergency hearing was set. Before this hearing my daughter-in-law informed my son she wanted a divorce. From that day forward we lost any contact with Kelsey, as Grandparents we did not have rights. My son had been injured in a truck accident in Iraq and with the news of his divorce he was allowed to return home one month early.

[*Lance's original tour of duty was said to be eighteen months. He allegedly arrived in Kuwait in May and he arrived back in the states in August or September. How could that be "one month early"?*]

He was only able to keep his spirits up with the thought of seeing Kelsey. He contacted DHS to let them know he was returning. Arrangements had been made for Kelsey to be at the airport. This was to be a big moment for us.

On October 11th, I received a call from a friend that Kelsey had been taken to the hospital. I contacted the CASA worker and asked her to check on the situation. I called her again and she told me Kelsey had a seizure and she would call me back. She never did. We heard from a friend at the hospital that Kelsey had died. My son called thirty minutes later from Ft. Benning, Georgia and I had to give him the news that would change his life forever.

Our family was never contacted by DHS. They did not make any effort to call the Red Cross to notify my son that his only child was gone. We made the calls necessary and got Lance home that night. A few days later we got the news, it was listed as a homicide. How could this have happened? So many people were allegedly watching over her. Not a week went by that our family was not contacting someone for help. Not a week went by that we were once again ignored. The day after Kelsey died everyone wanted to talk to us. Pott. County DHS called and wanted us to come in so they could open an investigation, but it was to little to late. So many people could have made a difference and they chose not to. People in the business of helping abused children ignored this child, but maybe because they let Kelsey down they will listen when the next child cries for help.

When Kelsey was born months after her parents were divorced I knew she must have a purpose and I wondered what it was. When my son was sent to war I feared he was not coming home and her purpose was for him to live on through her. Lance came home and Kelsey was the one who did not make it. That is when I knew her purpose; it is to send a message for change in our state and to save other children. We need new laws; we need an agency with authority over DHS. Grandparents need rights to fight for these children when their parents are not capable of making good decisions.

While my son was at war trying to protect the rights of another country, his own rights and those of his child were violated. This tragedy that could have been prevented has forever devastated our family. We did everything we knew to do within the law. Many failed Kelsey. Our elected officials could have and should have taken action when they heard our cries. If we do not have their attention now they should not be re-elected.

I ask each of you to take the time to write or call your state officials and ask them what they intend to do to help the helpless in our state. It is to late to save Kelsey, but there are hundreds of children in homes today with broken bones and bruises that were not accidents. Not only should the perpetrator be held accountable, but everyone who had knowledge of the abuse and those who failed to help."

# 11 A Ray of Light- Someone Speaks the Truth

"Kelsey's memory is entitled to have the real picture of her story exposed: a picture of deceit, and a picture of converging storms from which DHS and her mother could not protect her." ~ U.S. Observer

For almost two years after Kelsey's death, all that could be found were stories such as the previous one from Kathie. Finally, in June, 2007 a brave reporter stepped up and wrote about the untold events surrounding Kelsey's life in a newspaper that is dedicated to fighting injustice. The *U.S. Observer* has given me permission to reprint its article entitled, *"Kelsey Smith-Briggs - Murder and Exploitation – Prosecutor Smothermon Presses False Charges?"* as follows: [17]

---

[17] *US Observer* "Kelsey Smith-Briggs - Murder & Exploitation - Prosecutor Smothermon Pushes False Charges?" by Barry Jon, Investigative Reporter

*There is no more horrible, there is no more irreparable story than that of Kelsey. The unnecessary death of a child pains and shocks communities to the core and its effects ripple into lives distant and unconnected. We hold our own children more closely and we demand answers.*

(Kelsey Smith-Briggs, a child, not a purpose)

*Kelsey's memory is entitled to have the real picture of her story exposed: a picture of deceit, and a picture of converging storms from which DHS and her mother could not protect her. A tremendous amount of time and effort has been put into our research and interviews; documents have been poured over and countless people have shared their knowledge to piece together the true story of the life and death of Kelsey. The lack of evidence to support the loudly publicized rendition of Kelsey's abuse is as compelling as the evidence of what actually happened.*

*What stood out as our investigation progressed was how the system has been manipulated through deception and frequently told, outright lies. In the end, the amount of information compiled could easily fill another Grisham novel set in small town Oklahoma. A battle forged in Lincoln County became drawn unnecessarily along family lines. Every branch of state government, several agencies and countless people far from the town of Meeker have been directly affected by this saga, even if only on an emotional level. Yet the main characters around which this sad story revolves can be distilled down to six people: Kelsey herself, Kathie (the paternal grandmother), Mike Porter (step-father), Lance (biological father), Raye Dawn (mother) and Richard Smothermon, District Attorney.*

*Our biggest problem in writing this article wasn't finding people willing to talk, and it wasn't gathering verifiable documentation or information contained in records; it was how to tell the story as concisely as possible. This tangled story is entirely about Kelsey, but we determined the best way to tell it would be to untangle it one person at a time.*

***Lance: Biological Father***

*A father should never have to bury his child. It chills the bones to even conceive of such a painful ordeal. In the process of unraveling Kelsey's story we cannot forget the hurt surely felt by people in her life. Yet, in the unraveling we cannot fully understand Kelsey's ordeal without uncovering the world into which she was born. That world, whether he wanted it to or not, very much included her father, Lance.*

---

*"You want to play games? You decide!" – Lance Briggs*

---

*Research has shown that an intact and happy home is by far the best scenario for children. Why then did Kelsey's mother, Raye Dawn, divorce Lance in the first place? Wouldn't Kelsey seeing her mother and father together have been best? It was a long record of physical and mental abuse that preceded Raye's escape. Make no mistake; Lance is a vicious physical abuser with a long laundry list of offenses.*

*Lance threw Kelsey's mother against the wall and choked her with his arm for not* ***"super-sizing his McDonald's Value Meal."***

---

*Lance reportedly, violently punched the pregnant abdomen of Kelsey's mother causing a miscarriage in the summer of 2000. Police were called repeatedly during the marriage for assaults on Kelsey's mother and advised her more than once to get a protective order. Lance pled to assault charges and was court ordered twice to attend anger management classes for his assaults on Kelsey's mother and later on with [a former] girlfriend... The final blow, according to police records, came in May, 2002 when Lance threw Kelsey's mother against the wall and choked her with his arm for not "super-sizing his McDonald's Value Meal." What a hero! The injuries to her collar bone and neck were observed and photographed by police. When Kelsey's mother, Raye Dawn, filed for divorce, her pregnancy with Kelsey was so early on she was unaware of it. According to witnesses, Lance repeatedly, and against a temporary relief order, broke into her house and destroyed and stole personal items of hers only to leave them to be found in a nearby field and creek. On one occasion, his mother even returned items that had gone missing when Lance claimed to have had no involvement. Yet he kept leaving notes asking her to take him back or threatening, "You want to play games? You decide!"*

*Lance's second marriage...was so terrible that the divorce was finalized only one month after the death of Kelsey. However, Lance doesn't confine this physical and mental abuse to his wife. Lance was arrested just last year for assaulting two women when he broke into a former girlfriend's house and dragged her by her hair into the front yard and now yet another protective order is in place. Police records reportedly show he even had a loaded gun with him. How many charges and how many protective orders have to be filed before a pattern of violence is established and properly dealt with?*

*When Kelsey's mother, Raye Dawn, discovered her pregnancy, she attempted to shield this child from the chaos of the Briggs family. In the end, it was Kathie, not the father, who pushed for paternity testing. Originally, Lance didn't want anything more than standard visitation. He didn't push for custody; he didn't show up for hearings and he even reportedly told people that he hoped the baby wasn't his so he could move on with his life. These are not the actions of a loving father and certainly not the wonderful man he's been portrayed as. Lance even admittedly lied to authorities regarding his military movements to avoid suspicion.*

*Upon Kelsey's death, authorities attempted to contact Lance with the terrible news of his daughter's death, but were unable to locate him. We hear over and again of how Lance discovered the news of Kelsey's death right after getting off the plane from Iraq. Horrific news, but Lance and his mother Kathie appear to have been lying regarding his location and status as an American soldier. Lance wasn't fresh from Iraq, but rather sources inform us he had been testing positive for drugs and was spending time in a military drug rehab center at Fort Benning, Georgia. Sources go on to tell that he was being threatened with a dishonorable discharge if he did not voluntarily leave due to possible military drug charges and physically assaulting a superior officer in Germany. Lance claims to have received an honorable discharge, but according to an Observer source he was discharged for being "no longer fit for military service." Lance was initially scheduled to be back well before Kelsey's fatal day with Mike Porter, but was fighting his own demons and not for our freedom. We encourage Lance to release his unedited DD214 and his full military records to disprove our military sources – a small task for the hero his mother claims.*

*Not only should we be angry that the disgraced military service of Lance is being hoisted to war hero status, but we should be livid that it is being done on the memory of a slain little girl. This illustrates the level to which the Briggs have dropped in their attempt to use anything to pull at the public's heartstrings to fulfill their agenda – an agenda of vengeance towards Kelsey's mother, Raye Dawn, for divorcing and filing charges against an abusive man. This is a man who couldn't even protect his own marriages from himself.*

### ***Michael Lee Porter: Death by Deception***

*Michael Porter swept in as a confidence artist in shining armor. He was college educated (so he said), brilliant in his business dealings (miserably false) and had his own home (in foreclosure). Kathie has admonished Kelsey's mother for not verifying all of this, yet she herself publicly denounced one of her own "would be" supporters for attempting to do the same thing regarding her.*

*Sadly, it wasn't until after Kelsey's death that Mike Porter's house of cards came crashing down. Even before Kelsey's mother knew of the suspicions surrounding Kelsey's death she called for an autopsy because she "wanted to know what her daughter died from." Yet, Mike Porter immediately questioned the need. Mike Porter faked heart attack symptoms not once, but twice as the events following Kelsey's death unfolded. He raved to DHS and investigators in a letter on what a wonderful mother Raye Dawn was, but plea-bargained to "allowing abuse" as if someone was left unpunished. Even after his arrest Mike Porter was quite comfortable having Raye Dawn and her mother watch over his own children. Yet, sources tell us that Richard Smothermon, the District Attorney may be calling him to the stand as a "credible" state witness stemming from his plea agreement.*

*It's been reported to us that Mike Porter's own daughter shared with a school guidance counselor that her father told her "not to talk about what goes on at home" and that he would act loving towards Kelsey when her mother was around but would hit Kelsey when Raye Dawn was gone. She watched as her father hit Kelsey's head against a brick wall when her mother was gone. One of Kelsey's young cousins once witnessed him take Kelsey into a room and close the door and when they came out Kelsey was crying. This monster closely guarded his abusing secret like he did so many other lies.*

***Kathie Briggs: For the Love of Money***

*Kathie spent so much effort getting DHS, CASA, and the judge to chase Kelsey's mother that sadly the gathering darkness of a real killer slipped in almost unnoticed.*

*When police in our nation's capitol focused on tips that a shooter was using a white mini-van to randomly execute innocent people, the real killers went unnoticed until police changed their focus. Scott Peterson had family and friends so sure of the great man he was, all the while hiding a financial downfall that ended with him killing his own wife and unborn child. Even Ted Bundy, one of America's most notorious serial killers, was able to keep his family in the dark, yet Richard Smothermon wants us to believe that trained DHS and CASA workers could overlook Mike Porter but Kelsey's mother, Raye Dawn, "should have known." Raye Dawn was forced to focus on protecting her life and daughter from the manipulations of Kathie and Lance.*

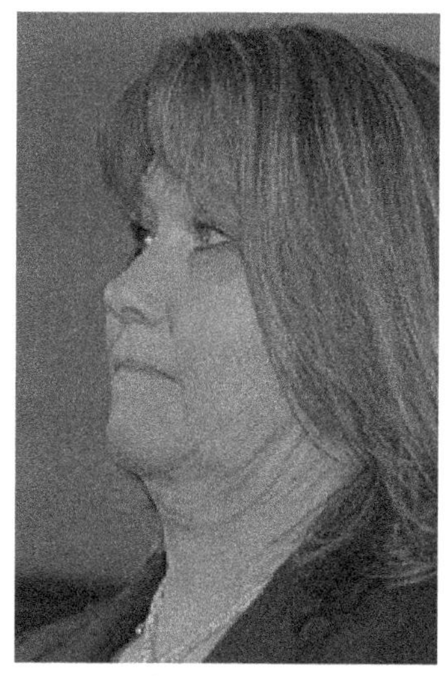

*"Take these kids or I will kill every one of them!" – Kathie Briggs*

*All too often when marriages fall apart the love and the feelings of extended family are shut out of the debate. The blessings of grandchildren are ripped from the nurturing wisdom of grandparents and these relationships are left empty and broken. But in contrast there can also be the meddlesome mother-in-law that has reached mythic proportions in every culture on the globe. Kathie wants you to focus on the dejected grandparent concept and prays her exploits as the meddlesome in-law (that appears to have been taken to criminal proportions) will go unnoticed. Three things tell us about the nature of a person: past record, actions and motives. We are directly questioning her record, her actions and her motives regarding her persecution of the mother of Kelsey, Raye Dawn.*

*Even though Kathie publicly questioned why anyone would "take the time to verify" details of the case, we decided to do just that and began to compare what was being said with what our investigation uncovered.*

*Kathie claims she was the one who sought out DHS for help with her own children when they were young. She argues, "This decision was my own and not court ordered." This is correct. In fact, according to witnesses, she drove down to the Pottawatomie County courthouse with her four young children and exclaimed, "Take these kids or I will kill every one of them!" DHS records and a sworn and signed affidavit attest to this. She is exactly right; it was her decision to abandon her own children, but once she threatened their lives in front of DHS workers it was no longer her choice.*

*Kathie spent two years (uncommonly long) working her DHS plan to get her children back. She was frequently given gas money and even driven by [a] health department worker, just so she would visit her own children. Kathie also claims that the judge in charge of her case praised her as a shining example when, in reality, Judge Carter never did so. This is her past record with DHS; this is her record with her own children, and this is how she revises truth.*

*Kathie has become the queen of revisionist history. She likewise affirms, "I am very proud of the children I raised and the adults they have become." So you're proud of a son who pleads no contest to assault charges on more than one occasion with more than one woman, who attends "court ordered" anger management twice, who reportedly gets beaten up for groping a woman in a bar, who admits to lying to authorities regarding his whereabouts, who doesn't show up for custody hearings, who gets relieved of military service for drugs and assault?*

---

*"The information known by Kathie Briggs demonstrates knowledge gained through hara-ssing/stalking activities." - Meeker Police*

---

*Kathie sued for the same visitation rights with Kelsey that she was already freely receiving without court intervention – any other statement is a verifiable lie. Kathie stalked Raye Dawn, following her to work, to her school and to her house long before she ever claimed Kelsey had any signs of abuse. In fact, in the report to the District Attorney when DHS was first called to investigate, Kathie stated "she had not seen bruising on Kelsey on any occasion prior." Yet, she would now have us believe that a nurturing mother of two years with no history of abuse or violence suddenly turns on her daughter. When DHS was called in after Kelsey broke her collar bone (the most commonly bone broken in children) Kathie called the Meeker Police and stepped up her stalking and harassment. Sources at DHS have stated that their offices received so many calls from Kathie that proved blatantly untrue they began to disregard them. Some of the calls reported abuse during times that Kathie didn't even know a DHS worker was present. And these calls haven't ended with the death of Kelsey but have continued, only now stating abuse of Raye's son, whom she has never seen outside of DHS supervised visits due to the malicious prosecution by Richard Smothermon, the District Attorney.*

*Kathie would also call in erroneous police reports as well. On one particular occasion, police stated they received a call from Kathie claiming that Raye Dawn was driving erratically and at excessive speeds. Kathie didn't realize an officer was on that exact road and he saw nothing to substantiate Kathie's claim. Kathie even alleged that Raye Dawn had the wrong license plate on her vehicle having switched it with another, which was likewise proved false. Moreover, in the official police report of the incident, the officer stated, "I believe that Kathie is continually following and stalking Raye Dawn in attempts to gain any information possible to use against [her] in the custody battle for the child. The information known by Kathie demonstrates knowledge gained through harassing/ stalking activities."*

*Kathie lists three main points in her abuse claims regarding Kelsey's mother, Raye Dawn: broken color bone, two broken legs and bruises from head to toe (the mother is not suspected in the abdominal injury resulting in Kelsey's death). Let us examine those three points from the position of evidence and not innuendo.*

*The mother took Kelsey to the emergency room when she complained of pain and was unable to use her arm freely. The broken collar bone and bruises were attended to and she was released from the hospital with no suspicion of abuse. The Briggs family, who were locked in a heated custody battle, returned her to the same ER and the same doctor four days later and complained of abuse. The doctor documented all bruises and the collar bone and referred it to the police to investigate. When questioned at the preliminary hearing if he thought abuse had occurred, that same doctor stated it was "not my job to determine what happened. That's for the police." He was required by law to contact authorities simply because the Briggs used the word abuse. Both the police and DHS investigated the incident and cleared Kelsey's mother of all suspicion, having determined the break to be nothing more than a childhood accident.*

***Time lines show Kelsey's legs broken while with Kathie Briggs; reason why DHS removed her from Kathie's custody?***

*Even more compelling is the evidence surrounding Kelsey's two broken legs. Evidence and DHS time lines substantiated by Kathie show that Kelsey was delivered to Kathie with a doctor x-rayed and diagnosed sprained ankle, but very much walking. Kathie herself states Kelsey "took three steps and fell down, then didn't walk the rest of the week" but sources tell us that Kathie took her to gymnastics classes several times during her stay. If Kelsey "stopped walking" why did Kathie take her to gymnastics, refuse to take Kelsey to the doctor and just give her back to her mother? Worried, the mother (not Kathie) reported this to DHS and took Kelsey to the ER where her legs were discovered fractured. The doctor diagnosed their cause as "complications from the sprain due to overcompensation" and cast both legs. Back in Kathie's custody Kelsey was taken under false pretenses to another doctor where Kathie had Kelsey's casts removed seeking a different diagnosis - what did Kathie know that the mother didn't? Then Kathie returned Kelsey to her mother without casts. The maternal grandmother then took Kelsey immediately back to the doctor to have the casts put back on so her legs would heal properly, and the doctor who removed the casts is part of the DHS investigation. At this point, DHS began to suspect Kathie, or at the least someone in her house, but realized there was almost no way to prove it. This is why DHS specifically removed Kelsey from Kathie's guardianship to place her in foster care. Very important to note is that three doctors directly disagree with one another on the fractures. Dr. Barrett and Dr. Koons examined Kelsey and determined their cause was over-compensation due to the sprained ankle, but the doctor that Kathie sought out, Dr. Sullivan disagreed. However, because one doctor said there was a possibility of abuse, DHS was required to act. Kathie once again was using anything possible against Kelsey's mother, but this time it backfired because timelines show Kelsey was with Kathie when the fractures occurred and not with her mother.*

*As for the bruises from head to toe, the pictures that Kathie has amassed are a showcase of every scrape and scratch, every bump and fall that a two-year-old can do over an 8-month time span and culminate with the results of an auto accident. The photographs that Kathie has plastered anywhere she can find a flat surface are from what she even called "a very active child." Even the blood vessel burst in her eye was a direct result of the auto accident.*

---

*NO ONE from the Briggs family bothered to show up for Kelsey's final "public hearing"*

---

*During the next several weeks, all of Kathie's and the mother's visits were monitored at a DHS facility. Here is yet another red flag; during all of these monitored visits with Kathie, Kelsey was documented to have continually hidden from Kathie, thrown things at her, run away from her, yelled at her and tried to bite her, until finally on July 6, 2005 Kathie, without warning, simply did not show up for her scheduled visit with Kelsey. When questioned, April, Lance's former wife stated Kathie "would not come to the office because DHS told in court what a bad person she was and she did not want anybody to state any more bad things."*

*Interestingly, DHS workers continually tried to gain contact information for Lance from Kathie, but she kept avoiding the request stating that he was moving around so much in the military this wasn't possible. However, during many of the supervised visits at DHS, Kathie would receive phone calls from Lance. Somehow he was able to coincide calls during visits, but could not keep in contact with DHS. In fact, Kathie spent so much time on the phone talking to various people during several visits with Kelsey that records show observers finally had to reprimand her for it.*

*So let us cast our eyes on the documented visits with Raye Dawn, the mother. Kelsey played games with her, laughed, snuggled next to her to watch movies and was notably happy with her visits that ended in "hugs and kisses." What did Kelsey know that we didn't? Kelsey's actions were not erratic during these visits; they were consistent with both her mother and with Kathie. We have heard the proverb that children are good judges of character and this child spoke volumes.*

*Kathie even purposely lies about her access to Kelsey after she was given back to her mother in June of 2005. Kathie claims that the court blocked the Briggs family from seeing Kelsey, yet our investigation revealed that this is an outright lie. For being as vigilant as she claims, how could she overlook her access for three months before Kelsey's death? In reality, NO ONE from the paternal family showed up to a public hearing to discuss restricting overnight stays outside of the mother's home because doctors were concerned about what might have been seizures that began to manifest. But Kathie knows she had access. It is in the court documents and she even exercised this once after an auto accident where Kelsey was in the car.*

---

*Kathie's front – Kelsey's Purpose - reportedly slapped with **"cease and desist"** order by Attorney General for **"misuse of funds."***

---

*What Kathie doesn't want the public or her supporters to know is that the DHS record does not show a pattern of abuse by the mother, because that abuse was never there. It shows a pattern of her own deceit and manipulation of the system which she learned with her own children. We already know, according to Kathie's testimony and others' to DHS, that Kelsey was not being abused before DHS involvement. Judge Craig Key and DHS workers poured over the records for countless hours before Kelsey was finally returned to her mother in June of 2005. Yet now the DHS worker is being ridiculed by Kathie out of one side of her mouth while telling reporters that her testimony at the preliminary hearing was, "the most compelling." You cannot have it both ways.*

---

*The Briggs family openly mocked DHS worker during preliminary hearing testimony!*

---

*Now, here is the real kicker; Kathie and Lance have filed a $15 million lawsuit against DHS for allowing the abuse and death of Kelsey. If they win, they will have to give half of the settlement to the mother, Raye Dawn. However, if Raye Dawn is convicted of anything regarding the abuse/death of Kelsey, then Kathie and Lance get to keep it all. You don't think $7.5 million dollars isn't a motive? The squeaky wheel gets the oil, or in this case, the cash. Kathie's embellishments and outright lies are out of revenge and she now seeks to destroy the life of a* *grieving mother while lining her own pockets. Even her attempt at a non-profit has been sent a "cease and desist" order from the Attorney General for "misuse of funds." A fact she has tried to hide from supporters, but is finding several in her ranks are discovering this for themselves. Call and ask her how her son, Lance, continues to purchase more and more possessions while remaining unemployed.*

*Beware a mother scorned. That's what stands out. Even in the father's seeming lack of interest, Kathie sought and seeks anything she can set her hands on to destroy Raye Dawn's life -attempting to gain any information possible and revising history to use against her. The police even saw this. These actions had nothing to do with the well-being of a child. It had to do with the selfish nature of an individual who was so angry for having been seen through that she came out spitting venom. Of course, we're sure she'll simply say the evidence is lying.*

***Richard Smothermon, the District Attorney***
***The Prosecutors: Reason takes a Holiday***

*The name "Mike Nifong" has quickly become synonymous with the zealous prosecution of the innocent bordering on the criminal. The fact is politics and ladder-climbing can play a powerful role in the justice system, and if left unchecked, can wallow in our own backyard. Richard Smothermon, the District Attorney wants to be Attorney General even if it takes the sensational prosecution of an innocent person.*

*Do you not find it fascinating that Mike Porter, Raye Dawn and DHS are all being accused of "allowing abuse" but no one seems to have actually committed anything according to Richard Smothermon, District Attorney? Richard Smothermon is now prosecuting Kelsey's mother, Raye Dawn, at the political behest of Kelsey's paternal grandmother, Kathie Briggs. Richard Smothermon even apparently told several witnesses that Kelsey's mother had nothing to do with harming Kelsey. The evidence doesn't warrant charges, but the Kathie Machine has forced his hand, and he cannot ignore it without suffering politically.*

---

*Richard Smothermon reportedly tells room of witnesses he thought the mother had nothing to do with abuse.*

---

*What is truly sad is that Kathie has amassed a small army of very good people around a swirling story of innuendo, half-truths, omission and even outright lies. Because Kathie's supposed "non-profit" calls for the reduction of child abuse by imprisoning Kelsey's mother, Kathie is attempting to see to it that an untainted and fair trial is all but impossible.*

*Seeing such a weak case, but no way out, Richard Smothermon, rather than directly attaching his own name to a no-win case, has hired a vindictive and reportedly dishonest private practice attorney to prosecute. When is the last time you have heard of a DA bringing in a hired gun and turning down the chance to directly prosecute the highest profile case in his district? A case with both statewide and national recognition. A case that could have his name and face on front pages and TV screens giving free publicity to his Attorney General aspirations. Even though he desperately wants the free camera time showing him prosecuting a child abuser, he distances himself from the media. The reason is because he wants to be at least arm's length when that ship sinks. The special prosecutor even saw how weak the case was and the first thing she did was attempt to stack charges in the hopes that something, anything, would stick. Prosecutors know that often a jury will see several charges and believe that where there is smoke there is fire and convict on at least one charge.*

*DA Smothermon and Patricia High now push the laughable charge that Kelsey's mother was abusing her long before DHS was ever involved based on a photograph given to them by the mother herself. However, the Briggs family and Kathie have given sworn statements to both DHS and police that they never saw anything questionable before January of 2005. The fact that Kathie doesn't stand up and let her own statement be heard is further evidence that the prosecution of Raye Dawn isn't about justice.*

*Most importantly, the DA has to prove intent or at the very least neglect. Notice that the DA has dropped the charge of neglect. Richard Smothermon knows that after all the DHS documentation he would not be able to prove neglect, so he amended the charges to Abuse and Allowing Abuse. However, the DHS record doesn't point to the mother as either abusing or allowing abuse. The DHS record does the exact opposite. It attests to the care, love and cherished relationship this mother and daughter shared. It shows how she jumped through every hoop to do what she thought was best for her daughter.*

*Thousands of dollars are being wasted on a case that has no business being pursued (outside of politics). Richard Smothermon, District Attorney has continued to offer plea agreements to Kelsey's mother in the hopes this case will go away as quietly as possible, but Raye Dawn has completely refused anything other than her innocence. Why would Kelsey's mother turn down an offer of only 5 years in prison to risk 30 years or more from a court? Her unflinching statement of innocence and Smothermon's waffling tell the story.*

***Raye Dawn: The Mother***

*When Kelsey's mother, Raye Dawn, was aggressively being que-stioned by investigators regarding her daughter's suspicious death, she shared with the investigators that her father told her as long as she told the truth everything would turn out alright. They told her, "Not this time."*

*We cannot simply try people on the basis of "guilt by association." Raye Dawn may have brought Mike Porter into her life, but she also brought Lance into it as well. The fact that Mike Porter turned out to be a more intelligent liar and a more secretive abuser than Lance does not make Raye Dawn an abuser or an enabler. Remember, two county DHS offices and CASA "should have known." They were trained and they had unrestricted access. Kelsey's mother, Raye Dawn, divorced Lance because she refused to allow herself to be abused. This fact, a stack of DHS documentation, sources inside DHS, and the courts as well as members of her own community tell us that this mother would never have knowingly allowed her precious daughter to be abused, let alone be the abuser.*

*There is no evidence in the DHS record that points a finger at Raye Dawn that does not also point at Kathie. Let me repeat that – there is NO EVIDENCE pointing to Raye Dawn as having committed any abuse. The record and sources in DHS point to Kathie making so many fabricated reports of abuse surrounding childhood scrapes that they told her to stop calling simply to build a custody case.*

*Kathie stalked Raye Dawn for two years and never reported to a single soul that she even thought the mother was abusing her child. Kathie's own testimony and that of other members of her family to both DHS and law enforcement stated that they had never seen bruising on Kelsey before January of 2005. But in the heat of a custody battle, that was not going her way so she whipped her family into a frenzy and called DHS over a broken collarbone (did we mention that this is the most frequently broken bone in children). Doctors investigated, DHS investigated and law enforcement investigated and not one of them found any reason to believe abuse was involved. Why? Because there was no abuse by the mother! But now the Kathie would have us believe that a loving, caring, nurturing mother would, after two years suddenly start abusing her child. There is NO history; there is NO motive. The DHS records show that from the time Kelsey was returned to her mother until Mike Porter killed her there was not one report of abuse, and DHS, having free reign, was able to drop in completely unannounced. This absence of false abuse reports to DHS directly coincides with Kathie no longer pursuing visitation with Kelsey.*

*Imagine, if you will, escaping from a violently abusive man, and discovering that you now have a precious child growing inside of you. Would you readily share that with a monster? Would you readily share that with a man who allegedly caused your miscarriage by punching your pregnant abdomen? Kathie and Lance have so maliciously sought to scar the life of a loving mother who only wanted refuge for her and her daughter. Kathie now does so for fame and fortune.*

*When we are too lazy to search for the truth and simply call for the hanging of all in the vicinity, it is painfully evident that we have no, or cannot conceive of, empathy. Lashing out with hatred and anger does not produce justice; it is simply blind vengeance. And just because we cannot imagine abuse and murder occurring, hidden from all but the victim and a sole perpetrator, does not mean it didn't happen. The writers of "CSI" and "Law & Order" have conceived of far greater twists.*

### *Kelsey: A Child, not a Purpose*

*Truly, the most important element to the Kelsey story is Kelsey herself. At the heart, the very core of this saga are the collected memories of youth and the bundled essence of a child - a child who was not born to simply be on a bumper sticker or plastered across a billboard. A child whose "purpose" was to giggle and climb monkey bars, to run through summer afternoons with dreams streaming in her hair. This child's inheritance was not a "purpose" to die.*

*One thing that cannot be forgotten and should not be eliminated is the fact that the "purpose" of a precious 2 year and 9 month old child was taken, not fulfilled. The murderer, Mike Porter, did not give Kelsey a purpose; he took her purpose from her. The grandmother, Kathie, does not give Kelsey's life a purpose; she uses it. The mother, Raye Dawn, did not obstruct Kelsey's purpose; she sought it and now mourns it.*

*If we are religious, we remember only one child was born so that others would be saved. If we live outside of faith, we remember the focus of our founding fathers and mothers and their assertion of the right to life, liberty and the pursuit of happiness. If we believe in the rule of law, we remember that guilt and innocence are proved by evidence, not innuendo or motives for financial or political gain. If we believe in the memory of Kelsey, we remember her purpose to prosper, and not a purpose to die.*

*In short, a precious child was used as a pawn by her vindictive [paternal] grandmother and physically violent father to deal out revenge on an ex-wife for filing divorce and assault charges. They then had Kelsey's mother, DHS, CASA and the courts so chasing their tails that a killer slipped in under the radar. Witnesses may lie, but the evidence doesn't. Every turn we made and every person we contacted drove us to this destination, including the Briggs themselves.*

Though the newly-published information was damaging to the story that had been created by Kelsey's paternal family, it didn't even cause a ripple in the continual tide of one-sided media coverage. Kathie and her family members and supporters personally collected the newspapers that had been distributed throughout their small town and publicly threatened to have a senior citizen who is a member of Kelsey's maternal family arrested for leaving a newspaper in the local beauty shop. These underhanded tactics as well as threats and other efforts would ensure the playing field would remain uneven and nobody would dare alter the untrue story of Kelsey that had been told.

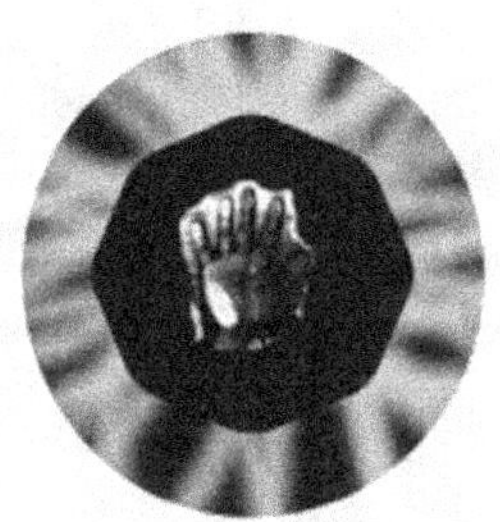

# 12 Day One - Trial Media Coverage

"The unfortunate truth is that today, each murder has many victims, and high-profile murders can hurt innocent people who get burned by the spotlight, whether or not they sought it out themselves." ~ Mark Fuhrman[18]

During the eight-day trial, the media coverage moved at a frenzied pace with a nonstop assault against Raye. There were approximately 478 news reports from the start of Raye's trial to the final interviews after the trial (not including all of the print articles). That's an average of 31.8 clips about Raye per day in that short time period, heard by all Oklahomans (including the jurors, according to witnesses).

[18] From the book *The Murder Business* by Mark Fuhrman. Copyright©2009. Published by Regnery Publishing, Inc. All rights reserved. Reprinted by special permission of Regnery Publishing Inc., Washington, D.C.

Not long after, I spoke to a local reporter who told me that during the trial, reporters were left feeling like "a fish out of water" if they weren't "buddied-up to Kelsey's paternal family." It was obvious from this reporter's viewpoint that two reporters in particular had "time invested" and had built a relationship with the Briggs family—the reporter for FOX 25, Ms. Follett, and Ms. Ballard with KFOR Channel 4, our local NBC station.

Ms. Ballard had built a close friendship with Kathie and her family. So close that she had Thanksgiving dinner with them. Ms. Follett's relationship seemed to become just as close, as she described her feelings for Kelsey and her paternal family in her blog that was published to her network's Web site with her notes on the trial testimony updated every day of Raye's trial.

I wasn't able to attend Raye's trial so watching the news each day kept me informed about the day's events. At the time, I was new to the case and had not yet figured out the dynamics between Ms. Follett and the Briggs family.

Unjustly, Ms. Follett's blog has been promoted as "official documentation," even though it's just notes from a reporter who was fresh out of school at the time of Kelsey's death, and was sadly biased against Raye.

The maternal family had no clue that Ms. Follett and Ms. Ballard were writing a book while covering the trial and yelling accusing questions at Raye in front of the jurors such as, *"Why did you kill your daughter?"* As the district attorney himself pointed out in the trial, and repeated in a town hall debate in July of 2010, Mike Porter sexually assaulted and murdered Kelsey. The maternal family had no idea why such inflammatory claims were made by the media when evidence to the contrary was at hand and seemed ready to be acted upon by those in positions of power. Now it's distressingly clear.

The following witness statement describes the atmosphere at Raye's trial and the fact that the jurors heard and saw everything inside and outside of the courtroom, including the media harassing Raye and other witnesses with questions of her alleged guilt.

**I, [name withheld for privacy] of lawful age, being duly sworn, state upon oath as follows:**

**The jury trial was held in...a fairly small one-story courthouse that takes up only about a half of the block, including the surrounding parking lots and county offices.**

**Inside the courthouse are various offices in between very narrow hallways and only the other courtroom aside from the one where the above proceedings took place. Just outside this second courtroom is the front entrance to the building, which is located on the west end of the block. The courthouse faces north.**

**The media camped out in lawn chairs every day on the front lawn of the courthouse just a few feet from the front entrance to the courthouse, which is on the west side. I also saw several jurors gathered at this same front entrance by the benches in the mornings before trial and during breaks from trial.**

**At the front entrance, the media was positioned each day with their cameras. More people from the news**

**media would arrive in the afternoons. Across the street, taking up half of the parking lot, were the satellite live trucks, i.e., tractor trailer rigs, from each television channel in Oklahoma. There were also several news media vans. There were at least 15 to 20 people from the news media present each day…There were several newspaper reporters present also, including reporters from the local…newspaper and *The Oklahoman*.**

**The jurors were not sequestered during the trial and were free to roam inside and outside of the courtroom along with trial witnesses, lawyers, family members from both the Smith and Briggs family, news media, and the public at large. During the eight-day trial, the jurors were allowed to return to their homes at night and were permitted to go home over the intervening weekend. Jurors shared the same restrooms as everyone else and took their breaks at the same time as everyone else. There was only one restroom in the entire courthouse. The jurors parked in the same parking lot as everyone else.**

**Jurors took breaks at the same time as everyone else. Sometimes the jurors would go to the jury assembly room, but most of the time they joined everyone else outside in the halls or outside the courtroom. I would pass jurors in the hallways, in the restroom, on the street at lunch, and eat in the same restaurant as jurors. The jurors would use the front entrance to the courtroom to enter and leave each day and during breaks just like everyone else did. Again, the Briggs family and news media congregated at this front entrance on the west side of the courthouse. The news media would interview members**

**of the Briggs family at this front entrance throughout the trial.**

**Each day there were approximately fifty people inside the courtroom watching the proceedings. The number of observers grew each day. The news reporters filled the first row. Many of Kathie Briggs's followers from the Internet Web site titled "Kelsey's Purpose," which she established, were present as well.**

**This was a highly publicized case before trial and during trial. It received so much publicity in the news that the judge granted a change of venue to Bristow, which is a small community with a population of roughly 4,300 people. Jurors, trial witnesses, news media, the Smith family and Briggs family would all eat at the same restaurants at noon each day. There was one barbecue restaurant…that was very small. Persons from the news media were seated at a large table in this restaurant. Jurors were seated at surrounding tables in the same restaurant. Other restaurants where I saw members of the jury and people from the news media eating included the Subway and a Mexican restaurant...**

**At the front entrance of the courthouse and certainly within hearing distance of where several of the jurors gathered at break time by the benches, the Briggs family were interviewed by the news media every day. The media interviewed Kathie Briggs, the paternal grandmother of Kelsey; Lance Briggs, the biological father of Kelsey; [Jack] and [Susan], both relatives of the Briggs family. Both Kathie Briggs and [Susan] testified for the prosecution.**

**After Lance Briggs was escorted out of the courtroom and cited for misconduct, he spent his time lounging in lawn chairs with the news media on the front lawn of the courthouse.**

**I observed several news reporters attempt to obtain statements from Gayla Smith, Raye Dawn's mother and a testifying witness for the defense, every day. Gayla Smith would continuously refuse to make any statement. I specifically remember Cherokee Ballard from KFOR News channel 4, Britten Follett from FOX 25, and a news reporter from *The Oklahoman* trying to secure statements from Gayla Smith. Other members of the Smith family were also approached for interviews and statements, but they all consistently declined to comment. I, myself, was not approached by anyone from the news media.**

**Cameras were not allowed inside the courtroom, but I observed the cameramen from the television news stations and those from the print media taking pictures and capturing television video through the windows and glass doors of the courthouse.**

**The news media interviewed other trial witnesses aside from the Briggs family, as well. The witnesses would be on the news each night after they had testified that day. I specifically remember the news media's interview with [the doctor], the child abuse expert that testified for the State. It was televised that night after he had testified earlier in the day at trial.**

At some point after Kelsey's death, Raye felt it was time that she issued a public statement. It was becoming clear that she had been badly misunderstood and misrepresented by everything else that was being released in the media. On July 8, 2007, the KOKH FOX Oklahoma City 9:00 PM News aired the following segment from Raye's previously taped statement:

*"I think I'm a pretty good mom. It's not something I've always thought about like, 'Am I a good mom?'"*

Her words were sincere and naked. It would be obvious to an unbiased listener that this young woman was not an abuser, but rather a mourning, young mother who was sorrowfully dealing with far too much pain to even defend herself as the loving and caring mother she had been.

However, the Briggs family was present in any audience's mind and quick to respond before a listener could give Raye the shadow of a doubt. The media let the Briggs' voice continue to drown out the innocence and sincerity that had been expressed by Raye where naked grief and an offering of genuine connection had been made. Once again, labels and accusations shut any doors that might have been opened. A Briggs family member stated:

*"It takes an evil person to do what they did, as much as I'd like one of them to come out and say 'I hit her this time. I broke her legs. I did this to her. I'm the one who punched her in the stomach and beat her. I'm the one who murdered her.'"*

When, in fact, Mike Porter had been arrested and charged with first-degree murder nine days after Kelsey's death.

Even Ms. Follett seems to forget this fact at times. She added, *"A year and a half later, we still do not know who killed Kelsey."*

Ms. Follett added, *"The medical examiner said Kelsey died of a blow to the stomach, had bruises all over her body, and between her legs. Mike Porter had told the judge he did not kill Kelsey. But his bond was set at one million dollars. Two months later when prosecutors asked for more time, the judge reduced his bond to $250,000 and allowed Mike Porter to spend Christmas at home."*

Having time with family is not something the Briggs are concerned about when it comes to Raye. Though, they were willing to see Mike Porter protected, and he avoided a trial.

Currently Mike Porter is in prison somewhere for enabling child abuse, protected and probably under a false identity, and with a much lesser crime than his original charges. He's under the protection of the district attorney, reportedly as part of his plea deal. Raye was offered this same protection, but she refused. Family visits were more important to her than her own safety.

The district attorney who is allegedly protecting Mike Porter is the same district attorney whom Kathie threatened if he didn't charge Raye with "something."[19] The excuse for the plea that was reported in the media was that "Lance couldn't handle the trial" so they worked a plea deal for Mike

[19] See Appendix B – Exhibit 6

Porter. This is further evidenced in the e-mails between Kathie Briggs and her daughter with Mike Porter in which they discuss a possible plea deal.

The question then comes to mind *"What about Raye's trial?"* Lance was certainly strong enough to handle *her* trial. Though, as you read in the witness statement, he was removed from the courtroom due to inappropriate behavior and he camped outside with the media for most of the trial.

On March 5, 2006, Kathie stated on her Web site, "Our DA has already stated on camera his case against Mike Porter is strong." After Mike Porter's plea, a *Shawnee News-Star* article reported, "If it wasn't for the Briggs family's desire to accept the agreement, Richard Smothermon said he would have taken this case to trial."[20] Just to be clear – that would be the case for sexual assault and murder! Not the one they allowed him to plead out to for thirty years on a lesser charge. Kathie also stated on her Web site on March 5, 2006, "We heard another rumor today that a deal could be made for the mother. This is not justice for Kelsey if that happens..."[21]

It seems so confusing at this point to a rational mind. Why would this family be so obsessed with going after Raye if they were willing to let Mike Porter accept a less severe punishment when their concern is for justice for their dear Kelsey? Alas, it does create a question in the logical mind.

---

[20] Morava, Kim. "Kelsey's Father Gets Deferred Sentence for Domestic Violence." *Shawnee News-Star*. May 24, 2010. <http://news-star.com/stories/011307/new_46279.shtml>. (online article has since been removed from website.

[21] See Appendix B – Exhibit 7

And we see that same confusion in the media accounts. There is a statement of allegations toward both Raye and Mike Porter. Some having her already condemned for months of abuse as though it were a fact and others showing that Mike Porter had the status of a verified state witness against her. She seemed to be somewhat behind the eight ball before she even made it to the courthouse.

At noon on July 9, 2007 KWTV of Oklahoma City reported, "...jury selection is underway in the trial of Raye Dawn Smith. She's accused of abusing her daughter Kelsey who died nearly two years ago...The trial...was moved because of extensive media attention."

At 4:00 PM that day, a reporter with KWTV in Oklahoma City stated, "A jury of seven women and five men will hear the trial of Kelsey's mother. The jury was chosen today for Raye Dawn Smith... She's charged with child neglect and enabling child abuse in the 2005 death of her two-year-old daughter Kelsey. Raye Dawn's ex-husband, Mike Porter, is serving a thirty-year prison term after pleading guilty to enabling child abuse."

KJRH Tulsa at 6:00 PM: "Nearly two years after a toddler died of child abuse her mother is seeing her day in court. The story is new at six. Raye Dawn Smith is charged with child neglect and enabling child abuse of two-year-old Kelsey Smith-Briggs..."

KOKH FOX Oklahoma City at 9:00 PM: "It's been a year and a half since someone murdered Kelsey Briggs and today the trial begins for Kelsey's mother, Raye Dawn Smith. But once this is over, will we ever know who murdered Kelsey? The twelve people who will decide Raye Dawn's fate have been chosen. Fox 25's Britten Follet was in court all day and tells us what the jurors heard." By Ms. Follett, "A jury of five men and seven women will decide whether Raye Dawn either abused her two-year-old or allowed someone else to. Before the jury went home for the night, this is what lawyers told them. Lawyers spoke because Kelsey is not here to." By Lance Briggs, "My daughter is gone and that's why we're here." By Ms. Follett, "District attorney, Richard Smothermon started by telling jurors the end of the story, that...someone beat Kelsey to death. She died when her pancreas burst. Only two people were around Kelsey between 1:30pm and 3:30pm that day—Raye Dawn Smith and Mike Porter. One of them killed her. Smothermon told jurors it is their job to decide who. Prosecutors told jurors they would see pictures of bruise after bruise, injury after injury, for ten months before the state says either Mike Porter or Raye Dawn beat her to death. Jurors learned Mike Porter will spend the next thirty years in prison because he admitted he did not protect Kelsey from abuse. [The district attorney] says Mike Porter will testify he witnessed Raye Dawn abuse Kelsey on numerous times and did nothing to stop it. Raye Dawn's lawyer argued Kelsey was a victim of a custody battle, while Mike Porter, the only person ever charged with her murder stood in the shadows. For ten months, caseworkers, police, doctors, even the district attorney's office watched Kelsey's case. Her attorney says if Raye Dawn 'should have known' Kelsey was being abused, everyone else should have known too." By a paternal family member, "I'm glad the trial has finally started. It's been a long time coming. Now it's up to the jurors to hear the evidence and make their decision and I'm confident they'll make the right one." By Ms. Follett "The judge moved the case...in hopes of getting a fair trial. It took thirty potential jurors for lawyers to decide on the twelve members of the jury and two alternates. More than ten people told the judge they had seen Kelsey's story on the news. Only one of them said they knew so much about the case they could not give Raye Dawn a fair trial." By anchor, "Britten has put all of her notes from the trial on our Web site so you can read all of the details of what happened in court today. Just log onto our Web site at okcfox.com and click on daily links. Last night we asked you if Raye Dawn Smith could get a fair trial... Here is what some viewers had to say: [name withheld for privacy] from Moore says, 'Doubtful! The primary caretaker of a small child is the mother! If she isn't directly responsible, she had to know what was happening.' [name withheld for privacy] from Marlow said, 'I think Raye Dawn will get more of a fair trial than Kelsey did. She was supposed to protect her and didn't do it.'"

KJRH Tulsa at 10:00 PM: "The mother accused of neglecting and allowing the abuse of two-year-old Kelsey Smith-Briggs spends her first day in court. Attorneys for twenty-seven-year-old Raye Dawn Smith say she was not at home the day Kelsey was beaten so badly that she died. They say Mike Porter, Kelsey's stepfather, is responsible for delivering the fatal blow to her stomach. He's already serving a thirty-year sentence and will testify in Raye Dawn's case. With opening statements complete, Kelsey's father says he's glad the trial is underway. He stated, 'It's been a long time coming and now it's up to jurors to make the decision and I am confident they are gonna make the right one.' Witness testimony will begin tomorrow."

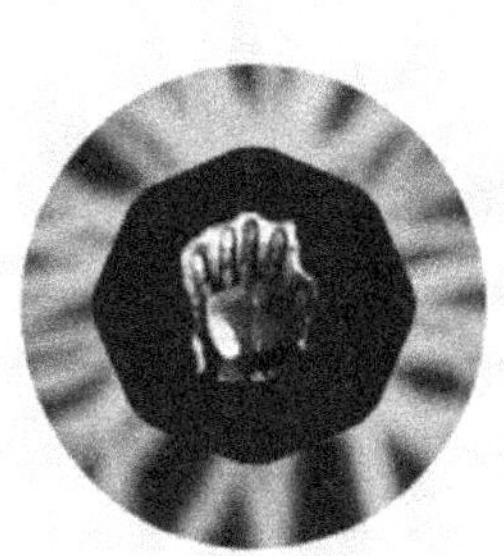

# 13 Day Two – Trial Media Coverage

"There are only two forces that can carry light to all corners of the globe...the sun in the heavens and the Associated Press down here." ~ Mark Twain

It was day two of Raye's trial, and the most brutal day for Raye and others who loved Kelsey. Although Kelsey's autopsy photos had no relevance in the trial because it was not a murder trial, they were allowed as part of the state's evidence. These photos were misleading and should have never been allowed in the courtroom. The following is from Raye's appeal: *"[The physician's assistant] estimated that Kelsey had been down for about 45 minutes when she arrived...at 3:59 p.m. They continued to 'Code' Kelsey for another 45 minutes before they called time of death. [The physician's assistant] called her time of death at 4:45 p.m. Raye Dawn requested that an autopsy be performed because she wanted to know what happened to her daughter. Mike*

*Porter, on the other hand, objected to an autopsy being performed. [The physician's assistant] testified that Kelsey had two small bruises on her face and one on her shin, which wasn't anything out of the ordinary. She testified that she did not notice any unusual bruising on Kelsey, and that she examined Kelsey's entire body and turned her over to look at her back. In fact, the first evidence of trauma is post-mortem. The autopsy photographs were misleading because they show post-mortem lividity and trauma caused by medical manipulation, which to a lay person appears to be evidence of intentional trauma or abuse."*

In layman's terms, first responders and EMT's worked to revive Kelsey from the time they arrived on the scene at 3:27p.m. until the time they arrived at the hospital at 3:45p.m. Upon arrival, a physician's assistant and her team worked on the small child for another 45 minutes. Photographs and statements from multiple witnesses prove that Kelsey *was not* covered in bruises, unlike what the autopsy photos displayed. The state used those photographs to back up their claim that Kelsey was covered in bruises and injuries at the time of her death. They posed the question: *"How could Raye not have known Kelsey was being abused?"* with evidence that did not accurately portray Kelsey's physical state when Raye left her home.

The facts lead us in a different direction, one in which Kelsey had three "normal, childhood looking bruises" at the time of her death. Which scenario would inflame a jury more: The facts—three bruises; or the smokescreen—the result of seventy-seven minutes of medical manipulation by several adults on a two-year-old's body? Because the autopsy photos did not prove anything related to Raye's charges—"should have known"—they should not have been allowed in her trial.

It seemed Raye was taking blow after blow from the system in which she had put her faith to see past the scorn and to the truth. Testimony was paused as Raye sobbed uncontrollably when faced with the pictures that no mother should ever have to see of her child.

On July 10, 2007 at 5:00 AM, KOCO Oklahoma City started off the reports with the following statements: "This morning a jury will hear evidence against a mother accused of child abuse. The child is two-year-old Kelsey Smith-Briggs. She died in October of 2005 from child abuse. Her mom's trial started yesterday and a jury will decide if Raye Dawn Smith is guilty of abusing Kelsey or allowing the abuse to happen. The trial could last up to two weeks. Kelsey's stepfather, Mike Porter, is already serving a thirty-year prison term and he could be a witness in this trial."

KJRH Tulsa at 11:00 AM: "Today jurors hear testimony in a mother's neglect and abuse trial after her two-year-old daughter died from blunt force trauma. Attorneys for twenty-seven-year-old Raye Dawn Smith say she was not home the day Kelsey was beaten so badly she died. They say Mike Porter, Kelsey's stepfather, delivered the fatal blow to her stomach. He's already serving a thirty-year sentence and will testify in Raye Dawn's case. Smith's trial was moved…because of pre-trial publicity."

KWTV Oklahoma City at noon: "Testimony is back underway today in the trial of Raye Dawn Smith after being put on hold this morning. Raye Dawn is accused of child abuse in the 2005 death of her daughter, Kelsey Smith-Briggs. Taking the stand today—a volunteer firefighter, physicians assistant and a medical examiner. The ME was testifying about Kelsey's extensive wounds when the trial had recess because Raye Dawn began sobbing uncontrollably. The volunteer firefighter and physicians assistant testified earlier that Kelsey was blue, had no pulse, and wasn't breathing when they first saw her the day she died."

Also on July 10, 2007, an article in *The Oklahoman* stated that Raye's sobs grew so loud that the judge called for a break. The medical examiner testified about Kelsey's injuries and the fact that she had suffered genital injuries, but in her opinion, it wasn't clear if they were from a sexual assault. However, an autopsy was performed by an Indiana medical examiner who determined that Kelsey had been sexually assaulted.

The second autopsy, which determined that Kelsey's body exhibited signs of "repeated forcible sexual assault," was performed after Kelsey's body was exhumed in April of 2006. This autopsy was scheduled at around the same time that Mike Porter's computers were confiscated and were said to have contained child pornography as well as videos and pictures depicting anal sex, which correlates to what was alleged to have happened to Kelsey. Raye and her family were put through this second autopsy in an effort to get justice for Kelsey, which came with the added charge of sexual assault for Mike Porter who had already been charged with Kelsey's murder. However, the results of the second autopsy were not presented to the jury at Raye's trial. This only added to her heartache...her daughter's grave had been disturbed and her body had been put through further testing, but because the evidence gathered pointed to Mike Porter as the perpetrator of Kelsey's abuse and murder and he never went to trial, the evidence was not used.

This same article spoke of the selected members of the jury, which included a highway patrol secretary, a contractor, a retiree, a stay-at-home mom, a hospital employee, a restaurant employee, and a former counselor at the local boys' home. Raye's private investigator later uncovered that two of the jurors had alleged abuse charges against them. One juror, Celia, allegedly spanked her child with a clothes hanger. This same juror was said to have "bragged about drinking with her underage daughter" in a statement from another juror. *Could this juror have been projecting her own feelings of failure as a parent onto Raye?*

KSBI Oklahoma City at 5:30 PM: "The prosecution called several witnesses today, including Kelsey Smith-Briggs's stepfather, Mike Porter, who is currently serving thirty years for enabling the child abuse of Kelsey." [Reporter:] "Mike Porter testified of three instances dating back to January 2005 where he says he saw Raye Dawn abuse Kelsey. He stated one of those times he witnessed Raye Dawn punching Kelsey in the abdomen. He went on to say he willingly lied to authorities several times to protect Raye Dawn. Prior to his testimony, the day began with the first responder who tried to help Kelsey and a physician's assistant from the Prague hospital. The third witness a forensic pathologist. After her testimony, we broke for lunch. It was when everyone returned that Mike Porter took the stand."

The district attorney told Mike Porter while he was on the stand, "You know I believe you murdered her [Kelsey] and sexually abused her [Kelsey]...I still believe you to be guilty." Media ignored the statement with their focus on Mike Porter's accusations against Raye instead of the district attorney's charges against the state's witness, Mike Porter.

The following letter was submitted to the court in 2005 when Raye's parenting was called into question. It was read on the stand during the trial where Mike Porter claimed it was a cover-up for Raye.

*"TO WHOM IT MAY CONCERN: I, Mike Porter, met Raye Dawn on or about October 15, 2004. Since beginning as friends, I have been present and witnessed many interactions between Raye Dawn and her minor child, Kelsey. We often spend time together watching TV, eating dinner, and playing with Kelsey and my two children. It is because of this time I have spent around Raye Dawn that I can make this statement unequivocally- Raye Dawn WOULD NEVER HARM Kelsey. I know for a fact that Raye Dawn loves Kelsey more than life itself. This fact is apparent to anyone who spends more than 5 minutes with the two of them. Raye Dawn is the kind of mother that ANY child would be lucky to have. I have never seen Raye Dawn administer discipline that would even come close to child abuse or neglect. In fact, there is a long running joke between Raye Dawn and myself that Kelsey is the most spoiled child ever. Raye Dawn puts Kelsey first in every thought and action. Raye Dawn provides Kelsey with clothes to wear, food to eat, a roof over her head, and all the love a child could ever need. She does all this while attending school (until this fiasco) and working to support herself and her child. If these qualities constitute an unfit mother, then we should all be so lucky to have unfit mothers. Raye Dawn has raised Kelsey from her birth until the time she was taken, and done a fine job by all accounts (except those of her ex-in laws.) From my understanding the paternal side of Kelsey's family has had little to do with Kelsey's upbringing besides visitation. One only has to do a*

*little research in the town that both families reside in to find out what kind of people are involved. I am aware, as everyone is, of the history of domestic violence involving Raye Dawn and Kelsey's father. Try as they may to blame the abuse on Raye Dawn, the fact of the matter is there is never an excuse for a man to hurt a woman. By making wild claims of abuse it would seem the plaintiff is casting rocks while living in a proverbial glass house. I do not purport to know the plaintiff and her family well, but I do know that after it became known by the plaintiff (Kathie) that I was involved with Raye Dawn, I received numerous prank phone calls at my home number- followed by a threatening phone call. The next day I received a phone call from the plaintiff that, in my opinion, took a semi-accusatory tone regarding an 'allegation' of child abuse. I informed the plaintiff (Kathie) at this time that these were not charges to sling about without regard and that if she was attempting to implicate myself she would certainly hear from my lawyer. This information is included in a written statement with the Lincoln County Sheriff's department. My impression from the phone conversation with Kathie was that she is a petty person who is attempting to take advantage of a good, hard working mother and an unknowing innocent child. I know this whole ordeal has been very hard on Kelsey, as she has been taken from the only true parent she has ever known. I have no doubt in my mind that if Kelsey were old enough to articulate her thoughts clearly, she would make it known to EVERYONE what a travesty this whole ordeal is. Being a veteran of two custody disputes, I am very familiar with the definition of an unfit mother. I can say with a crystal clear conscious that*

*Raye Dawn is an antithesis of an unfit mother. I pray that this court will use it's best judgment and return Kelsey to her rightful place- INTO HER MOTHER'S ARMS. I swear that the above statements are true and accurate to the best of my knowledge."*

KTUL Tulsa at 10:00 PM: "There was lots of finger pointing and accusations...today where the trial of Raye Dawn Smith is underway. She's charged with felony child abuse in the death of her two-year-old daughter Kelsey Smith-Briggs. Today, Kelsey's stepfather, Mike Porter, took the stand. He told jurors he saw Raye Dawn punch the child and that he helped cover up the abuse..."

Mike Porter's testimony was also contradicted in the OCCY findings as follows:

"Mike porter was also interviewed by [two DHS workers] on Friday May 20, 2005. Mike Porter said that he had pictures of Kelsey standing on both legs, dated Monday April 18. The worker wrote: 'Mike reports that Raye has a very close connection with Kelsey and that when they first started dating he was intimidated by the intensity of their relationship. He reports that Raye places a lot of her sense of self worth on her ability to be a mom and that he has seen Raye's self esteem drop since she has not had Kelsey.'"

Kelsey was picked up
from Kathie's four days
after this picture with
two broken legs.

# 14 Day Three - Trial Media Coverage

"The most important service rendered by the press and magazines is that of educating people to approach printed material with distrust." ~ Samuel Butler

On July 11, 2007 at 5:00 AM, KFOR in Oklahoma City started the daily reports with the most-discussed witness, Kathie Briggs. She was the face and name that had been in hundreds of reports since Kelsey's death. She's who members of the media had grown to trust to give them a story that would sell. They reported: "On crime watch the trial of Raye Dawn Smith continues today...The prosecution is expected to call Kelsey's grandmother Kathie Briggs. You'll remember she made numerous calls to DHS officials trying to alert them to Kelsey's abuse..."

A clear distinction in the reporting styles from the various media outlets is the fact that Ms. Follett's and Ms. Ballard's television stations continually called Kelsey, "Kelsey

Briggs" even though her legal name was Kelsey Smith-Briggs.

KOKH FOX Oklahoma City at 5:00 AM: "Day three of the child abuse trial involving Kelsey Briggs begins this morning. Yesterday they saw pictures of her lifeless body, pictures on the autopsy table. The judge told everyone to take a break when Raye Dawn Smith burst into tears and began weeping out loud as jurors watched her. Mike Porter came from prison and went straight back after telling jurors he knows Raye Dawn killed Kelsey. [by a paternal family member] 'I thought all along she did it.' The man originally charged with the murder says he saw Raye Dawn beat Kelsey three times. [by a paternal family member] 'I think she's the person that did most of it. I honestly think she is violent.' In July, 2005 he [Mike Porter] heard a door slam, a scream."

KOKH FOX Oklahoma City at 6:00 AM: "He [Mike Porter] walked into the bedroom and saw Raye Dawn holding Kelsey down with her legs while she hit her with a closed fist in the stomach...Two days before Kelsey was killed he saw his ex-wife drag Kelsey out of the truck, drag her to the house, and throw her in a chair saying she was being a little brat. He says he lied to case workers for ten months to protect his wife because he loves her." [Paternal family member:] "I think he is telling the truth. He's not going to get anything out of this...I hope she will get on the witness stand and try to say her side of it. I don't think she will. I don't think she has the nerve and guts to get up there. I would love to see her get on the stand."..."

KJRH Tulsa at 11:00 AM: "Testimony resumes today in the trial of Raye Dawn Smith. She is accused of child neglect and enabling child abuse. Her two-year-old daughter, Kelsey Smith-Briggs, died from a fatal blow to the stomach in October of 2005. Raye Dawn's ex-husband, Mike Porter took the stand yesterday. He denied any involvement in Kelsey's death and places the blame on Raye Dawn."

KAUT Oklahoma City at 9:00 PM: "...pictures Kelsey's stepmother took after she found the bruises on Kelsey. After discovering the marks, she took Kelsey to the hospital and called DHS...Kelsey's grandmother on her father's side, Kathie Briggs, was on the stand today for three hours answering questions about the animosity between the families, DHS's involvement in the case, and a meeting she had with Mike Porter, Kelsey's stepdad. Kathie said she had met with Mike Porter to get information from him about Kelsey's life and the abuse. Raye Dawn's attorney criticized her for that meeting."

Kathie's testimony is an excellent example of the many misleading statements made by Kelsey's paternal family. I'd like to address two of them: 1) The misstatement that Kathie didn't suspect Kelsey's legs being broken was abuse related until the doctor told her, and 2) The claim that Kathie's visits were taken from her.

To address the first claim--that Kathie was shocked to learn that Kelsey's broken legs were caused from abuse—I present a statement by the Judge who presided over the custody battle of Kelsey and who wrote a book about the final months of her life from his perspective on the bench:

*"[Kathie's aunt] accompanied Kathie to take Kelsey to see a specialist about Kelsey's legs after Raye Dawn had them casted. According to the aunt's testimony, Kathie told the doctor that Raye Dawn was suspected to have been abusing Kelsey."*[22]

---

[22] Key, Craig. *A Deadly Game of Tug of War: The Kelsey Smith-Briggs Story*. Garden City, NY: Morgan James Publishing, 2007.

In regards to the second misstated claim—that Kathie's visits were taken from her—Kathie's last supervised visit with Kelsey says it all. During this visit, Kathie was reportedly reprimanded for talking on the phone instead of spending time with Kelsey. According to witnesses, she became upset and told the DHS worker that she would not be at the next visit and that she would send someone to "check on Kelsey."[23]

On May 10, 2005, Kathie had a conversation with a DHS worker in which she was reprimanded for being on the phone during her visits with Kelsey. Kathie allegedly stated to the worker that she "knew Gayla and that she kicked Raye Dawn out of her home and wants no kids around her home and she will dump Kelsey with relatives." The worker reportedly asked Kathie if she knew this was happening. The worker reported that Kathie admitted that she did not, but "someone else might know of these types of instances." Kathie then demanded that her family get to spend time with Kelsey without supervision "like the Smiths."

After the hearing in June, 2005, April, Kelsey's stepmother, called DHS and told them that she was informed that the paternal family would no longer have visits with Kelsey. DHS reportedly informed April that wasn't true, and that supervised visits could still be arranged. According to witnesses, April eventually informed DHS that Kathie didn't like what had been said about her in court and that she would be taking over the supervised visits with Kelsey, in Kathie's place. (This is also evidenced in Kathie's deposition from

[23] See Appendix B – Exhibit 8

2009—Kathie's statement can be found in Appendix B - Exhibit 3 as well as Exhibit 8.)

As further evidence, following is another excerpt from Judge Key's book, *A Deadly Game of Tug of War: The Kelsey Smith-Briggs Story*:

*"From May 3rd to May 5th when Kelsey was taken into DHS custody, the Briggs family had supervised visitation. Their visits were also supervised when Kelsey was placed with Gayla while in DHS custody.*

*Kathie visited Kelsey for two hours every week at the DHS office. The CASA worker was provided notes from DHS workers who had supervised the visits between Kathie and Kelsey. The notes showed that Kelsey bit, pinched, hid under blankets, tore up books, and sometimes screamed at Kathie when she would visit Kelsey at the DHS office. Kathie claimed that wasn't true and that Kelsey screamed because she had taken scissors away from her. Kathie also claimed Kelsey scratched her when a DHS worker tried to take her away from her for a doctor's visit. She denied being bitten by Kelsey while being observed and claimed that Kelsey scratched her and acted cranky when she would get tired. Yet again, in Kelsey's obituary, she stated among Kelsey's favorite things to do was biting. All of the documentation by DHS directly contradicts Kathie's claims regarding Kelsey's reactions to her during supervised visits. But DHS noted that Kelsey always ran to and loved on her mother, Raye Dawn, during her supervised visits, some on the same day as Kathie's visit. Yet, Kathie wanted to regain guardianship of Kelsey until Mike Porter and Raye Dawn had classes or they figured out what happened to Kelsey. DHS did not see the Briggs home as an appropriate setting for Kelsey due to the questions about Kelsey's fractured legs and Kelsey's reaction to Kathie's visits.*

*In addition to Kathie's visits, [April] and Royce Briggs, [Lance's stepfather and Kathie's husband] shared in some of the supervised visitation with Kelsey, even though they were not specified visitation in the court order. Based on the DHS case worker, it was her recommendation that guardianship of Kelsey would never be returned to Kathie.*

*The DHS investigator also witnessed Kelsey losing her hair to the point that she had a bald spot the size of a baseball while living with Kathie. As soon as Kelsey was taken into DHS custody in May and then placed with her maternal grandmother, Gayla, she gained weight and her hair stopped falling out and eventually began to grow back. Kelsey continued to show physical signs of improvement while she was living with her maternal grandmother, Gayla."*[24]

On July 11, 2007, the third day of Raye's trial, Ms. Ballard reported on the KFOR Oklahoma City 10:00 PM news, "Difficult testimony today in the trial against an Oklahoma mother accused of abusing her child. The jury heard about repeated phone calls and reports to DHS warning them that someone was hurting Kelsey. Prosecutors believe that someone was Kelsey's mother, Raye Dawn Smith." [Ms. Ballard yelling at Raye at the courthouse:] "Why did you punch Kelsey in the stomach? Mike Porter said he saw you hold her down!" [Ms. Ballard:] "Raye Dawn

---

[24] Key, Craig. *A Deadly Game of Tug of War: The Kelsey Smith-Briggs Story*. Garden City, NY: Morgan James Publishing, 2007.

wouldn't answer questions about yesterday's testimony. That's when her ex-husband told jurors he saw her punch Kelsey in the stomach twice. Jurors also heard from the woman who took this picture of Kelsey's bruised bottom, her step-mother. She says she and others repeatedly told DHS officials that Kelsey was being abused."

To address the continual claims made by media and others that Kathie "did everything she could to protect Kelsey," in a sworn deposition that was taken on August 18, 2009, Kathie was asked, "How many reports did you make to DHS concerning Kelsey?" She answered, "Most of the reports that were made, I think I made one, maybe two. I think most of them were made by [April, Kelsey's step-mother]."[25]

The truth is that Kathie willingly gave up her supervised visits with Kelsey in June of 2005 because "she didn't like what DHS said about her." *How is that doing everything possible to save a child? Should not the needs of the child come before her feelings?* She addressed the following e-mail to over one hundred people after she quit visiting Kelsey. This e-mail has been promoted as her effort "to save Kelsey," but as you'll see from the language, the only concern she had was avoiding supervised visits for herself and Lance. This e-mail also clears up the issue of whether or not Kathie could appeal the Judge's decision to return Kelsey to Raye's home. This is a question that has been given many excuses and explan-ations while Kathie looked for the one that would stick. In this e-mail, she admits that her attorney told her she could appeal, but that she just couldn't afford it. The e-mail was—

[25] See Appendix B – Exhibit 9

as are all of Kathie's messages—lengthy. So, it has been cut down to just the issue at hand.

*"We need your help in clearing the name of a soldier fighting in Iraq... The mother returned Kelsey to me on Apr 14th with a sprained ankle. She went to the zoo with an aunt and fell off her platform shoes...The mother picked her up the following morning to take her to DHS for an assessment and kept her for the weekend. She was returned on Apr 18th and we were told her foot was still bothering her...On Mon the 25th the caseworker called and said the mother would be late bringing Kelsey home. She was in their office and both of Kelsey's legs were swollen and hot to touch. The mother said that was how she was four days earlier when she picked her up...The DHS worker told the mother she could keep her another day and take her for the cast the following day. I questioned how they had the right to let her keep her when I was the legal guardian, but it did not matter. The casts were put on and we went back to our schedule. During this ordeal, Kelsey was having some hair loss. The mother took her for blood test and everything was normal...[Someone] had her office make a referral to [Dr. S.]... I asked the mother if she would like to take her. She said "yes"...The mother had a death in the family and could not make that appointment and wanted me to reschedule. They could not see us for two weeks so I took her. [Dr. S.] told us that Kelsey did not have toddler fractures, and they were not stress fractures, but that some one had broken Kelsey's legs...I did not expect to hear this. I called...DHS the following morning to tell them what the Doctor said. That afternoon they called and wanted us to bring Kelsey to them and were placing her in a foster*

*home…they gave her to the maternal Grandmother. We went for a just cause hearing and it was determined that the broken legs could have happened at either house and since the mother had pointed a finger at us she could not be left in our home…My husband and I were given 4 hours per week of supervised visitation at the DHS office for the next month. The mother was given the same thing. During this time DHS was conducting an investigation…We went back to court on June 14th…[The CASA worker] stated when I visited, Kelsey screamed, kicked, pinched, and bit me. This was not all true. She also recommended that Kelsey be given back to the mother and we get one hour supervised visitation per month. She also recommended my son be given the same visitation when he returns. She also stated that Lance was allegedly in the Army because they did not have his address and she could not locate him through Government agencies. I really knew we were doomed at this moment. The DHS report was given to our attorney when court started. We were shocked at some of the things in it. There were many allegations made towards my son, his wife, and me that were unbelievable…In the DHS report it stated I had broken a court order when I let the mother have Kelsey for the make-up visitation so I failed to protect…The next morning the Judge came in and without explanation dissolved the guardianship and stated he over ruled anything the DHS recommended and he was returning the child to the mother and the grandparents would not be allowed to see her. The next court date is July 14th. The way I understand it that is when he will tell us if we have to take any classes…At this time I'm fighting to clear his [Lance's] name from all of this. They have him listed as an alleged perpetrator…I feel they are slandering his name while he's off fighting another war and when he comes home he may not be able to see his child. We were also told he might have to take classes as well. When he and the mother were married they both drank too much and did drugs. They battled constantly and she states he was abusive and I cannot deny or confirm that…Now he is fighting two wars…Our attorney says we can appeal this decision and is shocked at how the ruling went…We want to appeal, but at this time our financial situation will not allow for that. My son knew while he was gone he could save money for his family and get his truck fixed.*[26] *So far everything extra he would have had has gone to legal fees. Then when he comes home he will have his name attached to a deprived child petition and have to fight to see his child all over again. I do not believe this is how our military should be treated and I've talked to DHS and was told there is no appeal process for their reports. How can this be fair?… Raye Dawn has told the DHS many stories claiming abuse by Lance and even claimed he caused her to lose her first baby…She is trying to get sympathy from these workers and it is working…They have written these allegations as fact in this report, which seems like slander. We need help to clear my son's name and would like to see Kelsey again. It is not easy to ask for help, but my son has given up his freedom to fight for us and someone needs to fight for him…I have contacted almost every elected official in our area. [Rep. S.] and [another Representative's] offices are the only ones in Oklahoma who shared any concerns. I had*

[26] Emphasis by book author

*to get a Congressman from Nevada to give us any guidance and that is very sad. I feel it is time for the elected officials or someone, anyone in this state to help clear this soldier so that he may see his child when he returns home without restrictions. Since I first wrote this letter DHS contacted my daughter-in-law and told her she could visit Kelsey at their office for 2 hours per month supervised. They also told her when Lance returns home he will get the same visit. [April] has been given a service plan that she is more than willing to comply with. We were told Lance would have to have a service plan even though he was not here. That means if he gets a 15-day leave as some soldiers do he will see his 2-year-old child for one hour. We really feel she should be at the airport to see him arrive home...*

*Updated 8/3/05*

*[April] saw Kelsey...for one hour. My son was able to call her cell phone and talk to Kelsey for the first time in six weeks. When shown a picture of her Daddy, Kelsey did not know who he was right away. How sad is this?...She stated Kelsey looked well and seemed well adjusted."*

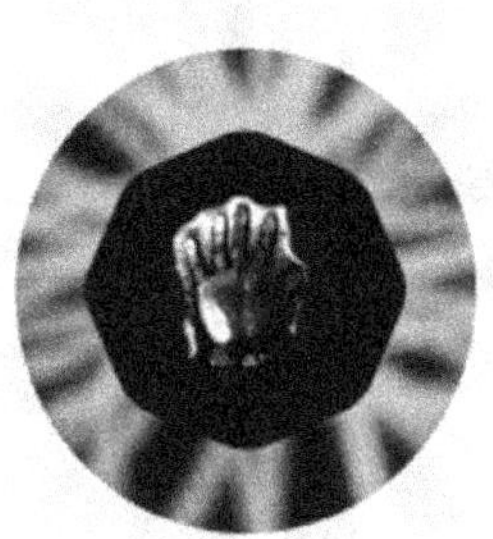

# 15 Day Four – Who Knows Who?

"A petty reason, perhaps, why novelists more and more try to keep a distance from journalists is that novelists are trying to write the truth and journalists are trying to write fiction."
~ Graham Greene

On the fourth day of Raye's trial, members of the local media droned on. Still having nothing positive to report didn't stop them from reporting. No matter what testimony was heard, the focus was still on the fiction the paternal family had pushed on the public, starting with the night Kelsey died. According to a witness, a sheriff appeared at the hospital after Kelsey was pronounced dead and asked, "Who's related to the governor?" and then stated, "The paternal grandmother called and said it was murder and the mother did it." Kelsey's step-mother's step-father is the cousin of the First Lady of Oklahoma. This is a tie that Kathie used to her advantage during her hate campaign, but it has since been severed by the step-family after the realization they were deceived by Kathie.

Also, at that time, and for days after her death, everybody thought Kelsey's death was caused by a seizure. Without knowing any facts or details because she wasn't in Kelsey's home at the time of her death, Kathie began building a case against Raye immediately, and the case continued to build from there.

On July 12, 2007, the KWTV Oklahoma City news at 5:00 AM reported, "Today is day four of the child abuse trial against Raye Dawn. Remember she's the mother of two-year-old Kelsey who's accused of enabling child abuse. Testimony has been emotional as family members from Kelsey's biological father's side took the stand yesterday. They talked about injuries they found on Kelsey's body and for months documented them. They took pictures of her bruises, two broken legs, and made calls to DHS. Kelsey's stepmother explained how she saw Kelsey deteriorate. 'It was very hard. It was plain as day something was wrong. At the time I felt like it wasn't going to be much longer before something happened to her.' Testimony from the prosecution's witnesses will continue today."

KJRH Tulsa at 11:00 AM: "A mother accused of neglecting her little girl before her death is hearing some negative testimony from her own relatives. Raye Dawn is on trial... The grandmother of little Kelsey [Kathie, the paternal grandmother] testified for the prosecution yesterday. She says Kelsey 'lost her spirit' and was neglected weeks before she died in 2005. Meanwhile, Kelsey's stepfather who's serving thirty years in prison for enabling child abuse testified he witnessed Raye Dawn harming the girl. The trial continues today."

In the following news clip, Ms. Ballard reports the other side in acknowledging the fact that a police officer testified that he believed Kathie was guilty of abuse. However, this report was given before Ms. Ballard and Ms. Follett chased the police officer down the street and mocked his opinion while the cameras were rolling.

KFOR Oklahoma City at noon: [by Ms. Ballard] "The trial of Raye Dawn continues... Today two former co-workers of Raye Dawn were called to the stand. They testified about a time when Raye Dawn told them she beat her daughter, Kelsey, with a hair brush through her diaper. A police officer who investigated bruises to the...toddler testified he suggested Kelsey's grandmother, Kathie, was the one responsible for the bruises to the child's bottom. The prosecution is expected to call state workers who were in charge of Kelsey's case to the stand today."

As a side note, I personally believe the police officer's scenario in that Kathie was responsible for the red marks on Kelsey's bottom. Kelsey had been with Kathie for at least two hours before Lance and April arrived at her home, and when the "injuries" were found, they were bright red. Kelsey had been at daycare all day that day and was only with Raye for thirty minutes to an hour before she went to meet Kathie. How could DHS automatically accuse Raye of causing the red marks when Kelsey hadn't been with Raye most of the day?

KWTV Oklahoma City at 4:30 PM: "It's now 4:30 and time to get up to speed on today's headlines. Kelsey's mother's trial continued today with her former boss taking the stand. Raye Dawn is facing abuse charges in the death of her two-year-old daughter in 2005. Today her former boss testified that Kelsey told her that Raye's boyfriend, Mike Porter was mean and then Raye Dawn replied that her daughter had a quote "attitude" and was jealous. Raye Dawn later married Mike Porter. They divorced after Kelsey's death. Mike Porter pleaded guilty to enabling child abuse and is serving thirty years. He testified earlier this week."

There were several media sources that ran this basic story. And then there are two media outlets that are very intriguing in that they report detailed versions of the events surrounding the version of a police officer's testimony and recollections. He both opines about his theories of how the events went down regarding abuse allegations and puts forth the theory that no one murdered Kelsey at all.

KOKH FOX Oklahoma City at 9:00 PM: [by Ms. Follett] "The...police officer who investigated Kelsey's broken collarbone and the twenty-nine bruises and abrasions on Kelsey's rear told the court he still does not think anyone abused Kelsey. In fact, he's not convinced she was murdered." [Ms. Ballard and Ms. Follett chased the police officer, Matt Byers, down the street and mocked him for his opinion—by Ms. Follett to Officer Byers] "How did the hairbrush get on Raye's bedroom floor?" [by Office Byers] "I don't know." [by Ms. Follett] "January 14, 2005 Officer Byers says Raye Dawn told him Kelsey broke her collarbone when she fell out of her crib and hit a plastic slide by her bed. As for the bruises, he told jurors it was his opinion Kelsey fell on a hairbrush he found sitting in her bedroom." [by Ms. Follett to Officer Byers] "I guess we should have had Kelsey in the Olympics if she can go from a slide to the middle of the room by the door to a hairbrush." [by Ms. Follett] DHS workers told jurors for every bruise Kelsey was in Raye's care. Despite all of those bruises on June 16th Judge Key says he was following the law when he let Kelsey go home with Raye Dawn against DHS recommendations. A decision one caseworker says she's never seen before." [by reported boyfriend of Ms. Follett--to Judge Key in a previously taped clip

(Judge Key was not allowed to testify at the trial)] "Can you tell us which law it was you said forced you to give her back?" [Judge Key] "No." [Ms. Follett] "Where did he get his information? This...police officer could not name the law on the witness stand but says he met with Judge Key in his chambers and told him he had to return Kelsey to Raye Dawn because the law required him to." [Ms. Follett to Officer Byers] "What is your relationship with the Smith family?" [Officer Byers] "Very brief, very little." [Ms. Follett] "DHS workers told jurors about Kelsey's life after Judge Key's decision. They say she was hurting herself, would not eat, lost weight, and the bruises continued. When a caseworker noted a tear on Kelsey's eyelid, she says she had a hard time believing Raye Dawn when she said she washed Kelsey's hair with adult shampoo and Kelsey rubbed her eye raw with a towel. On October 7th, that same caseworker says she saw Kelsey naked. She had no bruises. Four days later the medical examiner says she was murdered and covered with bruises." [Ms. Ballard to Officer Byers] "How can it not be homicide? You don't think someone killed her?" "The legal definition of a homicide is death by the hand of another." "You don't think someone killed her?" [by Officer Byers] "No." [Ms. Follett] "In a meeting without the jurors, the judge decided to allow testimony from another caseworker. Tomorrow we expect to hear from a woman who says she recorded Kelsey telling her mom, 'Daddy Mike hurt my legs' and Raye Dawn said, 'He could not have. You haven't been around him.' Back to you." [by anchor] "You can read all of [Ms. Follett's] notes on the testimony of Raye Dawn's co-workers. Just log on to our Web site at okcfox.com and click on daily links."

The far-reaching nature of the trial coverage may be seen in this next piece. Everyone seemed to be sharing some blame—police officers, the Department of Human Services, and so on. Overall, I think the shocking autopsy photos and the violence of the verbal assaults and overall clamor that were surrounding the spectacle left no question in anyone's mind, though, *surely Raye was guilty of something*. It was simply too much to take in that anyone could be innocent in a situation where a beautiful little girl had lost her precious life.

KJRH Tulsa at 10:00 PM: "Day five of Raye Dawn Smith's trial begins tomorrow morning. She's Kelsey Smith-Briggs's mother accused of enabling child abuse and neglect. Today prosecutors tried to prove that a...police officer showed preferential treatment regarding Smith's possible abuse to Kelsey. Defense attorneys tried to prove mistakes by the Department of Human Services when it failed to alert police of abuse. Kelsey's family says the system as a whole failed her." [by paternal family member] "It confirms what we have thought all the months with Kelsey and the time since that there was very incompetent people handling this." "Kelsey died at her home in 2005. Smith's attorneys claim Kelsey's stepfather, Michael Porter was responsible for her death."

# 16 Day Five - Trial Media Coverage

"The man who reads nothing at all is better educated than the man who reads nothing but newspapers."
~ Thomas Jefferson

On July 13, 2007, KFOR Oklahoma City started its news day with the 5:00 AM report on Raye's trial: "Raye Dawn Smith is accused of child abuse in the death of her two-year-old daughter, Kelsey...Testimony continues today with more people involved in Kelsey's case expected to testify."

Ms. Follett didn't skip a beat on her mission against Raye, even during the trial's weekend break. On Sunday, July 15, 2007, at 9:00 PM, Ms. Follett made another lengthy report on Raye's trial:

"Witnesses and family members involved in the trial have made Bristow, Oklahoma their home for the last week and they will be back tomorrow morning. First on FOX tonight, this small town has become home for a very big trial. Sidewalks Kelsey likely never walked down...her mom uses to walk to and from the courthouse where twelve people will decide if Raye Dawn walks away in handcuffs, or just walks away." [by a paternal family member] "There's a great possibility there are twelve people who are as ignorant about it as I am." [by Ms. Follett] Twelve people who walked into the courthouse wondering why television stations from across the state were in town." [by a bystander] "When I saw your car over here, I thought what would they be doing here in Bristow?" [by Ms. Follett] "The judge moved Raye Dawn's trial from Chandler to Bristow in hopes of finding a fair jury..." [by a bystander] "There are probably a lot of people in this town who don't know a thing about it." [by Ms. Follett] "The high-profile trial brings in lots of out-of-towners." [by a bystander] "Them things can happen anywhere's, you know, but that's the first one I've had happen here you know." [by Ms. Follett] "4,325 people live in Bristow." [by a bystander] "Farmer's town, used to be." [by Ms. Follett] "When something happens, the locals hear." [by a bystander] "Every time I see the police cars at somebody's house, my friend and I, we get in the car and run over." [by Ms. Follett] "People driving around in Bristow this week, notice squad cars lining the courthouse." [by a bystander] "I think people are very busy here." [by Ms. Follett] "Deputies are busy escorting witnesses in and out of Raye Dawn's trial." [by a bystander] "On this street right here, there's a lot of traffic—a lot of traffic here." [by Ms. Follett] "Traffic from Kelsey's stepfather, Mike Porter, who came from prison to testify...a trip each morning and evening from Raye Dawn and her mom to see the jury who will decide if her final trip will be to prison. Deputies are stationed outside the courthouse. To get inside the courtroom, you have to walk through a metal detector. Deputies say it's because this is a highly charged case with families who have a history of not getting along. So far we can report there have been no problems...."

Even though this reporter was obviously working very hard to acquire the various thoughts and feelings of many of the townspeople and those directly involved in the case, she seems to be unaware of just how insatiable her own appetite and – it seems from this story – everyone else's in this small community's were for the drama that was unfolding amidst them and their need to take part in the way that it unfolded. This kind of situation makes it impossible for people to remain objective and we see that in this reporter's words and actions throughout the time period of the trial and since. She has co-authored a book with another reporter (Ms. Ballard) regarding this trial and the experience she had with it in her own efforts to express her feelings and views about the case. Ms. Ballard admitted in a radio interview that the book was authored by the two reporters at the request of the Briggs family. These reporters have remained far from neutral or professional in their views and writings.

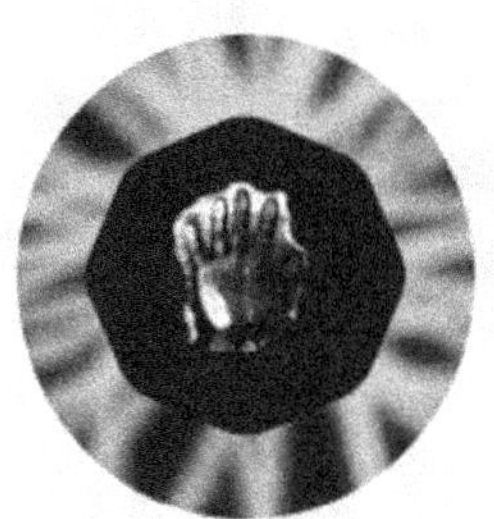

# 17 Day Six - Trial Media Coverage

"The advertisements are the most truthful part of a newspaper." ~ Thomas Jefferson

The second week of Raye's trial started with anticipation of a full week of defense testimony. However, since Raye's family couldn't afford expert witnesses and the judge denied the defense's request to allow the Judge who had heard the arguments during the final months of Kelsey's life to testify, the defense fell short with just friends and family testifying on Raye's behalf.

In a similar case in which a mother was wrongfully convicted after her son's murder and she spent three years in prison before an innocence project secured her release, Representative Paul Froelich raised the point that in serious cases where a defendant doesn't have sufficient funds to defend oneself, one is often at a disadvantage because the state has more than sufficient funds to prosecute but the defendant has neither the experience nor the funds to finance such a situation and, as such, is poorly suited for an equitable battle to take place.[27] This unfair battle is what Raye still faces to this day.

On July 16, 2007, KFOR Oklahoma City news at 5:00 AM reported, "Ahead, the trial of Raye Dawn continues this morning... She's accused of child abuse in the death of her daughter Kelsey..."

KWTV Oklahoma City at 4:00 PM: "The defense's case is next in the felony child abuse trial of Raye Dawn. The prosecution rested today after hearing from an orthopedic surgeon who examined Kelsey and says he has no doubt she abused two-year-old Kelsey who died in October, 2005. Raye Dawn denies the charges and her attorneys blame Kelsey's death on Smith's ex-husband Mike Porter who is now serving a thirty-year sentence for enabling child abuse. He testified against Raye Dawn last week."

During the trial, this doctor admitted that the information that led him to the conclusion given in his testimony had come directly from Kathie. He did not verify it with any source other than Kathie's statements to him. This is explained in detail in Raye's motion for a new trial, which is presented in a later chapter.

KJRH Oklahoma City at 10:00 PM: "It's the second week of testimony in the Raye Dawn Smith trial. She's accused of neglecting and enabling the abuse of two-year-old Kelsey. Today, Raye Dawn's mother took the stand. She says her daughter did not abuse the girl. Smith's attorneys say Kelsey's broken collarbone and several cuts and bruises could have been accidental, but

---

[27] http://wrongfulconvictions.blogspot.com/2006/08/julie-rea-harper-cases-raises.html

prosecutors say otherwise. Smith's attorneys say her ex-husband, Mike Porter, took Kelsey's life in 2005. He was charged with murder, but is serving a thirty-year sentence after pleading guilty to a lesser charge of enabling child abuse."

# 18 Charged!

"Truth is like the sun. You can shut it out for a time, but it ain't goin away." ~ Elvis Presley

Kathie and her family members have admitted that Mike Porter is a "liar," "monster," "murderer," and "disgusting." Yet, the focus is always on Raye. *Why?*

Among evidence against Mike Porter was a report on the contents of his computers. The report showed that on one of the computers numerous pornographic images were found with many of the pictures displaying acts of anal sex (an act that investigators and the district attorney reportedly believe that Mike Porter committed on Kelsey while Raye was picking his daughter up from school). Pornographic videos of anal sex were also found. Among the pornographic pictures were several pictures labeled with Mike Porter's name and they featured an erect penis. One picture, in particular, showed semen in the palm of a hand and had a baby bib on the floor in the background.

On May 16, 2005, less than a month after Mike Porter married Raye, "pdaddy_44" was his alleged chosen screen name in several Yahoo chat sessions with an unidentified person in which graphic language was used and his avatar was a picture of an erect penis with the picture labeled "Mikecock."

The same e-mail address that was used in some e-mail conversations with Kathie was also used to sign into AOL in online sessions during which the Web address www.-porno.com was typed directly into the search bar. This would not be the only pornographic site he reportedly visited. Some Web sites had the name "teen" in them as well as "sex," and he made multiple visits: 979; 740; 447; 424; 102; 60; and 15. In addition to porn, Kathie's Web site featuring Kelsey's picture along with plans to hold rallies and write letters to ensure that Raye was charged was visited on 711 occasions.

Aside from the evidence linking Mike Porter to Kelsey's alleged sexual assault and murder, witnesses state that Mike Porter appeared to be guilty at the hospital immediately following Kelsey's death. Among other eyewitness accounts, Mike Porter was reportedly seen by a police officer pounding his fist into a vehicle and yelling, "She'll never forgive me! She'll never forgive me!"

Though eyewitness reports and evidence verify that the correct charges were filed against Mike Porter (sexual assault and murder), he was supported by Kathie and her family members within days of Kelsey's death with e-mails and letters claiming that Raye had murdered Kelsey and that

Mike Porter was only guilty of "not protecting" Kelsey. The charges against him reflected the fact that investigators and the district attorney clearly did not agree with their point of view. However, this damaging evidence against Mike Porter was not presented at Raye's trial.

# 19 Day Seven - Trial Media Coverage

"Hastiness and superficiality are the psychic diseases of the twentieth century, and more than anywhere else, this disease is reflected in the press." ~ Alexander Solzhenitsyn

KSBI Oklahoma City at 5:30 PM: "A pastor testified today in the trial of Raye Dawn Smith. The pastor said Raye Dawn cried out to him at the hospital after her daughter died, asking, 'Why did God take my baby?'...he was the sixth defense witness called during the child abuse trial. Smith's attorneys today continued to try to show she did not behave like someone who would abuse or kill her daughter."

KFOR Oklahoma City at 6:00 PM: "They said in the trial the...mother accused of abusing her own child, little two-year-old Kelsey... Witnesses have testified she was a rambunctious and happy two-year-old....Today, Smith's attorneys presented witnesses who said they believed the father's family was abusive to Kelsey and they pointed the finger at Mike Porter, Kelsey's stepfather." [Witness:] "Mike Porter was a little bit strange at the funeral, not overly strange, but he came in and was holding the teddy bear, and he was being comforted by a teddy bear and I felt that odd. Everybody does their own grieving in their own way." [Anchor:] "Mike Porter is serving a thirty-year sentence after pleading guilty to allowing the abuse. The defense tried to get Craig Key called to the stand. You may remember, he's the Judge who sent Kelsey back to her mother months before her death, but the state protested, saying it would create a circus atmosphere. The presiding judge agreed and denied the testimony."

The following report was a rarity in the media coverage surrounding the case. In this news clip, the anchor uses the phrase, "chance to prove her innocence." Every other news report focused on the negative aspect of the trial with words such as "abuser," "neglect," and so on.

KFOR Oklahoma City at 10:00 PM: "Tonight on crime watch an Oklahoma mom accused of beating her own child gets a chance to prove she's innocent. Today Raye Dawn Smith and her lawyers were able to put their witnesses in front of the jury. Many of the family members who defended her saying she never disciplined her daughter, Kelsey, much less abused her. They pointed the finger of blame at the extended family of Kelsey's father. They say Kelsey would return home with bruises after visiting that side of the family. Yet, no one on that side has been charged with any crime in connection with the death. In fact, they were the ones who contacted DHS asking for an investigation. Also, today Smith's sisters testified Raye Dawn always cooperated with DHS by completing the programs the state required after numerous complaints of abuse. A pastor also took the stand to testify for Raye Dawn..."

# 20 It All Comes Down to Money

"Early in life I had noticed that no event is ever correctly reported in a newspaper." ~ George Orwell

Wednesday, July 18, 2007 was the last day of Raye's trial. Many Oklahomans were glued to their televisions for any word on the outcome of the case. Those who didn't want to watch it on the news showed up at the courthouse, leaving standing room only. After the guilty verdict was announced, the paternal family celebrated and, according to witnesses, ran through the hallways of the courthouse yelling that they wouldn't have to share the $15 million wrongful death lawsuit with Raye since she was convicted. (The lawsuit had been filed by Lance against the state immediately after Kelsey's death.) Lance's family and supporters celebrated their victory while others were crushed and felt as if there had been a second death in the maternal family, myself included.

A short news clip of Raye exiting the courthouse was shown continuously on every news channel. She was led from the courthouse with her hands cuffed behind her back, screaming, "I don't understand! I love my baby!" Many people shared her confusion. Plain-clothed police officers who were amongst the audience throughout the trial told Raye's attorney, "There is no way this girl will be found guilty." The sentiments were seconded by courthouse employees. But at the time, nobody realized just how tainted the jury had allegedly become by members of the media who had spent ten days reporting only the prosecution's (a.k.a. the paternal family's) version of events, nor had they heard the claims by witnesses that members of the jury had made their judgments based on outside sources.

Mark Fuhrman described this type of reporting on page 66 of *The Murder Business: How the Media Turns Crime into Entertainment and Subverts Justice*. Fuhrman stated, "...The vast majority of people in the media are not concerned with truth, justice, and the American Way. They're concerned with scooping the other channels. Many of the young producers of these shows don't have the worldliness even to understand the implications of what they do. They're producing shows that cover law enforcement, but they generally know nothing of how law enforcement works. This all started with the O.J. Simpson case. The media discovered how covering crime can be a low-overhead, massively profitable reality show. They don't have to pay for any actors or backdrops or anything. And it sells like crazy."[28] And in this case it did...

On this final day of trial at 4:30 PM, KFOR Oklahoma City aired the following report by Ms. Ballard: "A tense afternoon in Oklahoma...jurors are behind closed doors at this hour deciding the fate of Raye Dawn. Will she go to prison for felony child abuse in the death of her daughter, two-year-old Kelsey?"

Just an hour and a half after her former broadcast, Ms. Ballard stated, "Tonight will be the first night that Raye Dawn spends behind prison bars...Apparently, the jury agreed with the district attorney and the prosecution in this case and slapped her with this guilty verdict for enabling child abuse and sentenced her to twenty-seven years in prison...justice for Kelsey is what the family has been fighting for all along." Her choice of phrase, "slapped her with this guilty verdict," to me, showed her emotional reaction to the verdict.

KTUL Tulsa at 6:00 PM: "A jury has just reached a verdict in a child abuse trial. Raye Dawn Smith is charged in the death of Kelsey Smith-Briggs. She was found guilty. They deliberated swiftly, guilty of felony child abuse. A recommendation of twenty-seven years... Family members and friends are now able to speak. The gag order has been lifted."

KOKH FOX Oklahoma City at 9:00 PM: [Ms. Follett:] "Raye Dawn Smith was quite emotional when she heard the verdict....I have to remind you that there is a guilty verdict here but no one has been convicted of the murder of Kelsey. She was convicted of enabling child abuse." [Anchor:] "Twenty-seven years in prison...how big of a surprise was that to people in the courtroom?" [Ms. Follett:] "There was a lot of discussion over whether

[28] From the book *The Murder Business* by Mark Fuhrman. Copyright©2009. Published by Regnery Publishing, Inc. All rights reserved. Reprinted by special permission of Regnery Publishing Inc., Washington, D.C.

or how much she would get if she was actually convicted, especially when the district attorney told the jurors he believes Mike Porter is the murderer so how much would the jury come back and give her as a sentence if they found her guilty of either child abuse or enabling child abuse? Even Lance, Kelsey's paternal father, said he couldn't believe it when they said twenty-seven years. He kind of looked to the side and said, 'Is it two? Is it seven?'" Ms. Follett briefly smiled and then regained her professional composure as she relayed the number of years of Raye's sentence.

KFOR Oklahoma City at 10:00 PM: [Ms. Ballard:] "...Minutes after the verdict, Raye Dawn Smith left the courthouse in handcuffs crying, screaming, 'I don't understand! I love my baby!' Her tears came too late. Raye Dawn's attorney disagrees with the jury and says his client didn't do anything wrong." [Raye's Defense Attorney:] "There was a lot of pressure to prosecute this girl. It came from the media. It came from the Briggs family. I think it took four months. Why did it take four months for the district attorney to file charges?" [Ms. Ballard:] "...Tonight, she is sitting behind bars, spending her first night as a convicted felon."

Witnesses who attended the trial state that the judge ordered the jury to reach their decision by 6:00 PM that evening, leaving very little time to reach a consensus. From outside the jury room screams and yelling could be heard. One juror in particular, "Celia," joined Kelsey's Purpose and posted immediately after the trial. During deliberation, she held up Kelsey's autopsy photos in an attempt to persuade the jurors to give Raye a life sentence and screamed, "this is a life sentence!" causing the jurors to make an emotional decision, not one based on facts or evidence.

The autopsy photographs were only part of the deception. This was evident in the media's focus, which was clearly not on the full story, but on the negativity toward Raye and her family that had been promoted since Kelsey's death. There were many things never discussed in the press, such as the evidence through witness testimony and pictures that told the factual story. Members of the media ignored what was presented in the trial and trudged ahead with the "paternal family approved" message. As Kelsey's story swelled into something malformed and grossly severed from the actual events of her life, so did the message. The news reporters abandoned the facts and adopted the story from the paternal family without questioning, investigating, or discovering the truth behind the smokescreen of lies. Statements have been made such as "ten months of documented abuse" and "[Kelsey was] tortured for ten months" and "[Kelsey had] a lifetime of bruises and broken bones." There is no basis for fact in any of these statements. Any attempts made to try to correct the media's overblown story have been met with denial and silence. Sadly, in turn, Kelsey will always be remembered in the minds of Oklahomans as the girl with the bruised cheek, red eye, and two broken legs. The facts behind the injuries; the hit and run by a drunk driver; the proven fact that her legs were reportedly broken while with Kathie—these facts will never be shared in the Oklahoma media. The fact-based details of Kelsey's life and death will be silenced because the story concocted by Kathie and Lance sells better than the truth. This is a fact, and a hard lesson learned by those who love Kelsey and want her remembered as who she really was.

## *REALITY HITS HOME*

On the morning after the verdict, I was still in shock over what had happened. I had last spoken with Raye's mom, Gayla, just a day or two before the final verdict, and she was in good spirits about the expected outcome. During the trial, Gayla and Raye were staying in a camper they had parked in an RV park somewhere near Bristow, and they had no access to television or other media reports. They were at peace, cut off from what the rest of Oklahoma was seeing. Also, the district attorney had offered Raye another plea—a blind plea for admitting she spanked Kelsey with a hairbrush through her diaper. Like the previous plea offer of five years in and five years probation, Raye turned it down. She wasn't going to admit to anything she didn't do, not even to receive less time in prison. To Raye and Gayla, this seemed a promising sign that Raye would be found "not guilty." *How could she be found otherwise?* The facts did not prove the case that Kathie had worked so hard to build against her.

Unlike Raye and Gayla, I watched the news. I wanted to know what the media was saying, and it wasn't good. They focused solely on the negative testimony from Raye's trial. They had nothing good to say, and with the constant coverage and what I had recently discovered on the Internet, I knew she would be found guilty. However, twenty-seven years was a sentence I never expected, and it was a devastating blow. My family told me I acted like someone had died. I couldn't eat. I couldn't sleep. My heart was broken for Raye and her family.

The feelings of despair were compounded with a news report the morning after the verdict that showed Lance discussing his feelings about Raye's fate. He stated, "I hope prison is hell for Raye Dawn…I hope they put Kelsey's picture all over the prison to remind her of what she did so that the prisoners will beat her every day." I couldn't believe that a reporter actually allowed this side of Lance's character to be displayed on the news. Though mean, the statement didn't surprise me. I'd read the police reports that clearly proved Lance's violent tendencies. The shocking part of the report is that I've never seen nor heard anything similar to those thoughts from Lance directed at Mike Porter. If Raye is "equally as guilty as Mike Porter" as Lance stated on camera, why has he never publicly displayed any dislike or ill wishes for him?

Also, Kathie has stated, "Kelsey is smiling down from heaven now that her mother is in prison." This is a sad statement from a grandmother and a mother, to think a child would be happy that her mom is locked away.

Several days after the verdict, the maternal family received a card from a woman who had been a potential juror, but ultimately wasn't selected. Her kind words were comfort to Raye's family when they needed comforting the most. They needed an outsider to see what they saw—a grieving mother who loved her child. She did. She had decided to stay and watch the entire trial. She saw the same testimony and evidence as the jurors. Yet her verdict would have been much different than what was given based on her observations and the facts. This person was appalled by what she witnessed in the courtroom when the verdict was passed down, along with the rest of us who knew the truth.

In September of 2007, this anonymous post was left on a random blog from that same woman:

"I was called for jury duty but not one of the final 12; however, I attended every day because when I found out what the case was about, I had to know what really happened. You see I am vehement when it comes to child abuse and must admit the first 2 days of the trial, (I previously knew nothing of the case nor any of the people concerned on either side....I do not get OK Cy area news where I live) I just had to see what a vile and horrible person Raye Dawn must be and how could she???? Well let me tell you, by the 3rd day of the trial after listening and observing families on both sides and seeing the arrogance and hearing Mike Porter's testimony (he wanted Raye Dawn to suffer as he was by going to prison).

I saw and heard all the evidence presented on both sides as well as having the opportunity to mingle outside during breaks with those who were in the courtroom.... namely Lance and his 'supporters'...I saw by his actions each day as he flirted with all the pretty girls and buddied up to the reporters while he strutted around trying to impress anyone who was dumb enough to fall for his act, that he definitely was not there out of love and concern for his darling Kelsey....he could have cared less...

But Raye Dawn was a quiet, scared, nervous girl whose family was steadfastly standing beside her...quietly remaining out of sight rather than jumping in front of the cameras and reporters hungry for news. By the end of the 4th day, I knew in my heart that any grandmother that would put her 'beloved' grandchild (I have 3) through the turmoil and pulling back and forth that Kathie put Kelsey through could not have been truly concerned about the child. I saw proof that the timeline of dates showed Kelsey was with her aunt at the zoo when the first leg was fractured and with g'ma Kathie when the second one mysteriously came up showing a fracture also. I saw the evidence and testimonies of how while in DHS custody, Kelsey reacted during visits with Raye Dawn by running to her and hugging her and played happily with her during their visits. When her g'ma Kathie came to visit, she hid and kicked, bit her and ran from her trying to get away.....those actions spoke multitudes to me...what would you come away with after reviewing that? Of course Raye Dawn didn't want to admit that she might be carrying Lance's second child...after all he had killed the first one with a punch to her pregnant belly! Would you want him to know? DHS was in the home as well as CASA and CHUBS observing Raye Dawn and Kelsey regularly during the investigations....they never saw any indications of abuse by Raye Dawn to Kelsey...rather a loving mother trying desperately to keep a jealous grandmother from taking her child away because she had rejected the abusive father of that child. Raye Dawn had her hands full trying to do anything she could to do whatever was asked of her to keep Kelsey. When handsome Mike Porter came alone [*sic*] she was vulnerable and saw him as a knight in shining armor who could help. [Name deleted] | 09.02.07 - 8:22 pm"

# 21 Motion for a New Trial

"Justice denied anywhere diminishes justice everywhere." ~ Martin Luther King Jr.

Raye's family members leaped into action immediately following her conviction. They hired a new attorney—the man who had defended one of the Oklahoma City bombing conspirators and who is practiced in high-profile cases—and a motion for a new trial was submitted. Excerpts from that motion are as follows:

The State of Oklahoma v. Raye Dawn Smith, Case No. CF-2007-134 Defendant's Amended Motion and Brief in Support of Defendant's Motion for New Trial and Request for Evidentiary Hearing

October 22, 2007

COMES NOW Raye Dawn Smith, by and through her undersigned counsel, Stephen Jones, and moves this Court to grant her a new trial pursuant to OKLA. STAT. tit. 22 sec. 952. Having timely filed her Motion for New Trial on October 10, 2007, and to file a brief in support of a motion for new trial, together with supporting affidavits and other evidence and all parties and counsel having signed an approved order memorializing same and this Court granting same, submits this Amended Motion and Brief in Support to show that her substantial rights under the United States and Oklahoma Constitutions were prejudiced. Ms. Smith will present evidence in support of her motion at the evidentiary hearing concerning the factual matters set forth herein. In support of same, Defendant Raye Dawn Smith shows this Court as follows.

***INTRODUCTION AND OVERVIEW***

There is reason to believe that the case brought against Raye Dawn Smith may have had sufficient irregularities as to call into question the basic fairness that is the linchpin of our system of justice. An innocent woman has been convicted of a crime she never committed. In addition, she lost both of her children, one to death (most likely a homicide) and the other to the bureaucratic sweep of the Department of Human Services. These miscarriages of justice are, happily, only occasional, but they do happen. In this case, the miscarriage was not accidental or inadvertent. It was the result of a deliberate plan which was instigated from the venomous hatred of the Defendant by her former mother-in-law, the bizarre, erratic, and unsettling behavior of her abusive former husband, and insatiable appetite of the hyenas of the media built on sensational and untrue rapid fire "coverage" as "news" so that they shaped the events and public perception, and finally the trial itself. If there is a parallel to another recent case, it would be the Australian woman Lindy Chamberlain who was convicted in 1982 of killing her 9-week-old daughter, Azaria. There, as we now know all too well, half-baked and overstated incriminated forensic evidence and a profile infused with innuendo – including a media circus, and an unprofessional prosecutor – she was convicted and given a sentence of life. Four years later, she was released. The "evidence" proved to be "cooked" and "unsafe." Americans are, of course, familiar with the story through the talents of Meryl Streep, who played Chamberlain in "A Cry in the Dark." That case, and this one, are cautionary notes on how flawed evidence, perjury, overzealous prosecution, and a public campaign of vilification together with intrusive rampaging media which practiced no restraint of truth telling, objectivity, balance or fairness can influence unfairly the outcome and skewer justice. Like the plague of locust, the media descended upon all participants and simply ran over those in their path, egged on as they were by a self-seeking and self-promoting ex-husband and ex-mother-in-law.

...In summary, what occurred is this. The evidence suggests, quite strongly, that Kelsey Smith-Briggs was killed as a result of the actions of Michael Porter. Mr. Smothermon (the district attorney) has said as much...But, the Briggs family were less interested in Michael Porter than they were in prosecuting Raye Dawn Smith. But, there was little evidence to answer to by Raye Dawn Smith unless Michael Porter became a State's witness. So, incredible as it is to believe, the charged murderer of a two-year-old innocent child escaped justice by false testimony against his wife, the child's mother, and Mr. Smothermon and [the hired prosecutor] were party to this disgraceful, immoral, illegal, unconstitutional and unprofessional travesty. The evidence was clear that Michael Porter lied about Raye Dawn Smith. He not only contradicted half a dozen different oral and written statements (both sworn and unsworn), but his testimony was not supported by any medical evidence and could not be, honestly. So, he bought himself escape from the possibility of a death sentence, of life without parole, to a sentence that might be modified in the future, or even if not, would eventually result in his release, assuming a normal life expectancy. Mr. Smothermon facilitated this because by so doing he escaped the political wrath of Kathie Briggs. He had to have known that Kathie Briggs would come after him, as she did Judge Key, unless he went after Raye Dawn Smith. To prosecute Raye Dawn Smith, *it was necessary to let Michael Porter walk away from murder of a child.*

As disappointing as these actions were, they do not begin to compare with the lack of professionalism of the so-called medical witnesses who egregiously and unprofessionally dishonored themselves by manipulation of the honest medical evidence to support their view of alleged "child abuse." There was in reality little evidence that Kelsey Smith-Briggs had ever been abused until the day she died. The photographs of the alleged bruises and marks are not those of abuse. The fractures on her legs are not resulting from abuse nor is the collarbone break.

For Kathie Briggs knew from her own experience and observation that the Department of Human Services always opens a file and creates an investigation on a "referral." So, when she appeared in Dr. [S's] office, she immediately prejudiced the medical history of the child by talking about the mother and her "counseling" in "anger management." Dr. [S] having heard the magical words, decided that the child's injuries were the result of possible abuse and took the casts off. No primary treater of the child imagined child abuse. And then, to add to the coup de grace, Dr. [B] appears, a man who exaggerates his credentials and ability in trials, who attacks physicians personally and professionally who testify to contrary opinions, and who even files complaints against lawyers who have dared to challenge him. Less known is the other [B]. The carping critic, the angry polemist who writes articles for "peer review" which mainly consist of scathing and unprofessional comments against a host of doctors more experienced, more qualified and more talented than him.

All of these coming together—a benign court, a politically motivated district attorney, an available "assistant," a media in a highly competitive environment, and a grandmother who sought to bring herself to the center of the controversy—all resulted in a failure of due process of law.

We end as we began, an innocent woman was convicted of a terrible crime. We cite here the authority and the evidence which leads to no other conclusion than that.

On July 18, 2007, the jury returned a verdict of guilty of one count of enabling child abuse against Raye Dawn Smith and recommended a 27-year sentence of imprisonment…

**PROPOSITION 1: THE INFORMATION FILED AGAINST THE DEFENDANT WAS NOT FILED IN SUBSTANTIAL CONFORMITY WITH THE LAWS OF THE STATE OF OKLAHOMA AND IS VOID IN THAT IT IS NOT SIGNED BY A DULY ELECTED AND QUALIFIED DISTRICT ATTORNEY OF POTTAWATOMIE AND LINCOLN COUNTIES**

Under the Oklahoma Constitution and Statues, the prosecution of a criminal case must be brought in the name of the State of Oklahoma and must be signed by the duly qualified and elected district attorney for the district in which the alleged offense was committed…On February 24, 2006, an Information was filed and signed in the name of the "State of Oklahoma, County of Lincoln" by Richard L. Smothermon against Raye Dawn Smith for two felony counts…At the bottom of the first page of the Information, Mr. Smothermon signs his name purporting to be the District Attorney for Lincoln County, which is in District 23. This Information is void on its face; it is a false document. Mr. Smothermon may have very well taken the oath of office as district attorney for the Twenty-Third District, but his legal residence is in Oklahoma County, which is District 7. He is not the qualified district attorney…Pursuant to OKLA. Stat. tit. 19, sec.

215.2(B), to qualify as a candidate for the office of district attorney a person must have been a resident of the State of Oklahoma for two (2) years, the district for three (3) months, a duly licensed attorney for five (5) years, and be at least twenty-eight (28) years of age, prior to the date of filing for office. Richard Smothermon was elected to serve District 23 as district attorney in 2002 and 2006. District 23 encompasses two counties—Pottawatomie and Lincoln. Contrary to the statute, Mr. Smothermon was not a resident of District 23 when he filed his Declaration of Candidacy…

The Court in Lincoln County never had jurisdiction to try the case against Raye Dawn Smith because neither the Information or Amended Felony Information were signed by a duly qualified and elected district attorney of District 23 or his legally constituted assistant. Therefore, the Court did not have the jurisdiction and power to move the case to Creek County, Bristow Division on a change of venue motion. The Information issued against Raye Dawn Smith is void and her conviction and sentence are also. The Office of District Attorney of District 23 should be declared vacant and a duly qualified individual appointed as district attorney.

[Mr. Smothermon moved into District 23 shortly after Raye Dawn's attorney brought his residency into question.]

**PROPOSITION 2: A SPECIAL, HIRED PRIVATE PROSECUTOR WAS ALLOWED TO PARTICIPATE IN THE TRIAL IN VIOLATION OF THE LAW**

[Ms. H] was an active participant in the prosecution of Raye Dawn Smith. Disguised as a "part-time assistant district attorney for Lincoln County," [Ms. H] signed the Amended Felony Information for Raye Dawn Smith on March 16, 2007….Touted by the news as a "private practice attorney" and "hired prosecutor," [Ms. H] was hardly a backseat driver at trial but rather an integral part of the prosecution…In fact, [Ms. H] conducted 80 percent of the trial herself. She conducted voir dire. She took an active role in questioning and cross-examining the majority of the witnesses, and she delivered the State's first closing argument…Under Oklahoma law, however, [Ms. H] never should have been involved in the investigation or prosecution against Raye Dawn Smith. Moreover, she had no authority under the law to sign the Amended Felony information.

The laws authorizing the appointment of special prosecutors in Oklahoma was declared invalid in Driskell v. Goerke, 1977 OK CR 123, 562 p. 2d 157…

If one were to assume for argument's sake that [Ms. H] was a duly authorized part-time assistant district attorney for the Pottawatomie County District Attorney's Office, there is still one problem that cannot be explained away no matter how it is dressed up. And that is, under Oklahoma law, [Ms. H] cannot serve as a part-time assistant district attorney and a private criminal defense lawyer.

The State contends she is a part-time assistant district attorney. Yet, on March 26, 2007 and August 2, 2007, [Ms. H] filed entries of appearance in two separate criminal cases in Oklahoma County on behalf of the criminal defendants in those cases. See Oklahoma County Case No. CF-2007-840 and CF-2007-4046…Both of these cases are pending, and [Ms. H] entered her appearance at a time the State District Attorney's Council and Mr. Smothermon asserts she was employed as a part-time assistant district attorney in Lincoln and Pottawatomie Counties. She entered appearances at a time when she was assisting in the prosecution against Raye Dawn Smith. [From Howerton v. State, 1982 OK CR 12, 640 P. 2d 566, 567: A member of the bar who is a part-time district attorney may not be appointed to defend persons within or outside of the jurisdiction in which he serves as assistant district attorney. A district attorney represents the State of Oklahoma to enforce its criminal laws. His first and foremost duty is to represent the State in criminal proceedings, and, he cannot represent a defendant where the State of Oklahoma is the opposing party. One cannot adequately serve two masters; these positions are inherently antagonistic and irreconcilable.]…As evidenced, the Court did not have jurisdiction to try the case against Raye Dawn Smith because there was no verified Information signed by an executive officer empowered under the laws to prosecute; therefore, her conviction and sentence are, in effect, void.

**PROPOSITION 3: THE JURY RECEIVED EVIDENCE OUT OF COURT, WAS NOT PROPERLY SEQUESTERED DURING THE TRIAL AND IN VARIOUS RECESSES WAS PERMITTED TO BE**

**EXPOSED TO MEDIA COVERAGE AND TO CONVERSATIONS WITH MEMBERS OF THE BRIGGS FAMILY**

It goes without saying that this was anything but a typical criminal case. It is a case that achieved national attention. It is a case one might be reminded of every day, driving down any street in Oklahoma and see pink heart-shaped stickers on back windows and rear bumpers of automobiles with Kelsey's face on them. In fact, one legal analyst for KOTV News Channel 6 in Tulsa asserted on the second day of trial that "The case has received as much publicity for a local case as any case in the State with the exception of the McVeigh and Nichols trials." He added that "the public has already heard much of what will be presented in the trial for Kelsey's mother, Raye Dawn Smith."

This tragic saga started long before February 2006, when the accused was charged. Litigation involving the life of Kelsey Smith-Briggs started more than three years ago when Kathie Briggs, Kelsey's paternal grandmother, petitioned for grandparent visitation rights in September 2004. The custody battle began to heat up in January 2005 when the Department of Human Services became involved.

Lance Briggs and Raye Dawn Smith were married on July 15, 2000. It was a tumultuous marriage that involved serious physical abuse by Mr. Briggs toward Raye Dawn that resulted in domestic abuse charges. Mr. Briggs pled guilty to physically assaulting and battering Raye Dawn and was ordered to attend anger management and pay various fines. The marriage was short-lived, and the two divorced in July

2002. At the time of their divorce, Raye Dawn did not know she was pregnant with Kelsey. After the divorce, Mr. Briggs broke into Raye Dawn's home several times, vandalizing it and leaving threatening letters. On December 28, 2002, Kelsey was born...After Kelsey broke her collarbone in early January 2005, the custody battle ensued full-throttle, and from that point forward clear up until Kelsey's death on October 11, 2005, until the conclusion of the criminal trial against Raye Dawn Smith, Kathie Briggs made it her mission in life to destroy Raye Dawn's life.

[Footnote states as follows: Kathie Briggs has not been shy at expressing her animosity and hatred toward Raye Dawn. Even after the trial and sentencing, Ms. Briggs has continued to post slanderous comments on her Web site about Raye Dawn and members of her family. Moreover, she continues to accuse members of Raye Dawn's family of committing crimes. Following Raye Dawn's sentencing hearing, Kathie Briggs told *The Tulsa World* that Raye Dawn was "demented" and that she "Now believes she is God."]

Moreover, Dr. [G] testified at trial that this [the collarbone] was the most commonly broken bone in the human body. Yet, from that point forward Kathie Briggs, who reportedly showed up on the courthouse steps in Pottawatomie County with her own children years ago and said she could no longer take care of her children and who took almost two years to complete her treatment plan and to have her children returned to her by DHS would bring Kelsey to the Emergency Room for every little bump, bruise or scratch. See

Craig Key, *A Deadly Game of Tug of War: The Kelsey Smith-Briggs Story,* p. 18...Kathie Briggs and her family made referral after referral to DHS....Kathie Briggs admitted at Raye Dawn's trial to pushing the criminal case against Raye Dawn. According to Judge Key, Kathie Briggs and her supporters picketed the office of Richard Smothermon until the political pressure grew so strong that on February 24, 2006, criminal charges were filed against Raye Dawn...She admitted also that she had reported Raye Dawn to the Meeker Police Department for an expired tag....In May 2005 Officer Matt Byers from the Meeker Police Department investigated Kathie Briggs for stalking and harassing Raye Dawn...

The case has received an enormous amount of publicity both before trial, during and after. According to transcripts of close captioning of local news provided by Newslink there were 910 stories reported on Kelsey Smith-Briggs on local television channels...from Kelsey's death in October 2005 up until the date the defense filed its change of venue motion on May 11, 2007...The number of stories ran were the equivalent to almost two stories daily since the start of the case. Along with the extensive television coverage, *The Daily Oklahoman* Newspaper was shown by Newok.com to have produced at least 59 stories about Kelsey Smith-Briggs prior to May 11, 2007...The *Shawnee News-Star* also provided extensive coverage by publishing at least 62 articles in its newspaper and Web site chronicling the events of the case...On KWTV News Channel 9's Web site at newsok.com, there is still a continuing coverage link that takes the public directly to stories about the case.

Sealed DHS records concerning Kelsey were “leaked” to the press…Pictures of Kelsey following an automobile accident in August 2005 were given to the press and stories were ran claiming her injuries from the automobile accident were abuse.

In conjunction with the news media before trial, Kathie Briggs and the rest of Kelsey’s family on the paternal side actively voiced their opinion and bias through the use of the Internet. Kathie Briggs established the Web site titled “Kelsey’s Purpose,” shortly after Kelsey’s death in October 2005. The Web site’s stated purpose includes seeking “justice for her killer(s).” Since Kelsey’s death in October 2005, the Briggs family have used Kelsey as a poster child for money. They have continued to exploit her sad death for their own financial and emotional gain and gratification. On May 18, 2006, Lance Briggs filed a $15-million dollar lawsuit in Oklahoma County District Court alleging a systemwide failure to investigate who was abusing Kelsey. See Oklahoma County Case No. CJ-2006-4125. The case was moved to federal court in Oklahoma City…See also U.S. District Court Western District of Oklahoma Case No. CV-06-00677-HE. On June 5, 2006, Lance Briggs filed a second civil suit in Pottawatomie County Case No. CJ-2006-506. On October 12, 2007, Pottawatomie County District Judge Douglas Combs dismissed the case against the two doctors and the clinic, ruling that the lawsuit filed by Lance Briggs had no legal standing and was based solely to garner sympathy.

Kathie Briggs and members of her family also used the death of Kelsey to influence Judge Key's re-election in Lincoln County. The overriding outcome in the judicial election hinged on the events of the case. A letter written by Kathie Briggs expounding the bias viewpoint of members of the paternal family was distributed throughout Lincoln County through door-to-door delivery, passed out through political rallies, and mailed to all registered voters… Hundreds of fliers and thousands of bumper stickers were passed out at numerous rallies held by the organizers of Kelsey's Purpose…Further, billboards with Kelsey's face plastered on them were placed on Interstate 40 west of Shawnee in Pottawatomie County and on Highway 18 just north of Meeker. Kathie Briggs admitted at trial that she sponsored Sheila Kirk to run against Judge Key…

Sheila Kirk also exploited the death of Kelsey in her run for judge against Judge Key. For example, in late October 2006, she did a direct mailing showing Lance Briggs in his military uniform looking down on Kelsey….Kathie Briggs called every voter in Lincoln County several times with a pre-recorded message asserting that Judge Key had returned Kelsey to an abusive home against the recommendation of the district attorney and DHS and asking voters to vote for Sheila Kirk as Associate District Judge on November 7, 2006 because she had promised Kelsey to seek to hold those who failed her accountable…On November 7, 2006, Judge

Key lost his bid for re-election. Sheila Kirk represented Raye Dawn as the attorney in her divorce case against Lance Briggs. Clearly, Ms. Kirk owed an ethical duty to Raye Dawn as a former client to remain conflict free and not use or reveal information relating to that representation to the disadvantage of Raye Dawn. See e.g. OKLA. Stat. tit. 5, Ch. 1, App. 3-A, Rule 1.8(b) and 1.9(c). Clearly, exploiting an attorney's former client – without legal authorization – to get elected judge is not in the best interests of that former client, and, in the very least, has an appearance of impropriety. Joining forces with your former client's ex-in-laws (one of whom was a party against whom Ms. Kirk represented Raye Dawn) whose sole mission in life is to send your former client to prison for the rest of her life is not professional...

Legislation in Oklahoma was passed in Kelsey's name, i.e., The Kelsey Smith-Briggs Child Protection Reform Act, House Bill 2840. Kathie Briggs was instrumental in getting this legislation passed. She testified at trial that she lobbied at the Legislature...She also testified before the Senate Judiciary Committee which approved the measure in March 2006.

On June 27, 2007, just days before Raye Dawn's criminal trial, former Judge Key announced publication of his book, *A Deadly Game of Tug of War: The Kelsey Smith-Briggs Story*. As of June 27, 2007, the book was available online at www.judgekey.com. [Books were being pre-sold, but copies were not delivered until the end of Raye's trial.] Judge Key was a proposed witness for the defense with relevant admissible evidence, but this Court ruled that he could not even take the stand despite the fact that he had written a book about the case, the book had been released, he had no immunity, and his testimony would have directly contradicted testimony from the State's witnesses. [A footnote states: Note that Ms. Smith's trial counsel made an offer of proof on July 16, 2007 concerning this issue.]

The newspaper and television are not the only negative image delivery system in the market that has carried reports on Raye Dawn. Rather, the public has received an inordinate amount of other negative media impressions of Raye Dawn through radio, alternative publications and web "bloggers." The blogging traffic on this case has been extreme in language and quantity…One posted message by a female named [JB] discloses that Ms. [B] handed out over 100 fliers and stickers on the "Kelsey cause" to fellow classmates at the University of Oklahoma…Other posts report floats in parades and booths at festivals statewide were sponsored in Kelsey's name. The speech given by Kathie Briggs at the "Justice for Kelsey" rally on the steps of the state capitol was published in Post No. 2 by "Aunt Bean" on the site. The statements by Kathie Briggs in these blogs alone are appalling, and these statements were made while she was under a gag order….The following are only a few, but they certainly demonstrate Kathie's hostility, hatred and mission to ruin Raye Dawn.

"If ever anyone could plea insanity, it could have been her. She seems to have come by it honestly as her family shares her views." By Kathie Briggs

"Raye Dawn is just plain backwards if she as a mother could not see her child was in trouble…Raye Dawn's daughter is dead and she did NOTHING to stop it. Playing DUMB is not an excuse." By Kathie Briggs

People on Kathie Briggs' site personally attacked Raye Dawn's mother and 74-year-old grandmother. These persons accused both Raye Dawn's mother and grandmother of crimes, including child abuse, assault and battery, embezzlement and obstructing justice.

On June 28, 2007 the Honorable Paul Vassar granted defendant's motion for a change of venue and transferred the case to Creek County, Bristow Division, because of the inordinate amount of pre-trial publicity and inability to obtain an impartial jury in the Twenty-Third District. While this Court allowed for a change of venue, it refused to sequester the jury during Raye Dawn's trial, and conducted a limited and superficial voir dire.

On February 15, 2007, a "gag order" was issued in the case against Raye Dawn. Pursuant to the order, this Court ruled that none of the lawyers in this case or any persons associated with them or any person listed as a witness for either the State or defendant "shall release or authorize the release of information or opinion about this criminal proceeding which a reasonable person would expect to be disseminated by any means of public communications, if there is a reasonable likelihood that such disclosure will interfere with a fair trial of the pending charges or otherwise prejudice the due administration of justice." On October 25, 2006, a similar order was issued in Michael Porter's criminal case. The Honorable Dawson R. Engle, Special Judge for Twenty-Third Judicial District Court, found that repeated violations of the gag order entered in Mr. Porter's case had occurred despite strong warnings to both Mr. Smothermon [the DA] and Mr. Sutton [Mike Porter's attorney]. The trial court should have monitored and enforced this order....[29]

No one can reasonably dispute the fact that the news media had a tremendous impact on the outcome of Raye Dawn's trial. District Attorney Richard Smothermon, himself, admitted that the news media was a detriment to the trial. In an exclusive interview with KOKH FOX 25 on July 23, 2007, on the 9:00 news Mr. Smothermon was interviewed. He had the following to say about the trial and how the media handled the case:

"The media, no offense, the media took this case and really gave it a life that I wonder whether it should have had. I found it odd that the media became so consumed and so feverish about this case, and it was a detriment to the case. The media is never helpful to the case in my opinion because I would rather go in front of 12 people and give them the facts and let them make the decision. The media just influences it

[29] See Appendix B – Exhibit 10

by the way you report it, whether it's accurate or whether it's not."

***Few argue with that opinion.***

The 12 people who sat as jurors in Raye Dawn's case were influenced by the news media as well as members of the Briggs family. This brief will show that jurors received evidence out of court. Attached to this brief [excerpts are presented in the following chapter, The Witnesses] in support of a motion for a new trial are affidavits from 12 people who were at the trial, watched the proceedings and also observed what went on outside of the courtroom. These affidavits all evidence that members of the jury interacted with members of the Briggs family and were present just a few feet away while the news media conducted interviews with numerous members of the Briggs family and other trial witnesses...

Two witnesses report seeing a male juror sitting at a table right next to the Briggs family in a burger place in Bristow one day of the trial. This same male juror was observed watching the noon news on a television in the restaurant, which broadcast details of the trial. This was just minutes after the jury had been cautioned by the judge not to watch television.

Several witnesses distinctly remember [Celia] as one of the female jurors that congregated at the front entrance by the benches with members of both the Briggs family and news media. This is particularly important because [Celia] was an apparent leader in the jury in terms of emphasizing Raye Dawn's alleged guilt and responsibility and voicing the opinion that she deserved a life sentence. This is evidenced by comments she has made to the television and print media. For instance, in one television news interview with KOKH FOX 25, ran just a few days after the trial, [Celia] indicated that two of the jurors only wanted to give Raye Dawn a year in prison. [Celia] said she held up a picture of Kelsey's dead body saying this is eternity. [Celia] told *The Daily Oklahoman* that one male juror suggested Smith get only a year to which she responded to by holding up a picture of Kelsey and saying, "This child was given life in a cold grave."

It is also clear that [Celia] received evidence outside of trial. In an interview with KOKH FOX 25, [Celia] told Britten Follett the following:

"Who killed Kelsey? In my eyes, Raye Dawn did. The child was already in the process of dying whenever she left her there with Michael Porter, what set her off, or what caused her to do the injury, we don't know, but we feel she did it. If murder would have been down there as a possible deal, that's what we would have went with. It's not over with, because I know she's going to get out one day, she's going to breathe air, she's going to have life, what's Kelsey getting?"

Contrary to [Celia's] assertions on the air, it was never in dispute who killed Kelsey. In fact, Mr. Smothermon himself said on the record that he believed Michael Porter murdered and sexually assaulted Kelsey. Clearly, [Celia] thought she knew more about the case than what she disclosed in voir dire. [A footnote states: [Celia] did not raise her hand when the Court asked whether any of the potential jurors had heard about the case prior to coming to court that day.] She certainly received evidence out of court. A jury's verdict must be based on evidence received in open court and not from outside sources...Her comment that "the child was already in the process of dying whenever [Raye Dawn] left her there with Michael Porter" is absurd. Such evidence was absolutely not brought out in trial. Perhaps, she received this information while smoking with the Briggs family by the benches at the front entrance.

As soon as Raye Dawn's trial was over, [Celia] joined the Briggs' "bandwagon" and jumped on the "Kelsey's Purpose" Web site. [Celia] wrote the following on this site concerning "The Trial for Raye Dawn Smith":

"As one of the jurors in this heart felt trial, I have let my thoughts be known to many people. I have told Kathie that I believed Raye Dawn Murdered Baby Kelsey, and also I was one of few who wanted to give Raye Dawn a LIFE SENTENCE!!!!!! I BELIEVE SHE SHOULD HAVE GOTTEN A DEATH SENTENCE. I TRULY HOPE THAT SHE GETS SOME BEATENS JUST LIKE THE ONES SHE GAVE. I WILL NEVER FEEL THE PAIN THAT THE BRIGGS FAMILY HAS FELT, BUT I HOPE IN THE NEXT 27 YEARS IT GETS BETTER. GOD BLESS THE

BRIGGS FAMILY…SEE YOU ALL AUG 23 AT 1:30 PM …. FLY Kelsey FLY"

And, this individual was allowed to sit on the jury!

Due process requires that an accused receive a trial by an impartial jury free from outside influences…If publicity during proceedings threatens the fairness of a trial, a new trial should be ordered. The following are just a few selected comments that ran on the air during Raye Dawn's trial: [See trial media chapters]

[Two United States Supreme Court cases were discussed that established that the defendants were denied their constitutional right to a fair trial and they were Sheppard v. Maxwell, 384 U.S. 333, 86 S. Ct 1507, 16 L. Ed.2d 600 (1966) and Estes v. Texas, 381 U.S. 532, 85 S. Ct. 1628, 14 L.Ed.2d 543 (1965).]

As evidenced above [in the two cited cases], several of the witnesses in Raye Dawn's trial were interviewed both before and after they testified. This Court had total control of the courtroom and courthouse premises. It could have prevented the negative impact the news media had on Raye Dawn's trial. This Court's attitude in handling this aspect of the trial resulted in Raye Dawn receiving an unfair trial…Moreover, reporters would broadcast on television what the anticipated testimony would be for the next day. [See trial media chapters.]

"Had the judge, the other officers of the court, and the police placed the interest of justice first, the news media would have soon learned to be content with the task of reporting the case as it unfolded in the courtroom – not pieced together from extrajudicial statements." Sheppard, 384 U.S. at 362.

Like the Sheppard case, Raye Dawn's case was also appealing to the media because there was a murder of a small child; a possible sexual assault of a child; one family i.e., the Briggs family, that was more than willing to speak with the news media on a regular basis; two families that had been involved in tense relations for years; a so-called war hero who had allegedly returned from serving just a seven-month [evidence and Lance's own statement show four to five months] deployment in Iraq to find his daughter had died; a judge losing his re-election over the case; effectively two defendants, the stepfather and the mother; a paternal grandmother who was instrumental in passing legislation in the child's name; and multi-million dollar lawsuits filed against several state agencies and the Oklahoma Department of Human Services…It was every news reporter's dream. And, like Sheppard, Raye Dawn did not receive a fair trial by an impartial jury as due process mandates.

From Sheppard, 384 U.S. at 362-63: "Due process requires that the accused receive a trial by an impartial jury free from outside influences. Given the pervasiveness of modern communications and the difficulty of effacing prejudicial publicity from the minds of the jurors, the trial courts must take strong measures to ensure that the balance is never weighed against the accused…[W]here there is a reasonable likelihood that prejudicial news prior to trial will prevent a fair trial, the judge should continue the case until the threat abates, or transfer it to another county not so permeated with publicity. In addition, sequestration of the jury was something the judge should have raised sua sponte with counsel. If publicity during the proceedings threatens the fairness of the trial, a new trial should be ordered…The courts must take steps by rule and regulation that will protect their processes from prejudicial outside interferences. Neither prosecutors, counsel for the defense, the accused, witnesses, court staff nor enforcement officers coming under the jurisdiction of the court should be permitted to frustrate its function."

…Raye Dawn's case took on a "celebrity" status long before it went to trial. The news media locked in on Raye Dawn as if she was the bulls eye on the target very quickly and never inquired in the Briggs family or why Lance was only in Iraq for [four months to five months]. In essence, the news media became family publicists for the Briggs family and their cause but placed a scarlet letter on Raye Dawn's chest because she was the child's mother, i.e., she should have known, although admittedly several state agencies, including the Department of Human Services, numerous doctors, and each and every family member from both sides did not suspect Michael Porter. [A footnote states: At the conclusion of the Fox 25 Trial Transcript…is a letter written by a news reporter [Ms. Follett] that attended the trial. This letter evidences the obvious bias the news media had against

Raye Dawn and the intimate association it had with the Briggs family. This letter indicates that within two days of Kelsey's death at least one news reporter [Ms. Follett] from this local television station had called a member of the Briggs family, not the Smith family, and told them of the medical examiner's ruling the death a homicide. The reporter writes in part, "A year and a half later, a law has Kelsey's name on it; a judge is out of office; Kelsey's stepfather is in prison; her mom will soon join him; and there are pink heart stickers that dot car windows throughout Oklahoma." This was not a trial. Justice was blind, alright, but not because she was blindfolded, but because the lights from the television crews blinded her. Much of the media's conduct in this case is covered with shame. A lynch mob mentality settled over the case, and those charged by law to safeguard the halls of justice as civil sacred grounds utterly failed.]

...Bottom line, no one can deny the negative impact that the media coverage had on Raye Dawn's trial. Even District Attorney Richard Smothermon admits that the news media "was a detriment to the case." The jury in Raye Dawn's case should have been sequestered or protective measures should have been taken by the Court to ensure that jurors did not mingle and interact with trial witnesses, members of the Briggs family and the news media. Raye Dawn did not receive the fair trial she is entitled to under the United States and Oklahoma Constitution. As such, she should be granted a new trial with jurors uninfluenced by the news media.

**PROPOSITION 4: A JUROR WHO HAS NOT HEARD ALL OF THE EVIDENCE IN THE CASE BECAUSE THEY ARE SLEEPING IS GROSSLY UNQUALIFIED TO RENDER A VERDICT**

Several witnesses who were present at Raye Dawn's trial observed several jurors sleeping intermittently throughout the trial. [See The Witnesses Chapter] One observer reported as many as nine jurors who were nodding off or dozing during the trial. Apparently, the judge had to admonish the jury several times to pay attention and keep their eyelids open. One juror that was identified by at least two witnesses as sleeping continuously throughout the trial was [Celia]. [Celia] reportedly "sat slouched in her seat and wore a NASCAR fleece blanket draped over her body from head to toe." One witness said the "jurors appeared to be watching the trial as if they were seated in their own living rooms."

"A juror who has not heard all the evidence in the case is grossly unqualified to render a verdict." People v. Simpkins, 792 N.Y.S. 2d 170 (N.Y. App. Div. 2005 holding the Supreme Court should have dismissed as grossly unqualified the juror who was repeatedly observed sleeping during the trial.) A sleeping juror is arguably more prejudicial to a defendant than an inattentive juror, and courts have held that a juror's inattentiveness is a form of juror misconduct, which may prejudice the defendant and require the granting of a new trial. See e.g. Lester v. Kentucky, 132 S.W.3d 857, 862 (Ky. 2004).

Hasson v. Ford Motor Co., 650 P.2d 1171, 1185 (Cal. 1982) (internal citations omitted) "[A] jury's failure to pay attention to the evidence presented at trial is a form of misconduct which will justify the granting of a new trial if shown to be prejudicial to the losing party. The duty to listen carefully during the presentation of evidence at trial is among the most elementary of a juror's obligations. Each juror should attempt to follow the trial proceedings and to evaluate the strengths and weaknesses of the evidence and arguments adduced by each side so that the jury's ultimate determinations of the factual issues presented to it may be based on the strongest foundation possible. Were the rule otherwise, litigants could be deprived of the complete, thoughtful consideration of the merits of their cases to which they are constitutionally entitled." "It is said that the misconduct of one juror, so far as it may affect the verdict, in contemplation of law, is the misconduct of all." Brown v. State, 36 N.E. 1108 (Ind. 1894)...As evidenced above, a sleeping juror is an uninformed jury member, and therefore, he/she is grossly unqualified to render a verdict.

**PROPOSITION 5: THE MEDICAL EVIDENCE IN THIS CASE DOES NOT SUPPORT PRIOR ABUSE**

The medical evidence in this case simply does not support prior abuse. The physicians that testified for the State overstated the medical evidence. The State primarily relied upon two injuries – the broken collarbone and the two leg fractures. Dr. [G] testified that the collarbone is the most commonly broken bone in the human body...The Meeker Police Department investigated Kelsey's broken collarbone and did not file charges against Raye Dawn, ruling out abuse…DHS also ruled out abuse to the collarbone…Without more, a collarbone break is not concerning at all. Such an injury is common to a child Kelsey's age. Further, Raye Dawn's older sister, Janet Gragg, testified that her child had suffered not one, but two broken collarbones. There is no evidence that Ms. Gragg abuses her children.

Then there are the two leg fractures. It was established by evidence at trial that Kelsey was not with Raye Dawn when she sprained her ankle at the zoo…Rather, Kelsey was with her aunt. Therefore, one cannot blame this injury—which was not abuse—on Raye Dawn. She was not even around. Second, there is the issue whether the leg fractures, or one of them, were sustained while Kelsey was in the custody of Raye Dawn or the custody of her paternal grandmother, Kathie Briggs. [The timeline is discussed and references to the chart are made.][30]

…What is disconcerting about these facts is that whenever Kelsey suffered any small bump or bruise before or after this Kathie would make a DHS referral and take Kelsey to the emergency room. Yet, Kathie claims she does nothing in these four days where Kelsey refuses to walk…This lack of action is very suspicious. On April 25, 2005, Kelsey is diagnosed with bilateral tibia fractures…

The defense, after trial, sent the X-rays of Kelsey's right and left shins and feet to [Dr. K, MD], former Chief Pediatric Radiologist at Santa Clara Valley Medical Center in San

[30] See Appendix B – Exhibit 11

Jose, California for her review. [Dr. K] is Board Certified in Diagnostic Radiology and has trained and worked in pediatrics, general radiology and pediatric radiology for 15 years...She is not an advocate for either side, has no interest in the outcome of the litigation, and is unrelated personally or professionally to any party. She is what [Dr. S] and [Dr. B] are not: a witness who testifies as to what the medical evidence is to a degree of reasonable certainty. It is clear that [Dr. S] overstated the evidence. [Dr. K] asserts that the X-rays show "bilateral oblique fractures of the infant's right and left tibial shafts." "These are more commonly referred to as 'toddler's fractures.'" She further asserts that peak occurrence of these fractures is between nine months and three years of age and that such fractures are "usually associated with falls from swings, slides, trees, etc." Kelsey was less than 2 ½ years old when she sustained these fractures. This places her directly within the peak occurrence age for normal toddler fractures sustained through accidental causes. [Dr. K] also indicates that while fractures of this nature are common in child abuse, they have a "low specificity because of their common occurrence in accidental injury." As evidenced, the fractures to Kelsey's legs are non-specific at her age for abuse, i.e., not suggestive of abuse, much less evidence of abuse within a reasonable medical certainty.

Contrary to [Dr. S's] assertions, these leg fractures were not spiral fractures...Rather, they were oblique, slanted or tilted in layman's terms. No one grabbed this child in anger and twisted her legs...The leg fractures were not the result of abuse, either from the Briggs or the Smith families.

Kelsey could have well sustained these fractures through an accidental injury.

On cross-examination, [Dr. S] addressed the formation of callous, i.e., the healing of the bone...He testified that callous will form and become visible in an X-ray within a week to 10 days. He further testified that there was callous on both of Kelsey's legs and emphasized that callous does not form overnight. This testimony placed the date of Kelsey's fractures occurring at a time when Kathie Briggs had exclusive custody and control...

[Dr. S] admitted at trial that his facts as to what happened came solely from Kathie Briggs, who is hardly an objective source. He contacted no one—including the treating physician, the mother, or the child's regular physician—to substantiate those facts. [Dr. S] took a story—a story invented by Kathie Briggs—and manipulated the medical evidence to fit that story.

[Dr. B] testified at some length about the so-called bruises to Kelsey's backside that are visible in pictures taken by the paternal family on January 14, 2005. He testified that abrasions to this area are suspicious because they are in a place where they usually are not seen. He also indicated that a child's backside is padded and that these bruises pointed to a patterned injury. Independent medical review of the pictures of these so-called bruises indicates that these "bruises" are most likely not bruises or abusive wounds but rather the result of a child being kept in a soiled (feces) diaper too long. The evidence produced at trial supports this conclusion.

[April], the stepmother, testified that she took these pictures of Kelsey on January 14, 2005, while Kelsey was in the bathtub. [April] said Kelsey had been in Kathie Briggs' care that night at a birthday party, and that the birthday party started at 6:00 p.m. [April] said Kelsey had not been given a bath until sometime after 8:00 p.m. [Known timelines show it was around 10:00 p.m. when Kelsey was bathed.]

Kathie Briggs testified she was taking care of the birthday party, so she did not change Kelsey's diaper during that time. She also testified that no one else did either. [Susan], [April's] mother, testified also that no one changed Kelsey's diaper until [April] gave her a bath that night. Therefore, the evidence at trial shows that Kelsey could have sat—while with the Briggs family—in a dirty diaper for at least two hours that night if not longer.

In summary, there is no medical evidence to support abuse by the hand of Raye Dawn. Both the Meeker Police Department and DHS ruled out abuse as the cause of the collarbone break, and [Dr. G] testified that it is the most commonly broken bone in the body. Second, Kelsey sprained her right ankle under the exclusive control and custody of her aunt…Raye Dawn was at work. Third, the leg fractures date back to a time when Kelsey was under Kathie Briggs' absolute control and custody. Moreover, [Dr. K] has reviewed the films and has found that these injuries are not indicative of abuse in a child of Kelsey's age at the time. Finally, the so-called bruises to Kelsey's backside in January 2005 are most likely the result of her lying in her own feces for more than two hours because none of the paternal family members would change her diaper because they were too busy at a birthday party. For months, Raye Dawn was under the careful eye and watch of numerous individuals, state agencies and her all-intrusive ex-in-laws, the Briggs family. Raye Dawn did not abuse Kelsey.

**PROPOSITION 6: THE STATE KNOWINGLY SOLICITED FALSE TESTIMONY AND ALLOWED KELSEY'S REAL KILLER TO ESCAPE JUSTICE**

On October 11, 2005, Michael Porter killed Kelsey. No one else was present in the home. Richard Smothermon, the purported Lincoln County District Attorney, knows this. On February 2, 2007, Smothermon allowed Kelsey's killer to escape justice. Porter chose a 30-year sentence and a conviction of enabling child abuse over a life sentence and convictions for first-degree murder and sexual assault on a minor female child. Porter did not go to trial because he thought he could be found guilty. Smothermon himself stated on the record in open court that he believed Porter murdered and sexually assaulted Kelsey. Porter also admitted under oath that he was aware of the medical examiner's report that cited multiple sexual abuse. Porter claimed that Raye Dawn was responsible for what happened to Kelsey. Smothermon again stated on the record in open court that he disagreed with Porter. In putting a convicted felon and liar on the stand, Richard Smothermon also knew he was soliciting false testimony. [A footnote states: Porter may have lied to Raye Dawn and her family numerous times. He told them he had a college degree when he did not. His house was being foreclosed on, and he kept this a secret from Raye Dawn and Gayla Smith. Porter also had written a series of hot checks and cashed in his IRA.]

On October 20, 2005, Michael Porter was arrested for the murder of Kelsey Smith-Briggs. The Oklahoma Medical Examiner's Office ruled Kelsey's death a homicide. Kathie Briggs and her supporters picketed the office of Richard Smothermon, the District Attorney, until the political pressure grew so strong that on February 24, 2006, criminal charges were filed against Raye Dawn. It took Smothermon more than four months to charge Raye Dawn. Smothermon knew that without Raye Dawn placing Kelsey alive at the house when Porter showed up on the afternoon of October 11, 2005, he had insufficient evidence against Porter to convict him of murder. Raye Dawn agreed to testify at Porter's preliminary hearing without any agreement with Smothermon concerning any charge against her. Prior to Porter's preliminary hearing, Smothermon had Kelsey's body exhumed and a second autopsy was performed by an out-of-state pathologist, [Dr. H]. Following the second autopsy, Smothermon filed an Amended Information against Porter charging him with murder and sexual assault. Porter's preliminary hearing was held on August 23, 2006, amid the continuing media circus that encircled the Lincoln County Courthouse. News stations were reportedly stationed on every corner of the block with live feed trucks. At Porter's preliminary hearing, Raye Dawn testified that she had never seen Porter physically abuse Kelsey. At the conclusion of the preliminary hearing, Porter was bound over for trial for the crimes of murder in the first degree and sexual abuse of a child. His trial was eventually set for February 2007. It was during this time that the attorney for Porter learned that Porter had corresponded with the Briggs after Kelsey's death…Just five days before Porter was set to go to trial on first-degree murder and sexual assault charges he reached a plea agreement with Smothermon and pled guilty to enabling child abuse and received a 30-year sentence…The plea bargain meant no one would ever be prosecuted for Kelsey's murder and that Kelsey's probable real killer, Michael Porter, had escaped justice for her death.

Following Raye Dawn's trial, Smothermon was interviewed by KOKH FOX 25 concerning his decision to put Porter on the stand. Smothermon had this to say, "It was a decision I made against the advice of some other people that were trying the case with me. There was a great deal of risk putting him on the stand because it put the face of the monster in front of the jury. He's such a huge part of the evidence in the case I thought it improper for me to not present him to the jury." Smothermon was certainly right when he said it involved "a great deal of risk" to put Porter on the stand. In doing so, Smothermon knowingly and directly violated Rule 3.3 of the Oklahoma Rules of Professional Conduct and Disciplinary Rule 7-102(A)(4), which provides that a lawyer shall not "knowingly use" perjured testimony or false evidence…He also violated Raye Dawn's constitutional right to due process under Article II, sec 7 of the Oklahoma Constitution and the Fourteenth Amendment to the United States Constitution…Where perjured testimony is crucial to a jury's decision, the resulting conviction is fundamentally unfair and must be set aside…

Porter's story the day of the murder is simply not plausible. Our consulting experts have advised that the story Porter told on the stand at Raye Dawn's trial simply does not comport with medical science. Smothermon allowed Porter to testify to a series of events on October 11, 2005, that Smothermon knew were absolutely false…Porter testified that it struck him how quiet the house was that day after Raye Dawn left. We seek to prove that the internal injuries Kelsey suffered on October 11 are very symptomatic. Porter's story has no support. If Kelsey had supposedly sustained these injuries before Porter arrive home, as Porter claimed in his testimony, the house would have been anything but quiet. Kelsey would have been curled up in a fetal position. She would not have wanted to move, and she would have been crying and screaming. Abdominal trauma is immediately symptomatic from the moment of injury. Contrary to Porter's testimony, Kelsey would not have been in the other room sleeping if she had suffered these injures at the hand of Raye Dawn before Porter got home. Rather, there would have been a marked change in her condition that would have been evident to any care giver. Kelsey, who was verbal at the time, would have been crying, screaming and saying, "I'm hurt" or "My tummy hurts." She would have been complaining of pain. Clearly, the house would not have been quiet as Porter asserted in his testimony at trial. He had exclusive control and custody when he murdered Kelsey, and no one else was present in the house.

[Ms. B] from Comprehensive Home Based Services testified at trial that she was at the home with Raye Dawn and Kelsey on October 11, 2005 from 12:00 to 1:30 p.m. Kelsey had a purple bruise on her cheek, a band-aid on one finger and the little toe on her right foot was red and sore. Ms. [B] testified that when she left the house that day Kelsey was alive and Raye Dawn and Kelsey were sitting on the front porch playing with a turtle. It was after Ms. [B] left that Kelsey had an accident and urinated in her panties before her nap. Raye Dawn put Kelsey to bed wearing only a long black biker T-shirt with no panties or pull-ups on. The two laid down to take a nap together around 2:00 p.m. Porter testified that he left work around 2:35 or 2:40 p.m. and got home around 2:45 p.m. [He told investigators that he left work between 2:15 and 2:30 p.m.] He came home, and Raye Dawn woke up. Porter said Raye Dawn offered to go pick up his daughter…from school. Raye Dawn leaves the house and tells him to take care of her baby. It is at this point that Porter claims he went out to the garage to clean some tires but decides not to and comes back inside the house. After coming back inside the house, he claims he rounded up the laundry in the house, cleaned the kitchen counter and made himself some water. It is here where he says he noticed how quiet the house was. He testified he walked around the sofa to turn on the television and heard a noise from the bedroom—a noise he describes as an exhale, a guttural sound, an unnatural sound. He testified that he ran into the bedroom and saw that Kelsey was blue and was not breathing. Porter alleges that he tried to resuscitate Kelsey by asking her what was wrong.

Next, he went into the kitchen and called Gayla. The first person Porter calls is Gayla Smith, Raye Dawn's mother. He doesn't call the police. He doesn't call 911. He calls the child's grandmother. Gayla told Porter to call 911. Porter said he called 911 after talking to Gayla. Porter said he next placed Kelsey on the kitchen counter and tried to give her CPR. But it is what Porter does next that is truly remarkable and very significant. He says that he takes a pull-up that is sitting on the counter and puts it on Kelsey because he doesn't want anyone to see her like that. Picture that for a moment. There is a 2 ½ year-old child lying on the kitchen counter in a long T-shirt that her mother put on her after she had an accident and urinated in her panties before her nap. The child is reportedly not breathing, and what does Porter do but place a diaper on her. [A diaper that Raye states was in a bathroom closet and not on the counter as he claimed.] He placed the diaper on her because he had sexually assaulted her and he didn't want the paramedics to see the evidence. Porter told OSBI investigators that he circled the living room with Kelsey in his arms. He was circling the living room because he had done this terrible thing and he was trying to figure out what to do. Porter claims that he did not call 911 immediately because he "didn't want to believe how bad it was." Gayla arrived shortly after and took Kelsey.

Gayla testified at trial that Porter called her that day between 3:10 and 3:15 p.m. and said something was wrong with Kelsey. Gayla said that Kelsey squeezed her hand just before she handed her to the responders. The EMT's were dispatched to the house at 3:16 p.m. That gave Porter almost 30 minutes alone with Kelsey—sufficient time to murder and, perhaps, sexually assault her. [Mr. J], one of the EMT's testified that Raye Dawn was not at the house when he arrived. Raye Dawn did not arrive at the house with Porter's daughter until after Gayla and the paramedics arrived. [Mr. J.] also claimed that the child's body temper-ature was still warm to the touch. When the OSBI came back into the house to investigate the water in the kitchen sink was running. Most likely, Porter left the water running when he put Kelsey on the kitchen island to clean her off after he murdered and sexually assaulted her.

Porter's actions in the days following Kelsey's murder are certainly indicative of guilt. At the hospital, Raye Dawn wanted an autopsy performed because she wanted to know what happened to her daughter. Porter, on the other hand, objected to an autopsy being performed. [Mr. P], who has been a minister for 35 years, testified that he was called to the hospital in Prague on October 11. He observed Porter throwing himself against the wall and shouting…[Mr. P] thought Porter was overreacting and it bothered him that Porter was not comforting Raye Dawn. While Raye Dawn rocked Kelsey, Porter was in the hall yelling out, "Oh, my God!" [Mr. P] said that Porter blamed himself and said, "I hope I wasn't too rough with her." [Mr. P] thought Porter was feeling a tremendous amount of guilt. Officer Morrison, a Prague Police Officer, testified that Porter said, "She's never going to forgive me," while pacing back and forth outside the hospital. Morrison testified that Porter then fell to the ground and was staring up at the sky, but he was not unconscious. Porter was taken inside the hospital on a stretcher complaining of chest pains. The physician's assistant testified that she checked Porter for injuries and cleared him. According to [the physician's assistant] Porter did not console Raye Dawn.

That night at the house Porter ate a good meal while Raye Dawn refused to eat. One or two days after Kelsey's death, Porter faked a suicide attempt with a bottle of [Tylenol]. Raye Dawn's sister found 12-13 pills under the bed. Rachelle Smith testified that Porter got a gun out of the night stand and threatened to commit suicide. [Raye's cousin] testified that she took Porter to the hospital in Prague after his suicide attempt with the Tylenol, but Porter refused to go inside because Kelsey had died there. [Raye's cousin] talked him into going to the hospital in Shawnee. She dropped him off and went to pick up Rachelle, and when they returned to the Shawnee Hospital the hospital informed them that no one under Porter's name had ever checked into that hospital. When Porter was being questioned by OSBI investigators about the case he almost passed out. Porter told investigators the he had never seen Raye Dawn beat Kelsey or ever lose control with Kelsey. When asked by investigators whether Raye Dawn could beat Kelsey until she was dead, Porter said, "Never, never. She would never hurt her." The agents asked him this over and over again, and Porter always gave the same answer. His words exculpated Raye Dawn, but his demeanor and behavior incriminated himself…

Porter testified under oath before Judge Key that Raye Dawn was a fit parent. Five days before he was set to go to trial for first-degree murder and sexual assault, he pled to enabling child abuse against his wife, in contradiction to his sworn testimony, his voluntary statements to law enforcement officers, and his written statements. Porter admitted at trial that he left his own children alone with Raye Dawn. Rachelle Smith testified that Raye Dawn took care of Porter's kids five days a week while Porter was away at work. Further, [Ms. B], the CHBS worker, testified that it was not unusual for Raye Dawn to be alone with Porter's children. Presumably, if Raye Dawn was an abuser of her own child, Porter would not have left his children alone with her.

The key to all of this miscarriage of justice is that Porter met with Kathie Briggs less than 90 days after Kelsey's death. Kathie Briggs had a face-to-face meeting with Porter, the man accused of murdering her granddaughter. Moreover, Porter and Kathie Briggs corresponded by e-mail at least a dozen times after he was charged with Kelsey's murder. Kathie Briggs is a person who has made it her mission in life to ruin Raye Dawn. Kathie writes on her Web site that she was just using Porter for information. Undoubtedly, information to use in her quest against Raye Dawn.

[The e-mails between Mike Porter and Kathie Briggs and her daughters had not been read by Raye's new attorney at the time of this motion. They are included in later chapters in this book and the language is clear—she wanted Raye Dawn charged with murder and she didn't care what it took.]

Kathie Briggs has an insatiable habit to draw attention to herself, to create drama in which she is the leading lady. Ironically, it was the tragic death of an innocent child that brought a form of emotional and psychic gratification to Ms. Briggs to be the center of attention. Kathie Briggs is too real to be fictional, even for a William Faulkner novel, and Lance Briggs hoped for a financial windfall from his child's death. Both Porter and Kathie Briggs had something to gain by meeting and corresponding—Porter got the plea deal of a lifetime and Kathie Briggs got lies to assist her in her conspiracy against Raye Dawn.

Among the most telling facts is Porter's own 7-year-old daughter's statements that she made about her father to her school counselor on October 17, 2005. [Porter's daughter] told [the counselor] that she heard Kelsey getting a spanking upstairs, and when she looked inside the doorway she found her father spanking Kelsey "real hard." [Porter's daughter] said her father spanked Kelsey so hard it left her bottom "real red." [Porter's daughter] said her dad spanked Kelsey until she threw up. [Porter's daughter] added that when people were around her dad, he was nice to Kelsey. But, when no one was looking her dad would be mean to Kelsey. [Porter's daughter] also told the school counselor that she saw her dad hit Kelsey's head up against a brick wall outside on the house. [Porter's daughter] told [the counselor] that Kelsey would cry for Raye Dawn and would crawl to Raye Dawn and cling to her legs.

Mr. Smothermon iterated a number of times throughout the trial that he believed Michael Porter murdered Kelsey and the he believed Porter was lying on the witness stand. Richard Smothermon violated his ethical duty as a lawyer—an officer of the court—by calling Michael Porter as a witness against Raye Dawn...Worse, he proclaimed that he didn't believe him when he [Porter] denied murdering Kelsey and thought he was the murderer. Mr. Smothermon apparently did not notice the inconsistency in his statements (or perhaps he did) for if he believed Porter killed Kelsey, then how was it possible that Raye Dawn could enable his homicidal tendencies for a child already under supervision of DHS, subject to unannounced home visits from caseworkers, and the intrusion and curiosity of the Briggs family. For Kelsey to die, it had to be a sudden and forceful outburst. As such, Raye Dawn's conviction should be set aside and she should be granted a new trial. See Hall v. State, 1982 OK CR 141, 650 P.2d 893, 896-99. "The knowing use of false or misleading evidence important to the prosecution's case in chief violates the Due Process Clause of the Fourteenth Amendment." See Omalza v. State, OK CR 80, 911 P.2d 286, 307. Porter's testimony was not only misleading it was entirely false. Raye Dawn was not home when Porter murdered Kelsey. Porter had exclusive control and custody of Kelsey at that time. He was alone with Kelsey in the house for almost 30 minutes. Moreover, as evidenced above, his story simply is not supported by any medical science or teaching. Porter's accusations that Raye Dawn was the abuser are an absolute fraud to give Smothermon and the Briggs and to escape life in prison or a death sentence.

On June 15, 2005, Porter testified under oath that Raye Dawn was a fit parent. Porter testified at trial that the first incident of abuse he witnessed by Raye Dawn toward Kelsey was in January 2005. Yet, five months after January he testifies under oath before Judge Key that Raye Dawn is a fit parent. He leaves his own children with Raye Dawn five days a week while he is away at work after January 2005. His own 7-year-old daughter identified him as the abuser, not Raye Dawn. Further, Mr. Smothermon improperly admitted on the record in open court numerous times that he did not believe Michael Porter, and he believed Michael Porter to be Kelsey's murderer and the person who sexually assaulted her. Certainly, Porter's testimony was damaging to Raye Dawn and was material to the jury returning a guilty verdict. He was the only witness that testified that he had seen Raye Dawn abuse Kelsey. "When the prosecutor knows or should know that its case includes perjured testimony, a resulting conviction 'is fundamentally unfair, and must be set aside if there is any reasonable likelihood that the false testimony could have affected the judgment of the jury.'" See Gates v. State, 1988 OK CR 77, 754 P.2d 882, 886. See also Binsz v. State, 1984 OK CR 28, 675 P.2d 448, 450 (failure of the prosecutor to correct the testimony of the witness which he knew to be false denied the defendant due process of law in violation of the Fourteenth Amendment). "A lie is a lie, no matter what its subject, and, if it is any way relevant to the case, the district attorney had the responsibility and duty to correct what he knows to be false and elicit the truth." See also Mooney v. Holohan, 294 U.S. 103, 112, 55 S.Ct. 340, 342, 79 L.Ed. 791 (1935) (prosecutor's deliberate use of perjured testimony to obtain a conviction violates due process and denies the defendant a fair trial)...

**PROPOSITION 7: HIRED PROSECUTOR [MS. H'S] CONDUCT TOWARD THE DEFENDANT IN CLOSING ARGUMENT WAS HIGHLY IMPROPER AND PREJUDICIAL**

In delivering the first closing argument for the State, [Ms. H] engaged in highly improper conduct by screaming, yelling and pointing at Raye Dawn Smith. According to observers at the trial, [Ms. H] was screaming so loudly that she was red in the face. In Mitchell v. State, the prosecutor in his closing argument of a re-sentencing hearing yelled and pointed at the defendant as he addressed the defendant directly. See Mitchell v. State, 2006 OK CR 20, paragraph 101, 136 P.3d 671, 710. The Oklahoma Court of Criminal Appeals held that such conduct "was highly improper and potentially prejudicial."

The presentation of [Ms. H's] closing argument "was carefully calculated to inflame the passions and prejudices of [Raye Dawn's] jury." Yelling until one is red in the face and pointing at the defendant numerous times throughout a closing argument is the equivalent of expressing an opinion of "utter contempt and disdain." Such behavior is improper during voir dire and at any point during a trial. Such conduct violated Raye Dawn's constitutional right to due process and a fair trial. See U.S. Const. Amends. VI and XIV and OKLA. CONST. Art. II, sect. 7 and 20.

[Ms. H] used other methods in her closing argument to attack personally Raye Dawn and to associate her with Kelsey's real murderer—the murderer that Richard Smothermon and [Ms. H] allowed to escape justice. [Ms. H] referred to Raye Dawn Smith throughout her closing argument as Raye Dawn Porter. Raye Dawn Smith was on trial, not Raye Dawn Porter. The Information was filed in the name of Raye Dawn Smith. Michael Porter and Raye Dawn Smith's divorce was finalized on March 7, 2006—more than a year before Raye Dawn's trial. Raye Dawn was restored to her maiden name during the divorce litigation. This was simply another tactic by [Ms. H] calculated to inflame the passions and prejudices of the jury…

**PROPOSITION 8: WITH PRE-TRIAL PUBLICITY SO WIDESPREAD, VOIR DIRE SHOULD NOT HAVE BEEN COMPLETED IN ONLY A HALF A DAY**

The partial trial transcript reveals that voir dire took roughly a half day to complete.

[At the time of this motion, Raye's attorney did not have a trial transcript. The trial transcript was not complete until almost a year after Raye's trial. The attorney had to rely on Ms. Follett's notes that were posted online every day during Raye's trial.]

Jury selection started after 9:00 a.m. on July 9, 2007. Two 15-minute morning recesses were taken during that time. Peremptory challenges were exercised and the regular jury panel was formed before lunch. Everyone was told to return at 2:00 p.m. for the selection of the alternate jurors. After 2:00 p.m., the alternate jurors were selected. The Court gave some instructions and an afternoon recess was had. Everyone returned at 3:40 p.m. for the reading of the Information and the State's Opening Statement.

In the words of one reputable and experienced Oklahoma news analyst, "The fact that jury selection took only a half a day is appalling. Clearly, there is no way in just a half a day it could be determined that the 12 jurors on the panel had no prior knowledge of the case."

Ms. Briggs established a Web site, titled, "Kelsey's Purpose," shortly after Kelsey passed away. "The blogging traffic on the site is unreal." See affidavit [in The Witnesses Chapter]

The only publicity questions asked of the potential jurors at Raye Dawn's trial were asked by the Court. The questions were restricted primarily to three questions: (1) whether the potential juror had heard about the case; (2) from what news medium and when; (3) and through hearing about the case, had the potential juror formed an opinion as to the defendant's guilt or innocence.

One juror that was ultimately selected, [Ms. T], indicated that she had read about the case in the *Lincoln County*

*Newspaper*. She assured the Court that she had not formed an opinion about as to the defendant's guilt or innocence as a result of reading the newspaper. That was the end of the Court's inquiry with [Ms. T] on this particular issue. Neither the prosecutor or defense inquired of [Ms. T] any further. Therefore, it is undetermined what specifically she read about the case. Another juror that was selected [Ms. B], indicated she had heard about the case that morning on the television. She, too, assured the Court that she had formed no prior opinion as to guilt or innocence. That was the end of the inquiry with her from all parties involved. Finally, [Mr. H], another juror that was selected said he had heard about the case on the news some time ago. He also claimed he had not formed an opinion as to guilt or innocence. The others claimed to have never heard anything about the case prior to trial.

The only way such a statement can be true is if these other nine jurors have been living in a vacuum for two years. Their disclaimers were not credible and a much more searching voir dire should have been conducted. This case has received news publicity of mammoth proportions…

"Study after study emanating from high-profile cases indicates that media scrutiny has a profound effect on the attitudes and expectations of potential jurors, which is especially troublesome during the pre-trial period when reporting tends to be pro-prosecution oriented." "Further, research indicates interpretive bias is magnified in high-profile cases. In short, the difficulties for potential jurors to do an honest and fair job are greatly increased when pre-trial publicity like that with which Ms. Smith faced was present." [See affidavits]

"Studies show that in high-profile cases jurors will answer questions a certain way in an effort to get on the jury. Most persons want to serve as jurors in high-profile cases."

**PROPOSITION 9: THE COURT SHOULD HAVE ALLOWED FORMER JUDGE KEY TO TESTIFY AS A FACT WITNESS**

Raye Dawn's trial counsel made an effort of proof on July 16, 2007, concerning the testimony of defense witness and former judge, Craig S. Key. This Court heard the matter and denied the right to even call Mr. Key as a witness to the stand. In denying Raye Dawn that right, this Court directly infringed on her constitutional right to present a defense and to call witnesses to testify in her defense. See U.S. Const. Amends. V, VI and XIV and OKLA. CONST. Art. II, paragraphs 7 and 20. Craig Key was a fact witness who could have given relevant and highly material evidence that would have supported the defense...Mr. Key would have testified consistently with his book, and as evidenced below, his testimony would have been clearly relevant at trial and would have directly countered the testimony of witnesses for the State. Defendant proposes that Mr. Key would have testified to the following:

That in June 2005, he went to the court lobby to see Kelsey for himself. He writes, "She looked like a totally normal child, no bruises, nothing. She had been hopping around, almost bubbly."

"None of the evidence, allegations, or testimony that I had seen from the time I had made the decision to return Kelsey to the custody of her mother, Raye Dawn Smith in June, until October 11th had caused me to doubt whether or not I made the right decision. I had questioned DHS workers on several occasions to find out how Kelsey was doing, and I was continuously told she was doing well and that she was continuing to grow her hair back and gain weight."

"In fact, the placement of Kelsey in Raye Dawn's home was going so well that at the September 8th hearing to stop visitation of the paternal side of the family, the Assistant District Attorney and Kelsey's court appointed attorney wanted to dismiss the entire case against Raye Dawn."

"[E]verything I'd seen confirmed that although this case did involve allegations of child abuse, there was no definite perpetrator identified. It was apparent to anyone who was involved in investigating the case that Raye Dawn loved and wanted Kelsey. She fully cooperated with the authorities to gain back custody of her child. Further evidence was the fact that even after the June hearing, Raye Dawn continued her complete cooperation with the agencies that watched out for Kelsey."

At Pages 41-43, Judge Key writes about an incident between [Kelsey's daycare provider] and Kathie Briggs when Kathie came to pick up Kelsey from daycare. According to

Judge Key, "Kathie jumped out of the car, instantly became angry, and started yelling at [the daycare provider]. [The daycare provider] held Kelsey as Kathie grabbed [Kelsey's] little arm and tried to rip her loose. [The daycare provider] was afraid that Kathie would hurt Kelsey by pulling on her in that manner, so she let Kathie take little Kelsey."

"On at least three occasions, during the time Kathie had temporary guardianship of Kelsey, she took Kelsey to DHS and Kelsey was asleep and would not wake up for the worker to fully examine her. It has been alleged that Kathie continuously had Kelsey on unnecessary medicines and that Kathie took Kelsey to the doctor repeatedly. DHS workers noted that while in Kathie's custody, Kelsey seemed lethargic and slept most of the time."

"Although she was in protective custody, it was apparent that Kelsey wasn't adjusting to being in the Briggs home. A red flag was raised for me, as a judge, when DHS told me Kelsey's hair began falling out in clumps while in the care of Kathie Briggs. Kelsey's hair was falling out to the point that she had a bald spot on the back of her head the size of a baseball. She began self-mutilating by biting her arms, and as clearly stated in Kelsey's obituary submitted by the Briggs, she was apparently biting the Briggs family as well."

"After visitation when it was time for Raye Dawn to return Kelsey to the Briggs, she would cry and cling to her mom and say she didn't like 'Mommy [April]' and she didn't want to see 'Kafie.'"

"DHS was only able to narrow the time line to show that the fractures occurred when Kelsey was in the care of Kathie Briggs from April 18th to April 21st, or with Raye Dawn Smith from April 21st to April 25th, during which time, multiple people had access to Kelsey.

That it bothered him that Kathie did not take Kelsey to the doctor during that time she refused to walk. "When Kelsey could not walk, Kathie saw no need to get a second opinion." Judge Key emphasized that this inaction on Kathie's part for the four days she had Kelsey made no sense given that Kathie would send numerous e-mails to DHS any time she found a bump, bruise or scratch on Kelsey.

Mr. Key would have testified that there were "red flags" raised in his mind while Kelsey was under the care and custody of Kathie Briggs, and that the child began to thrive once she was returned to her mother, Raye Dawn, in June. Mr. Key's testimony was certainly relevant and material to Raye Dawn's defense. The fact that he was a former judge did not preclude him as a witness. Relevant evidence is generally admissible. Nor was his status as a former judge, or even the judge in another matter related to the criminal case, a bar to his competency as a witness. Even if the offer of proof of defendant's counsel was inadequate, it was plain error to bar him from the stand as his ability to testify to relevant and admissible evidence was clearly known by the Court. He should have been permitted to take the stand, then objections to specific questions could have been raised and ruled upon. To keep him off the stand entirely is sufficient, standing alone, to grant a new trial. It was and is plain error which was not harmless. He had personally observed the child in June 2005, and Kelsey had no bumps or bruises. She was happy.

Mr. Key would have testified that even Kathie Briggs was not concerned with Kelsey being around Michael Porter during late March and into April 2005. Finally, he could have impeached Kathie Briggs' credibility. Briggs testified as a witness for the State. Mr. Key would have impeached her credibility. Kathie Briggs told numerous DHS workers and Key that Lance Briggs was away in Iraq, and this was his reason for not attending the hearings involving Kelsey. Each time DHS wanted to contact Lance Briggs about the investigation, Kathie Briggs would say he was unreachable. For months, DHS had not heard from Lance and he had not contacted them to find out what was going on with his daughter. Kathie Briggs claimed Lance was in Iraq this entire time, but when the struggle over Kelsey was at its peak in April 2005, Lance was reachable on his cell phone and he told workers he was driving around Shawnee, Oklahoma.

It simply defies due process to suggest that former Judge Key would not be allowed to testify because he might attract the media's attention. It is the Court's duty to control the trial and media within constitutional limits and to see that the process is fair. The judge is not the "mere moderator, but the governor of the trial." See Herron v. Southern Pac. Co., 283 U.S. 91, 95, 51 S.Ct. 383, 75 L.Ed. 857 (1931). Surely, what media that was going to be present at the trial was already there. It appears that every local television station from Oklahoma City and Tulsa were present along with numerous newspaper reporters. In any event, the Court could have taken adequate measures to ensure that the news media inside and outside the courtroom did not detract from the proceedings.

The records of this case demonstrate that the trial court and counsel failed to exercise control over the abusive conduct of witnesses, potential witnesses, prosecutor, and members of the Briggs family, as well as the media. The jury was allowed to roam about almost at will, the prosecutor was allowed to engage in unprofessional conduct throughout the investigation, charging process and trial, witnesses were allowed to go far outside the evidence. The result was that the defendant's rights of fair process to due process and to effective assistance of counsel—all as guaranteed under the Fifth, Sixth and Fourteenth Amendments of the United States Constitution and Oklahoma Constitution—were denied and defendant was prejudiced by this denial.

### *CONCLUSION*

Raye Dawn Smith was denied her constitutional right to a fair trial. She was convicted by the media before she ever stepped foot in the courtroom. For the reasons set forth above, Raye Dawn Smith moves for a new trial. The Information charging her with alternative counts of child abuse and enabling child abuse was not signed by the duly elected and qualified district attorney for Lincoln County. Mr.

Smothermon also called on [Ms. H], as he does in many high profile cases to prosecute Raye Dawn Smith. [Ms. H] is a special prosecutor. The State can call her what they want, but nothing can disguise the fact that she is operating a thriving private law practice and on monthly salary with the State in violation of Oklahoma law. Raye Dawn's jurors did not adhere to the oath they took as jurors or this Court's admonitions. The jurors were continually exposed to news interviews with the Briggs family. Jurors were caught sleeping during trial, and one juror was seen watching a noon broadcast of the trial on the news. This jury should have been sequestered or kept together and subject to the watchful eye of the bailiffs, and in the very least voir dire should have taken longer than a half day to complete...One juror has demonstrated her obvious bias by taking no time at all in joining forces with Kathie Briggs. This juror has been interviewed numerous times, and her interviews reveal that she received evidence out of court....Finally, other evidence in this motion that supports Raye Dawn Smith obtaining a new trial is the medical evidence. The State's witnesses manipulated the evidence to fit with a story—a story that Kathie Briggs told them. Dr. [S] admitted at trial that his facts came solely from Kathie Briggs and that he did not contact anyone to substantiate those facts. This child was not grabbed by someone in anger and twist or slung around. These were bilateral oblique fractures. These are normal toddler fractures that are usually associated with falls from slides, swings, trees, etc. Kelsey was an active, playful child at the peak age for normal toddler fractures. Raye Dawn is entitled to a second trial—a trial that conforms with those rights and privileges she is granted under the United States and Oklahoma Constitution.

Respectfully submitted, Stephen Jones

*The trial judge denied this motion. In his answer, he cited an affidavit by Kathie's husband, Royce Briggs, and took his account over that of thirteen witness affidavits for the defense.*

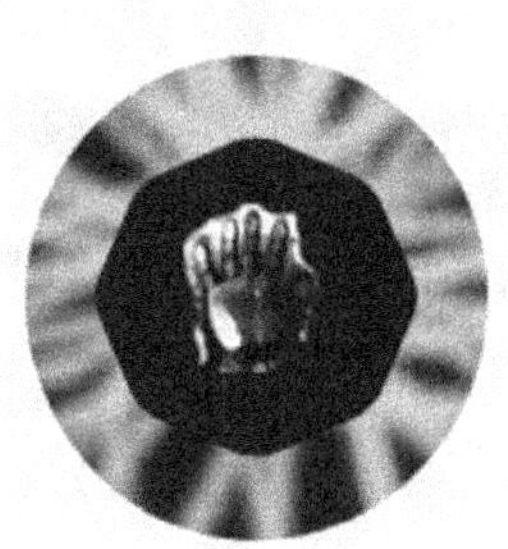

# 22 The Witnesses

"Journalism allows its readers to witness history; fiction gives its readers an opportunity to live it." ~ John Hersey

Oklahomans had seen the case against Raye play out in the media, so they were, unfortunately, blind to the injustice of her trial. It was like nothing our state had ever seen. Allegations against Raye were heavily discussed by the media before, during, and after the trial and the case is still a regular topic on the news to this day, three years after the verdict. Because of the amount of media it received alone, the possibility of the trial being fair was very slim. Almost five years after Kelsey's death, one would think the public would be tired of hearing about it. Unfortunately, Oklahoma media love the story the paternal family members created. Though attempts have been made to correct the false reporting, certain members of the media have stuck with the fictional story that Oklahomans seem to prefer to hear.

As Mark Fuhrman put it on pages 8 and 9 of his book, *The Murder Business*, when discussing the public's fascination with the Caylee Anthony case, "The Very Cute Innocent Child and the Very Bad Wicked Mother had now been minted as characters in this drama, and products—clips or pictures—that fed those images were in high demand. Hundreds of thousands watched each Caylee Anthony clip, and commented passionately about each gurgle and word she uttered. Thousands wrote in and swore they loved her as much as if she were their own child…Everybody settled into a comfortable seat to watch the show, which not only must go on, but on and on and on, spinning off the very axis of facts and forensic evidence that, in the normal world, would bring the case to a screeching halt. This is the first real problem of Murder in the age of Mass Media…"[31]

Fuhrman's description of the misrepresentation of evidence in order to create a show is sadly what has happened with Kelsey. I've seen hundreds of posts and comments from people who never met the toddler but claim to love her.

Members of Oklahoma media were taken for a ride as the "show" became focused on the end result of putting Raye behind bars and promoting Kelsey as a child who was unloved by her maternal family. Witnesses began speaking up immediately after Raye's trial, but their first-hand

---

[31] From the book *The Murder Business* by Mark Fuhrman. Copyright©2009. Published by Regnery Publishing, Inc. All rights reserved. Reprinted by special permission of Regnery Publishing Inc., Washington, D.C.

eyewitness accounts went ignored. Thirteen brave witnesses shared their observations with the maternal family and their attorneys in sworn statements that were presented to the trial judge in an attempt to garner an evidentiary hearing for a new trial. The hearing was ultimately denied based a single eyewitness account from Kathie's husband. *Why did the judge consider his statement more credible than those of thirteen other people?*

One sworn statement is as follows:

"The jury trial was held in…a small one-story courthouse that takes up only about a half of the block, including the surrounding parking lots and county offices. The courthouse faces north with four doors leading outside. There are two doors on the north—the one on the west end is the main entrance. There is a third door on the east side of the building and a fourth door on the west side that no one used.

Inside the courthouse are various offices and only one other courtroom aside from the one where the above proceedings took place. The Briggs family along with their friends took over this second courtroom. Just outside this second courtroom is the front entrance to the building, which is located on the west end of the block. The Briggs family used this front entrance, lobby area and the second courtroom as their staging area.

Each morning one had to pass through both the news media and the Briggs camp to get to the courtroom where Raye Dawn's trial was being held. There was only one public restroom in the entire courthouse, and it was located across the hall from the main courtroom. When court would recess, there was no choice and everyone had to walk through members of the news media and Briggs family.

The first day of trial metal detectors were set up at the door. As the trial progressed, the sheriff's deputies became much more relaxed with security.

Lance, the biological father of Kelsey, was cited for misconduct and removed from the courtroom very early in the trial for making statements under his breath. After he was removed from the courtroom, Lance spent his time lounging in a lawn chair under the big shaded oak tree on the front lawn of the courthouse with members of the television and print media.

[Jack], the spokesperson for the Briggs camp and also relative, sat on the right side of the courtroom on the front row just a few feet from the jury. [Jack] made several inflammatory comments directed at Raye Dawn and the defense while trial was in progress. Many of these comments were audible for me to hear, and I was sitting on the opposite side of the courtroom in a position where I could observe everything that was going on. Certainly, the jury that was only a few feet from where [Jack] was sitting could hear his comments. After a few days of this, someone wearing a badge, possibly an officer of the court or someone with the prosecution, moved near [Jack] and then [Jack] moved to the second row after that, sitting behind the man, and refrained from making statements aloud in the courtroom from then on out.

[Jack] did not refrain from speaking with the news media outside. None of the Briggs family did for that matter.

There were between 50 to 100 people present inside the courtroom each day. The number grew as the trial progressed. The Briggs camp sat on the right side of the courtroom, the side closest to the jury. The Smith family sat on the left side. The first two rows on the left side of the courtroom were full of news reporters. The last day of trial the courtroom was packed with several people standing up in the back.

Throughout the trial, members of the Briggs family would pass notes to the district attorney. During every break, the district attorney would speak with the Briggs family in the other courtroom. It was a regular event for the district attorney to be seen speaking with the Briggs family.

Several of the jurors appeared to be watching the trial as if they were seated in their own living rooms. I observed at least nine of the jurors nodding off or dozing during the trial at different times. One female juror, [Celia], sat slouched in her seat and wore a NASCAR fleece blanket draped over her body from head to toe. I observed her sleeping several times. The judge admonished the jury over and over again about paying attention, keeping their eyelids open, not to speak about the case with anyone and not to watch television, listen to the radio, or read the newspaper. The judge cautioned the jurors at the beginning of each day and at the end of each day.

The jurors were not sequestered during the trial and were free to roam inside and outside of the courthouse along with trial witnesses, lawyers, family members from both the Smith and Briggs family, news media, and the public at large. During the eight-day trial, the jurors were allowed to return to their homes at night and were permitted to go home over the intervening weekend. Jurors shared the same restrooms as everyone else and took their breaks at the same time as everyone else. The jurors parked in the same parking lot as everyone else.

At break time, several jurors would sit outside on the benches at the front entrance, both smokers and nonsmokers alike. Once Lance was removed from the courtroom, he would sit here, as well. The Briggs family would camp out at the front entrance with the news media also.

The media camped out in lawn chairs every day on the front lawn of the courthouse just a few feet from the front entrance to the courthouse, which is on the west side, and only a few feet from the jurors. The news media would interview trial witnesses and members of the Briggs family right there in front of the jury, and these jurors had to hear everything that was said. [Jack] gave statements to the press on a regular basis. His wife, [Susan], was also interviewed. Kathie, Lance, and [April], were interviewed as well. The media tried to interview just about everyone that testified at trial.

At lunch time, the jurors ate at the same restaurants as the news media, trial witnesses, and members of the Briggs family. I had lunch at a burger place one day, and I observed one male juror sitting at a table right next to the Briggs family. The same male juror was also watching the noon news, which broadcast details of the trial. This was just minutes after the jury had been cautioned by the judge not to watch television.

The number of jurors that sat outside at the front entrance varied each day. It seemed that about ten of the jurors would rotate outside in this spot. The jurors would sit, smoke, and visit less than ten feet from where the news media was conducting interviews.

One morning when I arrived, I observed two female members of the jury conversing like old friends in the parking lot. One of the female jurors I recognized as [Celia] and the other had tight, curly, permed hair. They were talking over a car, and one cameraman pointed his camera on them, but abruptly turned the camera away.

It was apparent that one female juror, [Celia], received information from an outside source. She was interviewed by FOX 25 out of Oklahoma City within 48 hours after the verdict was returned. I watched this interview, and [Celia] discussed evidence in this interview that was not presented at trial. Again, she was one of the jurors that would congregate at the benches at the front entrance with the Briggs family and news media. In her interview with FOX25, [Celia] claimed that the evidence at trial showed that the child was in the process of dying before Raye Dawn ever left the house that day... [Celia] further claimed that Raye Dawn set Mike Porter up to take the fall. I was present throughout the entire trial, and contrary to [Celia's] assertions it was never in dispute that Mike Porter was the perpetrator. The evidence at trial was that Mike Porter murdered and sexually assaulted Kelsey. The district attorney himself said that he did not believe Mike Porter and that Mike Porter was the murderer.

Jury selection was short. It only took a half a day. Each juror claimed not to have heard about the case prior to trial, while some said they only heard about it on the news that morning.

The news media was well represented. Television News Channels KFOR News Channel 4, KOCO News Channel 5, KWTV News Channel 9, and FOX 25 all out of Oklahoma City were present throughout the entirety of the trial. Channel 2 from Tulsa was also present. Reporters from *The Oklahoman, U.S. Observer Oklahoma*, and *Shawnee News-Star* were there, as well. The parking lot across the street from the courthouse was filled with media vehicles. There were at least three live satellite trucks parked there. At any given time, there were at least four cameras set up at the front door. The last day there were a dozen cameras. Many of the cameramen would use their long telephoto lenses through the windows and glass doors to capture pictures and video of the Smith family inside the courtroom.

This was a highly publicized case before trial and during trial. It received so much publicity in the news media that the judge granted a change of venue…In spite of the inordinate amount of pre-trial publicity, jury selection only took a half a day. In my opinion, Creek County was not far enough away.

Each morning Raye Dawn would arrive with her mother. The car they were riding in would drive under the covered awning on the east end of the courthouse where the sheriff deputies would meet them. They had to be escorted inside due to reported threats from the Briggs family. The news media soon became aware that Raye Dawn was using this other entrance in the mornings, and they would run from the west end of the courthouse to the east end just to capture video footage. The reporters tried every day to get a statement from Raye Dawn, but she continuously refused.

The news media would chase Raye Dawn and her mother inside the courthouse each morning. The news media would take pictures of Raye Dawn and her mother as they got out of the car each morning. I observed several news reporters [Ms. Ballard and Ms. Follett] yelling out very inflammatory statements toward Raye Dawn, including, 'Why did you kill your baby?' They would ask Raye Dawn how she thought the trial was going."

Another witness stated the following (only original statements will be repeated):

"I was present every day of the trial. I was called for jury duty, but my name was never called by the judge and I did not sit on the jury panel. I chose to stay and observe the trial proceedings once jury selection had concluded. It only took a half day to pick the jury…

The news media camped out every day on the front lawn of the courthouse just a few feet from the front entrance to the courthouse, which is on the west side. Every day, the media was positioned at these front doors with their cameras in place just waiting for someone involved with the trial to enter or leave the building. The Smith family kept to themselves at the other end of the courthouse. The Briggs family, however, mingled with the crowd and used every opportunity available to speak with the news media. The Briggs family was very willing to talk to the media, but of course, the news media was more than willing to seek them out, as well.

Lance, the biological father, was interviewed several times by the news media at the front entrance of the courthouse. [Jack], who I believe was a step-grandfather to Kelsey, was interviewed several times, as well. At each break, [Jack] would come out and talk to the news media first thing. It seemed that the news reporters would always turn to him for comments…

Each day there were approximately 50 people inside the courtroom watching the proceedings. Lance was present at least one day with several young girls.

Satellite trucks, i.e., tractor trailer rigs, from at least four different television channels were parked in the parking lot. There were also several vans parked there with their respective channels advertised on their sides.

Everyone was allowed to leave for lunch at the same time, including the trial jurors. I do not remember seeing any jurors at lunch, but I normally ate at the Pizza Hut and I believe that most people ate elsewhere.

One morning as I was driving up to the courthouse, I saw Raye Dawn and her mother being escorted into the courthouse through the back door on the east end. I observed the news reporters flock and run from the west end of the courthouse to the east end where Raye Dawn and her mother were entering in an effort to capture video, pictures, or possible comments. I was in my car, so I did not hear what was being said. Some members of the jury would take smoke breaks on this east end of the courthouse. Each day, court would break once in the morning, at lunch, and once in the afternoon.

The final day of trial was certainly a media frenzy. While everyone was waiting for the verdict to be returned, the news media was on edge. The news reporters and cameramen stationed at the front entrance would race to the other side of the courthouse if they saw anyone leaving the building. After the verdict was handed down, the news media again raced to the back entrance to catch video footage of Raye Dawn leaving the courthouse with the sheriff's deputies."

Yet another witness added the following to the previously stated eyewitness accounts:

"...At least 10 jurors would gather by these benches each morning, along with members of the Briggs family and the news media.

...The trial jurors in Raye Dawn's case would not immediately go to the jury assembly room during the breaks or before trial each day. Rather, they would congregate outside by the benches on either the west or east end of the courthouse—both smokers and nonsmokers alike. Essen-tially, the jurors were treated like everyone else.

The jury trial of Raye Dawn was a media frenzy with news reporters literally chasing people in and out of the courthouse each day in an effort to obtain information or attempt to conduct interviews with trial witnesses and family members. There were easily 15 news reporters and at least seven cameramen present each day. There was not a day when there was less than a dozen reporters even when it was raining outside.

The courtroom was at least three quarters full most days, and as more and more people testified or were released from their trial subpoenas it became more crowded each day. For the majority of the trial, 15 news reporters were inside the courtroom and at least 10 of those filled the first row each day of the proceedings while a few sat farther back. Each day there were approximately 60 to 75 people inside the courtroom watching the proceedings. Many of Kathie's followers…were present, as well.

I observed Kathie during several days of the trial while proceeding were in progress pass notes to the Assistant District Attorney or another woman assisting the prosecution. Kathie used members of the news media as intermediaries in order to pass these notes to the prosecution.

Satellite trucks, i.e., tractor trailer rigs, would come from Oklahoma City from at least two television news channels each day. They would set up around 10:30 a.m. for the live broadcast at noon. Again, jurors that congregated at the benches at lunchtime could hear the noon broadcast and interviews conducted by the news media with members of the Briggs family.

…I observed members of the jury eating in the same room with members of the news media. Other restaurants where I saw members of the jury and people from the news media eating and interacting together included the Subway and a Mexican restaurant.

The final day of the trial the courtroom was packed. It was standing room only the last day. People who had not been present in previous days were present the last day of trial.

The news media would interview the Briggs family right in front of the jurors seated on the bench or congregated just outside the front entrance of the courtroom. Just a few feet away and certainly within hearing distance of the jurors congregated outside, the news media interviewed witnesses that were subpoenaed for trial by the prosecution, including the biological father of Kelsey, Lance, and the paternal grandmother Kathie. Media interviews were conducted throughout the trial in front of the jury. The media also interviewed the spokesperson for the Briggs family [Jack] during the trial several times. At least one member of the Briggs family was on the news each night.

After Lance was escorted out of the trial room and cited for misconduct, he spent his time lounging in lawn chairs with the news media on the front lawn of the courthouse. Again, only a few feet away was the jury when they took their breaks.

The cameramen who were banned by the sheriff from being inside the courthouse after the first day of trial took pictures through the windows and glass doors of the courthouse.

The Smith family stayed on the east end of the courthouse while most of the media and jurors congregated on the west end.

The news media would chase Raye Dawn and her mother inside the courthouse each morning. On this east end of the courthouse, several of the jurors would also congregate each morning. There is a smoking area and a soda machine on this east end. The news media would take pictures of Raye Dawn and her mother as they got out of the car each morning. And with jurors standing by, the news media would yell out to Raye Dawn questions, including, 'Why did you kill your daughter?' and 'Why did you punch Kelsey?'"

The next witness observed everything that the previous witness observed, and added the following:

"The news media stopped at nothing in their attempts to capture footage of Raye Dawn and members of her family. For example, a photo of Raye Dawn and her mother sitting together on a court bench captured through a surveillance camera in the courthouse was leaked to the television news media and *The Oklahoman*."

Several witnesses repeated the same statements of what they observed. One witness added the following:

"I observed members of the Briggs family and several female jurors smoking and sitting together on the benches at the front entrance. This went on several days during the trial. The news media was always close by. Every day at break time, there would be a big congregation of people at the front entrance. It was primarily the female jurors that sat outside on the benches, usually four or five female jurors.

One day the sheriff's deputies moved the news media across the street. This did not last long and by that afternoon they were back over on the front lawn camped under the big shade tree. Several cameramen took pictures and captured video through the windows and glass doors of the courthouse since they were not allowed inside. I specifically remember the cameramen doing this the day Mike Porter testified.

Pictures of Raye Dawn and her mother, Gayla, were taken by the security camera inside the courthouse and leaked to the press.... I observed news reporters yelling out very negative comments toward Raye Dawn, comments that implied they believed she was guilty...This video footage and the news reporters' comments were broadcast on the evening news.

I had served on three criminal juries before, and I was surprised at how loose the judge was with confining the jury. During my prior jury service, we used restrooms that were inside the jury assembly room. If we wanted something to drink, someone would get it for us. The jury in Raye Dawn's case used the same restroom as everyone else. There was a time when I was in the restroom with a couple of the male jurors. They ate at the same restaurants as everyone else. They took smoke breaks with members of the Briggs family and persons from the news media. Moreover, I was dumbfounded at how fast the jury was selected. It only took a half a day to pick the jury. I sat on a murder trial once, and it took two days to select a jury. With this being such a high profile case, I thought the jury selection would have taken longer and I thought the jurors would have had stricter requirements.

Every juror during jury selection claimed not to have heard anything about the case in the media prior to trial. A few said they heard something about a trial on the news that morning. Neither the attorneys nor the judge seemed to explore the issue any further after the jurors claimed not to have heard anything. This was clearly not the truth. [Celia], one of the female jurors, was interviewed after the verdict was returned. She made statements in this television interview that indicated she had received information from somewhere besides inside the courtroom. For instance, she said that the child was dead before Raye Dawn ever left the house. This evidence was never presented at trial. I remember specifically that she was one of the jurors that sat outside on the benches with the Briggs family and the news media during the trial.

Although the judge cautioned the jury every day not to discuss the case with others or watch the television, listen to the radio, or read the newspaper, it was impossible for those jurors that sat outside on the benches not to hear the media interviews conducted with the Briggs family."

Another witness added:

"At any given time, there were camera people everywhere. There was at least one cameraman for each news reporter. There were at least five television stations present with reporters and cameramen. The news media was stationed outside when everyone arrived in the morning, they were there at breaks, during lunch, and at the end of each trial day. The news media tried their best to capture footage of Raye Dawn.

On the east end of the courthouse, there is an overhead drive-up area where Raye Dawn and her mother would drive up every morning with deputy escorts. The news media would try to capture footage of Raye Dawn as she entered and left the courtroom each day.

Although the judge cautioned the jurors before breaks not to discuss the case with anyone, the jury was not sequestered and was allowed to go home at night where they had access to television, radio, and newspapers. There was always a morning break, a break for lunch, and an afternoon break.

I observed Kathie, the paternal grandmother, during several days of the trial while proceedings were in progress pass notes to the District Attorney and his assistant. Kathie would lean over the rail and speak with the prosecution attorneys frequently during the trial."

One witness in particular was a professional journalist. Raye's trial was one of many he had attended, and in his professional opinion, something had clearly gone wrong. He stated:

"I am a legal resident of Oklahoma County and am familiar with the case involving Raye Dawn. I make this affidavit in support of a motion for a new trial to show the biased news coverage on Raye Dawn both before, during and after the trial and to establish that jury selection should have taken more than a half a day to complete given the widespread media coverage of this case that began within days after Kelsey passed away.

I received my Bachelor's Degree in journalism from the University of Oklahoma in 1980, and began my consulting business in June 1983. Since then, I have developed strategies for clients on hundreds of public affairs/political and litigation issues, with specific focus on media strategies in high profile cases. I have consulted on some of the nation's highest profile regulatory, legislative political and litigation cases. In Oklahoma City, I serve often as a news analyst for both television and radio stations.

In 2001, I became among the first communications consultants in the United States to receive bar approval for Continuing Legal Education (CLE) ethics courses for legal counsel regarding their ethical responsibilities, specifically Rule 3.6 on trial publicity.

It is my professional opinion that the jury in Raye Dawn's case should have been sequestered. During trial the media coverage was at its highest. There is simply no way to rule out that none of these 12 jurors watched the television, read the newspaper, listened to the radio, or got online during the trial while home at night or during the day on lunch breaks. Moreover, jury selection should have taken more than a half a day to conclude given the enormous amount of publicity this case garnered in the three years prior to trial.

I reached those conclusions after interviewing hundreds of news accounts regarding this case. When reviewed in the light of high profile criminal cases over the past decade, arguably this case achieved "celebrity" criminal case status, or in other words, a "media" trial long before the case came to trial.

Leaving aside the newspaper stories, during trial alone and in the 48 hours that followed the verdict, there were 423 stories reported on Raye Dawn's trial on local television channels in Tulsa and Oklahoma City. This information was gathered through transcripts of close captioning of local news provided by Newslink. Trial witnesses were interviewed by news reporters as they hurried to their automobiles following their testimony. Some of these witnesses can be seen on news video being escorted to their cars by sheriff's deputies while the new media were in tow shouting out questions and comments. Members of the Briggs family were on the news daily throughout the eight-day trial.

Pre-trial publicity in this case was enormous. Prior to the change of venue…, there were at least 910 stories reported on Kelsey on local television channels in Oklahoma City.

Since the start of this case which began in the days following Kelsey's death in October 2005 up until the filing for the change of venue, there were two stories a day ran about this case. This case spans a three-year time frame. In those three years, the news media has ran coverage on the legislation passed in Kelsey's name and the multi-million dollar lawsuits filed by Lance against the Department of Human Services, other state agencies, and various doctors who treated Kelsey in the months prior to her death.

The newspaper and television is not the only negative image delivery system in the market. Rather, the public has received an inordinate amount of other negative media impressions of Raye Dawn through radio, alternative publications, and web "bloggers." The blogging traffic on this case has been extreme. It seems that almost every one has had a comment to make about this case. Judge Key losing his reelection...over this case has been played out in the media. Judge Key, himself, released his book, *A Deadly Game of Tug of War: The Kelsey Smith-Briggs Story* a little over a week before Raye Dawn's trial. His book was available online at www.judgekey.com as of June, 27, 2007, just 12 days before Raye Dawn appeared for trial.

Kathie, the paternal grandmother, has been an active voice of the prosecution and the excessive hostility toward Raye Dawn, her family and defense in the media. Kathie established a Web site, Kelsey's Purpose, shortly after Kelsey passed away. The blogging traffic on this site is unreal.

It is my professional opinion that the change of venue in this case...did nothing to alleviate the impact of the negative news coverage on Raye's case. The jury was not sequestered during the trial. They were allowed to eat wherever they chose to at lunch, and return to their homes at night and over the intervening weekend.

What is important about this media coverage is its one-sided nature. The media never inquired as to why Lance was only in Iraq for seven months.

[In reality, he was reportedly in Kuwait from May to August or September—closer to four months. His original term there was to be eighteen months. Kathie has stated that he arrived home one month early. Her explanation does not compute within any type of realistic mathematical equation.]

The media never inquired into the Briggs family at all for that matter. It has been reported that a prominent news reporter, Cherokee Ballard, from a local television station in Oklahoma City has spent holidays with the Briggs family. In essence, some of the news media have become publicists for the Briggs family.

No one can deny the negative impact that the media coverage had on Raye Dawn's trial. Even Richard Smothermon, the District Attorney admits that the news media was a detriment to the trial. Richard Smothermon was interviewed by KOKH FOX 25 within days after the verdict was returned, and in that interview he admits that the media "was a detriment to the case."

The one certainty of a "media" trial is that the media will provide detailed coverage of the trial and will indeed influence the trial in ways researchers are only beginning to understand. It has been documented that in the O.J. Simpson case, the media's rush to file stories produced potential evidence and witnesses for the trial. Because of media influence, high profile cases are not typical cases, and Raye Dawn's case attracted extraordinary news coverage.

In Raye Dawn's case prosecution witnesses "came to light" as the coverage of the case on the news increased.

Study after study emanating from high-profile cases indicates that media scrutiny has a profound effect on the attitudes and expectations of potential jurors, which is especially troublesome during the pre-trial period when reporting tends to be pro-prosecution oriented.

Most troublesome for the defense are the trends that normally exist whenever the Fourth and Sixth Amendments collide. For example, media coverage often places emphasis on facts and evidence the jury may never hear. Additionally, jurors are instructed to not draw conclusions until all evidence is presented. In Raye Dawn's case, with such massive pre-trial publicity, virtually every negative item has been presented numerous times, and it appears that arguably many in the media concluded her guilt before she was tried and convicted.

Further, research indicates interpretive bias is magnified in high-profile cases. In short, the difficulties for potential jurors to do an honest and fair job are greatly increased when pre-trial publicity like that with which Raye Dawn faced was present.

After careful study, it is my professional opinion that Raye Dawn did not receive a fair trial. The negative news media in her case was very widespread. The fact that jury selection took only a half a day is appalling. Clearly, there is no way in just a half a day it could be determined that the 12 jurors on the panel had no prior knowledge of the case.

Studies show that in high-profile cases jurors will answer questions a certain way in an effort to get on the jury. Most persons want to serve as jurors in high-profile cases.

The face of Kelsey is everywhere. Hundreds of fliers and bumper stickers were passed out at numerous rallies held by organizers of "Kelsey's Purpose," in the months leading to Raye Dawn's trial. Driving down Interstate 40, there is a billboard with Kelsey's face...On Highway 18…there is a second billboard.

This story was appealing to the media because you had one family, i.e., the Briggs family, that was more than willing to speak with the news media on a regular basis; you had a child that died; you had two families that had been involved in tense relations for years; a so-called war hero who had allegedly returned from serving just a seven-month deploy-ment in Iraq to find his daughter had died; a Judge losing his re-election over the case; effectively two defendants, the stepfather and the mother; a paternal grandmother who was instrumental in passing legislation in Kelsey's name; and multi-million dollar lawsuits filed against several state agencies and the Oklahoma Department of Human Services.

Sealed DHS records were leaked to the press. Pictures of Kelsey following an automobile accident in August 2005 were given to the press and stories were run claiming her injuries from the automobile accident were abuse.

During the trial, the local television stations gave very detailed reports on the case showing video and pictures of Kelsey's alleged injuries. Video of Kelsey in the pink and green casts saturated the news media market in the years following her death. During the trial, a few stations would talk about anticipated testimony in the days to follow before the witnesses even took the stand.

Following the trial, we have seen at least one juror who has not been the least bit hesitant to converse with the television and print news media in Oklahoma.

Throughout the trial, there was at least one local television station, KOKH FOX 25, who provided notes from the trial on a daily basis on its Web site.

I am not related to any of the parties in this case."

As mentioned in the statement, the paternal family's propaganda blanketed the areas surrounding their county during the months after Kelsey's death. Flyers were mailed to voters in an effort to promote the paternal family's candidate to replace the Judge who heard the abuse allegations in the custody battle over Kelsey. A full-page letter was included in their "message." It started with a misleading statement: "After 9 months of documented abuse Kelsey was murdered. Judge Key against DHS recommendation sent her back into an abusive home. Four months later she was murdered while her father was serving our country in Iraq..." and ended on the same deceptive note: "While he was fighting for us his daughter lost her fight to live." The letter stated:

"After 9 months of documented abuse Kelsey was murdered. Judge Key against DHS recommendation sent her back into an abusive home. Four months later she was murdered while her father was serving our country in Iraq. In Oklahoma Judges DO NOT have authority to place a child that is in state custody. Judge Key stated in court he knew he did not have that authority, but he was doing it anyway.

We lost Kelsey at the age of 2 years, 9 months, and 13 days. Cause of death is blunt force trauma to the abdomen. Her stepfather has been charged with first-degree murder and sexual abuse. The mother is charged with two felony counts of Enabling Child Abuse and Child Neglect.

Kelsey's Story:

Kelsey was living with her mother when her father was called to active duty. Abuse began in January with a broken clavicle, 29 bruises and abrasions. We received legal guardianship on January 24th. The mother had weekend visits, supervised for one month. After the next court hearing she received unsupervised visits each weekend and one day during the week. The mother was ordered to attend Parenting Class, Anger Management, and Alcohol Assessment. We asked that the boyfriend not be present during these visits. Kelsey was returned to me several times with bruises. In March I took Kelsey to the ER after she was returned with a swollen nose. On April 4th, her father returned home for his last visit before deploying over seas. This was the last time he saw Kelsey. On April 14th, Kelsey was returned with a sprained ankle. The explanation was plausible; however, given the history we called DHS. On April 18th the mother married. The mother took Kelsey to DHS five days after receiving her from me to say I had hurt Kelsey. DHS instructed her to take Kelsey to the doctor. The doctor Kelsey had been seeing during this time was later discovered to be the sister of the attorney retained by Kelsey's mother. The diagnosis was the sprained ankle had actually been broken and the other leg had a stress fracture. I took Kelsey to OU Physicians Clinic May 2nd for a second opinion. Her broken legs were diagnosed as abuse. Since the mother had pointed her finger at me DHS had to investigate and Kelsey was placed with the maternal Grandmother. We were given supervised visits before the hearing on June 14th. Without interviewing our family CASA recommended Kelsey be returned to her mother. DHS recommended Kelsey NOT be returned to the mother at this time. Judge Key ruled Kelsey was abused and he could not determine the perpetrator. He then contacted the mother's attorney prior to the hearing and told him he was returning Kelsey. In August my daughter-in-law, [April], was given a five hour unsupervised visit. The morning of the visit [April] was informed that Kelsey had been in a car accident and the visit was canceled. The accident was minor; Kelsey was taken to the ER for precautionary measures. The visit was rescheduled for August 27th. I planned on taking video to send to her Daddy. We were shocked to see bruises on her face and arm. She had retinal hemorrhaging, had lost weight and appeared heavily medicated. She remembered us, but she was not the Kelsey we had known. Her spark was gone and something was wrong. This would be our last visit with this precious child. I contacted DHS on Monday asking what was wrong with Kelsey? I stated if they did not help she would not live to see her Daddy. [Kelsey's doctor] then wrote Judge Key and recommended that the visits stop. I remind you she is the sister of the attorney representing the mother. An emergency hearing was set. Before this hearing my daughter-in-law informed my son she wanted a divorce. As Grandparents we no longer had rights and lost contact with Kelsey. My son contacted DHS to let them know he was returning. Arrangements were made for Kelsey to be at the airport. On October 11th, I received a call from a friend that Kelsey had been taken to the hospital where she died. My son called thirty minutes later from Ft. Benning, Georgia and I had to give him the news that would change his life forever. Our family was never contacted by DHS. We made calls and got Lance home that night. While he was fighting for us his daughter lost her fight to live.

This tragedy could have been avoided. Key broke two laws in our case. I believe Lincoln County needs change so another child does not die. We need someone that will follow the law. I ask that you vote for [his opponent] for Associate District Judge. Thank you, Kathie. For more on this story log onto [Kathie's Web site address was given]."

Along with the propaganda was a page with a picture of Kelsey and Lance with Lance wearing his uniform and

Kelsey peering up at him with her arms propped up on his legs and her face in her hands. This picture had been staged according to Lance. Kathie is a photographer, and she took multiple pictures of Lance with Kelsey. Alongside the picture was a campaign push along with "An Important Message from Kathie" that was also a misrepresentation of the facts.

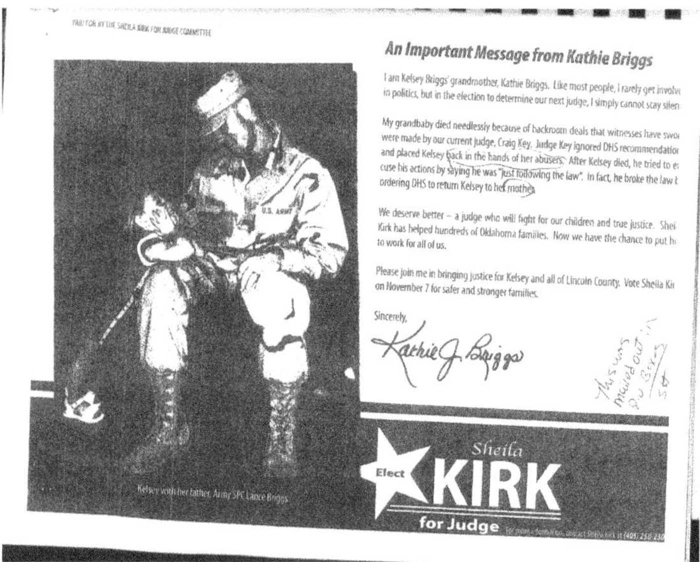

Kelsey with her father, Army SPC Lance Briggs

It stated: "I am Kelsey Briggs' grandmother, Kathie Briggs. Like most people, I rarely get involved in politics, but in the election to determine our next judge, I simply cannot stay silent. My grandbaby died needlessly because of backroom deals that witnesses have sworn were made by our current judge…Judge Key ignored DHS recom-mendation and placed Kelsey back in the hands of her abusers. After Kelsey died, he tried to excuse his actions by saying he was 'just following the law'. In fact, he broke the law by ordering DHS to return Kelsey to her mother. We deserve better – a judge who will fight for our children and true justice. Sheila Kirk [the attorney who represented Raye Dawn in her divorce from Lance] has helped hundreds of Oklahoma families. Now we have the chance to put her to work for all of us. Please join me in bringing justice for Kelsey and all of Lincoln County. Vote Sheila Kirk on November 7 for safer and stronger families. Sincerely, Kathie Briggs."

Misleading information and libelous statements such as these cost the Judge his re-election. They also compelled him to clear up the deception, which in turn, prompted my involvement in the case. Also, misstatements such as these that specifically targeted Raye as being the responsible party for Kelsey's death and created more drama and hate are what drove the paternal family's version of what happened to Kelsey into homes across Oklahoma. Because members of the media befriended the paternal family, nobody stepped in to put a stop to the misleading and untrue claims or questioned their lack of evidence.

The following statements are from the confidential OCCY report that was "leaked" to Kathie's media friends and prove that Kathie was also viewed as a possible perpetrator for Kelsey's abuse.

"The worker also documented concerns that the paternal grandmother was allowing visitation with the mother that was in violation of the court order, both in duration of the visits and Mike Porter was living in the home with the mother. The worker recommended that Kelsey remains in DHS custody and be placed outside the paternal grandmother's home and in the mother's home…After months of reflection and review, the…staff demonstrated an attitude of suspicion of the paternal grandmother, Kathie. The OJSO has considered the possibility that the paternal grandparents were somehow involved in one or more of the incidents reported. Within this context, after examining the evidence and DHS case history the following alternatives must be considered: a) Kathie was the perpetrator of some of the incidents of abuse and child welfare failed to adequately investigate and document her involvement. b) Kathie was not the perpetrator, but, by her demeanor, persistence, and/or irritation, was able to negatively influence DHS professional child welfare investigators so that her concerns were not properly investigated. c) DHS staff did not consider the danger to Kelsey significant to warrant a thorough investigation. d) DHS staff did not comprehensively review the case to consider the contextual evidence implicating a different perpet-rator."

The propaganda also mentioned the accident from August of 2005 when the truck Kelsey was riding in was hit by a drunk driver. The truck sustained more than $14,000 in damage with a shattered back window and a bent frame. Kelsey was in the back seat where the glass shattered. In Kathie's statements, she always refers to this accident as a "minor accident" or "fender bender" in an effort to justify the use of the pictures taken of Kelsey after the accident as evidence of abuse.[32]

Additionally, concerning Kathie's statement that they "lost contact with Kelsey," I present the following evidence that the paternal family willingly gave up their contact with Kelsey. On September 6, 2005 (two days before Kelsey's final public hearing) Kathie sent an e-mail to DHS stating:

---

[32] See Appendix B Exhibit 1

"After much consideration we have decided that no one from our family will be in court Thursday. DHS has been fighting any kind of reunification with our family since the beginning. Why hasn't the EEG been scheduled? She is the sister of Raye Dawn's attorney. She did have two night terrors while she was in my care. Kelsey seemed heavily medicated on her five hour visit last week. She seems to have lost weight. [April] can no longer take off work to attend such visitations so we will concede this fight and pick up again when her father comes home." From the language of this e-mail, does it sound like Kathie thought that Kelsey was dying—as she claims?

The following e-mail that was addressed to the head of Oklahoma's child protective services clarifies that Kathie's feelings were apparently higher on her priority list than her concern for Kelsey's safety. This rambling e-mail was sent in the middle of the night after Kelsey was removed from Kathie's home and Kathie had been reprimanded by workers for talking on her phone during supervised visits instead of spending time with Kelsey.

May 31, 2005 3:13 AM From: Kathie Subject: ...Kelsey

"I understand you have been contacted about this child by [Jack, Kelsey's stepmother's stepfather], cousin to [the state's First Lady]...On September 11, 2004 my son [Lance Briggs] was called to active duty and I applied for his visitation while he was gone...During this time Kelsey has come home with several bruises. Most seemed like something you would not be concerned with if you were in a normal situation, but it was almost a weekly occurrence. She would bang into things at my home and not bruise and be gone 24 hours and be bruised. Each time I had someone look her over for documentation purposes...When she was returned to me after a 24 hr visit she had a huge pump knot on her nose. The mother stated her seven year old stepdaughter had elbowed her in the middle of the night. After everything we had all just been through I chose to accept this explanation and did not call in. I took her to the ballgame that night and someone who saw her called in. The next day [the DHS supervisor] contacted me and he and [a DHS worker] came to my home for a visit. The knot was already gone, but we had taken pictures the night before for our records... These are the things [DHS] has done that makes me feel like I am getting an unfair investigation. I have strong feelings that they are befriending the mother and maternal Grandmother...I never dreamed when I took her for a second opinion that I would now be accused of neglect. I have seven Grandchildren and spoil them endlessly. I spanked one of them once and swore I would never do it again...this has been extremely devastating that someone already convicted of abuse could turn the table and [DHS] believe the allegations...It was extremely cruel to allow our family to believe that Kelsey was going to a foster home with strangers when she was actually with the maternal Grandmother. This would have been more comforting to us especially at [a] time that my son was landing in Kuwait on the same day. [The DHS worker] stated she had to many people to work around to schedule the supervised visits so my husband could be there at least once a week. We asked for the early appointment or late in the afternoon. During one of my 2 hour visits, [the DHS worker] came in after one hour and said she had just learned Kelsey had a Doctors appointment and took her. I received a couple of calls on my cell phone while visiting and I let Kelsey talk to my husband, since he could not be there, he would usually sing to her, and my son's wife called once. The next day I was told I could not use my phone during this visit. It was to spend time with Kelsey and that was taking away from my visit. I could understand if she were older and they thought people were trying to brain wash a child...[The DHS worker] came in and stated I was not allowed to use Kelsey's picture in the paper. I told her it had nothing to do with the case and it was only a military article we had been planning since the day he was shipped out. She still said, no. We then learned a release could be signed allowing this, but [the DHS supervisor] once again said, no. When I go in [the DHS worker] has been heard in the room with the mother and Kelsey laughing and visiting, but treats us as if we are criminals…I asked [the DHS worker] if my daughters could see Kelsey for 2 hours one weekend. The mother's family gets to see her anytime and they would really like a visit with their brother's only child while he is away at war. She stated she wanted Kelsey to be in a stable environment and our family probably would not see Kelsey for a very long time. Therefore my son will not have any contact with her either. My daughter then called [the DHS supervisor] to see if he would okay it and he also vetoed the idea. He also alluded to the possibility that Kelsey would be going home with [her] mother and no one in our family would see Kelsey unless supervised by the mother. He's already got that idea in his head without a fair hearing. I don't mind going through all the supervised visitation if that is what it takes to keep Kelsey safe, but I do not know how going to DHS three days a week with strangers to sit in a room for 8 hours a week then back to day care while the maternal Grandmother works is stable…On May 16th I pulled out behind the mother…she sat at the stop sign and would not move. While sitting there I noticed she had taken the tag off her vehicle and put it on her husbands. I reported this to the Meeker Police. They being friends with her and not investigating the original abuse for this reason along with the suggestion of [the DHS worker] filed harassment and stalking charges [to] be filed on me…[The DHS worker] never asked me for my side of the story. I knew as soon as I made the call it would come back to haunt me, but I don't understand how law enforcement officials can operate this way. Small town I suppose. I mostly don't know how [the DHS worker] can take it upon herself to suggest a charge be filed on me. The mother tried the same charges on my son's wife during their custody battle…"

The following was posted by Kathie Briggs on Kelsey's Purpose. It addresses Kathie's alleged stalking of Raye:

"At one point Mike Porter was driving a Suburban and Raye Dawn owned an Explorer. As I pulled out of my daughters driveway one day I got behind Raye Dawn. She pulled up to the stop sign in Meeker and would not go. After I sat there a few seconds I noticed she had the tag from her Explorer on the Suburban. I knew her tag number as I had seen it sitting on Main Street so many times at her work. I knew Mike Porter's tag started with a Q and this one was definitely hers. So I proceeded to have a high school moment and picked up the phone and called Meeker Police and reported it. Raye Dawn was letting several cars go and kept me behind her so I finally went around. Raye Dawn pulled into her grandmothers drive and later I found out she went in and called DHS to tell them I was stalking her. The...police officer...went to her grandmothers home to check out the report. He saw me drive by and told the DHS worker they needed to file a report on me. Then he proceeded to let Raye Dawn drive off in a vehicle that had a tag which expired six months prior and did not have insurance...I went on to the elementary school to watch the kids program. My main reason for making the call was to see if Meeker police would do anything that concerned Raye Dawn breaking the law and once again they did not. Later that day my daughter told her father-in-law about the incident. He was the Mayor of Meeker at the time and took some interest in our police department as he had several more complaints from other citizens. When he called the department and started asking the dispatcher questions this officer could hear her end and assumed it was me on the line. The Mayor could hear this officer in the background yelling for the dispatcher to 'tell Kathie to leave Raye Dawn alone.' She had to inform him it was not me on the phone. The following morning Mike Porter's Suburban was again parked on Main Street... This time it has the expired tag back on it. I figured they had purchased a tag since Mike Porter had called a friend of mine asking for an insurance quote that day. He told her he had not had insurance in nine months. I felt bad that I had made this call and put them in a financial bind. In reality I wasn't the one that put them in the financial bind, but I did make it worse with my call. If they had to take a tag from another vehicle they evidently were in a heck of a financial situation. Another day goes by and I get a call from a business in Meeker telling me flashing lights were sitting behind Mike Porter's Suburban. Once again they put the tag from the Explorer back on the Suburban and parked it on Main Street. The Mayor noticed it and personally went to the police department and told them they should take action. I couldn't believe they would have so little regard for the law... Mike Porter was allowed to walk down the block and purchase a tag and the vehicle was not towed in. When we went to Raye's trial I was questioned about this and her attorney made a big deal about my part in it. In reality she was the one that had broken the law and once again it was being blamed on me. I was not proud of the call I had made, but I made it and that was that..."

# 23 The Jurors

"The jury, passing on the prisoner's life, may in the sworn twelve have a thief or two guiltier than him they try."

~ William Shakespeare

November 16, 2007

Dear [Raye Dawn's current defense attorney]:

I am writing you today to clear my conscience. Recently, a co-worker served on a jury that convicted one of your clients, Raye Dawn Smith.

The juror, [Katrina], was called to serve on the jury and this was her third time to serve. She and I discussed her previous service and the upcoming date at which she was to report. While visiting with [Katrina], she recounted to me her boredom, inattention and lack of concern for the previous trials she participated in. [Katrina] said, "I was just sittin' there bored out of my head and looking for anything I could do to distract myself. I didn't care if the State wanted to take someone's property. I always picked the side I was going with by which lawyer I liked best. Both times, I already knew how I was going to vote from the start."

Eventually, [Katrina] went to court and found out she was going to serve on the Raye Dawn Smith case, which she quickly reported to me. She was excited and said this was the first criminal case she had sat on.

Practically every day during the trial, [Katrina] would call me during her lunch breaks and begin telling me about the case and what had happened that day. She would call in the evenings doing the same thing and admitted to me daily that she watched television news coverage of the trial and looked up the website for Kelsey, "just like everyone else on the jury has." [Katrina] also reported to me that she was bored during the proceedings as well and was even caught a couple of times playing with a gum wrapper or other piece of trash, just to pass time.

[Katrina] loves to be the center of attention. She frequently dresses flashily and is loud and boisterous. She claimed many times that she would arrive late or create the occasional disturbance in court creating laughter. [Katrina] did not take her responsibility seriously. After the verdict, she was contacted by News 9 in Oklahoma City and, in extremely bad taste, agreed to be interviewed. She asked me to accompany her, but I declined.

... I do not condone what happened to Kelsey and I do not know the full circumstances surrounding her mother's involvement in her demise. However, I believe in the importance of integrity and fairness in our adversarial, legal system. I find it hard to believe that, considering the actions of [Katrina], Raye Dawn could have received a fair trial. She deserves to have her case heard by, mature, responsible, people who will listen to and weigh the evidence against her.

Recently, [Katrina] contacted me to tell me that Raye Dawn's attorneys were questioning the integrity of the jury. She thought that was strange, was obviously worried and asked me not to mention any of the conversations we had to anyone. This is what prompted my letter. [Katrina] should be ashamed of herself and I hope that something can be done to right this wrong. Justice is required here for all parties involved.

If I can be of any assistance, please do not hesitate to contact me.-

Shortly after Raye's trial, her attorney hired a private investigator to check into the background of the jury and to visit them and see if any of the jurors would make statements.

When the investigator visited Katrina at work, he reported that he was asked, "Am I in trouble?" On the second visit, the investigator claimed that she refused to say anything, stating she had hired an attorney.

Following are the statements the investigator was able to obtain from members of the jury and other witnesses:

According to Juror number one (the juror numbers are not indicative of the jurors' positions in the jury box. The numbers are simply in lieu of names):

"[Fog] a fellow juror, slept continuously throughout the trial. I voiced concern to the judge's bailiff that [Fog] was not staying awake and was not paying attention. I was told by the bailiff to nudge [Fog] to keep her awake. I believe she should have been removed from the jury because she slept and did not pay attention. As jurors, we were allowed to keep our phones but had to turn them off during the trial. [Katrina], another fellow jury member, was always on her phone during breaks. I believe there were at least two to three jurors that should not have served on the jury."

Juror two stated:

"[Katrina], a fellow juror, was always on her cell phone talking the morning before trial, during the morning break, at lunch and during the afternoon break every day of the trial. [Katrina] was attention seeking and repeatedly late, sometimes very late. [Katrina] received numerous phone calls and sent text messages to a lot of people throughout the trial. When she wasn't on the phone, [Katrina] was chewing gum and passing out gum to the other jurors. [Katrina] told me that Raye Dawn had rented a trailer from someone...for her and her family to stay in during the trial. [Katrina] stated that the calendar introduced by the defense was absolutely boring and that she thought the calendar took too long to explain. [Katrina] referred to it as the 'damn calendar.' [Katrina] wanted to be the jury foreman because she had served on a jury before. [Fog], another fellow juror, slept throughout the trial. [Fog] told me she went to the hospital over the intervening weekend of the trial because of a potassium deficiency. [Fog] advised that this was causing her to fall asleep during the trial. [Fog], who was sick and slept all the time, wanted to know when we were going to be paid. Other jurors nodded off as well. I believe that ...another juror, already had his mind made up because he made comments that he did not need to see any more of the pictures or need to see the calendar or hear any evidence. I believe that [Celia], another juror who always talked about getting drunk with her underage children, had her mind made up that Raye Dawn was guilty before trial. From general conversation with [Celia], I believe that she based her decision off her knowledge of the case on the news before the trial. I also believe that she probably watched the news during the trial."

Juror three, Fog, stated:

"During the trial, I continually fell asleep and the woman next to me was told to nudge me to keep me awake. Several jurors nudged me off and on during the trial to keep me awake. Later, I discovered I was low on potassium. During the trial over the intervening weekend, my granddaughter took me to the Indian Hospital in Okeema. It was discovered that I was low on potassium, and my physician reminded me that I needed to remember to take my supplement. I have a prescription for potassium, but I never can remember to take it. I have been on potassium supplement and other medications since my open heart surgery in December 2006."

Juror four stated:

"One woman on the jury slept during the trial and several people tried to keep her awake. This woman was an Indian lady who worked at KFC...Some of the news media attempted to talk to me and other jurors during the trial, but we ignored them."

Juror five stated:

"Juror [Fog] fell asleep during the trial. Juror...spoke to the court clerk about [Fog] falling asleep during the trial. The court clerk told the judge, and the judge suggested to the court clerk that [the other juror] nudge [Fog] if she noticed that she was falling asleep."

Courthouse employees were among those who saw the injustice in Raye's trial. They also signed affidavits to that affect. Following is one witnesses' statement:

"I work in the city clerk's office...located in the same building that houses the...Courthouse...where the trial was held in the above-styled case in July 2007. During the trial, the paternal family sat in the vestibule inside the northwest entry of the building facing the courtroom door. This was the only entrance to the courthouse during the trial. The paternal family was loud, visible and available to the press during the final sentencing. I heard that after the verdict was announced, the paternal family came down the hallway shouting and bragging about how the guilty verdict would allow them to obtain $15 million from the Department of Human Services instead of only half that because Raye Dawn had been convicted. I heard that Lance, Kelsey's biological father, was kicked out of the courtroom for making duck calls during the trial. The jurors were not escorted by any court or law enforcement official at any time during the trial while they were on break. The jurors were allowed to go out the east door to smoke. Several of the jurors got on their cell phones as soon as they came out for a break. The press was always located on the east side of the building and inside the... Police Department covered parking area next to where the jurors took their break. The press was always around the building trying to get a picture or an interview. One juror came up to Richard Smothermon, the prosecutor, in the hall in front of my office and asked him "don't you remember me?" I could not hear his reply. The juror and Richard Smothermon had a short conversation, and then Richard Smothermon walked away. The jury always ate lunch at [the] Mexican Restaurant about one-half of a block east of the courthouse. The Briggs family and members of the press ate there every day, as well."

In May of 2008 Celia posted on Kelsey's Purpose in response to a thread in which members were "discussing" a letter Raye had written to lawmakers. Celia created a new screen name, "tomboy_88_94" and added to the flavor of the thread with the following post: "RE: Letter from Raye Dawn – Kathie, this is [Celia]. I hope all is well with you and your family.As far as Mike Porter and Raye Dawn,they both got some what they deserved. You know I was pushing for life on Raye Dawn.It's still hard for me to understand how a mother could either harm their child or let others harm them. I think what you have done to speak out about child abuse, is one of the most wonderful things you have done for and in memory of your loving granddaughter.I pray that it saves many babies lifes and keeps them from going through what Kelsey did . GOD BLESS YOU KATHIE AND KEEP PUSHING FOR ALL THE LITTLE ONES A SAFE LIFE ........"

# 24 The Blog

"Pray for the dead and fight like hell for the living."
~ Mother Jones

Searching Kelsey's name today produces something much different than what one would have found when conducting an online search before July, 2007. I should know because I conducted a search at that time, as some jurors allegedly did. Among hundreds of posts against Raye I counted sixty-three YouTube videos that were touted as "Kelsey's true story." The videos promoted Lance as a "war hero" and loving and attentive father, stating he was in Iraq at the time of Kelsey's death. According to witnesses, this portrayal was nothing but a smokescreen to garner media attention for the paternal family's "cause."

Lance's older sister, Wilma, confirmed this theory with the following post: Post date uncertain…print date December 12, 2005 "Did he [God] call Lance to active duty for the protection of his country in order to give Kelsey's story the edge that it needed for the media?" This post was made at about the same time a picture was taken of Lance in his fatigues at Kelsey's gravesite. The picture and another similar picture with him standing have been shared repeatedly in the media. It was said to have been taken by his mom. Lance had been out of the military for over two months at the time of this photo.[33] Some have questioned the authenticity of the uniform he wore in the picture, stating that the flag is on the wrong side and that the patch possibly belongs to a unit other than his own.

Picture taken by Kathie Briggs in December of 2005

What I believe to be Lance's true character was revealed when he was involved in an accident during the months that Raye was pregnant with his child. The following police report gives us insight into the man the news media portrays as a war hero:

---

[33] See Appendix B – Exhibit 13

"On 8-2-02 at approx. 15:45pm, I, Officer...and Reserve Officer... responded to a two-vehicle accident in the 200 block of West Main... Upon arrival I noticed a white male, later identified as Raymond Lance Briggs, walking away from one of the vehicles involved, a 1994 Blue Plymouth van. I then noticed two subjects, one white male and one white female in the other vehicle, a 2002 Blue Ford pickup. The white male walking around seemed to be highly agitated, he was walking with his hands in his pockets, looking at the ground, and scraping his feet on the asphalt. He was in pacing mode. I asked if anyone was injured and if an ambulance needed to be called. The white male threw up his hands and stated, 'Fuck yea, he does,' pointing at the subjects in the Ford pickup. I then returned to my patrol unit and requested first responders. I then had [the reserve officer] start traffic control. I then turned to the injured subjects to reassure the two parties that help was on the way and to find out what type of injuries they had obtained during the accident. As I was standing there trying to get some information, the white male (Briggs), started to walk up toward the injured subject. I asked the male subject to step back and I would be with him in just a minute. At that response, the white male (Briggs) looked at me, threw up his arms and stated 'Fuck you. I don't have to step back. Who the fuck do you think you are? Fuck this shit.' I advised the subject that I was the officer on duty to investigate the accident, and that I would be needing to speak with him in just a few minutes and obtain some information from him. The white male (Briggs) then started to approach my location. I advised the subject to remain by his vehicle and I would be with him in a minute. The white male (Briggs) then stated, 'Fuck you. I don't have to step back. What the fuck do you want? I don't have to tell you anything, Bitch.' The white male continued to pace, and continued to throw his arms up in the air. At this point, [the reserve officer] came over to my location for back up. I then advised the white male subject that if he didn't calm down and do what I asked him to do, I was going to place him under arrest for his safety as well as our safety. The white male responded by stating 'Fuck you. You can't arrest me. I haven't done a fucking thing. I know the fucking law.' He then approached [the reserve officer] and attempted to intimidate [him] by throwing his chest out toward him and flexing his muscles. [The reserve officer] then asked what I wanted to do. I advised, 'Handcuff him.' The white male (Briggs) then replied, 'Yea right. Fucking arrest me. You can't. You have no right. Oh, fuck this shit here.' At this point, he put out both his hands in front of his body in a motion, wrist by wrist, and stated, 'Fucking arrest me then, if you can.' Before another word could be said, another male subject walked up and advised this officer that he was the male subject's brother in-law and that he could take him aside and cool him down, and asked that I not arrest him. I advised the subject that I would give him the opportunity to take the subject off to the side by the curb, sit him down, and try to calm him, but if the subject continued to act in the same manner, I would have no choice but to arrest him. The white male (Briggs) jerked away from his brother-in-law and then stated, 'Who the fuck do they think they are? Fuck you and them. I don't have to do a damn thing. Fuck, leave me alone.' The brother-in-law finally got the subject out of the first responders' way and away from the scene. [The reserve officer] then returned to do traffic control. With first responders on scene trying to take care of the injured, I once again approached the white male subject for information. As I approached toward his direction, he immediately started in again, 'Now what the fuck do you want? Huh? Fuck you!' I advised the subject that I needed to see his driver's license and insurance verification on the vehicle that he was driving. The subject began to walk toward the van then reached into his back pocket and got out his wallet. He stated, 'Fuck, I don't have it, so fuck you.' I then asked if he had any other form of identification, so that I may know who his is. He then replied, 'I got a fucking military I.D. Do you fucking want it? No, fuck you. You don't fucking need to see it.' He then slammed his wallet shut. I then asked if I could have his name and driver's license number. He turned from the van and started to walk to the curb, continuously throwing his arms up in the air. He then turned and advised that his name was Lance and his driver's license number was...He said the number too fast for me to write it down and I had to ask him to repeat. He then turned around, threw his arms up in the air, and stated, 'What, you fucking can't hear either?' He then repeated the number. I then asked for his middle name, he advised..., 'shit, did you get that?' I advised, 'Yes, thank you.' Briggs then turned around and started walking toward the old gas station on the south side of the road. I then started to look at the damage done to the vehicle that he was driving and obtaining tag information. I attempted to see if the windows had been rolled down or if they had been shattered, when he started to walk up to the van. I turned and was attempting to ask him if he had had the windows down or if they had possibly been shattered when he interrupted by saying, 'What the fuck are you doing now?' Once I was able to finish my question, he replied, 'Fucking figure it out yourself, bitch.' It was determined that he had the windows down. I then returned to my injured subject to try and obtain information from them on their identities. I then exited my patrol unit and attempted to go back to the pickup and I noticed another disturbance in the location of where Briggs was located. [The reserve officer] and myself responded to the disturbance. Upon arrival, I observed Briggs screaming and yelling at a female subject standing by a car. As I approached, he turned away and started cussing another female subject who was sitting on the ground with two small children. It was learned that was Briggs's mother. I continued to stay between the female subject, a sister, and Briggs. I advised Briggs again that he needed to calm down. Again, I was informed by Briggs to fuck off and leave him alone. He had nothing to discuss with me and to fucking leave. Again, Briggs was trying to intimidate my reserve officer and myself by throwing out his chest and flinging his arms around. I then noticed a white pickup pull up and an older male subject get out. I walked up and asked if he was father of Briggs. He replied 'Yes, Royce Briggs [Lance's stepfather].' I then asked if he was the owner of the vehicle. He stated, 'Yes.' I then requested to see the insurance verification. [Royce Briggs] advised that he did not have any insurance on the vehicle, it was uninsured. I then asked the father to try to keep Briggs calmed down while we continued to investigate the accident. Mr. Briggs advised he was not sure he could do that, but he would try. I then returned to Briggs and asked that he come back with me to my patrol unit so that I could finish my investigation by obtaining further information. Briggs replied, 'No, I am not fucking going back to your car. Why the fuck?' I then noticed a slight hint of an alcoholic beverage coming from Briggs. I turned to his sister and asked if he had been drinking that day. She advised no, he had been at his great-grandmother's funeral today. I then returned to Briggs and advised him that we need to go to the patrol unit where it was cooler and try to cool down and that he would be getting a citation. Briggs politely states, 'You can go back to your fucking car and write my damn citation without me being there. Go the fuck back. I'm not going to your patrol car.' I spoke with the family and asked them to take Briggs home and get him calmed down."

This type of display was also evident on an occasion when Lance was arrested. According to the arresting officer, he threatened both the officer and his family members.[34] This is a claim that was also made by Judge Key and the DHS supervisor after Kelsey's death. From Judge Key's *A Deadly Game of Tug of War: The Kelsey Smith-Briggs Story*:

"I forced myself to go to work the day after Kelsey died. The last thing I wanted to do was deal with people's problems, but I felt obligated to do my job. The sheriff called me into his office that afternoon and informed me they had talked to Lance Briggs the night before to tell him of the death of Kelsey, and that he was in Fort Benning, Georgia. The sheriff indicated that Lance was in some type of a treatment center, and that Lance had made threats against my family and me. At that point, the sheriff was concerned because he told me he had spoken to people who were concerned with Lance's mental instability. The death threats that were made

[34] See Appendix B – Exhibit 15

had come directly from Lance. It was a threat against my children, as well as the supervisor for DHS and his family."[35]

As for the villain in their version of what happened to Kelsey, the focus was always on Raye as an uncaring mother who chose a man over her own child with statements such as "Kelsey was returned to the home of her mother..." However, it was never included that Kelsey's step-father, the man charged with her sexual assault and murder also resided in the home and had been home alone with Kelsey at the time of her alleged rape and demise. The way in which such statements were phrased cast a dark cloud over Raye, and sadly, the darkness is all the general public could see.

The voices trampling and trashing Raye were overwhelming and impossible to ignore. Therefore, Raye had few supporters outside her immediate family and close friends. As I soon learned, anyone who dares to stand up in Raye's defense is quickly shut down with threats of lawsuits or they're inundated with stories that aren't based on fact just to silence the opposing voice of reason.

Consequently, from the fall of 2005 to the summer of 2007, everything that had been attempted to aid Raye's defense or to repair the damage that had been done to her public image was immediately flooded and either shut down or taken over by those who opposed Raye. People were afraid of being added to the list of civil lawsuits or afraid of enduring a backlash of terror, and rightfully so. This fear was another catalyst for the lack of support for Raye, and it was

[35] Key, Craig. *A Deadly Game of Tug of War: The Kelsey Smith-Briggs Story*. Garden City, NY: Morgan James Publishing, 2007. p. 91.

echoed throughout the Web on every Web site where "Kelsey's story" was told.

During my search, I also discovered a blog that seemed to be actively discussing Kelsey's case. At the time, I didn't know much about Kelsey's Purpose and its followers, how many people were members, or who was involved with their mission. I just knew the facts. When I stumbled upon the blog, I didn't realize it was a temporary venue where Kathie's supporters were posting while her Web site was closed to new posts due to the trial. To me, it seemed to be random people sharing their opinions.

The blog began with the following intro: The "Other" Kelsey Posted on June 12th, 2007.

"Previously posted elsewhere on Tuesday, June 12th, 2007 8:32 pm Kelsey lived in a pack of wild dogs. And because she lived amongst these people, she did not live for very long: My Question is: Who is the Alpha Dog, the man who terrorizes women or the man who kills a toddler?"

After the introduction, the blogger listed an article that discussed Lance's two charges of domestic abuse from 2006 regarding his alleged attack on a former girlfriend who stated he had been stalking her before he reportedly drug her out of the house by her hair and then pushed her friend into a glass window that was said to have been broken by him.[36]

The blog owner seemed to want to present both sides, and he kept the conversation going with over 763 comments

---

[36] See articles and evidence at the following Web address: http://www.thetruthaboutkelsey.com/Lance/Lance%20Briggs%20Page.htm

in a month and a half—the amount of time that the blog was active.

Certain jury members could have read the blog posts according to witnesses who claim jurors were searching the case online. Also, the scenario that was introduced on the news by a juror, Celia, who posted on Kelsey's Purpose, was presented on this blog. The juror claimed Raye had murdered her own child and framed Mike Porter. Evidence of this scenario was not included in the evidence against Raye; she was not on trial for murder, but the juror seemed to quote verbatim some posts from the blog.

Following are a select few comments from the blog (Any use of actual names is not intentional):

**FYI** - July 3rd, 2007- "As for the observer. They should be sued. Along with the family pawn that has been passing the papers and the flyers out. I hope the Briggs have a good attorney."

**Karen** - July 5th, 2007 – "Kelsey wasn't breathing when Mike Porter went into the room. He said he heard a 'gurgle' sound and when he picked her up she wasn't breathing..."

**Jamie** - July 5th, 2007 – "Actually her statement doesn't even say he came in and woke her up, it just states that he woke her up. Is it possible that when he came into the house it woke her up?"

**[blog owner]** - July 5th, 2007 - "Jamie - you are correct - the part of the arrest warrant when MP makes a statement simply says: 'when Mike Porter arrived home Raye Dawn and Kelsey were sleeping in Raye Dawn's bed. Raye Dawn got up and Kelsey was still sleeping.' So Mike Porter did not say she was sleeping peacefully or that he saw her asleep at all. The idea that Raye Dawn started to abuse Kelsey out of jealousy is a possible theory - BUT WHERE DOES IT COME FROM? Since when does being a 'drinking, volatile tramp' make you a child abuser? At what point did the public decide that Mike Porter was innocent and Raye Dawn the abuser? This is an important fact for me in looking at the case. I am not saying Raye Dawn COULDN't be the abuser - she absolutely COULD be but I don't see in these reports conclusive evidence that she is except that Mike Porter is pointing the finger at her [as the abuser] - I read that the Briggs AND Raye Dawn were all cited as either being responsible OR not able to protect Kelsey but that didn't include Raye Dawn alone. All evidence that points to Raye Dawn directly comes from Mike Porter's own version of events. Where DOES Gayla fit in here? Something simply does not add up about these relationships. What does Gayla know that would settle the mysteries of this case? What did she see? WHy did all of the family trust her so much (to the point that Mike Porter called HER?) The unknown abuser theory, as frustrating as it seems, makes a little sense - DID ANYONE EVER SEE Raye Dawn ABUSE Kelsey? and they just aren't talking? DID ANYONE EVER SEE Mike Porter for that matter? Did Raye Dawn SEE Mike Porter or vice versa and they simply denied what they saw? Guess we'll never now I am just curious to know how onlookers can be so sure that Raye Dawn is guilty of the actual abuse (vs. enabling or failing to report it or intervene - still a hefty responsibility! AND if this is TRUE She COULD have saved Kelsey.) DId the Briggs make all those calls? and if so why are they being vilified since the abuse DOES seem to have occurred? is it because they are not cleared from inflicting the abuse? Suddenly I am wondering, why is the obvious answer not a possibility anymore: Mike Porter DID IT! Have all the mudslinging, divorce, custody, family-feuding and hatred issues clouded the obvious? I STILL need more evidence, not conjecture, that Raye Dawn committed the crime - I KNOW i could've missed something that makes others so sure - point it out to me!"

**Gracie** - July 5th, 2007 – "Just another tidbit of info..Raye Dawn moved out of her mothers house (which at that time also included her younger sister) around the same time she met Mike Porter. Which poses another 'theory' that having to care for a toddler all on her own may have been too much for her to handle."

The following post is reflective of the juror's statement to the media within hours of her verdict. This juror, Celia, convinced the jury to make an emotional decision.

**Jamie** - July 5th, 2007 – "Without a trial and evidence being shown, there is nothing that points at Mike Porter either except for Raye Dawn…From what I gathered, Mike Porter's doctor said Kelsey's injuries were inflicted several hours before he ever got home…As for the sexual abuse, the ME said he couldn't say whether it happened or not, the DA's hired doctor said it did happen, and Mike Porter's doctor said there was no evidence of sexual abuse. Who do you choose to believe? The defendant's hired doctor or the DA's high paid hired doctor? Both of them need to prove something…Since Mike Porter never went to trial, we will never know what made the DA so sure he was the one that did it. From what I understood, there was no medical evidence that pointed at either person and it was all circumstantial. Maybe when the gag order's lifted, the DA will show what he has that made him so sure it was Mike Porter."

The blog was so accessible and easy to find that the CASA worker who was listed as a state witness in Raye's trial joined the discussion DURING the trial.

**[CASA]** - July 9th, 2007 – "Please go Gracie June 19, 2007. then read the 33 page report that was in The Oklahoman this last week. Just put everything together."

**Karen** - July 9th, 2007 – " [CASA], aren't you supposed to be in Bristow today???"

**[CASA]** - July 10th, 2007 – "Who said I was going to Bristow??"

Although I suspect by the language of some of those who posted that Kathie was an active participant on the blog, she sent a message to the blog owner via e-mail alerting him of the trial notes that would be online nightly after the trial. Kathie's active forum was closed to new posts at the time, but members of the group seemed to always find a place to express their opinions, and Kathie always seems to know exactly where to find them.

**[Blog owner]** - July 9th, 2007 – "From Kathie Briggs: 'I hope you will let your readers know that each night after the trial Fox...will have a page of notes about the trial. Britten Follett, a reporter that has been on this case from day one will be in court daily. She will come home and give a more in depth look about the days testimony.'" A link to Ms. Follett's notes was posted.

**Jamie** - July 13th, 2007 – "I didn't think twice about the stalking allegations, until Kathie testified herself. How would you know if Raye Dawn switched tags on her vehicles unless you had known the previous tag numbers? How would you know a previous tag number unless you were stalking someone and writing it down? And then the officer testified the PD was getting phone calls about Mike Porter and Raye Dawn's whereabouts and what they were doing...I do not buy the testimony about the e-mails. There was a lot more to those e-mails and the meeting than what was testified to and if they had actually allowed the e-mail to be presented, I'm sure it would have shed some light. Someone else said on another blog that some of those e-mails contained several pictures of Kelsey that were sent to Mike Porter from the Briggs family. I'm not convinced it was a set up against Raye Dawn, but I do smell manipulative and vindictive. Against who? Who knows..."

**[Whit]** - July 13th, 2007 – "First off, Marcy and [Betsy], the point of this blog is for people to freely express differing viewpoints WITHOUT BEING ATTACKED. Attacking seems to be a Briggs (and supporters)specialty. If you have an opinion, i.e. that the

Briggs are unaccountable for the unraveling of this situation, then back it up with an explanation. Acting like an immature child that resorts to name calling when you disagree only discredits your opinion, character and intelligence. I'm not saying you are wrong or stupid, just that the explosive, irrational way you respond is coming off that way. Why do you assume every comment posted is made by a Smith family member? It only reinforces the hateful, assumptive mentality that people suspect of Kathie."

**Ellen** - July 13th, 2007 – "[Whit], I agree Craig Key is a IDIOT!! and should be as or more responsible in her death! hes a ASS-HOLE and i hopes he rotts in hell! [Betsy], I also agree 'officer Byers is the VILLAGE IDOT' I would like to see them both have the sh!! kicked out of them! I am appalled by both of their actions, they make me sick!"

The following post is definitely from a member of Kelsey's paternal family. The story about the "monitor" in the paternal family's home came from their overactive and paranoid imaginations and the story of Raye stalking the paternal family was supposedly told to Kathie by Mike Porter. Also, the "all cried out" phrase came from Raye's OSBI interview that the paternal family obtained illegally. At the time of Raye's trial, the paternal family members were the only ones who had any knowledge of what that interview contained. It was allegedly given to them by Mike Porter's attorney. After Raye's trial, Lance's sister, Wilma, passed out copies of the interview on DVD. One of the DVD copies that Wilma reportedly made was eventually passed on to me. It's a misdemeanor to distribute copies of a confidential inter-rogation, but the established pattern has been that nothing is done to bring justice to those who break the law when their actions are done by or on behalf of the paternal family.

**Jill** - July 14th, 2007 – "The stalking started with Raye Dawn stalking the Briggs home. She would sit across the road and 'monitor' everything that went on. She had a bug inside the house after a visit with Kelsey...Was she 'cried out' as she claimed...She is shedding more now for herself during the trial. Her out of control sobbing at the trial was so excessive that they had to take a recess. The moment the last juror walked out of the room, her uncontrolled crying ceased immediately. That's amazing that she's able to put her emotions back together so easily...Mommy will 'settle down' and cool off when she's in prison. Justice for Kelsey"

**Tony** - July 14th, 2007 - "OK, let me understand this, Raye Dawn has planted a wire tap in Kathie's home and sat outside her house with other spyware monitoring everything at Kathie's then she ran this 'game' on her whole family to get them on her side and now people have abandoned ship, right? Actually, it would appear to me that the pack of wild dogs have become rabied because they are not convincing people of their dillusional ramblings. Oh, they probably forgot to tell us about Raye Dawn's formative years in the CIA and the fact she helped Al Gore invent the internet. Was she around when the shopping cart was invented too or did her Dad have a hand in planning the Bay of Pigs invasion in Cuba? This sounds foolish and does not help anyone truly debate this case. I want to thank [the blog owner] for having this site and allowing some people to openly discuss this case. However, I will not be persuaded by 'JFK conspiracy theories'. Does anyone know why Fox 25 took all the prior days notes off their website? It appears to me from the notes that what the TV stations are reporting and what is in the transcript notes on Fox 25 are very diffrent. Look at [the DHS worker] saying really DHS thought Kelsey should have gone home with Raye Dawn, and the fact she didn't think Raye Dawn abused Kelsey, thats not what they said on TV though. Did anyone else catch [Jack] say that 'if they don't get Raye Dawn in Court then God will get her later'. I wonder if maybe it isn't going well for Smothermon?"

**Jamie** - July 14th, 2007 – "Tony, don't forget that Mike Porter's doctor says something totally different than the other 2, but I don't think the jury will see that either. Smothermon definitely won't introduce it because it blows his theory out of the water."

**ED** - July 14th, 2007 – "The facts of this case are that: Kelsey is dead, Mike Porter or Raye Dawn DID it, AND Mike Porter or Raye Dawn is HIDING it. No matter what happened with the family before the fact of death is really irrelevant. Raye Dawn is on trial for allowing someone to hurt her child. She knew and should have done something about it. Regardless of whether or not the families hate each other (which they do of course) that is not what is on trial here. I don't care what else is going on in your life, you TAKE CARE OF YOUR CHILDREN. I don't have any kids but my good friends do and I would put my life on the line for them, and they aren't even related to me. Why can't people realize that we need to take care of our kids? This is a sad case and it will never be a happy subject to talk about, but instead of attacking each other, the Briggs or the Smiths, or anyone else, why can't we try to work together and start preventing child abuse. This situation should have been stopped LONG before Kelsey died. No matter what, she should be here today."

**Jill** - July 15th, 2007 – "[Whit] stated that Meeker was no where land and Raye Dawn wouldn't have access to high tech spyware? Are you serious??? You're so uninformed it's pathetic. Anyone can buy a bug and place it in a house and listen from a short distance. Someone is feeding you a bunch of bull. You stated 'If Mike Porter had been tried for the crime he committed, instead of whittling down his charges in hopes of getting Raye Dawn, the evidence would have come to light at trial.' Whittling down? 30 years is whittling down. I'm sure that Raye Dawn's won't be whittled down. You are evidently related to that family and they have fed you a line sister!...Gayla is a big let down...She is like the "mother from Hell"...Gayla contributed to the hatred against Kathie and just added fuel to the fire to Raye Dawn. Party, in Raye Dawn's defense, she would have never hated Kathie so much if it hadn't been for her mother. Her mother didn't like her so Raye Dawn didn't like her. Monkey see monkey do."

The previous post was reminiscent of many posts that have been captured from various "bash boards." Why would random people on a blog worry about "who hates Kathie"? A question to ponder…

**Tab** - July 18th, 2007 – "Guilty!!!" [article posted]

**[Frances]** - July 18th, 2007 – "Mother convicted in child-abuse case Raye Dawn was found guilty of enabling the abuse of her 2-year-old daughter and given a 27-year prison sentence, a jury decided today. After the verdict was announced, Raye Dawn lowered her head into her hands and sobbed, 'I don't understand. Help me.'"

**Tiny** - July 18th, 2007 - "Wow, all the US observers in the state couldn't convince this jury that she was innocent."

**Tiny** - July 18th, 2007 – "I guess the old saying is true 'What comes around goes around. It went around TODAY. Thank God."

**[Whit]** - July 18th, 2007 – "[Frances] and Tiny, Where have you been the last week, why speak up now? To rub it in? Admirable."

**Tab** - July 18th, 2007 - "The 27 years isn't definite,only a recommendation by the jury.Ultimately,it is up for the judge to decide the length of her sentence.He could go less,he could go MORE."

**[Frances]** - July 18th, 2007 - "actually, i've been posting under the name karen. why?? because i felt i had the right to. it was in my best interest to do so, as i had been attending the trial and i don't know who reads what on these sites. and i'm sure i'm not the only one who has done so. and in all honesty, i thought i had put karen when i posted. forgive me. regardless, i've been here posting the whole time and telling what i knew to be fact."

The blog shut down within days of the completion of Raye's trial. The final post was from the blog owner explaining that it was time to let Kelsey rest in peace. Although I agreed with his statement, I felt that finding peace for Kelsey involved peace for her entire family, and in particular, Kelsey's mom.

# 25 Seeking the Truth about Kelsey

"You can bend it and twist it... You can use it and abuse it... But even God cannot change the Truth." ~ Mike Levy

Raye wasn't charged with any crime until four months after Kelsey's death. These charges didn't come from an investigation or newly-discovered evidence. They were the result of months of plotting, planning, and pushing the district attorney to charge her with "something." Kathie and her followers clearly schemed and plotted to ensure that Raye would be imprisoned. They threatened and harassed anyone who dared stand up in Raye's defense, such as I.

Many akin the actions of Kathie and her followers to those of the angry mobs during the time of the Salem witch trials. The witch hunts reportedly started not because there were actual witches running around in Salem and doing evil deeds, but because the Pilgrims had moved to a new country with a climate unlike their own with a different type of soil, and a whole new host of environmental factors. When things went wrong, their faith was so strong that they immediately blamed Satan and thought his work was being done through "witches." These people didn't factor in the environmental or regional differences they encountered while growing crops and building communities. When something went wrong and crops died, they jumped to conclusions and blamed, judged, and murdered innocent people. Through this tragic part of our history, we've learned that blame is at times associated with a specific, targeted person, not outside factors. When tempers get heated, the result is often the guilty walking free while the innocent is crucified. Someone has to pay and rational thinking is tossed aside in the name of "justice."

In the case of Kelsey, an innocent child was reportedly raped and murdered. The fact that this happened is appalling and disgusting and something that is heartbreaking for all. Consequently, the first thought that came to the minds of those following or closely involved in the case was to "burn the witch." Due to the hate that was already established for Raye from the paternal family, and since all of the fingers pointed toward Raye (aside from those who actually investigated the crime and were to prosecute the guilty party), she became the witch in this scenario.

In a typical case, one article can ignite a heated rage toward the perpetrator of a crime against a child. Multiply that rage by over 400 articles in print and in excess of 1,300 televised reports and imagine the amount of hate and anger and pure rage that has been centered on Raye...a mother who wasn't home at the time of her child's alleged rape and murder. As a logical person, wouldn't you question why the public was deceived in order to bring that type of hate for Raye while the torch-bearers worked to create sympathy for Mike Porter? I questioned this as well. I was an outsider who saw through the smokescreen and I was determined to bring the truth to light and fight the injustice that surrounded Kelsey's case. Therefore, in the last days of Raye's trial I started blogging about the facts as I knew them on a blog I created entitled "Seeking the Truth about Kelsey" and I invented the character "Truth Seeker." The character I created was a mixture of various people that I knew. I drew from their lives as a basis for details I would share about me. I didn't want my identity known. I feared that people who knew me would recognize me if I were myself. I had a strong desire to help Raye, but I wasn't ready to commit myself to being the main person who spoke out on her behalf. The truth had started coming to light with the article and the Judge's book. People were opening their eyes to the public deception. I viewed myself as nothing more than a messenger sharing the facts. I never dreamed it would grow into anything other than my original intentions. Within days of the trial ending my blog was flooded with members of Kelsey's Purpose.

My first post was titled, "Meet Kelsey." I never thought anyone would read the blog. I merely sent my thoughts into cyberspace about the things I knew as fact and my opinion. There were no pictures of Kelsey or anyone in her family. I wasn't sure what I could legally use, so I kept it simple in the beginning. This was the introduction:

"Meet Kelsey - She was a beautiful two and a half year old child who died of blunt force trauma to the abdomen. That much I know is true. All the other things I've read, I'm not so sure about. I do want to give my sympathies to her family. The loss of a child or grandchild is so hard to bear. My sympathies to you. My prayers are with Raye Dawn (Kelsey's mom) this week as she faces a jury for either abusing Kelsey or enabling abuse. I realize the hope of a fair trial has been tainted by the media and the paternal family out for revenge. I do hope the jury opens their ears and judges you according to the facts and not preconceptions. I began this blog after being outraged at the viciousness I've read on the Internet toward the Judge in the case, Craig Key, and the mom, Raye Dawn Smith. I would like to hear some constructive, truthful comments about what happened and suggestions or ways to prevent it from happening in the future. There doesn't seem to be a neutral site anywhere that I've found that isn't asking for money or ragging on someone who hasn't been found guilty and someone who was doing his job. If you've come here with those intentions, you've come to the wrong place. I am looking forward to the book that was written by the Judge. I think it's about time he told his side of this story. If you want to know more about Kelsey, go to [link given to the state newspaper's articles]. I look forward to your comments. I hope some of you out there aren't media zombies who believe everything you hear and read."

Soon after the initial post, my blog was flooded. Topics of conversation changed on the blog. It seemed that some came to the blog to discuss their beliefs and known facts, others only wanted to argue and find a hole in my statements that they could rip apart. Soon, my blogging turned into what I termed "rants." The nonstop arguing was getting to me. I'm not an argumentative person, but if I quit, I would be letting down Raye and her family. I was torn between doing what I thought was right and putting myself into a situation with people that were not the type I would invite into my life.

At one point, someone posted on my blog that I couldn't discuss the case without Lance's permission. After that post

I consulted with an attorney whom my parents had recently used in an unrelated issue. We had exchanged e-mails a few times regarding their situation and I thought he'd share his opinion with me regarding my right to free speech. In our short conversation, he told me that as long as I was discussing true events and not purposely lying or libeling anyone, I could in fact discuss the case. He also informed me that I could display a picture of Kelsey as long as I wasn't using it for profit. The blog soon changed its look and I added a picture of Kelsey with Raye. Those who came to my blog to start trouble were not happy that I didn't follow their orders. It wasn't long until threats of a lawsuit began circulating. To this day, I've been threatened so many times with a lawsuit that the words no longer have an affect on me. Despite the threats, the conversation continued as people came together to voice their opinions on the case, and others worked to silence our opinions. Although Raye had been found guilty of "should have known" and was convicted by a jury with a 27-year sentence, those who worked to put Raye into prison just couldn't let it go. It seemed like their hate grew stronger, especially as the facts they had spent years silencing were breaking through to the surface. Since Raye was in prison, the target for their hate soon became me…the one who dared to defy their orders to stop discussing the case and the one who ignored their threats. The battle that started over the custody of Kelsey soon turned into a battle of truth vs. lies. Each side thought their side was that of truth. It soon became clear who fought for the truth and who just wanted to fight.

Once our group moved to a forum, emotions were running high. People were outraged by the content of Kathie's

Web site and "bash boards." On many occasions they had tried to voice their opinions and state the facts, but found themselves censored and silenced. Things had been left unsaid and they were grateful for an open forum that was not controlled by Kathie's gang of cyberbullies. Therefore, for the first few weeks, nobody was censored. Our conversations were a continuous flow with hundreds of posts within days. Although at times things got out of hand when someone wanted to vent or the "others" came looking to start a fight, we were, at the core, a spiritual, open-minded group of individuals. We all had a different idea of what happened to Kelsey, but for the most part, respect was shown for a difference in opinion. Over one hundred active members participated, with only about one-fourth of those there for the wrong reasons. I was alone at the helm and I had no clue what I was doing. I made it clear in the beginning that I was new to forums and some participants understood and were, in turn, kind and helpful. Threats didn't come from any of us who were there to discuss the case or vent. The only threats were from the other side. However, Kathie and Lance were called to the carpet on their lies. On several occasions, they were boldly called "liars"—a term that seemed too "in-your-face" for me at the time, but it was a claim that I had also found to be true.

After moving to the forum, I reluctantly became acquainted with the cast of characters that had been posting on my blog. Some became confidants who, today, I consider my closest friends. Looking back, it's comical how hard I fought it in the beginning. I was lured into chat rooms, something I tried to avoid at all costs. I really didn't have time to socialize because my world was falling apart around me. I didn't want to like anyone, let alone trust them or let them into my world. I was the character that they all knew as Truth Seeker—the woman with several children who worked hard at being aloof, tough, and all of those things that in real life, I was not. I shared life experiences that were not my own in developing the character. I didn't want to remove the curtain or allow those who supported Raye and had come to know and like me to realize that I was a person who was in the midst of one of the most difficult times in her life. I was ashamed that I was failing miserably. I thought if they saw the real me—flesh, blood, and tears wrapped in a body that often betrayed me, they would no longer support Raye. I couldn't have been more wrong. I soon learned that some were also hurting and their lives consisted of different challenges from mine. They were searching for someone to throw them a life preserver and they found me—desperate, drowning, disappointing me. They didn't care that I wasn't the seven-foot-tall and tough-as-nails character I wanted everyone to see. The first time we met face-to-face, they expressed their relief that I was struggling, just like them.

Their image of me probably came from the avatars I had selected for intimidation. Unlike Kathie and her group who continually use pictures of Kelsey to be the face of their negativity, I chose a female warrior and then Keanu Reeves from the movie, *The Matrix* with his dark sunglasses and penetrating look. Kathie's supporters were hounding me with threats of lawsuits and constant harassment. I couldn't be the Girl Scout leader, Meals on Wheels driver, St. Vincent de Paul volunteer, homeschooling mom, former Mary Kay sales director that was the real me. I had to be someone who would be perceived as the type who wouldn't give in to the constant threats, someone who had been through hell and survived to tell about it. My intent wasn't for them to fear me; my character wasn't threatening. I just wanted them to know they had a true match in me. I wanted them to see me as someone who could not be threatened, someone who would not back down, regardless of how nasty their threats became, and they were constant and they were terrifying. The flood of hate mail had shaken me to my core, and I could only imagine what life had been like for Raye's family for the two years before I became involved. It was overwhelming for me and I was an outsider. My heart broke even more for Raye's family as the gravity of the situation started to set in and I realized what I was getting myself into by dueling with Kathie's supporters.

In essence, I had stolen a move from Kathie's playbook and I created a fictional character to play David to her Goliath. As David, I stood tall on my single area of the Web against Goliath, Kathie and her supporters, ranking into the thousands, with hundreds of Web sites and videos spreading their message of hate for Raye. I stood with my slingshot and pelted small snippets of truth at their massive army of haters who shamelessly used Kelsey as their shield. I was in a no-win situation. They had a dead child and a "war hero" they treated as mascots. I had a mom who loved her child but was blind to what was happening in her own home. Due to what some see as her blind trust in her husband, her child was allegedly raped and murdered. There was no winning that battle. All I had on my side was the truth and my integrity, and on that issue, I would not bend.

### *THE TRUTH CHANGES MINDS*

Some who came to the forum to destroy me, along with my mission, quickly opened their hearts long enough to listen to what I had to say and to them, it made sense. Many had questioned various parts of Kathie's story and they had seen her lack of integrity as her story changed with each lie in which she was caught. The difference in us was clear. She had been there and lived it. I never met Kelsey. I was piecing together the facts as I discovered them. Kathie had been a part of the madness that engulfed Kelsey's life. When pieces of Kathie's story didn't fit into the puzzle, they were changed until a piece was found that would fit. In the end, it was my integrity that won the support of those who had previously believed Kathie, or possibly it was the fact that I wouldn't back down and give in to the threats and hate that were thrown at me on a daily basis. Maybe they just wanted to support Kelsey's story and found a group of people who were open-minded and wanted to know the truth just as badly as they did, and their support had nothing to do with me. I'm not sure why the forum grew as quickly as it did, but I was thankful that it was no longer "David vs. Goliath," or myself against thousands. It soon became "us vs. them." Our numbers weren't as great because we refused to use Kelsey as a mascot or to feed into the constant negativity on which they thrived, but we soon took control of the forum and banned anyone who was negative, became threatening, or seemed unstable. Each day was a myriad of trials followed by never-ending drama. One never knew what to expect. At times, emotions and words were heated. It was like an uprising of the downtrodden. For two years, those connected with Kelsey's Purpose had ruled the Internet, but there was a new sheriff in town and we collective few were no longer going to sit by and watch people be destroyed by the hate. It was time for it all to stop.

# 26 A Bright Idea

"An idea that is not dangerous is unworthy of being called an idea at all." ~ Oscar Wilde

The first conversation I had with Gayla, Raye's mom, after the trial involved coming up with a "bright idea." Gayla was the only person in the family to whom I had spoken besides Raye. For months after my initial involvement, Raye's family members had heard of "Truth Seeker," but they didn't know if she was someone within the family or an outsider. My identity was a mystery to all. Not even my family knew. Since I didn't discuss business with my friends or family, they thought I was spending all of my time working. However, keeping up with the blog overwhelmed me and my business started to suffer.

Managing my business and overseeing all of the projects that were ongoing was an eighty-hour per week job. I had an assistant. She managed the contract labor and assigned projects, but I wanted to personally inspect every page of transcription that was presented to my clients because my name was on the work; it had to be perfect. Since I fell behind on my end, I found myself in the situation where I paid my contract labor thousands of dollars that they had earned, but I never collected from my clients. Every credit card was charged to the limit; my savings quickly became depleted; I was in a ship that was broadsided by a roaring tide of hate and I was swiftly being pulled into the darkness. Instead of putting myself, my family, and my business first, I never abandoned ship. I stayed on board with all hands on deck and lost everything I had worked so hard to gain in the process. Taking up for a person in need became stronger than my survival instincts, and looking back, common sense. To me, a person's life was worth more than all of the money in the world and I knew that one day I would be blessed in return, so I sacrificed in order to give. I didn't have any grandiose illusions that I could get Raye out of jail, but to assist her family in gaining support so they would no longer be smothered in the stifling hate was worth the risk.

Gayla told me, "We just need a bright idea."

Although I didn't know much about building Web sites, I could build one well enough to put up some facts about the case and start an online petition. Therefore, I offered to build a Web site and put up a form to collect petition signatures. Gayla was grateful and open to any suggestions, so *Free Kelsey's Mom* was created. The name was something that immediately came to me due to the fact that each corresp-ondence I had seen from Raye was always signed, "Kelsey's mom."

The text on the first edition of the Web site was limited. As a professional, I was reluctant to write anything that could be misunderstood or argued. I knew some facts in the case, but I wasn't confident that documentation could validate all of them. At the time I hadn't seen much in the way of evidence. If my identity were ever revealed, it was my reputation on the line and I didn't want to be put into the position that my character could be attacked because I got something wrong. In turn, the case information on the Web site was restrained and there were only a few pages with the petition and pictures.

The Web site had been uploaded for just a couple of days with no Meta tags or keywords so it was not searchable on the Internet. It also wasn't submitted to any search engines since I was still in the process of building it. The only way someone could have found it at that time was by clicking on a direct link or typing in the exact address. After testing the form for the petition, I forwarded the link to the site to Gayla, who then shared it with family members and friends. Signatures trickled in with loving words of hope and faith, which instilled a reassurance that I was doing something right and good. During a shopping trip with Mom and my daughter the tone of the signatures turned dark as hate flooded my Blackberry's memory. While reading the words I felt stunned at not only the amount of hate directed at Raye and her family, but also over the fact that the people sending me the nasty messages felt justified in doing so. Raye's family was grieving the loss of Kelsey as well as her younger brother, the son of Raye and Mike Porter. The baby boy had been taken by child protective services following yet another campaign from Kathie's group. Compound the loss of the two children with Raye's 27-year conviction—more than four times the amount of time the prosecutor thought she should serve (he offered her a five year plea), and just imagine the amount of pain the family felt. They were hurting. Why did these people feel justified in adding to their heartache?

I had no idea how to handle the situation so I created a post for my blog that included some of the nasty messages along with information that proved they had come from a link on Kelsey's Purpose. Following is an excerpt from that post:

"After being posted on Kelsey's Purpose, the administrator was slammed with mean, spiteful, and hateful messages with names like Charles Manson, Bullshit, etc. and messages like,

'This entire case was a horrible tragedy, caused by Raye Dawn and her then husband Mike Porter. May she burn in hell, starting the day before she's due to be released from prison. In my eyes, 27 years isn't nearly enough... perhaps we should petition the court to increase it?'

'This site needs to be shut down, she got what she deserved. There is no way she wasn't abusing or knew about the abuse... I hope someone kills her in prison, but slow and suffer like Kelsey did!'

'they should be serving life in prison!!!!!...i wish when they are in their jail sells someone abuses them just like they abused Kelsey!!'

'I have pictures of Kelsey too. Of course they are of her with two broken legs and bruises on her sweet little face. You also may want to mention to people that Raye Dawn was ALSO charged and sentenced for ENABLING!!!'

'If poor little Raye Dawn is so innocent, she wouldn't be sitting in a cell waiting for the transfer to her new home.'

'My only hope for Raye Dawn is that everyday of her life is spent thinking over and over again about how she allowed that little girl to suffer and die, whether by her own hand or her own will to let the abuse continue on through Mike Porter.'

'Maybe she can pen-pal with Susan Smith and Darlie Routier. You can delete this immediately, which I'm sure you will. It's obviously hard for you people to face the truth. Let me just say that I will save this message and start my own 'petition' for appeal denial and I guarentee my list is longer then yours!!!'

'i think she is giong to hell 4 what she did!!!'

'OK Hell no I do not support this at all, I can't even believe you have the gaul to have a petition!!!!! Besides the fact , that you have a picture of the murderer!!!!! Sick is all I can say! Oh and this is my Freedom of Speech!!!'

'I dont think the mom deserves anything but but to have her ass beat to helll sorry low life bitch why did you abuse that sweet baby?'

'HAHAHAHA!!!! SHE GOT WHAT SHE DESERVED!!!! HOPE SHE ROTTS IN PRISON!!!!!!!!!!!!!'"

A chart of traffic facts was posted that showed all direct links came from Kelsey's Purpose. Following are screen shots from the original report.

This first screen shot shows the date that traffic started on the Web site. I set up the traffic reporting as soon as I purchased the domain. Its original intent was to use for marketing purposes to determine what keywords were driving in traffic. That intent soon changed after the hate-filled messages started arriving.

Report created by Traffic Facts for http://www.freekelseysmom.com on 07-26-07

Summary

| Date | Visitors | Unique Visitors | Page Views |
|---|---|---|---|
| Jul 19, 2007 | 0 | 0 | 0 |
| Jul 20, 2007 | 1 | 1 | 2 |
| Jul 21, 2007 | 3 | 3 | 5 |
| Jul 22, 2007 | 37 | 18 | 268 |
| Jul 23, 2007 | 97 | 66 | 423 |
| Jul 24, 2007 | 20 | 19 | 111 |
| Jul 25, 2007 | 308 | 230 | 1,214 |
| **Total** | **466** | **337** | **2,023** |

Copyright © 2003 - 2007. All rights reserved.

The second screen shot shows where the traffic came from—what links or search engines were used to discover the Web site. As you'll notice, the majority of traffic came directly from Kelsey's Purpose with some also coming from links within e-mails and from search engines.

| | A | B | C | D |
|---|---|---|---|---|
| 1 | **Report created by Traffic Facts for http://www.freekelseysmom.com on 07-26-07** | | | |
| 2 | | | | |
| 3 | **Referring Domains** | | | |
| 4 | 2007-07-19 00:00:00 | 2007-07-25 23:59:59 | | |
| 5 | | | | |
| 6 | **Hostname** | **Referrals** | **Percentage** | |
| 7 | www.kelseyspurpose.org | 11 | 22.45 | |
| 8 | search.yahoo.com | 10 | 20.41 | |
| 9 | bulletins.myspace.com | 6 | 12.24 | |
| 10 | thetruthaboutkelsey.com | 4 | 8.16 | |
| 11 | blog.myspace.com | 3 | 6.12 | |
| 12 | kelseyspurpose.org | 2 | 4.08 | |
| 13 | us.f611.mail.yahoo.com | 2 | 4.08 | |
| 14 | bored.com | 1 | 2.04 | |
| 15 | mailcenter3.comcast.net | 1 | 2.04 | |
| 16 | search.live.com | 1 | 2.04 | |
| 17 | us.f357.mail.yahoo.com | 1 | 2.04 | |
| 18 | us.f635.mail.yahoo.com | 1 | 2.04 | |
| 19 | us.f802.mail.yahoo.com | 1 | 2.04 | |
| 20 | us.f824.mail.yahoo.com | 1 | 2.04 | |
| 21 | us.f829.mail.yahoo.com | 1 | 2.04 | |
| 22 | us.f831.mail.yahoo.com | 1 | 2.04 | |
| 23 | us.f836.mail.yahoo.com | 1 | 2.04 | |
| 24 | webmail.aol.com | 1 | 2.04 | |
| 25 | **Total** | **49** | **100** | |

The following screen shot shows that the only "key words" that were typed into a search engine was the actual Web site address. Therefore, this Web site was not discovered through a search. The Web address was known.

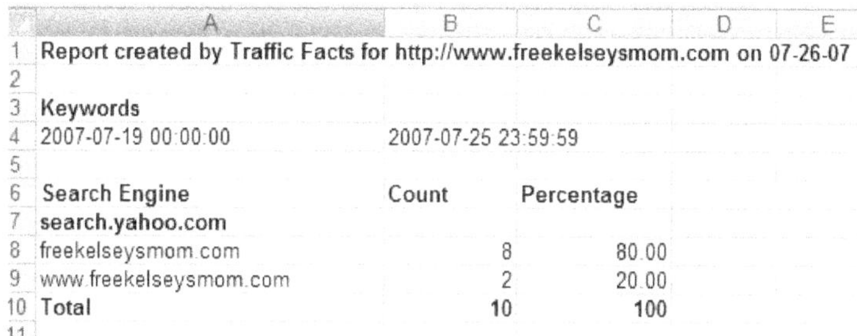

| | A | B | C | D | E |
|---|---|---|---|---|---|
| 1 | **Report created by Traffic Facts for http://www.freekelseysmom.com on 07-26-07** | | | | |
| 2 | | | | | |
| 3 | **Keywords** | | | | |
| 4 | 2007-07-19 00:00:00 | 2007-07-25 23:59:59 | | | |
| 5 | | | | | |
| 6 | **Search Engine** | **Count** | **Percentage** | | |
| 7 | **search.yahoo.com** | | | | |
| 8 | freekelseysmom.com | 8 | 80.00 | | |
| 9 | www.freekelseysmom.com | 2 | 20.00 | | |
| 10 | **Total** | **10** | **100** | | |
| 11 | | | | | |

The next screen shot proves that there were no keyphrases used to discover the Web site.

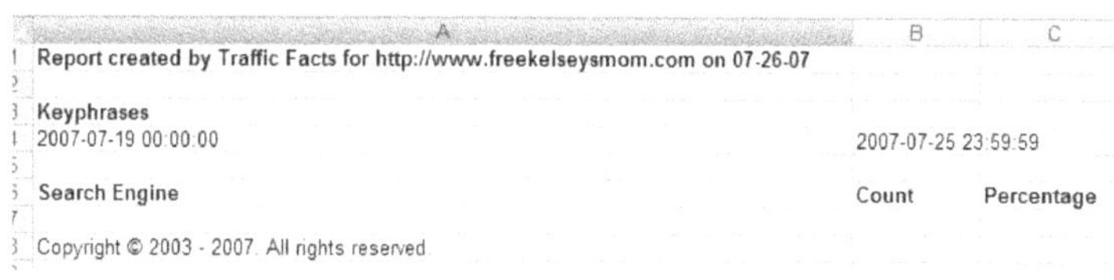

| | A | B | C |
|---|---|---|---|
| 1 | **Report created by Traffic Facts for http://www.freekelseysmom.com on 07-26-07** | | |
| 2 | | | |
| 3 | **Keyphrases** | | |
| 4 | 2007-07-19 00:00:00 | 2007-07-25 23:59:59 | |
| 5 | | | |
| 6 | **Search Engine** | **Count** | **Percentage** |
| 7 | | | |
| 8 | Copyright © 2003 - 2007. All rights reserved. | | |

The final screen shot shows the amount of traffic that the Web site picked up within the first few days, and before it was finished being built or submitted to search engines.

Report created by Traffic Facts for http://www.freekelseysmom.com on 07-26-07

**Hits**

| Date | Hits | Percentage |
|---|---|---|
| Jul 19, 2007 | 0 | 0.00 |
| Jul 20, 2007 | 2 | 0.01 |
| Jul 21, 2007 | 8 | 0.05 |
| Jul 22, 2007 | 1,064 | 6.51 |
| Jul 23, 2007 | 2,872 | 17.57 |
| Jul 24, 2007 | 847 | 5.18 |
| Jul 25, 2007 | 11,551 | 70.67 |
| **Total** | **16,344** | **100** |

Copyright © 2003 - 2007. All rights reserved.

The first response was from Lance's sister, Rita. She wrote, "I have just read the above comments that were posted on freeKelseysmom.com... When Kelsey's Purpose was started it was with the intent to make changes to help other children not suffer. A lot of the members feel very passionately about this cause and sometimes get carried away. I have spent a lot of time trying to keep our members focused on good and not get caught up in the rest, but they are all individuals...we have hundreds of guests that visit the site daily. Any one of them could have happened upon the other site just by browsing through ours..."

I can understand how she would want to explain away the nastiness that was being put upon Raye's family. But the reports were concrete evidence, to me, that Kelsey's Purpose members were behind the hateful messages.

In August, 2007 the Web site had just been completed when its existence was announced on the news. An evening broadcast on our local CBS station relayed the following:

[Anchor] "Raye Dawn Smith's friends and family are raising money for her legal fees." [Co-anchor] "They sat up a Web site and sent fundraising packets in the mail..."

[Reporter] "A woman called me after receiving these papers in the mail from Raye Dawn Smith's family and friends asking for money. That woman's not the only one bothered by this."

A clip of Raye being placed into the sheriff's vehicle after her trial flashed across the screen with Raye crying, "I don't understand. I love my baby!"

[Reporter]: "One month after this moment when a jury found Raye Dawn guilty of enabling child abuse."

[Kathie Briggs]: "I think desperate people do desperate things."

[Reporter]: "Raye Dawn's family and friends fight to pay for her appeal."

[Kathie Briggs]: "Had they fought this hard for a small child as they are for this adult who has been convicted of this crime, then we might not be here today."

[Reporter]: "Kathie, Kelsey's paternal grandmother, couldn't believe all of this. There is a Web site called, 'Free Kelsey's Mom' and letters going out to the community, both asking for donations to raise $25,000 to process Raye Dawn's appeal."

[Kathie Briggs]: "I would imagine that their legal fees are pretty expensive but I just don't understand why they would want the public to pay."

[Reporter]: "The letter signed by Raye Dawn's family and friends says she was dragged relentlessly through the legal system and media; that she will be exonerated because she is innocent, and that your donation will help right this terrific wrong in an attempt to provide a fair trial for Raye Dawn."

[Kathie Briggs]: "I understand that they want to support their family member, but they really need to acknowledge what Kelsey went through."

[Reporter]: "Our legal analyst…said this strategy is not entirely new."

[Legal Analyst]: "It's not unusual to see people find a way to raise money for a defense fund, but this organized of a manner, I've not seen it."

The Web site home page was shown.

[Reporter]: "According to the Web site, they have $4,000 so far. The battle won't end here."

[Kathie Briggs]: "And we know Kelsey fought and fought just to stay alive and now that she's not here, it's up to us to fight to make sure justice takes place."

[Reporter]: "I just talked to Raye Dawn's cousin who signed this very letter. She told me Raye Dawn did not get a fair trial. She said since the family has no more money for legal fees, they're reaching out to the community for support. The family does not want publicity and does not want to talk on camera."

[Anchor]: "Raye Dawn's lawyer…says he is not involved in the fund raising effort. He expects to file the appeal by the October 11th deadline."

I remember watching the report with a mixture of feelings including excitement that Raye's family's efforts in support of her defense were being shared, and angst over the fact that Raye's side of the story could never be told without someone else butting in with a negative opinion. It seemed to me that Oklahoma had forgotten the fact that Kelsey had two families who were suffering and grieving her loss. I questioned why the media didn't want to hear from the other grandma, the one who had shared in raising Kelsey.

With a feeling of hope that the public had watched, listened, and opened their hearts and minds to the other side of the story, I continued to work on behalf of Raye and Kelsey to ensure that her mom would no longer be crucified. I never imagined that the hate that had been building and brewing for years would soon turn on me. In 2007, I believed in the Constitution and my right as a citizen of the United States of America to have an opinion. I believed I should be able to voice my opinion without fear of retaliation or threats against me. However, since my opinion did not include hate or a public flogging for Raye, the rights I thought I had were soon turned against me with an underhanded and illegal plan from the opposition to silence me forever.

# 27 The Bullies

"In my opinion they are like an abuser, boiling waiting for the rage to come out uncontrollably then patching it over hoping it is forgotten or repressed. If not then they will intimidate to distract." ~ [Whit]

The reputation that Kelsey's Purpose members had created for themselves as being "bullies" was finally coming to light; the fictional story that had been created started to unravel with the truth being exposed through various sources, such as the Judge's book, in which he depicted a much different image of the paternal family than the fictional version that had been painted like one of Norman Rockwell's scenes.

To demonstrate how such a reputation was earned, I present the following statements taken directly from Kelsey's Purpose that Kathie personally posted as well as a few statements from her closest friend—we'll call her "Ursula":

"If ever anyone could plead insanity it could have been her (Raye). She seems to have come by it honestly as her family shares her views." Kathie

"In regards to the maternal family they need your prayers so they can realize Raye Dawn is not the victim." Kathie

"Gayla had the choice right then and there to save her granddaughters life and she made the choice to let her die." Kathie

"I wonder if our District Attorney does not get a conviction if this will be an issue in his next election?" Kathie

"We wanted Raye Dawn to be held accountable for her role and/or lack of action in Kelsey's death, ie: we wanted her brought to trial." Ursula

"I read the report a couple of days ago, and I would think the recommendation would stand. Uumm...the Judge knows everyone is watching this case...from ALL over. I believe **he probably remembers what happened to the judicial career of the last Judge** that did not pay attention to things related in this case. I believe he will sentence her to the 27yrs and not release her. **To do anything but** that, since it is also the recommendation from the investigators **would be suicidal to his judicial career**. I doubt he is going down that road." Ursula (emphasis placed by post author)

"I don't know how his [Judge Key's] wife sleeps beside him every night." Ursula

"As I have stated before **we have been harassed, stalked, physically assaulted, threatened, and slandered for almost two years."** This was posted by Kathie on August 19, 2007, one month after I became involved in the case. Yet, she later blames all of those same accusations directly on me.

"Mike Porter was originally charged with her murder and plead to enabling child abuse. We cannot call him a murderer or a sexual predator because he was not convicted of that crime." Kathie

"I cannot imagine how Gayla must feel knowing two of her children are facing prison. The fact is they are not in this position because of anything our family did." Kathie

"Her child is dead and she continues to focus on why people don't feel sorry for her." Kathie

These statements were made on a public forum that is dedicated to "preventing child abuse" where often their focus is on being cruel, criticizing, and threatening. Unbelievably there is an even more sinister side to Kathie and her followers. There is always a secret place where they show their true characters, under aliases and out of the public's eye. They label these places their "bash boards" and through their e-mails with Mike Porter we learned that Kathie is "addicted to" the morbid and unruly side of her "cause."

After reading the negative comments, the pure, unfiltered hate, and about what I believe to be crimes that Kathie and her group have instigated and participated in for years, you'll shake your head, as I do, and wonder how these people could possibly claim to be victims of a fight they started, and are still carrying on amongst themselves in a public venue for all to see, almost five years after Kelsey's death.

# 28 First Signs of Hate

"Those who hate most fervently must have once loved deeply; those who want to deny the world must have once embraced what they now set on fire." ~ Kurt Tucholsky

Our nation's founders created laws to protect our right to speak freely. As part of that freedom, we are allowed to express our opinions and feelings about a topic without fear of reprisal. But when that freedom is misused and turned into a campaign of hate, people who abuse their rights to publicly crucify someone should not be allowed to hide behind "anonymous" or "concerned citizen." They should be forced to put their name to the hate so that the victim can seek a resolution.

In 2005 a hate group was formed in Oklahoma. The members were bold and fierce in their comments; some posted under their real names, but most used "anonymous" or an alias. They didn't see themselves as a hate group, but to someone looking in, the hate is all that is seen.

Their first target was, of course, Raye. She's the woman they portrayed as the "evil mother" who didn't care about anyone but herself. Next on the list were Raye's mother and grandmother, two upstanding and respected women in their community—two widows who were portrayed as self-absorbed women who were too busy with their boyfriends to see what was happening with Kelsey. Then there was the Judge who was said to have "sent Kelsey to her death." According to these people, he's a monster who doesn't care about children. That is far from the truth.

I've read post after post where Kathie and her followers stated "if the Judge would just apologize, he would still be on the bench" or if Kelsey's maternal great-grandmother, Mildred, would apologize for not doing more to save Kelsey, then she would not be harassed. On one occasion, Kathie stated, "I know one day I should forgive Raye Dawn for what she has done. I hope I can, but how do you when that person won't take responsibility for her actions and then ask to be forgiven?" My question is: How does Kathie know what Raye has confessed or if she's asked God's forgiveness? His forgiveness is all that matters. Kathie claims to be a Christian. Shouldn't she know about forgiveness?

Kathie seems to have forgiven Mike Porter. She stated that Mike Porter showed remorse so instead of going to trial, he was given a plea. Instead of a lynch mob going after him with picket signs in-hand, prayer requests for him and his family were extended. According to witnesses, Kathie even had tears in her eyes at Mike Porter's plea hearing stating, "It's hard to see him like that." The man was charged with murdering and sexually assaulting Kelsey, but because he showed signs of remorse, he was to be forgiven.

### *THE HATE*

When putting this book together, I was given a stack of papers approximately two feet tall that was nothing but evidence of this hate campaign against Raye and her family. For the first few weeks, I was overwhelmed. Of course, I wanted to include every awful word, but it's just too much. After months of editing, I believe I've included just enough to clearly illustrate the intense hate targeted at Raye and others, and then at myself. Possibly, a companion book will be published at a later date that will expose it all.

While reading the following posts, one may see a family that desperately wanted justice for a dead child. However, known facts in the case, such as Kathie's accusations against Raye starting on the night of Kelsey's death, give us insight into the actions to come. Even with the arrest and charges of murder and sexual assault for the man who was home alone with Kelsey at the time of her alleged rape and murder, Kathie's initial thoughts of what happened never changed. Her mind was made up and she would work day and night to convince Oklahoma, and then the world, that she was right, despite the facts or the evidence. Is that "Justice for Kelsey"?

On November 11, 2005, just one month after Kelsey's passing, Kelsey's Purpose's home page relayed the following message: "My granddaughter Kelsey was born after her parents were divorced. I wondered why this child would be put on this earth after the two people who were not meant to be together had already gone their separate ways. I knew she had a purpose, but what could it be? When my son was called to active duty and sent to Iraq I was sure that I knew. God was giving Kelsey to us because her father was not coming home. I was wrong. Kelsey was the one who did not make it. She died just days before her dad was to return. After nine months of abuse, she joined the other little angels in Heaven. It was then that I knew her purpose...She was put here to make a difference – to make sure other children are protected. This website is still being developed. We plan to have more pictures and information about Kelsey, links to agencies and organizations who can help prevent child abuse, and a message board dedicated to sharing information between people who are dedicated to the welfare of children everywhere. Please check back soon!"

By November 18, 2005, the campaign was in full swing. The following e-mail was sent to sixty-one of Oklahoma's teachers:

From: Justice for Kelsey Subject: Justice for Kelsey Briggs

"Oklahomans are outraged by the senseless and preventable death of Kelsey Briggs. Please help get Justice for Kelsey and prevent other children from suffering from child abuse. A demonstration will be held on Monday, November 21, 2005 at the...County Court house at 11:30 am and then move to the...County DHS office at 12:30 pm. If you are wondering why Raye Dawn has not been charged in the death of Kelsey, contact the District Attorney's office at 275-xxxx or fax them at 275-xxxx. A website www.Kelseyspurpose.com has been set up with links to various websites to assist Oklahomans in holding the agencies and people that failed Kelsey accountable. Included in this e-mail are a poem written for Kelsey and a speech that was given by Kathie at the State Capital on November 8, 2005. The hope is that they will inspire Oklahomans to make their voices heard for Kelsey and other children suffering from child abuse. Please forward this e-mail to your family, friends, and coworkers to make a difference in a child's life. Thank you!"

Included in the e-mail was a poem about Kelsey that targeted Raye as the monster and a speech given by Kathie at the State Capitol. The speech gave details of Kelsey's life, according to Kathie.

At some point in November of 2005, a poll was added to the Kelsey's Purpose Web site that posed the question: "Do you think Raye Dawn had any doing in hurting Kelsey?" The possible answers were: "Yes- by not protecting her from Mike Porter," which garnered 16 votes or 57.14% as of December 12, 2005, and "Yes – by enduring it herself" had 9 votes or 32.14% with "No" obtaining zero votes and lastly "Not sure" with 3 votes or 10.71%.

One of the captured posts was from "LazyHusker" which stated, "…This is only an opinion…" The signature at the bottom of the post stated, "May Kelsey's Memory Live On! Keep Fighting For Kelsey! An Eye For An Eye!" As the button that I received from the Oklahoma Coalition to Abolish the Death Penalty states: "An eye for an eye leaves the whole world blind."

From the posts it was evident that people were joining forces with the paternal family, even though they knew nothing about either family or any details of the case other than what they had seen in the media and what was being shared on Kelsey's Purpose. A gag order was in place, but that did nothing to deter the witch hunt that was brewing. Weeks passed and torches were lit and nothing stood in their way.

Everybody else followed the rules and remained silent but the group was determined that Raye was going to be charged with something. Witnesses state that Kathie repeatedly said, "Raye has to go to prison, if only for one day! She just has to go to prison!"

Raye's family soon learned that Raye would have no claims to any monies awarded from Lance's multiple lawsuits if she was convicted of a crime in connection with Kelsey's murder. That meant Kelsey's paternal family would stop at nothing to get her convicted, even if that meant teaming up with the man charged with Kelsey's alleged sexual assault and murder.

# 29 Justice for Mike Porter?

"Whoever blushes is already guilty; true innocence is ashamed of nothing." ~ Jean-Jacques Rousseau

Mike Porter was arrested within days of Kelsey's murder. After the discovery was made that Kelsey's death wasn't the result of a seizure, as the maternal family had been led to believe by Mike Porter himself, the Oklahoma State Bureau of Investigation conducted interviews of both Mike Porter and Raye simultaneously and in separate rooms.

Mike Porter had been acting guilty with multiple phone calls to the medical examiner's office the day after Kelsey's death, demanding the results of the autopsy. He was reportedly upset that the autopsy would be thorough. At one point, the person he spoke with at the ME's office quit answering any questions, noting that only the person guilty of or charged with the crime would behave in the way that Mike Porter had on that day. Also, according to witnesses, Mike Porter pretended to attempt suicide on two occasions: first with a gun that he "overlooked" in a drawer he opened and then slammed shut when he threatened to shoot himself, and then with a full bottle of Tylenol he supposedly swallowed that was later found. He acted equally suspicious during his interrogation.

Raye was interrogated with the same amount of suspicion as Mike Porter because, as the investigator phrased it, Kathie was "calling everyone in the world and saying [Raye was] guilty." Investigators were supposedly presented with hearsay evidence of Raye's alleged "violent tendencies" in an effort to make her the main suspect for the crime. Days after Raye lost her child; she was treated like a criminal and told gory details of her only child's death with Kathie's finger pointing at her as the perpetrator.

As previously mentioned, I was given a DVD of Raye's OSBI interview that had been copied by Kathie's daughter and then distributed. For six heart-wrenching hours, I watched Raye as she begged for answers as to what had happened to Kelsey. The investigators had the same question of Raye. She cried out and screamed—the pain evident on her face and in her actions. Every answer was the same: she didn't know. She wasn't home. Raye informed them that she was there "to find out what happened." When the investigator mentioned the word "murder," Raye's entire body shook; she screamed and jumped out of her chair and crumpled into the corner of the room. This young mother had to learn her child had been murdered in the most awful way imaginable because of claims made against her by people who weren't there and didn't know anything about the turn of events.

At one point in the interview, the investigators realized they were getting nowhere. Raye had nothing to tell them. She was just as confused as they were. They decided to take a break, during which they spoke to the investigators interviewing Mike Porter. Once they returned, their tone changed from accusing to compassionate. The lead investigator gave Raye his business card and told her that if Mike Porter confessed, she needed to call him right away. He also stated that since Raye "lived and slept with" Mike Porter, she needed to be "scared to death" because he was "one sorry son-of-a-bitch."

Following is a partial summary of Mike Porter's interview:

Steve, the investigator with the Oklahoma State Bureau of Investigation, started Porter's interview by informing him that the interview was voluntary and he could leave at any time. Porter responded with the fact that he just wanted to know what happened to Kelsey and he would tell him everything he knew.

Steve noticed Porter was acting strangely. Steve asked if he was comfortable in the chair. Porter said that he couldn't breathe because "it hurt so badly."

Porter's flare for the dramatics obviously made an impact on some paternal family members while watching the taped interview that had been given to Kathie by Porter's attorney. Lance's sister, Rita, stated, "During Mike Porter's interview, he kept grabbing his heart and acting like he was having chest pains and he acted like he was going to vomit a time or two and was very dramatic. I have never seen such a drama queen. His body language was screaming guilt. He was beyond nervous and then toward the end he says he wants an attorney and he wants to see his wife. Watching is so different from reading it. I truly feel this man is responsible for the death of Kelsey."[37]

Lance stated, "Raye Dawn killed Kelsey. I know she did. I know she did," following Raye's sentencing. It seems he did not share his sister's opinion, despite the evidence.

Steve asked if Porter had a chance to discuss what happened with Raye, which Porter denied, stating they had "been too busy." As an afterthought, he added that Kelsey was a "special kid." When Steve pressed the subject, Porter explained that she made people feel like they "knew her for her entire life." He added he had "never had anybody touch him" like she had done.

Steve asked for an elaboration by asking about Kelsey's demeanor, if she was loveable, and liked to be held. Porter nodded in response.

Steve asked if Kelsey would crawl up in his lap and love on him. Porter answered "Yes."

Steve then changed the subject by again pressing the issue of Porter's and Raye's relationship since Kelsey's death. He asked if they had spent any alone time since Kelsey's death. Porter said he didn't know. Steve questioned his answer, to which Porter responded, avoiding a straightforward answer, saying that he thought sometimes Raye needed to be alone.

Steve asked if Raye had talked to anyone, like her mother. Porter interrupted, and skirted around the question

[37] See Appendix B – Exhibit 16

by saying they had all talked. Then he stated that they had been so busy that what had happened hadn't sunk in yet with Raye.

Steve questioned how Raye had been since Kelsey's death, to which Porter interjected himself into the answer by stating he and Raye had cried for two days and hadn't eaten or slept. Steve was questioning Porter about Raye. *Why did he interject himself into the answer?*

Raye's sister stated that Porter had no problem eating or sleeping. Porter and Raye stayed with her on the night Kelsey died and Porter ate well and then slept through the night while Raye cried all night and refused to eat.

Steve noticed Porter's answer and asked if they had both cried about the death of Kelsey. Porter became emotional and apologized because he was "going to try to be composed." Steve humored Porter, apologizing for having to put him through the interview, and told him, "Be whatever you need to be."

Porter stated that he and Raye just "wanted Kelsey back" and for someone to tell them what happened. Steve questioned Porter about Kelsey's injuries by asking about Kelsey's broken clavicle. Steve asked if it was in December of 2004 that it occurred.

Porter stumbled through his answer, stating that it was right after that. He explained that it happened on a weekend and Raye called him. He stated they took Kelsey to the emergency room and had her X-rayed and got a sling for her. He stated that they "did everything parents can do." Then he started to talk about Kathie when Steve interrupted him. Steve asked Porter if Kelsey was with Kathie when she applied for the order. Porter answered "yes" and stated they never got her back, and that Kathie had just "taken Kelsey." Steve asked if that occurred in December. Porter mistakenly answered that it was sometime around there. It was actually January, 2005 when Kelsey's clavicle was broken and Kathie refused to return her to Raye.

Steve asked Porter how long the Briggs had custody of Kelsey, to which he replied that the paternal family had her until May. Porter then went on to explain that DHS took Kelsey from Kathie in May and that he and Raye had to go to DHS and be supervised during their visits. He then explained that Gayla became Kelsey's foster parent and that Raye still couldn't see Kelsey.

Steve asked for clarification of where Kelsey had gone after leaving Kathie's home. Porter confirmed that after leaving Kathie's home, Kelsey went to Gayla's home. The investigator asked for confirmation of the month that Kelsey went to live with Gayla. Porter answered his question, but then offered more insight into Kelsey's physical condition during the time that Kathie had guardianship of Kelsey. He stated, "That was around May. I think, and that was when Kelsey started to return back to normal. When she was – from the period of January to May she slid downhill like I've never seen – like I didn't know a person could. My mom had cancer, and that's – that's what it was like. I mean, Kelsey, her hair fell out, she lost weight, and she just looked sick. I mean, her being away from her mom she just looked sick. I mean, it was – it was sad."

He explained that when Kelsey went to Gayla's home that she began to be normal again.

Steve then questioned Porter about Kelsey's broken legs. He asked Porter if Kelsey was with Kathie when her legs were determined to be broken. Porter confirmed his question. The investigator then asked Porter who took Kelsey to the doctor when her legs were broken. Porter responded that Raye had taken her both times. He went on to explain that Raye did everything for Kelsey. He explained that Kelsey had sprained her ankle at the zoo and that Raye and her sister-in-law took Kelsey to the doctor for an X-ray and it was determined that she had a sprain. He stated that if the doctor had X-rayed Kelsey's leg up to the knee, they would have seen a hairline crack in her tibia. Porter then clarified that Kelsey's leg injuries occurred during the time Kathie had custody of Kelsey. He further stated that he thought it was "overkill" to take Kelsey to the doctor for her injury, but that he and Raye wanted to be safe. He went on to say that every time Kelsey got medical attention, it was Raye that took her.

Steve then questioned when it was determined that Kelsey had a broken leg. Porter interrupted him and said that he and Raye followed instructions by making Kelsey walk because they thought it was just a sprain. First, he stated that when they tried to make Kelsey walk on the ankle that she wouldn't do it. Then, Porter stated, "Children are tougher than adults" and if they have a hurt ankle, they'll "push through their pain" and walk on it. He stated that when Kelsey's ankle hurt so badly that she could no longer walk on it, they knew something was wrong. He said that Raye noticed

Kelsey's ankle was swollen and had fever in it and Raye told him, "This isn't right."

Steve asked if they took her back to the doctor at that point. Porter answered that they had taken her back. Steve questioned what the doctor did. Porter replied that it was then that the doctors said Kelsey's legs were cracked. Steve asked if Porter meant both legs, to which Porter answered, "Yeah." He stated that Dr. K and Dr. B put the timeframe of the breaks as the first one happening when Kelsey tripped and fell at the zoo and the other break happened a week later while Kelsey was with Kathie. (This was also proven at Raye's trial.)

Steve interrupted Porter's rambling and asked if that was when they thought Kelsey might have brittle bones. Porter answered, "Yeah." He stated that a brittle bone test was ordered and that Kelsey had been put through several tests. In Porter's answer, he referred to Kelsey as "the kid." This isn't the last time he referred to Kelsey as "kid" instead of referring to her by name.

Steve continued with the questioning and asked when Raye regained custody of Kelsey. Porter answered that she never got custody, but "placement," and that Kelsey remained in the custody of DHS. Porter stated that after the "kid" was better…then he trailed off and stated that *basically* the Judge said he created this monster, referring to Kathie. In this statement, he explained that those were not the Judge's words, though Kathie repeats it as fact. He was paraphrasing what occurred at the hearing in June, 2005, according to him.

Porter continued to explain what Raye went through regarding the custody battle with Kathie. He stated that at the June hearing the Judge said, “You know what? I screwed up and I’m going to place the child back with the mother, back with the natural mother.” That was another statement the Judge did not make, according to witnesses. The investigator clarified with Porter that the hearing took place in June.

Porter then added that he and Raye had Kelsey in their home for four months and that Kelsey was doing much better. He stated that within a week of Kelsey being in Gayla’s home, Kelsey started to get back to normal. He stated that she gained weight and had regained the light in her eyes. Porter emphasized that when Kathie had custody of Kelsey, the light was gone out of her eyes.

Steve then questioned Porter about the agencies that were assigned to watch over Kelsey’s progress. The investigator asked when CHBS started their visits. Porter interrupted, stating they started immediately. He explained that the DHS worker went to visit on the day Kelsey went back to Raye. He stated that the DHS worker checked out the house, did a walk-through, and made sure everything was safe for the “kid.” He explained that everyone knew “this child.” He then started to complain about the hassle the agencies had been, and then stopped midsentence.

Steve returned to the subject of Kelsey’s legs and asked Porter if the doctors were able to determine how Kelsey’s leg was broken the first time. Porter stumbled and said the first break was consistent with Kelsey falling at the zoo and that they thought it was just a sprain. Steve asked about the second one. Porter answered that he didn’t know and that nobody knew. Steve asked for clarification on Kelsey's whereabouts when her second leg was broken and if Kelsey was with Kathie at that time. Porter confirmed that the timeframe they had gotten from the doctor would have put Kelsey with Kathie.

Steve asked if during that time Raye had Kelsey for week-long visits. Porter answered that she did not, and that it was a weekend. He then stated that Kathie said she was going to take Kelsey to Children's Hospital for a bone density test, but she was really getting a second opinion. He stated that Kelsey's casts were cut off, and the doctor said Kelsey's broken legs were the result of abuse. The investigator again asked for clarification that the doctor who said Kelsey was abused was the doctor Kathie took Kelsey to see.

Porter confirmed that it was the doctor that Kathie took Kelsey to that said it was abuse. He stated that the Children's Hospital doctor refuted everything that Dr. B, Kelsey's doctor said, and that he tried to discredit Dr. B.

Porter stated that he was told that Children's Hospital doctors are notorious for saying injuries are the result of child abuse.

Steve changed the subject and asked about Porter's and Raye's relationship by asking when Porter and Raye started living together, to which Porter stated they moved in together when they got married and with the custody battle Raye was going through that they did not spend the night with each other when Raye had Kelsey.

Steve asked if Kelsey was potty trained, to which Porter responded with an emphatic YES and once again, referred to her as a "kid." Porter then quoted Kelsey and said that she would say, "Mama and Daddy, I have to go pee" or "I have to go poop."

Steve asked, "Was she potty trained before you-all got her in June or…"

Porter responded, "Oh, yeah. Raye had her potty trained before they took her." He furthered his answer by adding, "She was a bright, bright kid. She was very intelligent."

Steve asked about Kelsey's disposition: "Was she colicky in any way? Crying? Whining?"

Porter stated she had been a happy "kid" before Kathie got custody of Kelsey, but that her disposition changed and she became cranky during the time she lived with Kathie. He stated, "[W]hen she was with Kathie, yeah, she was miserable, I mean. But as far as colic where you just cry for no reason, no. She had a reason. I mean, she was mentally – she was very upset. You could tell."

Steve pointed out to Porter that children Kelsey's age did not know what was happening when they went to other homes, to which Porter replied that Kelsey knew.

Steve clarified that at the time Kelsey went to live with Kathie that she had just turned two years-old. Porter stated that she was smart for her age and he said they called her "an eighteen-year-old in a two-year-old body." Porter then explained that after Kelsey went to live with Kathie that Kelsey would ask Raye "What happened?" He stated that she didn't know what was going on, and then fumbled back to his original statement and said she knew that Raye would never hurt her. He stated, "She would just look at Raye Dawn, you know, when Raye Dawn would get to visit her after Kathie – after Kathie took her, she would look at Raye Dawn and say, 'Mommy, what happened?' She had no clue. I mean, she knew, you know, that her mom would never hurt her. And she would just look at her and say, 'Mommy, what happened?'"

Steve then asked Porter how they had disciplined Kelsey.

Porter responded, "No, I'm not going to say I never get on to them, but as far as physical punishment, never. I mean, in my – my thing is time-out. I mean, I have had to spank my boy before, because boys are just that way. I'll tell him to go to time-out, and he'll look at me and tell me no." He added, "But as far as her, no, she doesn't – she never whipped Kelsey. I mean – and I know she got whipped, you know, being raised and she just never did that. Even before all this started, even before December, I mean, when I was around her, she never had to. She never had to."

Steve asked if Kelsey was aware of what time-out was. Porter answered that she did. Steve asked if there was a designated spot for time-out.

Porter responded, "Yeah. Whenever – in our old house in Shawnee, after we got married, her time-out room was her room. We would say or Raye Dawn would say, or me, either one. 'Kelsey, you need to go sit on your bed in time-out until you're ready to be good.' And she'd sit in there for a couple of minutes. And we – she was smart. We left it up to her. We said, 'When you're ready to stop doing what you're doing, you can come out.'"

Steve questioned Porter about who would put Kelsey in time out. He replied, "Oh yeah, yeah. I mean, if she did something, Raye Dawn told me, 'Well, you don't think twice about sticking her in there.' But I mean, I rarely did. She – I don't know if it was my tone or what or she saw me getting onto my children, but she just – she just minded me."

Steve asked again if Kelsey was ever spanked, to which Porter replied that she had been given "spats" but that Raye had never spanked her. He stated, "No. Like I say, I've never seen Raye Dawn whip her." *This statement is much different from the story he presents later when saving himself from the death penalty.*

Steve asked when the family moved into their new home and Mike Porter stated that they started moving in on October 1st. Steve asked if they had lived at the same address in Shawnee to which Porter nodded and gave them the address.

The investigator asked if there was a specific place for time-out in the new home.

Porter said, "Yeah. We'd usually send her to the – we call it the fish room. It's the room closest to – it would just depend on where she was. I mean, if we were upstairs, it would be her room, or if we were downstairs, it would be the fish room usually, which is the room closest to our bedroom. And that's where – that's where I sent my kids."

*In Kathie's version of this interview, it stated that Kelsey was sent to a closet for time-out, which was included in the first version of this book, because I took some of the interview from what Kathie and Lance's girlfriend had typed. This is just one example of how changing a simple word can create a completely new version of the story, one even I believed.*

Steve asked if Kelsey was on any medication, to which Porter asked for clarification of a timeframe. Steve clarified from June to the day she died. Porter stated that she had been given nasal spray by Dr. K for inflamed nostrils and Phenergan for an upset stomach.

Steve asked if Porter took any medication, to which he answered "No." Raye told me that many questioned why Porter's eyes were always red. Raye stated that she also asked him that question and his excuse was that he had Glaucoma. I asked Raye if he used any eye drops and she stated, "Not that I ever saw." My grandmother and my cousin both had Glaucoma and they had to use eye drops daily. I told Raye about this and she stated that she did not realize that Glaucoma has to be treated daily. This is just one instance of deception where Raye believed her new husband.

Steve asked Porter if he could possibly be depressed. Porter answered, "I mean, God knows me and Raye – I mean, we've both been through enough to be, but no, we don't – I mean, we can't. We don't have a choice."

Steve asked if Raye was on medication. Porter answered "No." Steve asked if Raye were depressed or angry before Kelsey died.

Porter stated, "No, she was depressed before – whenever she had to go to DHS and see her baby for an hour. That was the darkest time I've ever seen. And then when she got her back, I mean, it was a 180. I mean, she lived to be that girl's mother, Steve. I don't know how else to say it. That was her heart and soul."

Porter was asked if Raye ever lost her temper, to which he replied, "Never."

Steve asked if she had lost her temper with Porter.

Porter stated, "No, I mean, we've had arguments. But as far – I've been in an abusive relationship before where she was abusive to me. And Raye Dawn never – she never crossed that line."

Steve asked if Raye had ever been abusive toward Kelsey or his children.

Porter answered, "Never. No, she loves my kids. I mean, frustration, yeah, but she has the ability to control it, absolutely."

Steve stated that children "push buttons" to which Porter agreed and stated that Kelsey was "good at finding buttons to push." He stated, "Kelsey was – she was the best at it. But then she could – she could do something that you just couldn't believe and you'd say, 'Kelsey, what are you doing?' And then the next minute she'd do something that just made it all go away. She would say something that just…"

Steve interrupted Porter and asked how Kelsey was from the time she returned to Raye's home.

Porter answered by stating, "She was home. That was the best way – the first day she got back, I mean, Kelsey – this is how grown up she was. She looked at her and she, 'Mommy, I am so proud of you. I'm so proud of you.' And she said, 'Mommy, I'm home.' That was it. She was back. I don't know how else to say it." He then added, "You could just see the relief in her face. Within a week, that gleam was back. In pictures, you can see it was back in her eyes. I mean, I know that's probably – you think that's a subjective thing, but I mean, there's – I can tell you I've only known Kelsey since October and I saw the difference when Raye got her back. I mean, it was just – it was like relief. 'God, Mommy, why did you take so long?'"

Steve asked what Kelsey had been eating. Porter responded that Gayla had gotten Kelsey to eat fruits and vegetables and that she preferred carrots over French fries. He said she would eat oranges, peaches, pears, and broccoli.

Porter continued, "And then if you'll just let me tell you this whenever they started – after Raye Dawn got her back and – well, I can tell you this, that whenever – whenever Raye Dawn was having to go to DHS for visitation and her ex-family-in-law had the option to do that, then they didn't do it. They would not go visit Kelsey. Whenever the chips fell down and it was time to see who really cared about Kelsey, they didn't show up. They didn't go see Kelsey."

Steve asked if Gayla gave the supervised visits to Raye. Porter responded that the visits happened at DHS. Steve asked if Raye ever visited Kelsey when she was not supposed to, and Porter answered that neither Raye nor Gayla would break the rules and that Raye never saw Kelsey while she was with Gayla. Porter stated that Raye got extra visits when Kelsey was with Kathie when the visits were allowed to be unsupervised.

Steve stated, "I was told that sometime you-guys would spend the weekend at [Gayla's friend's] house when Gayla had custody."

Porter stated that they never did. Steve said that he would be bringing that question up again later.

Steve asked if he watched Kelsey when Raye was not there, and he stated that nobody watched her but Gayla.

Steve asked if Gayla took Kelsey places for the evening after she went back to Raye's home. Porter stated that Gayla took Kelsey to the movies and out to eat. Porter added that the only other person Raye would want around Kelsey would be her brother, but that they had never gotten it approved. Steve asked if Gayla ever kept Kelsey overnight and he said that he didn't recall her staying overnight with Gayla and that Raye would miss her too much if she did stay overnight because she just got where she could go to the store or get Porter's daughter from school without taking Kelsey with her.

Steve asked about Kelsey's last planned outing with Gayla. Porter responded by telling him that Kelsey was going somewhere with Gayla on the day she was murdered, but he didn't know where.

Steve then steered the questioning back to the day that Kelsey died. He stated that Porter had told him that he gave either Kelsey or Raye a kiss—he wasn't clear in his statement—to which Mike Porter called it a "routine." Steve stated, "You dropped your daughter off – you-all got up that morning, and you couldn't really remember if those guys – if Raye Dawn or Kelsey were awake. And you kind of go in and probably nonchalantly gave her a kiss and then took off."

Porter responded, "It's just a routine."

Steve stated that Porter dropped off his daughter at school at around 8:00 a.m. and arrived at work at 8:30 a.m. Porter's co-worker and friend who was the first to arrive on the scene that day stated that Porter only spent an hour or two at work that day. *Where was he?* Porter, however, continued with his story that he spent the day at work.

Porter stated that he talked to Raye at 9:30 a.m. when she called him and he asked her why she was up so early. He clarified that she liked to sleep late and that she was around four months pregnant so she was tired.

Steve asked if Kelsey was awake when Raye called Porter. He stated that he believed she was.

Steve asked when it was decided that Raye would pick up Porter's daughter that day.

Porter stated, "Yeah. It was something that we had already – I mean, she had – maybe the week before that she would pick – I don't know. It was over the – sometime. It wasn't a big deal, you know. Maybe that morning she said – and she had planned on taking Kelsey, because we were on the phone one time and she said, 'Yeah. I'm going to go into town and pick up [your daughter].' Porter added, "And then Kelsey said, 'Mommy, I want to go.' And, you know, she got her shoes ready and everything else. So, I mean, it was known she was going to go pick up [my daughter], you know, earlier and Kelsey was going to go."

Steve asked about how many times Porter and Raye spoke on the phone that day. Porter stated that he had spoken to Raye several times. He stated that he even spoke to Kelsey during one of his calls. He stated, "I talked to Kelsey. What did she tell me? She told me she was eating some berries. And she was calling these raisins 'berries.'"

Porter added more dialogue, stating, "And she talked to me, and I said, 'Are you being good for Mommy?' And she said, 'Yeah.' And I said, 'Well, Daddy is going to be home after a while.' And she said, 'Okay. I love you, Daddy.'"

Porter stated that he had never seen Kelsey eat raisins, but that Raye was having a hard time getting Kelsey to eat that day and that she had sent Kelsey to time-out for not eating. Porter stated, "Kelsey said, 'I'm not hungry, Mama.' So Raye Dawn kept working with her and working with her 'You've got to eat something, honey. Come on.' So finally they were sitting in there and Kelsey said, 'Mama, I'm hungry.' So Raye Dawn sent her to time-out. She said, 'You need to eat something, so you go sit in there, and when you're ready to, you know, you can come out.' And then Kelsey, I guess, came from time-out and said, 'Mommy, I want some berries.' And they laughed about it. So we figured that Kelsey sat in there and thought about what she could eat."

Steve asked about the visit from CHBS. Porter told him that the CHBS worker was late and that he didn't know if she was there for the full two hours because he said she left at around 12:30 p.m. or 1:00 p.m. and Raye called Porter after she left. He said Raye wanted him to go home. He claimed that he wanted to and he was the owner of the company so he could make his own hours, but he didn't, so Raye and Kelsey took a nap.

Steve asked if Kelsey took daily naps. Porter stated that she did not have a set time for a nap, but she napped when Raye got tired and when Porter's son was there, they would all nap together.

Steve wanted to know how much Raye slept. Porter stated that Raye "sleeps a lot," but he didn't want it to be mistaken that she slept instead of parenting. He stated, "Yeah, she sleeps – well, when I say she likes to sleep, I don't mean that she will sleep through the day. I don't want that to be in any way construed as that she's, you know, an absent mom. I want to make that clear that I'm not saying that, you know, or that she sleeps through the day or anything like that. But, you know, she can go to sleep at – you know, we could go to bed at, you know, at nine o'clock and she could sleep until, you know, ten or twelve the next day. But that's just – I think a lot of that is just being pregnant."

He added, "Well, I just want – I mean, she sleeps regularly. We both worry about our kids, because that's a bigger house than we've ever had. And Kelsey and [my daughter] sleep upstairs. And, I mean, she worries. She worries, you know, about Kelsey coming down the stairs. But, you know, we check on her. I get up and check on her two or three times a night and so does Raye. And Kelsey, she mastered those stairs. I mean…" Porter stated that he would go upstairs two or three times a night to check on Kelsey, and then, as an afterthought, he threw in that Raye did too. Raye told me that she did not know he went upstairs. He never told her he did.

Porter added that Kelsey had mastered the stairs.

Steve pointed out that Porter said he talked with Raye on the phone after the CHBS worker left and that he left work at 2:15 p.m. or 2:30 p.m. Porter said it was approximately at that time and that he was running late.

Steve asked if Porter took the truck home so Raye could pick up Porter's daughter.

Porter stated, "We just got her Explorer out. It had been in the shop for a while. And when we were driving it home, we noticed it had a wobble and it's almost too much of a wobble for her to control. So that is why I said, you know, 'I'll just bring the truck home, and you can go get [my daughter].'"

Steve asked Porter what time his daughter got out of school. He stated, "She gets out of school at, I think, 2:55 but we always try to get there a little after three, because [the school], I don't know if you've ever seen it, the pick-up line will flow all the way out into the street. And a lot of time if you get there, even if you get there at 2:30, you don't get up there to pick them up until 3:05 anyway. We usually go about 3:05, I guess, and we can just drive right in and get her."

Steve asked how long it took to get from their home to the school.

Porter answered, "I'm guessing 20 minutes." Porter stated that Raye left the house at 2:45 p.m. so she would get to the school right at 3:05 p.m. Steve asked how long it took to get from work to home. Porter said, "Oh, yeah, I'm just right there. Five minutes."

Steve asked where Kelsey and Raye were once he arrived home. Porter said, "When I got home, Kelsey and Raye were in the bed still napping."

Steve asked, "Did you go in the room?"

Porter answered, stumbling over his words while describing what he did once he got into the room. He said, "Yeah. I walked in the room. And Raye, she usually sleeps pretty light, I guess, whenever Kelsey is in there, and she's ready to jump up at the drop of a hat. So I walked through the room, and I was going to…I was just going to go. And I said…you know, her eyes popped open. And I whispered…Kelsey was still asleep... 'I'll go get [my daughter].'"

He added, “And she said, ‘No, no, no….I told you I’d go.’

And I said, ‘Baby it’s all right.’ And I said, ‘Just lay down.’

And she said, ‘No’ she said, ‘I’m going to go.’

She looked over at Kelsey and she said…she said, ‘I’m going to let her sleep.’

And I said, ‘Well, she is going to be mad at you.’

And she said, ‘Well, I’m going to let her sleep.’

And she got up out of the bed, and we both walked into the kitchen. She put her shoes on and a couple of minutes later, she left.

I’ll never forget the last thing she said to me. She said, ‘Take care of my baby.’ I’m going to remember that for the rest of my life.

I don’t know if I can do it, Steve. I hurt so bad right now. And Raye feels like that if she had been there, that she could have got her out of it.”

*At the time of Kelsey’s death and before the interviews, it was thought that Kelsey died from a seizure. Raye thought she could bring Kelsey out of the seizure.*

So she said, “Take care of my baby,” and she left.

Steve tried to regain Porter’s focus by asking what happened when he walked into the bedroom. Porter stated, “Yeah, and I didn’t intend that she heard me walk into the room.”

Steve asked, “She woke up?”

Porter answered, “Yeah, I didn’t go over there and shake her and say, ‘It’s time to go.’ Her eyes popped open and I knelt down beside her and said, 'Baby, I'm just going to go get [my daughter].'"

*Raye told me that she had a feeling that someone was watching her, and when she opened her eyes, he was standing above her. She said that she had no idea how long he had been there.*

Porter said that her eyes opened and he knelt beside her and said that he was going to pick up his daughter. Steve asked Porter if he looked at Kelsey.

Porter answered "Yeah. She was just laying…she was sleeping."

Steve asked if she was snoring or making noises.

Porter stated, "I know that she was very deep into sleep, because there was hardly a time whenever….if Kelsey is sleeping with somebody and that person gets up, she will wake up. I mean, she has been through so much in her life that she…she had, you know, separation anxiety for a while. And that really affected her, and she was scared to death, you know, that she was going to be left or be taken away."

He added, "So she…this day, she just didn't wake up. I mean, Raye got up. And I know I thought it was unusual that she…Kelsey didn't wake up. I mean, she was okay. You know, that's the first time in awhile that I've seen Raye get up…and she'll tell you that. When she's laying with Kelsey and she gets up, Kelsey pops up. She wants to be…she wants to hang around with her mommy."

Steve asked what position Kelsey was in when Porter saw her. He answered, "She was on her back and she was laying on a pillow. And I don't know if she had half of her covered up. And it didn't look like she had rolled around or anything, which was strange in itself, because she…you know, there are kids that are rollers and movers, and she's…she will instinctively roll to her mom. I mean, that's just…you know, she'll roll until she finds her and then she'll throw a leg up on her."

*Porter told Rita, Lance's sister, that when he first saw Kelsey, Raye was gone and Kelsey was naked and positioned on a pillow with her bottom in the air. This is but another example of the stories that have been told in an effort to blame Raye. The most telling part in all of this is that the Briggs family continues to repeat this story as possible fact, just to create doubt of Porter's guilt in the minds of the unsuspecting public.*

Steve asked if Kelsey was breathing.

Porter answered, "I didn't pay attention. I mean, I couldn't tell. I don't know. I didn't get down and feel her chest. I just knew…I noticed that she didn't get up and I thought, 'Man, she must be out.' She must have been tired."

My guess is that she was tired. From descriptions of what took place that day and from Porter's deception about what he did that morning, I have come to the conclusion that he probably assaulted Kelsey before he left for work that morning, and it was most likely before he woke his daughter for school.

When Raye woke Kelsey, she had a towel under her head. *Why?* The first thing Kelsey told Raye that morning was that her tummy hurt. Porter later describes in detail how he took a "squealing" and happy Kelsey to bed with Raye that morning, yet Raye stated that Porter took Kelsey to bed with her every morning, <u>*except*</u> that morning.

On the ride home from the interviews, Raye's mind was flooded with questions as to what she had been told during her interview. She did not know whom to believe. First, the investigators told her that her child had been murdered, and then they accused her of doing it. They said that it had to be her in an effort to get her to confess. Later, they told her if it was not her, then it had to be Porter.

During the trip home, Raye refused to talk to Porter. She wanted to think. Porter asked her if she told investigators that he had taken Kelsey to bed with her that morning. She said she told them that he had not. Porter reportedly became agitated that Raye told the investigators the truth.

Once they arrived home, Raye packed her bag and left the home. She did not see Porter again until he showed up at Kelsey's funeral carrying a doll that had been Raye's as a child, and Raye had passed it down to Kelsey.

Porter did not comfort Raye at the funeral. As Raye was going over what she wanted to say about Kelsey, Porter snatched the paper from Raye's hands and questioned, "Why isn't there anything about me?"

Raye's eyes were opening to the truth about the man she had trusted with her daughter's life, and so were the investigators'.

The investigator asked if Kelsey normally woke up when Raye did.

Porter stated, "You know, it doesn't happen very often, but if she's really, really tired, then she'll sleep, which all that could have been was that she was up when I came in and took her down to sleep with Raye in the morning, she was instantly up waiting for me. She was so excited that morning too."

Steve questioned, "Kelsey was?"

Porter answered, "Yeah. I mean every morning when I come and get her the first thing, I'll say, 'Baby you want to go lay'…and she was up out of that bed just jumping. And she would have her legs wrapped around me and squealing. She was just so happy. And she'd say, 'Thank you, Daddy.'"

Steve asked again about the day Kelsey died and asked if Raye kissed Kelsey on the cheek before she left.

Porter stated, "I don't remember. We both just…we stood there for a minute and just made sure that she wasn't going to get up and cry, because Raye would have took her. If she would have woke up, we would have loaded her up."

Steve asked if Kelsey had woken up after Raye left, what would have happened?

Porter responded, "She probably would have walked in there and found me. And we would have had a talk, and she would have said, 'Where Mommy go?' I mean, her first reaction would have been, as usual…"

Porter pointed out that it was not fear that would make her react that way. He said, "Yeah. 'Where's Mommy?' I mean, it's not fear. It's just, you know, 'Where did she go?' That would be her first question. And she'd walk in there and do her little hands and say, 'Where did Mommy go?'"

Steve asked if Kelsey would have had a fit to the point that Porter could not control her.

Porter said "No." Steve asked if she would have cried. Porter, again, said "No."

Steve asked if Kelsey was upset if Porter would embrace her, and love on her, and assure her that her mommy would return.

Porter stumbled with his answer, stating that he had gained Kelsey's trust because Raye always returned when he said she would. He stated, "Yeah. She knows I can tell her…I mean, when I tell her Mommy is coming back, I've always…I made a point to…that was me establishing my trust with her…is whenever I promise her Mommy will be back, she comes back."

Steve asked if there were times when Raye was gone and it was just him and Kelsey.

Porter stated there was. He said there would be times that he would have Kelsey and his two children or just him and Kelsey or just him and his son. Steve asked if that was normal. Porter responded, "Not unusual at all. She trusts me. Kelsey trusts me, Raye Dawn trusts me. There's never a question."

Steve asked about what Porter did after Raye left. He stated that Porter had previously told him that he had cleaned up the kitchen and was doing laundry.

Porter stated, "Yeah, I was just tooling around. I guess I went upstairs. I don't…it wasn't immediately, but I went out…I know I had opened the door into the garage, and I was going to get those tires that I knew my friend was coming after work to pick up the tires. And I was going to pull those out, but then I didn't want to get all black and dirty, because I still had stuff to do in the house. So I shut the door and tooled around in the kitchen. I was just, you know, cleaning the kitchen sink. With kids, it stays so messy."

Porter added, "I went upstairs. [My daughter] was, I think, the last one down, and I wanted to make sure and turn all the lights off up there. So I was upstairs and turned out lights, and I just came back down and I was just doing normal…I mean, it's one of those routines that I just do it every day."

Steve asked if Kelsey's bedroom was upstairs or downstairs, to which Porter answered that it was downstairs in the north part of the house. He pointed out that it was "far away from everything." (Her bedroom was actually upstairs.)

Steve asked Porter where he was when he heard Kelsey grunt. Porter stumbled with his answer. He said, "I was…I guess I was in the kitchen. And I don't know if I was…I guess I was about to make me a glass of water, get a drink of water. And for some reason I just said…you know, it just sounded too quiet in the house. And for some reason I wanted to turn the TV on. And as I was across the couch…I walked to the left side of the couch and I heard….and I heard that noise."

Steve asked Porter if he knew where the noise was coming from.

Porter said, "I knew the only place it could be coming from. There was nobody there."

Steve asked how loud the noise was, because it must have been loud.

Porter answered, "As I walked around the couch, I'm right there. I walked by the doorway and it was quiet, and that's the reason I was going to turn the TV on."

Steve asked if he was talking about the doorway to the stairs. Porter stated the doorway to his bedroom he shared with Raye. He stated, "No, the doorway to the room. I walked right by it. And I don't know how long that noise had been going on."

Steve asked if it was upstairs or downstairs.

Porter stated, "No, it's downstairs. She was in the bed where we left…in our bedroom. And as I crossed the couch, as I went around the couch, I walked right by the doorway to our bedroom and heard it. And I didn't hear her walking up there. I didn't hear…I don't know how long…she could have been making those noises when I was tooling around upstairs and in the garage. I don't know."

Steve clarified the time that Raye left and asked if it was around 2:40 p.m. and Porter said it was somewhere around 2:40 p.m. or 2:45 p.m. Steve then asked how long it was after Raye left that he heard the grunt.

Porter stumbled around for a while. He stated, "I couldn't put a time on it. The only thing I can tell you is…leading up to that is just empty space. But after…that's when it gets…after I saw her, that's when…no, I don't know, because I was just…I mean, I wasn't looking at a clock. I wasn't on a schedule. I don't know."

Porter added, "I mean, if I had to guess, I'd guess….I couldn't put it down to within 5 minutes, I don't think. Fifteen, 25 minutes, I don't know. I know the best way to tell you how long it is, is when I called Gayla was right after I picked her up. And I tried to wake her and then I could tell that this was different. And my first reaction, I knew Gayla was the closest. And as far as we live out in the country, I panicked and I just called Gayla and said, 'Gayla, I need help.'" *Earlier in the interview, he stated that he carried*

*Kelsey around for 30 minutes. Now he's stating that he picked her up and immediately called Gayla.*

He further added, "And from whenever Raye Dawn left and when I called Gayla, that's how long, because as soon as I picked her up, after I…usually I can pick her up in my arms, and I can…and I said, 'Kelsey come on, baby. Come on…Wake up,' and she would kind of pop out of it, but she just didn't."

Throughout the interview, Porter's interactions with Kelsey are far different from the private moments that his daughter witnessed. She told her school counselor as well as an OSBI investigator that her father hit Kelsey's bottom until it turned "real red" and then Kelsey threw up and Porter went downstairs and did not say anything about it to Raye. His daughter also stated that he hit Kelsey's head on a brick wall and then he told his daughter, "She's going to throw up." Porter masked his evil side. Raye only saw the loving and caring side of her husband that he now described to investigators. However, his daughter knew the truth. Soon, investigators would as well.

Steve asked if Porter went into the room after he heard Kelsey grunt. Porter stated that he ran into the room.

Steve asked if she was in the same position as when Raye had left.

Porter stated, "She was in the same position. Her head was kind of…I guess she wasn't sitting up, but her body was. I don't know what the word is. Is it flexion or…her body was in…she was…I mean she was flexed a little bit up, is what she was, like all the muscles were contracting. And she had her tongue out. I mean, I knew the noise when I heard it, because me and Raye Dawn and Gayla, we've all heard that noise."

Steve asked if that was the type of noise she made when having a seizure. Porter answered, "It's a guttural. It sounds like she's either forcing....trying to force air in or out. It sounds like a...I can't think of what the sound is. It's just a..."

Steve asked if her tongue was sticking out and if her jaws were clenched the entire time. Porter said "Yes." Steve asked if Porter was able to separate her jaws.

Porter said, "I was able to separate it whenever...as I picked her up, she...she was rigid. I mean, she appeared rigid on the bed. But when I picked her up and I tried to wake her up, I was on the phone with Gayla and then she loosened up. And that's when I knew that...I mean, it was getting dangerous, because she loosened up and she just...I mean, she had nothing..."

Steve interrupted Porter and asked if he took her into the kitchen area. The water had been running in the sink.

Porter stated, "I walked in the living room. I mean I took her out of the bedroom, and I don't know. I was panicking. I walked her out and I was making my way towards the kitchen, but I walked around the living room and made a couple of circles around the living room. And the whole time, you know, I'm talking to Kelsey, 'Come on, baby. Come on.' And I'm trying to lift her head up, because you know at this point her arms were down and she was...I mean, her..."

Steve asked if she became limp when he was carrying her around the living room.

Porter answered, "Yeah. I mean….and it wasn't…she didn't become totally limp until I was outside waiting on the ambulance. But she was struggling to…I mean, I would say her motor control was severely…I mean severely limited, severely, I mean because I'd say, 'Come on, Kelsey. Wake up.' And she'd kind of give…I mean, it couldn't even be considered a response. I don't think it was a response, but it was kind of a 'uh,' so weak."

Steve asked Porter if Kelsey's eyes were open.

He responded, "Yeah, her eyes were…they were open, but they were closing, I mean, they were…when I…when I kind of tried to shake…I mean, that's what I normally would do. I would hold her and I would say, 'Come on, Kels.' And as I'd do it, her eyes would pop open, but then they'd just…"

Steve cut him off and asked how tightly he was holding Kelsey.

Porter stated that he didn't know how tightly he was holding her. He stated, "I was holding her underneath." Steve asked for clarification and asked if he were holding her under her bottom.

Porter said, "Yeah, under her butt, and she was…you know, usually she'll sit up straight. But the way she was, I had to hold her out and then she was kind of towards me, and so I had to kind of lift her back up so I could see her face, because you know, that was the only way I knew what was wrong was her face, because it was just…I mean, her lips were…I mean, she was blue…I mean, the color was fading."

Steve told Porter, "I think you told me before that when you were in the bedroom before you picked her up, you noticed that her lips were blue?"

Porter agreed and then stumbled again over his words. "Yeah. I mean, it just looked like she..."

Steve asked if he felt her heart.

Porter stated, "The first time I felt for her heartbeat was whenever I took her in the kitchen after I called Gayla and 911 and I laid her down on the island. And I took...I tilted her head back and I listened. And all I could hear was that little...tiny little 'uh.' I mean, it wasn't even that loud. It was weaker than that. I can't reproduce it."

Steve asked Porter if he laid Kelsey on the island before he called Gayla.

Porter stated, "No. I had her...I had her..."

Steve said, "You had her in your arms?"

Porter answered, "I had her in my arms. Yeah, because I was talking to...I mean, Gayla and Kelsey. And I said, 'Gayla, I need help.' And at the same time, 'Kelsey, come on, baby.' And having the phone in my hand, I felt like prevented me from doing the only thing I could do to help Kelsey at the time; which was to try to get her to come to."

Porter added, "I couldn't do it one-handed, because she was falling over on me. And the only way I could do it was try to sit her up, and then I figured out that, you know, with this arm taken up holding her, I couldn't do it. And that's why I took her into the kitchen and laid her down. And I listened, and then 911 is talking. And I picked the phone up and they're talking. 'Keep talking to her. Keep talking to her.' And I was trying to tell her...I was trying to tell this woman that I needed help, but, you know..."

Steve asked Porter to describe how he gave Kelsey CPR. Porter stated, "Her head was already tilted back and I just did what they taught me to do. I mean, I just pinched her nose and I held her…I held her jaw and made sure it was tilted back and tried to make sure her airway was open. And I blew and I waited and I blew and then I would do compressions. And I just did them the best…I was so scared, because they say you can crack ribs and stuff."

Porter went on to describe his "efforts to save Kelsey." He added, "No, I mean, not even enough to know if I was helpful or hurting her, but I do know that after two or three cycles of the compressions that I got a response. And the lady on the phone heard the response and she said, 'Is that her?'

And I was talking and I heard it, and I said, 'Kelsey, Kelsey. Come on, baby. Grandma is coming. Come on. Come on.'

And she said, 'Is that her?' I don't know if she made a noise or if she said…she never talked, but I guess she went 'uh' or something. I don't know if it was just air coming out or what. And the lady said, 'Was that her?'

And I said, 'Yes, that was her.'

And she said, 'Keep talking. Keep talking.' So at that point I thought that maybe she had…that maybe she had come back enough. And then I picked her up and…and I picked her up and I was talking to them and I was just trying to get them there.

And then as I walked to the door, I see my friend pulling up who was coming to get the tires. So I run outside, because I know that I'm not…I'm not telling…I don't feel like I'm helping 911 get there, because I'm so focused on Kelsey."

*Porter's friend stated that when he arrived at the home, Porter was already standing outside holding Kelsey.*

Steve questioned, "You had Kelsey in your arms?"

Porter explained, "I was holding her at that point. When I felt like she came back, I picked her up, I mean, whenever the lady told me, she said, 'You're doing the right thing. Keep talking to her.' So at that point, I picked her up."

*Why would a 911 operator tell him to quit doing CPR and to talk to Kelsey instead?*

Porter further described his version of the scene by adding the following: "And, you know, I'm talking and I'm saying, 'Come on, Kelsey. Come on, baby.' And then I started to go to the door, because I wanted to go outside and see if I could see them coming. And I see him coming up. And at this point, that's whenever…that's whenever she…she…When I went down the steps, she fell back…When I went down the steps on the porch, she fell back. And her arms…

And I forgot to tell you that the reason that I thought that I might have helped her was that after I picked her up, she seemed like she got a little bit of…I don't know, but she…when I laid down on her, I said, 'Come on, baby. Grandma's coming.' And I felt her push.

And that's why I thought that…you know, I knew I had to get outside and let somebody that could help her, because I felt like there was…but by the time I made it to the door, I mean, it seemed like maybe that was the last that she had, because when I went down the steps, she fell back and her head was…I mean, her head just went all the way back. And so I had the phone and I had to lean back with her to get her to come back to me.

And so I was still trying to talk to her and my friend pulls up and he sees what's going on, and he runs out. And I'm on the phone and I said, '[Friend],' I said, you know, 'she's not breathing.'

And he looked at her and saw her lips and everything and said, 'Oh, my God.'

And I hand…he tried to take her and I said, 'No.' I said, 'No.' I said, 'You take the phone and you get them here.'

So he took the phone and he said, you know…he tried to talk them into getting there."

Steve asked, "The training that you…the limited amount of training you had in CPR, how long ago was that?" Porter answered, "It had been over a year ago." Steve questioned, "Over a year ago?" Porter clarified, "I meant to go somewhere and refresh it with everything that she was going through, but every doctor that we've ever had…you know, that we'd ever seen for the seizures…"

Steve asked, "I mean, you know the difference of what kind of breaths and what kind of compressions you give to a three-year-old versus an adult?" Porter stated, "We had some training. I mean, we had limited training in that, because the majority of the people we were dealing with were adults."

Steve asked, "And what kind of breaths and chest compressions did you give to Kelsey?"

Porter answered, "I gave the only kind I knew how, which I gave the…I mean, I closed her nose off and gave her breaths and then I gave the compressions." Steve asked, "The breaths?" Porter confirmed his answer.

Steve asked Porter, "Now, I've had CPR training too, so maybe…you didn't practice on some babies and then on some larger mannequins?"

Porter stated, "No. I mean, all that was told to us was that, you know, you have to be a lot gentler with smaller people, because of their…"

Steve interrupted, "Their lung capacity?"

Porter completed his thought, "…their lung capacity. And I…as far as I know, I wasn't blowing. I mean, I know I wasn't blowing heavy-handed. I gave her small breaths."

Steve asked, "What about the chest compressions?" Porter started to answer, "I just…" Steve interrupted, "One-handed or two handed?"

Porter answered, "I gave her one-handed. I mean, she was on the island, and I should have put her on the floor but didn't…I didn't have leverage to do it two-handed. And all I could do was like that."

Steve then asked, "This is kind of disgusting, but did you hear anything crack or anything like that?" "No." "Where was your hand when you gave her the compressions?" "It was below the sternum, right where…" "Right here?" "Yeah." "Was it above that or below that?"

Porter explained, "I mean, my hand is her whole chest, but my palm was right…I believe right…it was…I think it was right on her…I mean, a little bit of it was on it and below it."

Steve asked, "And you didn't…you probably shouldn't give her two-handed anyhow, so it was probably a good thing that…" Porter interrupted, "No, and I didn't have…like I say…" Steve asked, "You didn't have a lot of pressure?"

Porter answered, "No, our island is tall and I couldn't. I mean, I didn't have any leverage. All I was doing was just…" Steve interrupted, "Those compressions were probably sufficient to…"

Porter further explained, "And I just did it enough to where I could see her chest. I mean, I didn't put any weight on it. It was just…she was so…so small." *He just said that he "laid down on her" and "felt her push."*

Steve then asked about the events that happened after Porter's friend arrived and how long after they arrived at the hospital until they found out that Kelsey was dead.

Porter answered, "Yeah, it was hours. And now they're saying in the paper…nobody would tell us anything. They're saying in the paper…we had to read in the paper that she was dead on arrival, but we were there for three hours, somewhere, two or three hours. And I had a little incident, so I didn't even…I found out after everybody else."

Steve asked how long after their arrival at the hospital did Porter have his "incident." Porter answered, "We were…everybody was just pacing and we were asking everybody and then I just kind of…I've had a mild heart attack before. I just got a chest pain and I woke up and I was back…they had me back there and they had a neck collar on me. And I guess I…I guess I fell over and hit my car and hit the concrete, so I don't know. And then I…and then I…I just kept begging them to just save her, just tell me what…I have to see her…so they did an X-ray, and I was fine. I told them I was fine."

*A witness stated that although Mike Porter fell to the ground, his eyes were open and he just stared at the sky.*

Steve continued the questions and informed Porter that Kelsey had been murdered, but not until after he committed to his story that he tried to "save Kelsey" and that he had performed one-handed CPR on her while she was on the bar. *When witnesses arrived at the house, the water was running in the sink by the bar. Why?*

Steve then told Porter, "The problem we're running into is with the report that the medical examiner has given. It appears…well, it doesn't appear; it's a fact that there were some internal injuries that Kelsey had that absolutely cannot be caused by chest compressions. They were abdominal injuries that were inflicted on Kelsey to the point of where they were so significant that Kelsey would have been in the fetal position right after they happened, okay." A medical examiner from Colorado also stated that Kelsey would have been in a fetal position and screaming from pain until she passed out just moments before her death. The medical reports did not correlate with the story that Porter was trying to sell to the investigators.

Steve further added, "The injuries were probably caused during a very short time period, okay. Now…and the injuries would have absolutely put Kelsey, like I said, in a fetal position where the pain would have been so significant that she wouldn't have been able to handle it and still be functional."

Porter claimed he didn't understand. Steve added, "There was bruising, a significant amount of bruising that they found underneath the skin, so it was…the bruising hadn't made it to the outer layer of the skin yet. What we have to try to determine here, Mike, is what happened to Kelsey, okay."

*Raye was later told by an investigator that Kelsey also had a bruise on her bottom like someone was "holding it open."*

Each time the investigator said that someone hurt Kelsey on purpose Porter brought up Raye and stated that she would not hurt her. During Raye's investigation, she never pointed a finger at Porter. She continually stated that she didn't know what happened.

Investigators offered Raye the opportunity to suggest that she could have hurt Kelsey by accident, and Raye said, "No way!" When the same offer was made to Mike Porter, he jumped at it by stating, "There's no way that any of the things that I did trying to help her, that I could have hurt her?" The investigator stated there was no way.

Mike Porter asked, "As small and fragile as she is?"

The investigator said, "No way."

Mike Porter asked, "What about me shaking her up on my shoulder?"

The investigator asked, "How tight were you holding her?"

Porter answered, "Well, I wasn't holding her tight. I had her under the butt and I was lifting her up."

The investigator explained that the injury was so severe, that Porter would have had to squeeze Kelsey very tightly. Then he asked Porter what was wrong. Mike Porter shifted the blame to Raye, again. "This is wrong, I know what happened and I know Raye didn't hurt her."

Porter feigned a heart attack, but soon recovered. The investigator went back-and-forth with Porter asking for help and saying, "This is wrong" and "That child was not intentionally hurt."

Porter went on to reason, "I was shaking her up."

Porter continued to make statements such as the following:

"As small and fragile as she is?"

"What about me shaking her up on my shoulder?"

"This is wrong, Steve. This is wrong. I know what happened, and I know Raye Dawn didn't hurt her."

*It was almost as if he was trying to lay blame on Raye. While Raye stated, "I didn't do anything" and "I never saw Mike hurt Kelsey" only when asked about his possible involvement, Porter first mentioned Raye as a suspect and he continually put the focus on Raye's possible guilt while trying to convince the detectives that he could have accidentally killed Kelsey while trying to save her. This was an option that investigators tried to give to Raye, but she stated there is no way she hurt Kelsey, not even accidentally.*

Porter then changed his story by stating, "The first time I saw her was when I picked her up out of bed." *Earlier he stated that he watched her for at least a minute with Raye to make sure she wasn't going to wake up before Raye left.*

He then added, "I don't know everything that I did…everything I did was to try to help that baby. And I don't know how…you asked me…I don't know how I was holding her. I don't know."

The investigator argued with Mike Porter for a few minutes. Mike Porter kept insisting that Kelsey wasn't intentionally hurt, and that there had to be another explanation. He repeatedly stated that Raye would never harm Kelsey, and that it must have been something accidental. When the investigator did not agree, Mike Porter quit talking and asked to see his wife.

At the end of Raye's interview, she was informed that Mike Porter had refused to take a lie detector test. Raye was willing to take one, but since she was pregnant, they wouldn't give her one. Since Raye had fully cooperated and repeatedly yelled, "Tell me what I need to do!" investigators brought Mike Porter into the room with Raye and discussed the fact that he refused the lie detector. Mike Porter stated, "It's not that I'm not cooperating. We're just at an impasse." After hearing his uncooperative stance, Raye stormed out of the room and the video of Raye's interview ended shortly afterward with the investigator trying to get more information from Mike Porter. He would not budge. Days later, when Raye returned to the OSBI office for her second interview, the first words from the investigator included an apology for how she was treated in the previous interview. The investigator stated, "I didn't know what happened. I only had the autopsy results."

Recent reports have been released claiming that during the simultaneous interviews, Mike Porter was writhing in pain due to his grief over the loss of Kelsey, while Raye was talking about her big house and great life, and basically being a cold-hearted, uncaring mother. This is untrue. From what I viewed, those things were never said during her interview. They also claimed that Raye never cried, yet, from the beginning of the interview, she continuously wiped tears from her cheeks. These reports have clearly been created just to promote hate against Raye—a hate that Mike Porter helped to build with misrepresented and untrue accounts of events.

Mike Porter is a smart man. He quickly learned how to play the game. After his release on bond less than two months after being arrested for the first-degree murder of Kelsey, he became an active member of Kelsey's Purpose. What had started as a cry for justice against both Mike Porter and Raye soon turned to a united roar, with Mike Porter a member of "team Kathie," doing her bidding. He even earned her trust to the point where she gave him a ride to her daughter's apartment for a private meeting with just herself and Mike Porter to discuss not Kelsey's death, but according to Kathie, possible civil lawsuits.

The Briggs and their supporters have threatened lawsuits against anyone who spoke up against them. Members of their family have played the role of victim, each time their version of Kelsey's story has been questioned, while the hate for Raye and her family has been a never-ending tide. For instance, shortly after Kelsey's death, one of Kathie's supporters left messages on the answering machines of Kelsey's maternal grandmother, as well as her great-grandmother.

The following was a message left for Mildred, Kelsey's maternal great-grandmother: "Now listen here you old pig!

You are spending all that money defending old Raye Dawg, why didn't you spend half a little of that money takin' care of Kelsey? You think the citizens of Meeker are hot? You ought to come up here to Oklahoma City, you old pig, and see how we feel. We are mad as hell! And we are going to do something about it! We are going to keep this out in the public and continue to fight for Kelsey till we don't have another breath in us! If you had took half the money you are spending on Raye Dawg and spent it on Kelsey! People like you make me sick!"

A few days after Mildred received this message, her phone rang and she answered. No one said a word. The only sound was that of a baby crying.

Gayla, Kelsey's maternal grandmother, received a message that was addressed to her male friend. The person stated, "I just want you to know I'm a grandmother from Oklahoma and the story on Kelsey Briggs has just upset me so badly. I talked to all of my friends and neighbors and we will never buy from [business name withheld for privacy]. You're harboring a murderer and you're harboring somebody who sat by and watched it and I hope that it cuts into your pocketbook, because maybe if it cuts into your pocketbook, you might get rid of both of them. I don't know what kind of guy you are, but someone who harbors a baby murderer tells me a lot about that person."

A second message soon followed: "Well, I can't believe you're still living with a (inaudible)…whore and a baby beater and raper. Good lord! Somebody was looking the other day and saw a real estate sign out there and somebody was taking down the name. One of the neighbors ran out and said, 'Don't buy that house! They harbor a baby raper!' Boy, you must be low. None of them ain't good looking. Hell, I think (inaudible) are better than old Gayla and Raye Dawn! Why don't you give one of them a shot? They haven't killed anybody yet. You sorry thing! Good bye!"

On December 9, 2005 a letter addressed to Gayla's friend arrived with a picture at the top of the letter of Kelsey that was displayed on Kelsey's Purpose. It read, "Look at that adorable innocent little face, so full of wonder, hope, magic and love. Children are so innocent, they believe in the tooth fairy, and Easter Bunny and Santa Clause. They have not learned to hate or show prejudice and everyone is their friend. They turn to the adults in their life for love and protection, without asking for anything in return. Children are our future. What kind of monster, punches a baby in the stomach, ending her life?? What kind of monster breaks both legs of a toddler??? I cannot imagine such an individual. I keep asking myself why, why, why???? And again, I ask myself, 'How could you protect and shelter an individual responsible for beating a toddler?' I hope you can sleep at night, knowing you have two women in your home, one abused Kelsey and the other ignored Kelsey's bruises and broken bones. I heard your girlfriend was too wrapped up in you and your money to pay any attention to what was happening to Kelsey. I am putting the word out to boycott your realty company to all my friends. Hope you guys enjoy the holidays together. A Grandmother."

Kelsey's great-grandmother, Mildred, received a message from another one of Kathie's supporters that was read from a pre-written statement that included accusations against Kelsey's maternal family. The message ended with this warning: "You'd better be doing something else and praying A LOT!"

As time went on and Kathie became a regular face on the nightly news, it seemed some of her supporters felt as if they were rubbing elbows with a local celebrity and only wanted to please her by generating more hate for Raye and her family. There was a unified roar for justice. Mike Porter's voice soon became the loudest of all. His $1 million bond was reduced to $250,000, allowing him to bond out of jail.

Pretending to be his sister, he became a part of the forum and later the paternal family's "bash board." In the beginning, he was blamed, along with Raye. Kathie and her family members wanted him to "pay." Once Kathie's forum was flooded with posts from "Mike Porter supporters," which coincidentally, started at around the same time Mike Porter was released on bond, the tone toward Mike Porter changed while the hatred for Raye grew even more intense. It's clear from communications that Mike Porter manipulated Kelsey's paternal family by sharing "stories" with them of things Raye and her family members had said and done. He knew exactly what they wanted to hear. Some posts by his "supporters" mimic statements he makes later as himself. Therefore, my suspicion is that it was actually him.

On December 5, 2005 "Malena" posted an opinion under the heading "Poll." "I hope I can voice my opinion here without hurting any of the Briggs' feelings. I also believe that Raye Dawn was the one the hurt Kelsey, she knew what was going to happen the day she left Kelsey with Mike Porter. Mike Porter and I have been friends since we were in elementary school, he was my neighbor for 12 years. My mother was also best friends with his mother, and worked at their company. I do not know Raye Dawn, but we have many mutual friends. These friends also know Mike Porter, and they ALL agree that she would do something like this, not him! Don't get me wrong, I believe that Mike had to know what Raye Dawn was doing to Kelsey and did nothing to help her, so he is also guilty. They both must be punished. I think that the police in Meeker just needed to make an arrest in the case, so they arrested Mike just because he was arrested and was the last one with Kelsey. I have talked to Mike Porter, very briefly, the day he was arrested and in my heart I don't believe he was the one that hurt that baby. I pray about Kelsey every night, that justice will be served and that the truth will surface. I know I wrote this before, but I can't believe that Raye Dawn hasn't been charged with anything, anything at all! She is walking around free right now, demanding this and that from Mike, while he sits in jail. Makes me sick! I would do anything to take that baby away from her! It does surprise me too that the Smith family isn't seeking justice for Kelsey. They are too busy trying to protect Raye Dawn and their reputation. When I saw her family on tv you could tell they are just trying to protect her, they act like they didn't see the bruises or that anything was wrong with Kelsey. If Raye Dawn has nothing to hide then why is she hiding so much? I know there are a lot of rumors going around and I don't know who has come forward and who hasn't. I have heard, though, that Raye Dawn got in touch with an old friend of hers the day after Kelsey died and told her two different stories about what happened. I know about this because the old friend and I have a mutual friend, who told me about it. I have tried to relay this info. To others, but I don't know if it has gotten to anyone yet. Lance, I read in the paper that you are bring a $15 mil tort claim against the state, GOOD FOR YOU! God bless!"

On December 7, 2005 a "Concerned citizen" voiced an opinion similar to "Malena's." "The chances of justice being carried out in this case are getting smaller by the day. As far as the OSBI is concerned I don't believe they have looked any further than Mike Porter. I grew up with Mike and I know he is no murderer or accomplice to murder. I've heard second and third hand stories that, if people had the guts to come forward with, would mean jail time for Raye Dawn. If everyone just sits back and keeps quiet they will convict Mike and Raye Dawn will be free to ruin another child's life. An innocent child is dead and many lives are horribly altered. The time for family, friend, employer loyalty is long past. Our only loyalty should be to the truth."

Lance's sister was apparently disturbed by the good reports regarding Mike Porter's character. She stated, "I am sorry but I just cannot sit here and listen to all of these people who say they knew Mike Porter and never thought he could be involved in the murder of my niece. I knew Raye Dawn through school as well and was even on our high school Pom squad together. I never thought I knew anyone that could ever be involved in hurting a child..."

"KJ3" expressed her feelings about Mike Porter with the following: "...I think people just want the truth and want to make sure the right person pays for the murder. I agree that know one thinks that their friend, neighbor, or family member could do such a crime, but the fact is we don't know. We just all want justice for your precious little Kelsey...They just want everyone to know the Mike Porter they know not the one that the media has portrayed..."

"JusticeforMike" seemed to be a less educated character in Mike Porter's sudden support system. "every time we asked Raye Dawn what was wrong with Kelsey she would always tell us Kelsey was sick or she had just went to the doctors and so on she always had excuses for us can anyone tell me what eveidence they have against Mike besides he was the last one with her. that dont make you guilty maybe he found her that way he says she was having a seizer...I just dont understand why they have arrested Mike and not investegated anyone else. Raye Dawn should be sitting right there in jail next to him intell the investagation is over."

Rita added, "As much as I hate to say this, there is evidence against Mike Porter that is not public knowledge at this time. OSBI has assured our family that they have the person who murdered Kelsey in custody. I know it is difficult for people to wrap their minds around the idea of Mike Porter being guilty. I know how easy it is to automatically think Raye Dawn is the guilty one, but none of you have seen the evidence. Yes, Raye Dawn is less than appealing to so many of us and yes, Mike appears to be a good father to his own children, but so was the BTK serial murderer. He was a strong member of his church and was wonderful to his own children. They did not know he was raping and murdering women his own daughter's age for thirty years...Again, if you feel you have information to prove otherwise, please come forward and contact the OSBI or the DA."

Wilma echoed the feelings of her two sisters by stating, "There have been many posts about the character of Mike. Our family understands how those who know Mike feel the need to support and defend him. Our family has felt the need to defend ourselves and our character against the lies that Raye Dawn, her mother, her grandmother, her uncle, her sister, and yes, her husband have said about our family for the last eleven months. They have spread many, many lies in order to make Raye Dawn look like the poor innocent victim of the 'evil, psychotic' Briggs family...Mike has behaved in ways that showed poor character with no appreciation for what is right and what is wrong. I do not doubt Mike Porter was a good son, a giving boss, a kind friend, or a loving father to his biological children. Yes, many think that Mike's character is wonderful, but they have not been in court against him, Raye Dawn, and her family. Even if he did not hurt or kill Kelsey, did you ever think that Mike was capable of allowing a two year old child to be mentally and physically abused? Yes, it would be very scary to have your fate decided upon in the...County Court system. Trust me, our family is very wary of the court system too. I am sure that Mike Porter is scared to death to have his fate sitting in the hands of the courts...My family suffered a great deal because of the actions of the...Police, DHS, the Judge, Raye Dawn, her family, AND Mike Porter....Whether Mike killed Kelsey or not, he contributed to her death. Period!"

"JusticeforMike" replied, "WELL SEE RAYE DAWN TOLD US YOU ALL WERE STALKING AND CAUSING TROUBLE FOR THEM THAT'S ALL WE KNEW WHAT ABOUT THE TROUBLE THAT WAS HAPPENING BEFORE MIKE CAME ALONG?"

One member of the forum didn't approve of the name "JusticeforMike." She stated, "I have a real problem with someone who posts under the name of 'Justice for Mike' on a website devoted to a precious, adorable toddler that was murdered. Mike Porter was the only person arrested and jailed for the murder of Kelsey. I believe that Raye Dawn needs to be occupying the jail cell next to her husband..."

"Concernedcitizen" kept the conversation going against Raye by claiming "...I've heard from those that know Raye Dawn and her mom well that they are world class manipulators. Why is it so hard to believe that they manipulated Mike? So he reacted to what Raye Dawn and Gayla told him without checking into it first...I'd be interested to know what lies Raye Dawn and Gayla told Mike about the Briggs family...For those of you that talk to the OSBI – are they even looking at Raye Dawn?"

On December 29th, Mike Porter stepped up his defense efforts by privately contacting Rita, Lance's sister, pretending to be his own sister. He stated, "Let me say our family's thoughts and prayers are with you everyday...The only thing that gives us any comfort is we know the truth – Michael DID not do this. I know that is a comfort that your family does not have right now. We also understand that Kelsey was taken from your family by someone and the same person is now trying to take Michael from us. However, there seems to be a great lack of interest in prosecuting the guilty party...What we should ALL be concerned about is the reluctance to prosecute other parties. We know what kind of person Michael is – proud, gullable, trusting, blind at times – yes. Capable of hurting a child – never. The truth is there – search your heart for it...We will continue to support your Kelsey and your family in our prayers and actions. We would like to keep the lines of communication open; and for that to happen our communications should be kept in confidence. I hope you will respect and honor this request. God Bless You and your family."

Rita immediately answered his plea. "You and I had a nice heart felt discussion and you made a request to me. I will not go into details because I do not know who all has access to this address because I know [a forum member] has access to it, but I will say this. I cannot help without getting the confirmation I need and only Mike can do that for me. I am not saying I have groundbreaking information, I do not, but I cannot grant your request without mine being granted."

The public and private conversations continued with Rita questioning Mike Porter's trustworthiness. She wrote the following words to the man charged with the murder of her niece: "...It is tragic what we all have had to endure at the hand of Raye Dawn. Mike, I truly understand your fear to speak with me. I would not blame you for not contacting me. I was just in hopes you might trust me to do so...I know trust is something you are probably not big on these days. I feel the same way. Just know my heart and prayers go out to your family, especially your precious children..." The e-mail ended with Rita's home and cell phone numbers.

Mike Porter, pretending to be his sister sent this prompt reply: "We all appreciate your discretion after you spoke with **ME** last time. We don't worry about anyone bringing us harm...The threats are constant and expected, and we know they do not come from anyone who loved Kelsey. The last thing Kelsey would want is more violence or heartbreak. What is the one thing you need to know, [Rita]? If it is in my power to tell you I will. Please understand that our phones are most likely tapped. Michael does not eat or sleep because he misses Kelsey, [Mike Porter's daughter and son] so much – not telling you that for sympathy, but because it is the truth. Many don't realize that this has destroyed so many families...How to explain to a 2 year old why someone would ever take any child's life? Especially their own? One they 'loved'?"

Rita responded, "I need to hear it in his voice. I have seen it in his eyes but I need to put the two together."

"In person would be best – but how?" Mike Porter asked, and then he answered his own question with the start of a plan...a plan to escape facing the death penalty. "We need to think about where and when. We all know why this will be a huge obstacle to overcome – trust is not something Michael feels he will ever be able to afford again – look at where trust in Raye Dawn has gotten all those who loved Kelsey. Trust is the main factor here – breaking confidence will not change anything that Michael is going to do – that will be done for Kelsey. All it will do is close down the lines of communication between our families – and that is never a good thing...Michael was pulled into this battle by Raye Dawn, and Raye Dawn always made it about a fight between families – and of course you would never believe the things he was told...Michael would give his life in a second for Kelsey to get to see her father again. But he refuses to give his life so the person who is responsible can walk free to do this again."

Rita seemed impatient for the meeting. "Do you feel up to meeting somewhere this evening? ... I posted a reply on the bash-board stating I had changed my mind in wanting to be contacted. Please disregard what I wrote. I just did that because I have already had a nosy person e-mail me to see if I had heard from him. I do not in any way want people to know what I am doing here. This is strictly between US!!! I have not and will not even mention it to ANY members of my family. This is from one big sister to another."

Rita eventually met with Mike Porter. She claims Mike Porter was worried about dying for what Raye had done. The district attorney was seeking the death penalty against him. Mike Porter also told her things Raye had allegedly said about Rita's family. Mike Porter is a manipulator who knows how to play Kathie, and he played her so well that he never went to trial and never faced the death penalty. The e-mails and the game continued as Mike Porter won over Kelsey's paternal family. He made sure that all of the negativity was directed toward Raye and her family instead of himself. The plot thickened as they soon became an important part of his defense team. Months before Kelsey's body was exhumed for a second autopsy that resulted in the added charge of sexual assault, Mike Porter saved his own life by using the family that had sworn they were only fighting for "Justice for Kelsey."

# 30 The Plot

"When evil men plot, good men must plan. When evil men burn and bomb, good men must build and bind. When evil men shout ugly words of hatred, good men must commit themselves to the glories of love." ~ Martin Luther King, Jr.

By January of 2006, it seemed the plot against Raye was in full swing. Rallies and protests were held to bring public awareness to Raye and the Judge, and their charge of "failure to protect Kelsey," a charge of which the paternal family thought they alone were innocent. Mike Porter seemed to stay under the radar with prayer requests extended for his family by Kathie and her daughters.

Posted by Kjbriggs, Kelsey's [paternal] Grandma "Two months ago yesterday we got the call that would change our lives forever. Our lives are now filled with questions, anger, and a mission for change. As I look back over the last two months I am amazed at all of the positives that have come out of this tragedy. We have heard from old friends and we now have new friends that have reached out to a family they have never met. Our family that has always been close has been our biggest source of strength next to the prayers that come from people near and far. To count our blessings would be an endless task. Yes, some days are long and hard, but we get through them together.

So many have shared their kind words on this site and we appreciate all of them. We have even allowed some to voice opinions we do not necessarily agree with, but at this time I am asking that some of that stop. This site was designed to honor Kelsey and the loved ones she left behind. It was not put here to defend or attack the ones who abused her.

I agree there are many questions that need answers. There are many facts that don't add up. The wheels of justice are way too slow, but we have no choice but to wait. I have to believe the truth will come out and justice will be served.

**In the mean time, Kelsey was not the only victim of this crime. I continue to not only think of how this has changed our family, but the lives of the Porter children. I also want to mention Mike Porter has two sisters ages 27 and 22 that are alone during this time. Their parents are no longer living and they do not have the support system we have. It breaks my heart to think what these two girls are going through. I would ask each one of you to remember them in your prayers.**[38]

Please remember this site is a memorial for Kelsey. We are interested in your views, but we would like you to be considerate of all of Kelsey's family when posting. Thank you, Kathie Briggs"

This post was last modified: 12-17-2005 10:26 PM by aunt bean.

Those closest to Raye had their suspicions that something odd was happening between Mike Porter and Kelsey's paternal family, but they did not know they were

[38] Emphasis by book author

communicating privately or that Kelsey's paternal family was aiding in his defense. A witness recently told me that Kathie confided in her by stating that the only way to ensure Raye would go to prison was to give Mike Porter a plea deal. While reviewing the evidence of the obvious plot against Raye that was formulated and implemented by Mike Porter and his new friends, Kelsey's paternal family, the actions of this group of unlikely allies now make sense. They substantiate the fact that their mission had nothing to do with Kelsey, but instead Kathie's desire to see Raye behind bars.

The sharing of information about the murder case against Mike Porter started with an e-mail Rita sent to him on Sunday, January 1, 2006. "Not sure if you know this but OSBI interviewed CG on Thurs. I will be willing to discuss this further later."

Mike Porter snapped at the bait. "I assume you mean Raye Dawn's ex? I hope he wasn't stupid enough to lie about things...Can you give me any more info?"

Rita obliged, "...He said OSBI was very mean and rude to him...He said Mike lost his temper and walked across the room and hit him across the face so hard it knocked him down. [Raye's ex] said he knew at that point he had two choices, get the @%*! Beat out of him or leave so he left. He said that Mike had gotten jealous over something to do with Lance..."

Mike Porter grew defensive. "that is a bald faced lie about why they had a disagreement...all these people that are lying are going to be in deep trouble when they get hit with obstruction of justice charges...you know the way I feel about the Smiths trying to trash other people? BRING IT...Let them talk their same old bullshit about them being the victims...[Rita], Michael knows the lies that the Smiths spread about your family – these will come out!!!! Let them act desperately...I HOPE they try to trash our family..."

Rita took Mike Porter's words as truth. "We kinda figured [Raye's ex] was not telling the complete truth...It shows so much of what kind of people we are dealing with...[Raye's ex's] intention with telling that story was to add to the fact that Mike Porter was 'very jealous of Lance and he has a temper'...I will not lie and say Lance was a complete victim and was not at fault, he was...She made him out of his mind crazy at times and she is going to exploit that for all it is worth. She is going to do the same thing to Mike...When the story in the paper comes out about Lance and Raye Dawn it is not going to be pretty. She stated that Lance beat her and tried to choke her because she forgot to supersize his french fries...Lance went to jail...Raye Dawn did not have any [injuries] except for the red mark where he put his forearm on her to keep her from hitting him...Mike Porter needs to be prepared for what is coming his way. They are EVIL people. Have you given any thought to us meeting?"

It seemed through their communications that Mike Porter and Rita were developing a bond from their mutual hatred for Raye. Mike Porter told Rita, "...Raye Dawn would always try to make Michael hate Lance...As far as Im concerned she can say what she wants about Michael – because there are enough people who know it is bullshit. She is the alcoholic, she is the one who is a sex addict – she is the one with anger problems, she is the jealous one, and she is the controlling, possessive one, and she is the one who killed Kelsey...She is fooling herself if she thinks badmouthing Lance, your family, or Michael is going to convince anyone that she didn't kill her daughter and that she gives a care that she is gone...If she says anything about Michael that is not a fact, she will be sued for slander and libel – I would recommend you all do the same. We will not let her try to destroy him – he is already accused of murder because of her..."

The topic skipped as Rita discussed the upcoming article. "...I am supposed to prepare a statement from our family and give it to them in the next day or two and Lance is doing the same...Lance is having a very hard time with it because it is going to make him look like a monster for hitting her over french fries...He just wants people to realize that after they split up he went through weeks of anger management and also checked himself into rehab...The comments about the supposed sexual abuse are quite hard to bear and I feel for Mike everytime someone makes a comment about his unborn child. I know people are just venting and do not mean any harm but man is it hard to read some of it. I do find some of it entertaining as well. I am not sure if you realize but 'hangemhigh' on the blog is [Wilma's mother-in-law]. I believe [Mike's attorney] has already spoken to her. I did not want you to think it was a new avenue to explore. I will warn you that she thinks truejustice is Mike and is trying to lure him out a little. Please continue to post on there, I think you are doing a great job with fueling the Raye Dawn talk. I have had more than one person e-mail me about it being him and wanting to know if I have been contacted by him...The person who started the blog is also trying to find out the identity. I told her I knew for sure it was not Mike and for her to leave it alone...No one has thought anything of 'ntersted inthetruth' I just knew for some reason it was you and thought I would take a chance... My mom said that she wished she could just let you guys know one thing...Sometimes there are things written on the website or blog by us that may seen anti-Mike and she does not want you to assume that automatically means any of us think Mike is guilty of Murder, it is sometimes necessary to say such things to try to get a reaction out of people to get them to talk, more specifically, to draw out Raye Dawn and her family....I have also talked to OSBI and have heard some things from them that are hard to take. I do want to warn you about a thing are two where that is concerned but not on here. I would also love to be able to give you some insight from the DA, but again, not on here..."

It was still January 1st and the conversation continued with Mike Porter defending Lance. "but he knows it is a lie – he knows he didn't hit her over french fries...If she truly didn't hurt Kelsey then she would be working with you – But her driving force is her hate for your family…I would love to know what your insight from the OSBI is. I do know that they very much WANT it to be Michael that did this, that was obvious from day one – of course they do not want to admit that they could be wrong…Insight from the DA would be great too – but I would be wary of anything the OSBI tells you, they've been very dishonest so far. The fact is, if there was CONCLUSIVE evidence that Michael did this, then they NEVER would have set a bond for him, much less reduced it. They are attempting to build a circumstantial case against Michael, and the DA has admitted as much. But my question is why? Why pick him? Because he was there? Why was he there? Why was he left there with Kelsey? Could he really have done everything they say in 15 minutes or less?"

Mike Porter was attempting to build doubt in Rita's mind about his presumed guilt. The next day she answered him. "I am not hesitant to tell you about the DA and OSBI necessarily because I am worried about the security of this website…I am needing to have my feelings confirmed before I can be too forthcoming with evidence to help him…I would not be able to live with myself if I thought I was helping Kelsey's murderer get out of being punished. I think you know how I feel where Mike is concerned but I still need to be a little more sure…I think it was great that you have started posting as anonymous on the bash board…Do not be too trusting. I would hate for someone to contact you who was up to no good…Again, I do hope you understand about my not giving you all of my insight just yet."

Mike Porter was trying to hold it together, but his desperation was coming to the surface in this message to Rita: "I certainly understand your position..I did not mean to imply that I wanted you to help Michael…I know he is no saint…but the things that they will say and are already saying about him are not true…the truth is the DA or the OSBI does not have conclusive evidence…not to say they won't do their best to build a strong circumstantial case against him…but if there was clear and convincing evidence at this point we both know he would not be out on bond… I wish more than anything that I could grant you some comfort by knowing or convincing you that Michael is innocent…but the fact remains if EVERYONE who has facts and truth comes forward then our brother will not be convicted of this crime…I try to imagine Michael if [the mothers of his children] killed one of his children...The only picture he can look at of Kelsey's is on your family's website...I don't know what he would do if that wasn't there...I honestly feel the public backlash is going to be huge against the Smiths...especially from what I have seen on the blogs...the DA will not be arresting her...so sad...It makes me angry so I know it has to anger your family..the thought that Raye Dawn could weasel out of this like she has everything else in her life....I know Michael is innocent and the thought that NO one will be held accountable for this makes me shudder...just because the DA and OSBI were swayed by God knows what? Do you want to meet?"

The e-mails that were turned over to the district attorney did not include any correspondence from January 2nd to January 10th. The conversation throughout all of the e-mails seems to be spotty. Either some of the e-mails were withheld by Kathie's family or the district attorney, or the communications were solely by telephone and in person during the obvious lapses in time. The logical answer is that some were withheld. A few of the e-mails are in answer of a subject to which there is no original message with the same subject heading, just an answer.

One of the stories that Mike Porter told Rita was of a listening device. He claimed that Gayla put something from the black market somewhere in Kathie's home so she could eavesdrop. Gayla and her family assume that this story developed from something Mike Porter had told them. Kathie seems to be paranoid and he played on that fact. On January

10th, Rita questioned him about the location of the alleged "device": "...Would you happen to know if it was possible for them to still use that listening device if it was still in the room? Or record phone conversations?"

Mike Porter answered, "I do not know if they could use it...but I know if it was still there you could find it. It wasn't a fancy one..I'm pretty certain the range was limited..."

Mike Porter and Rita discussed an upcoming rally for "justice for Kelsey" that he wanted to attend. He claimed his sister and daughter were on their way to the rally when his daughter got scared because of what people thought of her father. Rita responded, "...I have a question or two. Has your attorney requested the phone records for your home and Gayla's phone to see if she was making calls instead of sleeping? Do you know if it is true that Gayla was planning to take Kelsey to the movies that evening? And, you mentioned a 911 tape. We were told that one did not exist. They said Lincoln County does not record 911 calls. Do you know if that is true? My sister and I have come up with a plan to try and get something going with the DA. Not sure how successful we will be but I will let you know if anythig comes of it. The problem is Lance. He is the one who has to request certain things and he is still VERY angry. ..We are doing what we can. Keep your fingers crossed. I have let [Wilma] in on our conversations. She is just as trustworthy as I am I assure you. She is a very take charge and get some action done kind of person that I knew would be beneficial..."

Mike Porter focused on the possibility of a 911 tape. "I was so caught up in one part of your e-mail I missed another part. You were told that Lincoln County does not record the 911 calls??? Is this possible? How do they make sure they are doing the job correctly? I can't believe that if it is true..I will try to find out tomorrow if it is true...I know the 911 tape would open some eyes....."

Wilma joined the private conversation with a message to Mike Porter. "I posted this last night for everyone who is wanting Raye Dawn arrested right now-I posted it especially for Mike. 'We do not want to have Raye Dawn arrested before the time is right. I know that everyone wants her arrested RIGHT NOW!! Trust me, I do too. However, I do not want her arrested before the case against her is rock solid for the appropriate crime. I do not want the OSBI with sufficient evidence to support it. We just have to be patient and have faith that everything will work out in the end. We have to pray that God's will and his justice is served in this case. I have said on here before and I truly mean it—God may have arrested Mike first in order to open his eyes and get his heart and head in the right place for him to be used by God. I believe that God is using Mike to be Kelsey's voice and tell her truth. It is a huge burden to place on him, but Mike put himself in the position for it. Now God is giving Mike the chance to do the right thing and be used by God to be Kelsey's voice. As hard as it is, we must all be patient and let Him bring justice for Kelsey.'"

Mike Porter replied (still pretending to be his sister), "Michael did read and 'hear' it – there was a post that followed that said 'Spoken like a true believer. The love for Kelsey and the strength of the person is evident from this post..We will continue to have faith and be strong – thanks to posts like these.' I think that this post would echo Michael's exact feelings. Thank you for your advice. Michael cried like a baby after reading that....it could not have been said better."

On January 11$^{th}$, Mike Porter questioned Rita about the "bash board's" disappearance. Rita responded, "I had it shut down...I think it started out as a good thing, but I feel it has gotten out of hand. And honestly, I am worried about you. I am so afraid you are going to hurt yourself and your case. I do not want to see that happen. I hope you understand..."

The following day Rita vented to Mike Porter about her family's supporters. "...It is funny how people can hide behind a fake name and say all of the things they say but if they were to see you or Raye Dawn on the street, they would not dare. They would never have the nerve to say what they say on those blogs in person. I am sorry. I am just having a very poor attitude toward the whole situation right now...Especially the ones who are power hungry and the ones who suddenly want to be able to say they know any of us. The people are sick and they need to get a life."

Mike Porter turned the conversation back to his defense. "I understand what you mean....I hope the DA has what he needs to charge Raye Dawn now..he has all the reports he was waiting for."

Rita responded, "If [Wilma] was to talk with [the district attorney] is there anything that you would want him to know or anything you would want her to say that you feel he needs to know, but you cannot tell him yourself? He gave her his personal e-mail address...I hope you did not think I was telling you what to do or anything with that bashboard. I was just afraid [Enough] was getting a little too powerful with it and the knowledge she was gaining. I feel that if you and mom will stay off of there it will die out and she will lose out on that power trip of hers. Unfortunately, I cannot tell her what I think of her these days because she does have too much information and I do not want to make her too mad, but I would just love it if someone would call her out and post her name on there. I bet she would not find that too funny...How are you? I thought the medical report [Kelsey's autopsy] may be hard to handle for you. It was for me. have you read it?"

Mike Porter feigned sympathy, "...If anyone wants to really know what happened in those nine months – Michael knows...The site will die out, I agree. The medical report was unbearable. I could not sleep at all last night – I prayed all night that God would allow the DA to hold Raye Dawn accountable with the findings of the report. I can not imagine what she had to endure. I do not understand how any one could do that to Kelsey – and the thought of Kelsey looking at Raye Dawn and wondering why kills me. He needs to know that there is alot more to this story than whatever he has been told by Raye Dawn..."

Rita continued to protect Mike Porter. "Just so you know, you can change your identity all you want on the site but the host of the site knows who you are every time you get on there by your IP address. She lives in Meeker and she as a VERY big mouth. She knows it is you and she is telling people. Her name is [Enough]...You should really think before you get on there again."

Enough's mother-in-law was one of the main witnesses against Raye. She came up with a story that Raye admitted to abusing Kelsey after Kathie spoke with her. Her sister was in the same prison as Raye when Raye first arrived. She sought Raye out and apologized for the fact that her sister had lied in order to help convict Raye.

It was still January 12th when Rita contacted Mike Porter with what she termed "discouraging news." "... I must now add a bit of news that you may find somewhat discouraging...I have news from the DA. There will not be an arrest until the week of your hearing so quit hoping it may be next week. He apparently has another trial on Tuesday he needs to focus on. He does not seem to understand the importance o[f] this case, so I guess it is time to remind him. I am having everyone I know send him a post-card letting him know that this case WILL make or break his career. I will be urging him to get with the program and start making this case a priority. You might suggest doing the same to your supporters. Mom will be on the news at ten on channel 4 and 9 tonight. Please do not lose your faith. I have this hope for seeing Raye Dawn in her stripes being paraded into court they way you were except I hope there are cameras in her face when they do it. I know that hope will come to light. I know it will."

Mike Porter quickly replied, "...THAT SELFISH BITCH!!! the news about the DA is discouraging. I guess the most discouraging thing is it is hard to believe anything that the DA says anymore. For the last month it has been next week, next week, next week. Now he has everything he said he was waiting on, the OSBI report, the ME report, and he still stalls. If anything the ME report only makes it more obvious to me that Raye Dawn is guilty. How could I have done all that in 12-15 minutes??" [It was actually 30 to 45 minutes]

Mike Porter then contacted Enough, the person who controlled the "bash board" with the following message: "I hope that any information that you recieve from the website will be confidential and not be used in ANY way to jeopardize justice for Kelsey. This CAN NOT happen. I know the IP addresses of those who post are probably available to you. But my point is, I feel your heart is in the right place regarding Kelsey. I think I knew who you are, but the fact is it doesn't matter. I know that you may know people that are for Raye Dawn, but we all should want justice for Kelsey no matter who it involves. I hope you don't take this e-mail the wrong way, I just wanted to make sure your intentions were completely honest and you would never exploit any of the things that were said or any of the information obtained from the board to help someone who does not deserve helping. To many people this is our life and not something that is happening to someone else. I am in no way questions your motives, I just want to make my feelings clear. God Bless."

On January 13th Rita was eager to share evidence with Mike Porter. "what do you know about a hand print bruise?"

Mike Porter quickly responded with a question, "when would this bruise have been on Kelsey?"

"I am not sure. I really kind of need to talk to you because I am not sure I can tell you what I know in this e-mail. It is just a little too bazarre. I just wondered if a hand print bruise meant anything to you at all."

"the only thing that I know about a hand print bruise is very very old. Before me. If it is something recent then I have no clue what you mean. If you want you can call me at 602-xxxx."

On the same day, Rita contacted Mike Porter but this time the news was good. "I do not mean to tease you with this next piece of information, but we have been told by OSBI that the possible reason for the stall from the DA is that he is not just looking at making ONE arrest. He is looking at making multiple arrests. Now, you know how things are said and they may or may not come to light, but that would be a nice explanation as to why they are not moving quickly. I personally would love to see more than one person arrested. Be patient. I know that is hard to do..."

Mike Porter responded with his usual flattery. "We can only hope that people will be held accountable for their failures. We already know I will be and I will face that...You and your family continue to amaze me."

### *PUBLIC HATE*

On January 16, 2006 a letter was distributed to residents in the neighborhood where Gayla and Raye had taken refuge with Gayla's friend. The misinformed author repeated inform-ation that had been distributed throughout the media that has since been proven inaccurate and misrepresented. At the top of the letter were two pictures of Kelsey. In one picture, she had a bump on her nose. The other was of her with a big, white bow on her head with her face lying in her arms. On the second page was a picture of Kelsey in her swing after the hit-and-run accident caused by a drunk driver in August of 2005. All three pictures had been taken by her paternal family.

"Dear resident: I am a concerned citizen that would like to make you aware of a couple of people that you currently have residing in your neighborhood. They are residing with [Gayla's friend's name was listed as well as his home address]. Some of you may have heard recently in the news the story of little Kelsey

Briggs that was murdered in her own home." A list of "injuries" from the first autopsy was given. She continued, "Her step-father Mike Porter was arrested in October and charged with her murder, but was later bailed out in December. Her mother has yet to be arrested on any charges. The mother, Raye Dawn, is widely SUSPECTED to be the actual person that abused and killed Kelsey and not Mike Porter. It is expected that Raye's arrest will come in the near future, most probably in the next 3 weeks, for the murder of little Kelsey. You will have to read the entire story of the day of her death to make a judgment for yourself, however, it is also widely believed that it would have taken Kelsey more time to die than in the short amount of time that Mike Porter had her in his care that day, before he called 911. This would only leave one other person responsible for her death, Raye Dawn. It was also speculated that Kelsey had been sexually abused before her death; however, the Medical Examiner was unable to determine if this was actually the case, due to the extreme damage done to that area of her body. Raye Dawn and her mother, Gayla are still out living as free citizens, living their lives day to day as they want, and they are living IN YOUR NEIGHBORHOOD. Raye Dawn is pregnant again, due to give birth sometime in the next couple of months. The reason I am writing this to you, is to make sure you are informed that you have a SUSPECTED murderer and possible SUSPECTED child molester living in your neighborhood, especially if you have children. Both Raye Dawn and Gayla formerly lived and worked in Meeker, however, after the death of Kelsey they fled Meeker and are now living with [Gayla's friend]. It is SUSPECTED that Gayla helped her daughter cover-up the abuse, and manipulated and lied to people in order to get them to go to court for Raye Dawn and lie that she was a good mother and should get Kelsey back. It is also SUSPECTED that Gayla is now helping Raye Dawn cover up the murder of her daughter. [A link was given to Kelsey's Purpose] www.Kelseyspurpose.org is a website set-up by the paternal family...and is dedicated to finding justice in the death of little Kelsey, and also working to make reform of current child welfare laws so this does not happen to anyone else. They have been asking everyone to display the Justice for Kelsey signs in their yards and businesses, and they have stickers available to put on your car, or where ever else you wish. I am asking you to have it in your heart to display a sign in your yard for little Kelsey, and a sticker on your car. The stickers are small hearts with her picture on them saying 'Justice for Kelsey'. You can request both at the above website, and someone will send or deliver them right out to you. None of us can just turn our backs because we don't want to get involved or because we simply don't want to hear about this horrific case. Little Kelsey did not ask to be put through this, and I am sure she would have like to have turned her back as well. We all have to fight to find justice for this little girl, and all the other abused children in Oklahoma and around the nation. If you have any questions about the case, you can also go to the above website and the family will be glad to answer them for you. I AM NOT RELATED TO THE BRIGGS, SMITHS, OR ANY OF THE OTHER FAMILY OR FRIENDS INVOLVED IN THIS CASE. THEY DID NOT PUT ME UP TO THIS, NOR DO ANY OF THEM HAVE ANY KNOWLEDGE OF THIS LETTER. I HAVE TAKEN IT UPON MYSELF AS A CONCERNED CITIZEN TO INFORM YOU. As I have said, everyone spoken of in this letter is purely 'suspected', and everyone is innocent until proven guilty, however if you look at the case I think you will see everything I have stated is the truth. You can go to the above website to read up on the case, or any of the local news channels have plenty of articles on Kelsey's death. Sincerely, An anonymous concerned citizen of Oklahoma"

At approximately the same time this letter was distributed, Ms. Ballard did a newscast from the entrance of Gayla's neighborhood with a "Justice for Kelsey" sign as her focus. Ms. Ballard stated that the signs had been "spotted all over Oklahoma City" and surrounding areas. According to witnesses who collected the signs, the only area they were found was in that neighborhood. According to OKC.gov,

Oklahoma City covers an area of 622 square miles (an area larger than New York City, Houston, or Atlanta)[39]. How did Ms. Ballard just happen upon signs that were only present in one neighborhood, and do a report on it, if Kathie and her group knew nothing about the letter, as the author claimed? Also, how did Raye and her family stand a chance against a growing mob that had members of the media willing to cover "stories" that promoted their campaign against Raye?

On January 25, 2006, Gayla's friend wrote a letter to Raye's attorney. The tone of the letter clearly illustrates the frustration felt by Raye's family due to the negative, untrue media reports and the backlash of hate from Kathie's supporters as well as the fear of charges or arrest of Raye if the family dare speak up and put an end to the lies. Kathie was quickly gaining power in the state and everyone was afraid of her…and still are to this day.

"Dear [Raye's attorney]: As you know, Raye Dawn and Gayla live with me. You are aware of the letters and phone calls that have been directed at me over the past several weeks and now the letter sent to all home owners in my subdivision has taken me to my 'fight back' point.

I have watched both Raye Dawn and Gayla struggle with the loss of Kelsey and have felt bad for them every time Kathie has been on TV ranting and raving about how they need to 'arrest just one more person'. I have offered comfort to them and even though I have been approached by the news media, I have kept quiet. Now under attack by the cult from Meeker, it is time I defend myself.

I composed a letter that I have attached for you to review. Gayla says it will get Raye Dawn arrested. I don't think so. I think

[39] http://www.okc.gov/info_tech/gis/index.html

it will, if anything, get Kathie to put up or shut up. I have agreed with Gayla that if you think it will get Raye Dawn arrested, I will not print it. I am going to offer it to the Shawnee news paper and the *Oklahoman*. If they will not print it on their own, I will purchase space to have it printed. I will do this only if you think it will not get Raye Dawn arrested. I am not speaking for anyone in this letter other than me so I see no harm. I also am going to hand deliver the letter to [the district attorney] and to the OSBI and will mail copies to [the Judge] and last but certainly not least to Kathie.

They are attacking me and I WILL NOT allow it. I have done nothing wrong.

Your opinion is appreciated and I will be glad to talk to you about the letter. Feel free to call me anytime at my office or on my cell or at my home.

[Attached open letter] This is an open letter to Kathie and all of the misled people she has persuaded into thinking that Raye Dawn killed her child.

Because of a court order, Raye Dawn has kept quiet about the horrible tragedy of losing her child. Fact is Raye Dawn and the entire family is devastated. The family was cautioned about saying anything as not to jeopardize the justice system in its efforts to properly work the case. As a favor to them, I too have not said anything that may cause prejudice. That is until now.

Over the past several months I have been the target of harassment. Letters have been sent to my office. Phone calls on my answering machine accusing me of harboring 'sluts', 'baby killers' and 'child beaters'. Now someone has started sending anonymous letters to every home owner in my neighborhood with the same accusations. Kathie, I have done nothing to you. I hardly look at you when in public court. I have never commented publicly about you. That is until now.

I have a challenge for you. You pick the place and time for a public debate about Kelsey and Raye Dawn. I'll bring the cookies and Kool Aid. First though, I will arrange for a licensed person to give both of us a lie detector test asking us 15 questions of the other parties choosing. This test will be made public at the debate.

Ready yourself for questions such as 'who was Kelsey in the custody of when her legs were broken?' You say it was Raye Dawn but why was it that she wanted to crawl when Raye Dawn picked her up for Raye Dawn's scheduled visit? Who took her to the hospital to have the casts put on? We both know it was Raye Dawn. And who took Kelsey to the doctor to have them removed just one week after they were put on? The day you picked her up you took her to 'your' doctor to have them removed. Why? When Raye Dawn got Kelsey back, Raye Dawn took her back to the doctor to have them put back on. And 'why did Judge Key take Kelsey away from you in late April and give her to Gayla?' The public is going to love that answer.

[Actually it was child protective services that removed Kelsey, but the answer would be the same.]

You scream you want the DHS reports released to the public? No you don't. You say that only because you know they would not because the courts would not let them be released. You know, the reports that states what the DHS worker wrote while viewing the visitations. The ones that said that Kelsey could not wait to see her mother and they sat and played the entire hour while during your visits, Kelsey hid under a table. One time she had a blanket over her head. One time she slept during your entire visit. And one time she even bit you. I loved the blurb you put in Kelsey's obit saying she loved to bite. Here is a clue for you; she NEVER bit anyone from her mother's side of the family. You have painted a picture that depicts everyone on Kelsey's mother's side of the family as a group of people that sat around and beat on Kelsey. You ready for another shocker? Raye Dawn smacked Kelsey only once on her diapered bottom. Raye Dawn NEVER raised a hurtful hand to Kelsey. All of her bruises were accidents that are explainable and I plan on explaining them to you and to your followers.

Unless you want to open the files to your followers first and explain them that way. Remember, you were care taker from January thru April and all of Raye's visitations were supervised visitations. That means that at least one other person, not counting Mike Porter, had to be present at all times. Mostly there were two and three people around. Something that you forgot to tell the media when you had a microphone in front of you. And prepare to talk about your web site. The accusations that your group has made. I can set some of those rumors straight now. The truck did not get repossessed. It was sold. Raye Dawn has not been to any bar or casino in Meeker or the surrounding area and the baby she is carrying is Mike Porter's and not Judge Key's. I did not pay off Judge Key so Raye Dawn could get Kelsey. She is not having a 'fling' with someone with the OSBI, and that is not why she has not been arrested. Gayla did not get fired from her job. She quit to marry me. And to pick on Gayla's mother, Mildred, is really a long shot. That lady has more class and dignity, as does Gayla, in their little toes than you have in your entire being. Neither one of them had two children from two different men so close together that they went through school at the same grade at the same time. And neither of them is on or ever has been on welfare. Nor have they made one cent from Kelsey's death to spend on themselves. Can you make that statement? Hint: that will be a question on your test. Be sure to review your copy of the custody trial from last September. If you have lost your copy, I will get one for you. Everyone will absolutely LOVE this one as well. It really shows you for your true colors since you did not even show up at the hearing knowing what was going to be said. You can also answer the question as to why you want Raye Dawn charged. Since you were not there and have not a clue as to what happened that fateful day. Could it be because that if she is charged, you will be able to keep all of the money you have sued the DHS for, assuming you win, and if she is not charged, you will have to split it with her? Just for the record, I believe that DHS did its job properly and Kelsey's death was a random act of violence. But then, this is something that we can discuss later.

Now you can invite anyone you want to this meeting. Naturally we will want [the district attorney] there. At least he will be able to meet all who have been sending him all of the anonymous letters. I will also invite the OSBI. They have not interviewed Gayla, Mildred, Raye's brother and most of the family so they can hear what is said. You ever wonder why they have not charged Raye Dawn? Could it be that after interviewing Raye Dawn, and other key witnesses and viewing documents that they don't feel that she had anything to do with Kelsey's death? I will also invite Judge Key. He may not come and I would not be surprised if he did not but at least I will let him know that he is welcome. He may want to send someone else in his place to ask you questions and that will be fine with me. Naturally we will want [Representative S.] there to witness who he is representing in the 'Kelsey Bill' he will be sending to the House and Senate. Funny how there is not a drop of Briggs blood in Kelsey but the bill will be named after the Briggs. Let's also invite the Meeker police. I would love to hear what they say about your following Raye Dawn and filing numerous false reports on her. You said under oath in court that you did not do that. Another question for the lie detector. And bring your son. Let's ask him about his beating Raye Dawn and destroying her apartment after their divorce and before he joined the military. You can invite the news channel that seems to burn up the highway just to hear you throw fuel on a fire. You know, the TV station that was sued and lost a slander case some time back and paid over $800,000 to a restaurateur who promptly left Oklahoma. I'm not too fond of you inviting the reporter that works for that station either, but you can. You know the one that was arrested in California some time back but they managed to keep it under wraps here [Ms. Ballard]. I would really like to hear her definition of 'investigative reporting' since she has not talked to anyone from the mother's side of the fence. She did manage to drive out to interview a couple of your 'workers' at the entrance of my subdivision just to let people know where Raye Dawn lives. She did not have to do that. She could have called me and I would have given her permission to tell where I live. Be sure to invite the news paper people. They need to be there to get their story straight as well.

Anyway, you have the challenge. Any place. Any time. Lie detector first. Your 15 minutes is up. Time to put up or shut up. And I will do something that 99% of the letters to the OSBI and [district attorney] and 100% of the letters sent to me don't have. That being a signature. JUSTICE FOR Kelsey! With this meeting, Kelsey's family will have it, and if the court system does its job, she will have hers as well."

On the same day the above letter was sent to Raye's attorney, Kathie answered a Web site member: "Jerry or whoever you really are, I agree there were many negative comments toward Raye Dawn and I too was surprised at how many people felt the way they did. People are more than welcome to speak up on her behalf if they have facts to prove she is an innocent victim in all of this…My son has not posted anything and he has not spoken out in public. Neither has the mother…He is also adjusting to civilian life after serving his country for thirteen months…It is our belief the facts will speak for themselves once all of the arrests are made and trials begin. In the mean time you are welcome to introduce yourself to us at any of the rallies being held against child abuse. You are also welcome to show your support for Justice for Kelsey by sending me your address and I will in return send you a sticker for your automobile."

## PICTURES OF THE VICTIM SENT TO THE MAN CHARGED WITH HER MURDER

Mike Porter soon learned another way to get in with Kathie and her family…money. He offered to purchase a billboard for their cause. Rita sent at least 43 pictures of Kelsey to the man charged with her murder. Within months of receiving the pictures, Kelsey's body was exhumed for a second autopsy and a sexual assault charge was officially added to Mike Porter's Murder in the First Degree charge.

On January 17th Mike Porter told Rita, "I would like your family to pick the picture of Kelsey that will be on the billboard on I-40...She is so beautiful in all of her pictures but I want to use one that is special to your family..."

Wilma, Lance's older sister, e-mailed Mike Porter on the same day in an attempt to control him. "I am going to tell you the same thing that I just told my mother. Neither one of you have anyone to blame but yourselves when Raye Dawn's attorney can anticipate EVERYTHING that either of you (especially you) have to say on the witness stand. Both of you are handing their defense to them on a silver platter. I can get on the bashboard any day of the week and know who is who. Do you think that Raye Dawn, Gayla, or [Raye's attorney] cannot determine that either? I will be damned if I am going to sit by quietly and watch Raye Dawn walk away scott-free because two people have to communicate about this case via the Internet. Trust me-I would like all of the answers too, but I do not want them in a format where everyone, including my relentless, obsessed, mother-in-law and all of the rest of the free world can figure out who is who. Communication can be accomplished privately. It may be too late to salvage the damage that has been done. I understand the need to get one's story told, but telling it to Raye's defense attorney and obsessed freaks is not [the] place to go about it. We all know how strong their powers of lying and manipulation already are. Let's not give them any more power than they already have."

Mike Porter responded in agony. His emotions were obviously running high. "ARGG!!! I can't take it anymore. The DA is not going to charge Raye Dawn!!! God it is too much. I can't take not being able to speak these things. The fact is he should have all the evidence he needs to charge her. Nothing I can say will convict her. The truth will be told no matter what. But it seems like the burden is too much to bear sometimes. These things weigh on me everyday like a ten ton truck. I pray and pray, I guess I should have saved your post about about being Kelsey's voice. Damn!! you are right. I need you and [Rita] as big sisters also. I am sorry. I have faltered. It is so hard to bite my tongue, it makes me so mad at the justice system that the truth has to be rationed out or justice will not be served."

Wilma e-mailed a warning to Rita: "You, or, we, have got to get some people under control."

Rita responded by sending Mike Porter some false hope. "the psychic says it will happen tomorrow at 10. If it does that is going to freak me out but make me very excited at the same time. She will supposedly turn herself in. I guess we will see if she is right."

Mike Porter replied with information about Kathie. "that would be too good to be true. By the way, I was with my attorney today. Something I wanted you to know – I was told that Raye Dawn called [the CASA worker] and requested that she give her the info from your mothers old custody thing. I know that whatever Raye Dawn does or tries to do to your family one makes her look worse, I just wanted you to know...Why she would still think anything that your mother did however long ago even MATTERS I have no clue. It seems to me and everyone else that she is preparing her defense, almost trying to justify why she did what she did. I will say an extra prayer tonight that the psychic is right, but it will be scarier to me if she is right, I think, but scary in a good way. the things you told me the other night stuck with me, she knew things that NO one could know. She knew that I did not kill Kelsey and the only two people living that know that for a fact are Raye Dawn and myself. She knew about the handprint and today when I got to my lawyer's the FIRST thing they asked me for out of the blue was a HANDPRINT. There is pretty convincing evidence in my opinion that Raye Dawn's hands made the bruising on Kelsey."

Mike Porter was clearly falling apart emotionally. As the evidence against him continued to build, his time became limited. He had Kelsey's paternal family on his side, but how long would it last?

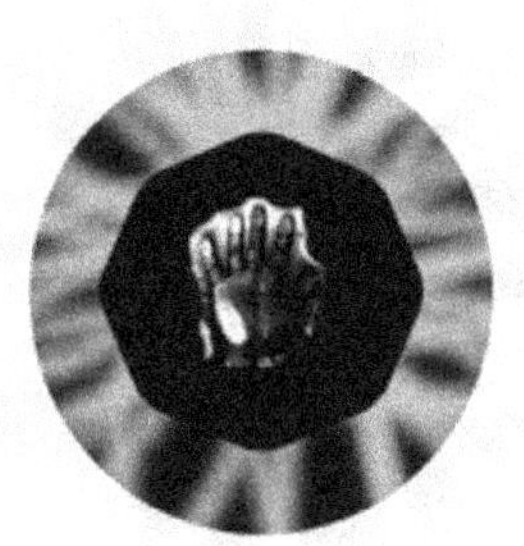

# 31 Civil Lawsuits

"I can't do literary work for the rest of this year because I'm meditating another lawsuit and looking around for a defendant" ~ Mark Twain

From the first mention of Kathie's desire to communicate with Mike Porter, her interests were clear. She wanted to know who she could sue and if she could take down Raye's entire family. On her forum she hinted at her intentions when answering a question about a possible lawsuit against Mike Porter. She stated, "RE: suing - That is a good question. Kelsey was injured and murdered in their home. I have been told the home was only in Raye Dawn's name so I would doubt Lance could sue Mike. They only lived there for a little more than a week. The house could have still been insured by Gayla."

On Friday, January 20, 2006 Rita wrote to Mike Porter: "My mom has a specific question she would like answered...She wants to know if you and/or Raye Dawn ever had Kelsey during the time that Gayla had her in her care...Mom is also interested in starting some private correspondence other than what you two are doing on the awful bashboard. If you are interested in doing the same to keep it out of public viewing you can e-mail her at...Do not sit by the tv today expecting an arrest. Mom's talk with Smothermon did not go well yesterday."

An hour later, Mike Porter responded to Rita: "I e-mailed your mother. She has not responded...Can you tell me about the talk with the DA?"

Rita answered, "Mom said she will not be on her computer until atleast 4:00 today. She said the DA is having a press conference at 2:00 so she is supposed to go to that. I guess he is going to pretty much say if you have info step forward, enough with the anonymous tips. Either put up or shut up pretty much. I don't think he is going to release any groundbreaking news or anything."

At ten minutes past four Mike Porter answered. He was still pretending to be his sister in some of the e-mails. He kept referring to himself in the third person. Perhaps this would be his defense if he slipped up and said something incriminating. He could claim, "I didn't say it." "Well the DA is sadly mistaken...he has only heard one side of the story, which is Raye Dawn's side...we both know that if the DA is fooled and does not file the correct charges against her, the truth will not make sure Raye Dawn is held accountable. Nothing that Raye Dawn can say will convict Michael. The DA was not convinced fromt he evidence that Michael did it...We can't do the DA"s job for him. If he ever wants the truth, then he will talk to Michael. He is trying to build a case to back up what he has already done, and that is wrong. He has already charged Michael, and rather than start form scratch, talk to Michael and Raye Dawn, and do a thorough investigation with both of them as primary suspects, he is gong to use Raye Dawn to build his case against Michael, which will seriously hurt the credibility of the whole case. He can't know the truth unless he talks ot Michael – Raye Dawn will never say anything that incriminates herself. It would be truly sad if no one was held accountable because the DA did not do his job and pursued a one sided case, which it looks like he is on course to do."

Thirty-three minutes later, Mike Porter e-mailed Kathie; "We had been wanting to contact you for some time now. There are so many things that need to be said, but I will just tell you that I will answer any questions that I can for you. We know that you all want and deserve the truth. I know the correspondence must be hard and many people would not understand but here goes..."

Kathie answered his e-mail later that same evening. "...First of all this is a little strange. Why we either one have a desire to communicate may seem strange, but when you grasp at straws for answers your willing to put yourself out there...I would like to sit and ask point blank questions and get very honest point blank answers, but I also don't want to take advantage of your situation. Basically there is nothing I can do to change the criminal investigation. Facts are facts and that is what it is based on. I am sure you know I am not convinced the proper person has been charged with the right charge...I am actually looking for answers for the civil case at this point...If there was enough information to put some others in jail for failing Kelsey then I would be willing to talk to the DA about deals. I am sure you know who all I am interested in, but mostly Gayla or any family member, Meeker Police, DHS, CASA, CHBS, Judge Key, [another judge], [Raye's attorney for the custody battle] and [Kelsey's doctor]...Don't answer anything you are not comfortable with, I am not trying to put you in a bad position. Even with the situation the way it is, I don't think it right to take advantage of you. You are young, you got caught up with a family that snowed you big time. I understand how that can happen. I honestly don't have much information on how the investigation is going. One minute I feel they are going after Raye Dawn for the right charge and sometimes I wonder what they are thinking...Once again let me say, you are young, you don't have the guidance of your parents, and I am trying not to take advantage of that. Part of me has compassion for you...I am not here to make you feel worse... I don't want my feelings for Raye Dawn and her family to over shadow my willingness to accept the fact that maybe they did nothing wrong. I had no idea they hated me and our family the way they do...At any point you are uncomfortable communicating with me, please let me know and I will understand your decision."

Within minutes of receiving the e-mail from Kathie, Mike Porter eagerly replied. "Well here goes. This is the hard part. The criminal investigation is being bungled severely. Every lawyer in the county knows this. The DA is destroying his case day by day...Raye Dawn was NEVER pursued as a primary suspect in this investigation – even these last two months have been them basically going through the motions...The fact is Richard Smothermon could just as easily charge Raye Dawn with the murder as me...Basically, his press conference sounded to me like he is already preparing people for the possibility that he may choose not to even file against her. He was passing the buck saying 'if you all don't give me info then I can't arrest her'. He has just as much evidence against her as me, and then he would have her actions since Kelsey's death, which speak volumes. I know you have been fooled in the past, we all were. I know you want people hels accountable, but it HAS to start with Raye Dawn. Anything esle is not justice. As far as the answers, I have them all. I would rather talk to you or someone in person...I never hurt Kelsey. Never did, never could, never would – in a million years...Basically by me being in jail for two months that made people who knew better think twice about my innocence...I am going to nail everyone to the wall that I can in the criminal case to see what they have to say...the thing you need to know is that I will give you the answers and I want people held accountable..."

A meeting must have been planned in an e-mail that was not turned over to Raye's attorney. The following day, Mike Porter told Kathie, "Would you still be interested in meeting tomorrow? I am not opposed to [Rita] coming. I feel the strongest need to talk to you. Let me know and I will plan accordingly. So many questions need to be answered."

The e-mails continued for several days as the tone between the grandmother of a murdered child and the man charged with her murder grew to be friendly, playful, and compassionate. It's not clear which one of them was the manipulator and who was being manipulated, but it appears they both thought they had the upper hand. Kathie's words reflected the tone of the many letters received by OSBI and the DA within days of Kelsey's death. They pressed to have Raye charged with murder, and it seemed that Kathie would not give up on her mission.

Kathie responded, "Tomorrow is fine...You should spend as much time with [your daughter] as possible since she has been through so much. I am supposed to take Richard a time line on Monday sometime, but I can work around that...I don't know what your transportation is like so let me know. I am pretty flexible. I will be up for another 30 minutes or so. I took a tylenol pm and it should be kicking in soon."

Mike Porter stated, "...Monday I will be at my office. I will wait to hear from you...As you know my life is pretty devoid of activity. I know you have much more to do so you tell me the day and I will work a time out...I can hand you your civil case on a silver platter...I want what you want. I will do everything in my power to make sure everyone who is responsible is held accountable – financially or criminally – no matter who that may be."

Wilma, Lance's older sister, sent Mike Porter, a suspect in a murder case, an e-mail from a governmental e-mail address. "I truly believe that [the district attorney] wants the truth and true justice for Kelsey. I believe that he is open to ANYONE who has evidence in this case. He has stated to me that he would rather see a guilty person walk free than a wrong person convicted. At this point, I have to believe that he really means that...Kelsey's voice needs to be heard and her true story needs to be told."

Mike Porter replied, "conversation with attorney was not hopeful. Bottom line is this – [the district attorney] knows who the single biggest source of information is. [The district attorney] has made NO attempt to talk to this person. [He] is placing weight on Raye Dawn's testimony when she is the other murder suspect. Better lawyers than him feel he is looking for a way out of arresting her. No good attorney would attempt to prosecute a murder case withour hearing all sides. Feelings were echoed of if [the district attorney] had any information he needed verified there is one source to have that done, whether it is info on Michael or Raye Dawn. Raye Dawn has had her chance to tell the truth, and she obviously has not done that or she would have been arrested. The feeling is that by placing the burden of proof back on "anonymous" tipsters, the buck is being prepared to be passed. The DA has put himself in this position. The truth will be told but I am afraid that our desire to believe that the DA is genuinely concerned with prosecuting the correct party may be in vain. If he was interested he would contact the proper parties and arrange it. It is HIS job to do this. Michael WILL tell the truth, but he will not be allowed to take the first step. If [the district attorney] wants to know the truth about Kelsey he will either file charges or contact the proper people."

On the following day, Kathie sent an e-mail to Mike Porter questioning him about his work schedule and providing him with information that makes her appear to have been stalking Raye and her family, an allegation she had faced in the past. "Do you actually stay at work each day?...You better not let you wife know you are working, she might want all of your earnings. I saw you mother-in-laws car at Mildred's again last Friday. They have come to town several times lately. You should get a giant sticker made for your window at work. That might send them over the edge...The bash board was interesting last night...I am going to [the district attorney's] later this afternoon...I hope he worked on the case over the weekend and is ready to sign the warrant...I read the e-mail Raye Dawn wrote to the DHS and it is almost amusing. There is no train of thought there. The things she brings up are crazy…We really thought we were rid of her until we found out she was pregnant...Let me know what day, time, and place is good."

Mike Porter's reply included his usual phrase of "murder suspect" in relation to Raye. The fact is that the only murder suspect was charged with Kelsey's murder. Possibly he was trying to convince himself as well as Kathie. He said, "it makes me as mad at the DA and the OSBI as anyone. They should not be deterred from speaking to people because the mother of a murder suspect convinces them that the people who will speak about them have a grudge. The biggest mistake [the district attorney] is making besides not talking to me is assuming Raye Dawn's testimony will have credibility with a jury when she is a murder suspect…If that doesn't show how much she hates your family…I had transportation but the Spawn of Satan has taken care of that for me. I do not want to be in a rushed atmosphere, and I know you don't either. Honestly you tell me the day and I will make it happen."

Kathie's response was filled with compassion. "Sounds as if you are having a particularly bad day. They seem to come more often and I understand, please feel free to vent here anytime. I do believe we were both mislead into thinking a lot of things…You are right our lives will never be the same. All we can do now is figure out what went wrong and make her pay. At this point I do believe Raye Dawn and Gayla are very evil and they have manipulated people to long. It has to stop before more innocent people pay the price. I do worry about your new baby and the life they will inflict on him/her. I also worry about the two children you already have. Raye Dawn has ruined so many lives all because she hated our family. The whole thing is she had no reason to hate as she did…[The DA] was busy when I took the papers in so I did not speak with him. Raye Dawn and Gayla were at Mildred's along with about four others cars today…They are up to something. They keep trying to pull stuff and it doesn't work. First they tried to put something in the paper and she would not do it. They got mad. Then they wanted the OSBI to banish the bash board and that did not work. Something is in the air and if they don't put the little hussy in jail soon we are probably going to be the target of their next scheme."

Mike Porter played on Kathie's sympathy: "Today was bad. I get more and more frustrated everyday, as we all do. I am so disillusioned with our justice system...Some days I feel like there are too many people who know the truth for it to be completely hidden, but [t]hen there are days like today when I think it doesn't matter what I or anyone else who loves Kelsey does, because evil always wins...I can meet with you tomorrow, I do not mind...I want your word I will not be recorded..."

Kathie responded with directions (for the man charged with her granddaughter's murder) to her (single) daughter's apartment and then stated, "There will be no recording devices, I know you are use to dealing with the Smiths, but the Briggs do not operate that way. I would like to take a few notes...If that will bother you I won't do that...We really don't have to meet there if that makes you uncomfortable. I know you may need to work and if you would rather wait I don't mind...I hope [your attorney] is having someone go through the reports and the stuff Raye Dawn has written to prove the girl is unstable. We can't be the only ones who see it. *I just read the three page e-mail from Raye Dawn in the DHS files again.* ***Everytime*** *I read it I am amazed.* She skips around, she is crazed. I had the OSBI go to [Raye's old job] and talk to the women there...[a state's witness] called me and talked for a long time about things Raye Dawn stated while working there. [Betsy] played right into their hands last night and then changed her name to Joan. She was so obvious. **I wish I wasn't addicted to that stupid bash board**, I know there has to be better things to do with my time...." [Emphasis by book author]

Mike Porter prepared Kathie for the emotional display he was saving just for her. "How does 1:00 sound? I see no need in waiting…[The DA] told [my attorney] today that he still ahs every intention of arresting her, he just does not want it to be for too little…I could have handed her on a silver platter, but since they let her clean out all the evidence like they always do, all I have left is my word…I will do my best to control my emotions tomorrow but I can't promise anything. I can't turn my feelings on and off like Raye Dawn. Although I did not kill Kelsey and I do not feel I should spend the rest of my life in prison, a part of me feels a great deal of responsibility and regret. I was already faced with the facts that I believed Kelsey died in my arms, but I would have coped with that because I knew I did everything I could THAT day to save her…"

Kathie seemed eager to meet. "Do you live close to something? I can meet you in the City. This should not be this hard. I don't have a problem with picking you up. It is not like I feel unsafe. I am up for a while…Don't chicken out, I don't bite, that was Kelsey's trademark…I don't know why I have compassion for your situation, but I do…You know how they [Raye's family] work so you should have an advantage, then again, knowing how sneaky there are can be scary. Gayla is the one that should be ashamed of herself for taking advantage of someone so young…They have been in Meeker so many times lately and that is odd. I think [the DA] does want to arrest her for murder, and at one time I thought it was a done deal…Let me know something. This should not be so hard, dang!"

Mike Porter's emotions took control in his reply. "…I will accept any responsibility that is mine in this. We all owe that to Kelsey. But I will not accept responsibility so the person who killed Kelsey can walk free. I really hope you have serious doubts about it, because if the DA chooses to prosecute me he will be prosecuting the wrong person for Kelsey's murder. I hope that shakes you to your core like it does me…I can tell you if [the DA] gets this wrong then THE PERSON WHO KILLED KELSEY WILL GO FREE. HOW DOES THAT MAKE YOU FEEL? THAT SHOULD SCARE THE HELL OUT OF YOU. IT SCARES THE HELL OUT

OF ME. SOMEONE KILLED KELSEY AND SO FAR BY AND LARGE THEY HAVE MANAGED TO ESCAPE SUSPICION FOR THE ACTUAL CRIME."

Kathie liked what she was hearing. Mike Porter was speaking her language. "**First of all, I want Raye Dawn in jail and I want her charged with murder...**I hope when I go in there tomorrow he will have read through more reports and he will have her phone records like I requested. I really wanted her in jail by now and the wait is making me nuts. Honestly I want her and Gayla in jail...If you are willing to help me do that I am willing to help you...Do you need me to park around the corner and drive you over there? Let me know..." [Emphasis by book author]

In a later e-mail, Kathie told Mike Porter, "... maybe tomorrow we will be together when we get the call she is in jail. 11:00 will be fine. You can call me at home if something comes up. I don't think my phone is tapped, don't know why it would be...I noticed several cars at the house on the news. Did Gayla and the other family members come up there or did they just ignore you?"

Kathie and Mike Porter exchanged several lengthy e-mails discussing the same issue—their mutual desire to have Raye arrested. Kathie also informed Mike Porter that a company was sponsoring the billboard that he was purchasing for Kathie, but she informed him of a place he could put his billboard in their small town. He replied that money was "no object" and that she could of course count on his financial support.

On January 26, 2006 Kathie thanked Mike Porter for meeting with her. She stated, "You are welcome, I enjoyed our visit. I know it wasn't easy for you...I did not get the feeling I wanted when I left the DA's office. He is going out of town all next week and it will be after that before he gets back to work on this case. My trust issues are flaring up again. Gotta go, I will check with you later."

More e-mails were exchanged in which Mike Porter focused on proving his innocence and Kathie continued to be nosey. On January 29th she stated, "I just had a report that possibly Raye Dawn and Gayla are staying with Mildred. You know how rumors are, but Gayla's car has been there for the past three days…"

By the end of January, their conversations suddenly seemed cold. Mike Porter wasn't providing Kathie with concrete evidence that he was telling the truth, and she had already expressed her impatience in having Raye charged and arrested. Mike Porter and Kathie continued their mission on their beloved "bash board."[40]

---

[40] Read the e-mails at www.RayeDawnSmith.com and www.FreeKelseysMom.com.

# 32 The "Bash Boards"

"When we judge and criticize someone, we are not describing them, but instead, our own true character."
~ Jody Ortiz

Originally, Kathie and her group started two separate "bash boards." There was one that focused on Mike Porter and one with Raye as the main topic of discussion. Since Mike Porter and his supporters were a part of the group, the Mike Porter board didn't last long, but the Raye board buzzed day and night with hate for Raye and her entire family. While Kelsey's maternal family members were still in mourning, her paternal family members were apparently having fun with Mike Porter and his supporters at Kelsey's maternal family's expense.

There are several posts in which they pretend to be Raye's family members, specifically her mother, in order to make fun of them. Following is just a sampling of the posts that were captured.[41]

Posted by "stinky pete" Friday, February 3, 2006 @ 12:04 AM "I wonder who all will be in the interview tomorrow night. Did they all meet at Mildred's again?"

Posted by "Webster" Friday, February 3, 2006 @ 12:05 AM "Could someone take a dictionary to their interview so they can look up 'seizure'"

Posted by a Gayla impersonator Friday, February 3, 2006 @ 12:08 AM "Hey, that is my house too now that [Gayla's friend] has kicked us out and traded me in for a new model. What is so wonderful about 60 year old women anyway?!?!"

Posted by another imposter, "The Real Gayla" Friday, February 3, 2006 @ 12:14 AM "excuse me but I am only 54!! And I think I have preserved well, considering I cake on 3 inches of make up daily. My nightly dips in formaldehyde help to slow the aging process. If it wasn't for those I would look 95."

Posted by "Raye Dawn is guilty" Friday, February 3, 2006 @ 12:15 AM "Where else would they do the interview? In the death trap?"

One question that was asked of Kathie at Raye's trial was if she and her followers bashed Mildred, Kelsey's maternal great-grandmother, on her "bash board" or Web site. Her answer was "Not to my knowledge."

Posted by [unknown person] Saturday, February 4, 2006 @ 12:33 PM "Mildred would be left out of it if she would just come out and tell the damn truth. If she would come out and say 'I am just supporting my daughter and granddaughter. I do not know what went on in that house. I know Kelsey was abused and I do not know what went on in that house. I know Kelsey was abused and I do not know who did it. I know it was not Lance or Kathie. I will support my family and that is all. I will not lie for them, or

[41] Watch for *"Bash board" Bullies* coming soon from Jody Ortiz to read more of the "bash board" posts

withhold information for them. I will tell everything that I know, even if it makes my daughter or granddaughter look bad. Yes, Raye Dawn is an alcoholic and yes I tried my best to cover it up. Yes she has slept around and treated people like shit generally. No she was not a good mother most of the time. But I do not believe she killed Kelsey so I will support her.' IF MILDRED SIAD THAT THEN I WOULD SAY 'EVERYBODY LEAVE HER ALONE AND BASH RAYE DAWN AND GAYLA.' BUT SHE WIL NOT DO THAT SO SHE DESERVES WHAT SHE GETS. SHE HAS DONE JUST AS MUCH TO COVER SHIT UP AS ANYONE."

Gayla noted on the printed page beside this next post, "I have never been on here. They are posting my name."

Posted by "Gayla" Saturday, February 4, 2006 @ 12:58 AM "NO, I do not live with Mildred. I am simply staying there for a few days. There is a good reason. I just can't tell you what it is. [Gayla's friend] and I are still together. He could never get rid of me even if he tried, which he has. I did not embezzle any money form my cousin's company. I simply permanently borrowed it. But I quit because I had a nervous breakdown. I am so worried and so scared because Raye DAwn did nothing wrong and we have NOTHING to hide. Me and Raye DAwn are so upset over this. It took us a whole 3 hours to get over Kelsey's death. I know we don't cry anymore, but we are just STRONG women. I have to go now, I have to take my mask off. It is staring to droop." In Mike Porter's e-mails with Kathie and her daughters, he frequently typed Raye's name the way it had been typed in this post. If I had to guess who this was, I'd say it was him. He obviously loved all of the negative attention toward Raye and her family because it diverted the hate away from him.

Posted by "Anonymous" Saturday, February 4, 2006 @ 12:59 AM "Granny Grunt should just marry…or what ever the heck his name is and move out of Meeker if she cannot handle the crap her daughter and granddaughter have created for her."

An e-mail from a family friend had some of the following "bash board" posts attached. In the text, this person stated, "Well, Kathie just could not stand not having a place to put Raye Dawn down. She has endorsed and even posted on a new blog...It is called 'How was Kelsey, let down?' It claims to not be a bashboard but the 1st post is a slam on Raye Dawn. Imagine that. Kathie is really a piece of work, she is so obvious in her manipulation."

Posted by kjbriggs [Kathie] Saturday, February 4, 2006 @ 12:30 PM "...Gayla was right. Mildred is 74 years old and no one should be calling her and leaving hateful messages...[Raye's sister] stated that they cannot grieve. Join the club, this family cannot either. I think the only difference is we are not consumed with the guilt of not fighting for Kelsey's safety. So I am asking that all hate mail and calls to stop...."

Posted by "Anonymous" Tuesday, February 14, 2006 @ 2:40 PM "Poor poor Mildred. They better hold a press conference for her. She needs peoples sympathy for her getting left out in the dark."

An e-mail from Gayla's cousin, Sherri, to Gayla on February 15, 2006 warned Gayla of Kathie's group's next steps in getting what they saw as "justice."

"Gayla, I just want you to know that I got this info from Kathie's website. You might want to inform your lawyer and possibly the DA. There certainly are a lot of strange people out there!!! Hang in there, we are still with you both~~~ xoxo"

The following post by "new" forum member, "Mygift9602" was attached regarding the topic titled "Peaceful Protest": "I have learned today, that there is going to be a grand jury hearing next week, in the later part of the week for Raye's charges. What they are, is unknown. This amounts to either, [The DA] cannot solve the case himself, and feels like he must do this, or he is taking the easy way out of this mess. We must question his motive in doing this. He needs to be reminded of his professional and humanitarian duties to Kelsey, and that if Raye Dawn gets off on whatever charges she is facing, his career as a D.A. is over. In my opinion, this case has been handled very unprofessionally, and sloppy from day one, and I don't think he is taking this for its seriousness. I am staging a PEACEFUL rally tomorrow at 3 p.m. at [the] D.A...I need at least 20 – 30 people there, with signs to join the protest. The more, the better. I also realize that this is VERY short notice, and it is hard for people with jobs, and kids, as I have both, but we HAVE to do this, and do it during business hours. If you are interested or have any questions, please private message me. I apologize for the last minute notice, but I JUST found this out. It will be on the news tonight. I think on all channels, but I do not know the time. PLEASE, anyone that can join us, please do so! We need to show [the DA] that we will not stand for Kelsey to have died in vain, and for her mother to walk free! He needs to be reminded of his duties, and reminded that he IS an elected official. All of you that say you want to help, THIS is your chance. Stand up for little Kelsey, and let your voice be heard! Let him know we will NOT stand for this injustice!"

On February 23, 2006 at 2:29 PM Wilma issued a paternal family statement. "Raye Dawn will be charged tomorrow morning with one count of enabling child abuse and one count of child neglect. Both are felony charges and could be punishable by up to life in prison. My sister received a disrespectful e-mail from one of our members questioning the intentions and integrity of our family in regard to the criminal proceedings in this case...It is my understanding that rumors are being posted on other sites regarding our family's dealings with the District Attorney and some of the responsible parties in this case. Unless you read a statement on this site that is posted by a Briggs family member, consider it a false rumor. Our family has not and will not entertain ideas of negotiating deals or plea bargains in this case. Kelsey was not given a deal and neither will anyone else. Those responsible for her death and abuse should be punished to the fullest extent that the law will allow...Our family is working hand in hand with our District Attorney... We stand behind him and support him. Today's announcement was just one more step in the long journey ahead..."

The post was followed by a statement from Kathie. "Raye Dawn, the biological mother, was charged with two felonies, One was Child Neglect and one was Enabling Child Abuse. After new evidence that came out charges were amended. She is now being charged with felony Child Abuse which is more serious than Child Neglect. In the alternative she is charged with Enabling Child Abuse. This means the jury will have a choice. She either abused her child or allowed her to be abused. Either charge can put her in prison for life. In Oklahoma life is 45 years. This is an 85% crime which means she could be eligible for parole in 37 years if convicted and sentenced to life. She would be 64 years old at that time. It is possible a jury would give her less time, but that will depend on the evidence presented..."

The "bash board" picked up on the news right away with a post by "sew&sew." "Quit bitching so much about what hasn't happened yet. If Raye Dawn gets off with a 'slap on the wrist' even after a jury trial I should think the folks you can 'thank' would be the jury-won't they set her punishment?...Why keep beating up the DA? Granted he may be worthless but at least TRY to be a bit more supportive-what would that hurt? A lot of you who bitching about what 'punishment' will or won't be dealt out to Raye Dawn were on here raising hell that Raye Dawn would never be charged in the first place (guess you were wrong). I know it's hard to see all this happen (especially when we think it could have been done differently)—but couldn't just one day be spent bashing Raye Dawn & Mike Porter & less bashing the 'system' that finally got off it's ass and is doing SOMETHING (which to me is still better than nothing). *&^%)%$#"

One day before the charges were filed against Raye, the district attorney held a press conference during which he stressed that the charges he had filed against Mike Porter and Raye were appropriate for their culpability. He stated that Mike Porter murdered Kelsey and Raye "should have known and could have prevented her abuse or death." Ms. Follett attended the press conference and stated that she heard that the district attorney was considering Murder One charges against Raye. The district attorney denied ever stating that as a possibility.

Posted by Anonymous Friday, February 24, 2006 @ 11:53 AM "Raye Dawn is out on $25,000 bond"

Posted by "Anonymous" Friday, February 24, 2006 @ 12:18 PM "She SHOULD have been brought in in handcuffs!"

Posted by "Anonymous" Friday, February 24, 2006 @ 12:19 PM "I think we need to start calling TODAY Judge...'s office and tell them this is a bunch of BULL****! Seriously, this is CRAP!"

Posted by [unknown person] Friday, February 24, 2006 @ 12:35 PM "Cherokee Ballard even sounded disgusted when she read how much bond was set at."

Posted by "pissed off bitch" Friday, February 24, 2006 @ 12:38 PM "Well its nice to know that the state of OK is great when it comes to law, welfare of children. But who cares what happens to these children more will be born right who cares is mothers beat or allow their kids to be beaten. Lets just keep giving them chances slap there little hands and tell baeting your kid is a no no. TO THE JUDGES IN LINCOLN COUNTY YOU SUCK ASS"

Posted by "sew&sew" Friday, February 24, 2006 @ 2:38 PM "If Mildred & [her male friend] was to be pissy I suppose that's their right. Would seem their Pissiness would be better spent though bitch slapping that worthless daughter of Mildred's and kicking Raye Dawn in the ass. Their vileness is sorely misplaced if you ask me. Their own family is what has brought them to their sorry state...if they want to pint fingers & start assigning blame they have no further to look than within their own gene pool!!!!"

Posted by "kjbriggs" Sunday, February 26, 2006 @ 12:24 PM "We have been fighting the tactics of the Smith families for so long and it is hard to plan for their next move, as we cannot think in the same manner as they do...They have accused us of threatening people, stalking, and harassing...That old man and woman obviously need therapy. I honestly feel bad for Mildred, she is 74 years old and her mind is slipping. Must be a difficult time to know her granddaughter has been charged with such a serious charge. But to still blame Kathie shows her mind is slipping. We should probably pray for her to get back to reality. What a sad thing it must be to put on the image of an ultimate Christian woman and then blow it in one encounter."

Posted by "kjbriggs" Sunday, February 26, 2006 @ 1:01 AM "I have had several people contact us about a protest. My opinion is this...it concerns me that Raye Dawn will never spend jail time. I do believe she needs jail time. She deserves no deals as Kelsey was not given a deal...We are having a town hall meeting on March 11th ...We have a billboard going up...on 177 in the next two weeks. We are also needing to get more and more people to commit to yard signs. We have distributed 14,000 stickers, yet there are so many cars that do not have them on them. We have received some donations and that has been amazing and we appreciate it. We have ordered close to 1000 stickers a week and still have a big demand. We were lucky to have an anonymous donor take $200 to the sign shop. ...Even though we don't post often, we do read as often as we can. Thank you."

A power struggle over the "bash board" that Kathie read, posted on, and was "addicted to" soon erupted with "Audrey," a Mike Porter supporter. Kelsey's Purpose members did not realize that the forum administrators could read private e-mails and reportedly, Mike Porter and Audrey had developed a friendship before Audrey took over the "bash board." Since the paternal family couldn't direct the conversation, they wanted it shut down. Rita posted their wishes on her family's Web site. "I would like to stress to everyone who visits our site, that the Briggs Family (me especially) in no way supports the bashboard that has been set up. When it was originally created with the permission of the Briggs Family but has since then requested it be removed. It has not been removed even though we were told it could be taken down anytime we felt it was not appropriate. Well, it is most definitely not appropriate and the Briggs Family is strongly against its existence. I have told everyone who will listen to me that it is nothing but a place for Mike Porter to twist his truth and get people to have reasonable doubt to keep him from being convicted of murdering our precious Kelsey…Anyone posting on it, I am afraid, could be asking for trouble. It is being monitored by many who are interested. I would hate for people to be on there posting stuff that should not be posted that could end up in court defending what they have said. Please, please take our wishes into consideration and join with me to ban this awful site. I do apologize if I have offended people by posting this, but so many other people are being offended by posting on the bashboard. I feel the emotions that came out in court last week may only be the beginning and I feel a lot of the anger that is being expressed between the different families involved is partly because of the hate that is being generated on that bashboard. Please consider what I have said…."

Kathie posted on the "bash board" as "Anonymous" and then changed to her actual name and posted the exact same post. She must have realized she blew her cover immediately after posting. Posted by "Anonymous" March 2, 2006 @ 4:19 PM "For the record…our family has in the past asked for this site to be shut down. Many innocent people connected all three families involved been hurt. Comments expressed have either been misguided rumors, opinions, meant as humorous, or just a need to vent. Once again we are asking for this site to be shut down. There are sites for more constructive methods of venting about this case and child abuse."

Posted by "kjbriggs" March 2, 2006 @ 4:21 PM "For the record...our family has in the past asked for this site to be shut down. Many innocent people connected all three families involved been hurt. Comments expressed have either been misguided rumors, opinions, meant as humorous, or just a need to vent. Once again we are asking for this site to be shut down. There are sites for more constructive methods of venting about this case and child abuse."

Sherri, Gayla's cousin and family spokesperson sent the following letter to Raye's attorney on March 16, 2006 in a desperate plea to control the building hate:

"We, as family members of Kelsey, find it appalling and sickening that Kathie is blatantly exploiting Kelsey's picture on interstate billboards, T-shirts, banners and buttons. Kelsey should not be the 'poster child' for abused children. We, as Kelsey's maternal family, feel victimized and harassed. Raye Dawn should have a say about where and how pictures of her daughter are being publicly displayed. She is the mother and had joint custody with the state of this child. Why have those rights been taken away from her? We understand she has been charged with enabling and neglect, which we disagree with. The truth will come out in court. In the meantime, what can our family do to stop this exploitation of Kelsey?? Kathie thinks Kelsey's purpose was to be an advocate for abused children. We witnessed the fact that Kelsey lived a happy life for 2 ½ years, full of love for and from her family. She should not be exploited as an abused child. Justice for Kelsey is being served with the stepfather who has been charged with her murder. Justice for Kelsey is NOT being served by corrupting the public's opinion of Kelsey's mother and maternal family. Raye Dawn has NEVER been charged with child abuse. She did everything in her power to work with the State to find out who and why abuse allegations were being made. The State could not even figure it out! Please help us protect Kelsey now as an abused child in the public eye. Her memory does not need to suffer anymore.

This unconsented exploitation should be discontinued immediately. [Attached were excerpts from the Oklahoma Constitution concerning harassment and stalking and victims' rights] Please advise us how we may protect Kelsey's memory and her victimized, emotionally distressed family members."

On March 17, 2006 the Governor included Kelsey's case in his executive address. It seemed to be never-ending and all one-sided. A letter to the editor of the local newspaper was posted on March 22, 2006 as follows:

"To the Editor: I am the ex-wife of Raye Dawn Smith's deceased father. I have known Raye Dawn her whole life and knew Kelsey too. Kelsey's violent death has affected this whole family in a profound and long-lasting way. We as citizens have a few questions. I'm concerned about the fact that the man charged with Kelsey's murder is free on bail. It seems all the TV media has been more about Raye Dawn, who has not been charged with murder, while little concern or TV media attention has gone toward the person who actually has been charged with her death. Little has been heard from the maternal side of Kelsey's family, yet we are forced to see ongoing footage and copy driven by her paternal side. Why? Why is the paternal family not voicing their concerns about Mike Porter, the individual who has been charged with first-degree murder? Fact: he had his bond lowered 75 percent. Fact: he is allowed to see his daughter with DHS supervision. Has that stipulation been followed to the letter of the law? Fact: Mike Porter was not to be in contact with any state witnesses. Is this stipulation being followed? Kelsey's paternal grandmother has stated on TV that she is concerned for his safety! I have never heard her or any of the TV media voice the same concern about Raye Dawn, Kelsey's mother. How can this be about justice for Kelsey? If this was all about justice for Kelsey, it seems we, as Americans, should all be asking these questions. Kelsey's maternal side would like to remind the media and the public that Raye Dawn has not been charged with murder. Is this justice for Kelsey? As a mother, grandmother and an American, I am concerned about our rights as citizens and the fact that anyone who has been charged with murder of a child is walking around free, in contact with children. Where is the justice here? I implore the people of Oklahoma to look at all the facts and not be caught up in the TV media hype that has surrounded this emotionally charged tragedy. Justice is an American freedom meant for all."

In this next post, Kathie states that at every Kelsey event, it rained. This brings to mind a conversation I had with one of Kelsey's family members who sat on the paternal side of the courtroom during Raye's trial. There was a downpour during Raye's sentencing. While the paternal family laughed and celebrated that Raye would be imprisoned for 27 years, this person, who I've since learned has a wonderfully caring nature about her, cried as she wondered if the downpour wasn't Kelsey crying over what happened to her mother. Now with the knowledge that rain seemed to follow Kathie's efforts, I have to wonder the same thing.

Kathie March 13, 2007 Re: Agenda and Events – 2007 "...It rained as has been typical for any Kelsey event."

Kathie and her supporters continued with their mission full speed ahead. Their "justice" stickers were on so many cars that one could hardly drive down the street without seeing a sticker. According to a close friend, the group visited a small town in the southern part of the state and stood on street corners, slapping stickers on back windows as cars came to a stop at stop signs. A family member of my friend rolled down the window and instructed the person that he did not want a sticker on his car. He had to repeat the order several times and then the person approached his window and shoved the sticker through the crack. Many people in the small town were reportedly upset about the fact that a sticker had been placed on their car without permission given. For those who had been watching the tactics of Kathie and her group, they knew that their mission seemed to have nothing to do with helping children. This became even more evident after Mike Porter's preliminary hearing when the "bash board" opened back up with the sole purpose of ripping apart Raye's testimony against Mike Porter. The fact that the district attorney presented new evidence of Kelsey's sexual assault and asked that Mike Porter's bond be revoked (which was later denied) seemed to escape this group because their only concern was a mention of a possible plea deal for Raye. Any attempts to bring up Mike Porter's new charges were squashed and the person who dared bring up the topic was threatened with expulsion from the board.

On September 6, 2006, the Kelsey's Purpose group put the following open letter in the local newspaper:

"This letter stems from news of the recent developments in the pending criminal cases involving the mother and stepfather of Kelsey Briggs. After watching coverage of the stepfather's preliminary hearing held on August 23rd, we were very disturbed by the news that Kelsey's mother is currently in plea negotiations with the District Attorney. This news is even more shocking given [the DA's] past public statements concerning the possibility of a plea negotiation between his office and Kelsey's mother. In that press conference, [the DA] spoke of society's demand that parents be held accountable when they do not uphold their moral responsibility to protect their children. He said that Kelsey's mother knew or should have known her daughter was being abused. His emphatic statements to the media made the recent development all the more surprising.

We would like to know why it seems that people who 'ONLY' fail to protect or enable their children to be abused are not considered to be as culpable as the actual abuser? Why would [the DA] even consider any kind of plea negotiation for this woman! What would the reasoning behind it be? Why would he even consider using her testimony?

Another recent child abuse case comes to mind, that of another very young child. The mother and mother's boyfriend were both charged in the beating of this child, arrested and each subsequently jailed on a $250,000 bond. The mother in that case was able to give a timeline for each individual bruise, and in exchange for her testimony she received a plea deal of two years from [the DA]. Two years for a mother that stood by and watched as her child was savagely beaten. This leads us to wonder how light the punishment for the mother in Kelsey's case will be? Why is [the DA] sending a message that it is not acceptable to beat children but it but it *[sic]* is acceptable to stand by and watch or not protect your child? More importantly, why are the citizens of the 23rd Judicial District allowing our District Attorney to send this message? We would encourage all of you to take the time to let your feelings be known. RICHARD SMOTHERMON, WE DEMAND JUSTICE. [The DA's address and phone number were provided.] Paid for by Concerned citizens of the 23rd Judicial District..."[42]

The group members made a plan to write the judge and the district attorney that there should be "no plea for Raye," yet not a peep about the man who was accused of raping Kelsey and who was out walking free. This double-standard continued through the time of Raye's trial and spilled over onto me. By the time we outgrew the blog and moved to a

[42] See Appendix B – Exhibit 16

forum, I still was clueless about the past actions of the hate group. I had no idea what I was getting myself into or how relentless some of the Kelsey's Purpose followers could be.

# 33 Man in the Hole

"If you want others to be happy, practice compassion. If you want to be happy, practice compassion." ~ Dalai Lama

Shortly following Raye's trial and arrest, I made the two-hour trip to visit her in jail. Members of her family held jobs that didn't allow them to take time off during the week, so I thought a friendly face might cheer up Raye on days her family was unable to visit. Also, doing something productive, such as working on her book, would keep her mind busy.

I'll never forget that first visit. The county jail was in a small building that didn't have an intimidating appearance from the outside. I parked in the mostly empty parking lot and approached the doors with only my driver's license and keys, as well as a pen and pad to take notes. The foyer reminded me of a doctor's office. It was sterile, cold, and uninviting. The most remarkable difference was the bulletproof glass that surrounded the reception area and the bank-like slot that was only large enough to slide my identification through.

Every head in the room reacted as I was forced to yell the name of the person I was there to see through the small speaker box. "Raye Dawn Smith!" I shouted and then quickly turned to see all eyes in the room on me. I wasn't the typical visitor. I was there to see a prisoner who was widely known in our state. I had a pen and a pad for notes. I had no children with me, and my appearance was maintained and clean. I'm not sure what the other people in the room thought of me. I felt as if I stood out from the crowd, but while I waited for the sheriff to bring Raye to the visiting room, I was entertained.

One woman in particular placed herself on the coffee table in front of me. I tried not to wince at her dirty, bare feet, cut-off shorts, and matted hair. "Is your man in the hole?" she asked me in a serious tone.

"What?" I replied, trying not to be rude.

"My man's in the hole." she proudly proclaimed.

"What's the hole?" I asked, curious about the new lingo I was learning. *Perhaps I could use it in a client's book*, I thought.

"He keeps gettin' in fights. He'll never get out." she informed me. "It's where they put the prisoners that don't follow the rules."

After a few moments of silence, she continued, "I've never been in the hole."

"Oh!" was all I could think to say.

She then explained why her feet were so dirty. Apparently, she had to be dropped off in the street by her friend who had given her a ride. She went on to explain that her friend had recently been released from jail, and for a certain number of days, the friend couldn't be on jail property. She furthered her story with the fact that she, however, had been out of jail for a long enough period of time that she was allowed to come onto the jail property and visit her boyfriend.

I'm not sure if she thought of me as rude, but I didn't know what to say or how to respond. This was a world unlike my own, and I was fascinated, but at the same time, repulsed. I smiled in response to her commentary and fielded her questions about the identity of the person I was there to visit. I called Raye "a friend" and left it at that.

Relief washed over me as my name was called and I was led into a tiny room with barely enough space for a chair, a small table built into the wall, and a phone. The door was locked behind me. On the other side of the glass partition, Raye looked tiny and helpless as she pointed to the orange receiver and raised her cuffed hands to pick up her end. My heart immediately went out to her and I grasped the germ-filled receiver and held it to my ear and mouth without thinking of the people who had touched it before me. My only concern was for the person sitting in front of me with tears streaming down her cheeks and pain visible in her eyes.

Before arriving at the jail, I had prepared myself not to cry. I didn't want to upset her more than she already was, and so I told myself over and over on the trip there that no matter what happened, I would not cry. Though tears streamed down her cheeks from the moment I sat down until the time I left, I remained calm and tried to cheer her up with stories of the forum and the characters that had become a part of her online support group. She enjoyed learning about the people who didn't know her and had never met her who were spending their time sharing the truth about what had happened to her daughter. She seemed to be grateful for the efforts of everyone involved. The conversation went well and I held it together until she told me about what the hate and the constant harassment had done to her. She stated that "if it wasn't for" her son, "things would be different." I knew what she was referring to and all of my Girl Scout leader training didn't prepare me for that moment. I was shocked and saddened that Kathie, Lance, and their group had driven her to that point, but I was disgusted when I thought of the pleasure that those same bullies would get if she had gone through with it.

I lost my internal battle and my eyes filled with tears as I asked for clarification. *Did she say what I thought she'd said?* She did. She told me, "I have nothing left. My baby is gone. She was my life. I lived for her. She was my best friend. How could he hurt her?! I don't understand how he could hurt Kelsey! She was perfect." She repeated through her tears, "She was perfect."

I hung my head in agreement with her disbelief. How do you understand what a monster like that is thinking? I didn't know how to explain it or what to say to alleviate her pain. I've always been more like a bull in a China shop when it comes to "touchy-feely" situations and I stick my foot in my mouth more times than not. I blurt out what's on my mind without thinking about the repercussions because I've always been taught that honesty is the best policy. For these reasons, I avoid funerals and anything to do with grieving, whenever possible. I don't want to be the one who causes more pain by saying something inappropriate. On that day, I was the only person on the other side of the glass and Raye was crying out for help and I felt terrible that she was stuck with me. *Why me, God?* I asked, trying to figure out why God would place someone like me in a situation like that. I was out of my element and I didn't know what to do.

Today, I can't recall everything I said and I'm not sure if I helped her or if I opened the wound even deeper. I wish I could remember. I just know that I cried with her and tried my best to be a shoulder for her (figuratively speaking, of course), if nothing else. The visit didn't last long. When it came time to leave, I was reluctant, but relieved. My only concern was to not cause her more grief. Her burden was already too much for her tiny body to handle.

I returned home and to the forum filled with both compassionate people and troublemakers and I didn't say a word about my visit. It was emotionally draining for me to realize that she was on the brink of suicide due to the hate she had endured, the same hate with which I had been dealing day and night, with no end in sight. I wrestled with what she had told me and wondered if I should pass on the information to her family or keep it to myself. In the end, I decided her family needed to know. If she was crying out for help and something happened to her after she confided in me, I would have been devastated. I would have held myself accountable. It was the hardest news I've ever had to deliver.

Making light of the situation with the "man in the hole" comment made it easier for me to make return trips to see Raye. I didn't want to abandon her, especially after my first visit. So, before my next visit, my daughter and I went shopping for what we jokingly termed, "Man in the hole" shirts. I wanted to make sure that I was dressed well enough that nobody would even consider that I was someone with a man in the hole. It worked. On each of my remaining visits I was ignored by all of the other visitors. I breathed a sigh of relief.

On my second visit, Raye had been spending a lot of time praying and writing, and although she still cried throughout the visit, she seemed to be in better spirits. She told me that she was worried about issues she was having with blood in her stool. I immediately thought she probably had an ulcer since her level of stress had been off the charts for quite some time, but since her father had died from colon cancer, she was concerned that she could have cancer as well. Raye's family worked with the sheriff's office and a scope was ordered. Raye told me that the nurse knew Kathie's story and that she was extremely rough when inserting her IV. She said that the nurse jabbed it into her arm so hard that it hit the bone. I winced as she described the cruel and unusual treatment she had received from the nurse, as well as from the person from the Pardon and Parole Board who interviewed her for her pre-sentencing report. It seemed certain people had judged Raye from what they had heard. Their minds appeared to be closed to the possibility that Raye was also a victim. It was terribly disturbing for me to watch the tyrannical turn of events unfold.

Kathie and her supporters, however, seemed to surpass everyone when it came to disturbing words and actions. They viewed Raye's possible illness as entertaining. They accused Raye of being pregnant and laughed at her. They relished in the fact that she was in pain. Granted, it was discovered that the pain was something minor that could be treated, but her diagnosis lends no excuse for laughing at a young girl whose life was ripped away from her.

I recall wondering at the time how Kathie and her followers knew about Raye's medical condition. Several times, Raye's family members and myself discussed the possibility of someone they trusted leaking information to Kathie. When we later discovered the e-mail tampering into Janet's, (Raye's sister's) e-mail account and other illegal means by which they gained inside information, things made sense. Raye's right to defend herself was in jeopardy due to the illegal measures that the Briggs and their supporters were taking. They were always one step ahead. They always knew the game plan before it was played. As I repeatedly reminded forum members in messages, "This is not a game! Someone's life is at stake." Looking back, I was so naïve. I had no idea that to some, it's only a game.

# 34 YouTube and Erin Brockovich

"For the first time in my life, I got people respecting me. Please, don't ask me to give it up." ~ Julia Roberts as Erin in the movie *Erin Brockovich*

Before working with Raye and her family, I didn't have a clue about YouTube or how to make a video. Once, a friend had taken a cute video clip of her nephew that she wanted to upload to YouTube and she thought I should know how to do it. I laughed and stated I had never heard of the Web site. That was less than a year before I met Raye. Within just a few short months, I found myself in a position where I had to learn how to make a video and upload it to YouTube. Just weeks after Raye's trial, it was brought to my attention that Kelsey's Purpose was gaining a large amount of supporters from videos. Something needed to be done to counter the negative videos being made that didn't reflect the true story. So, I opened an account and created a video using Word and

PowerPoint to create slides and then I incorporated the slides into the video software that came with my computer. It wasn't professional, but it was a video and it reflected the facts in the case. At the time, none of the other stuff mattered.

It wasn't long before I started receiving hate-filled messages on YouTube. One in particular accused me of trying to be the next Erin Brockovich. It was meant as an insult, but I took it as a compliment. Like Erin, I was fighting for the underdog and sacrificing everything I had in order to do so. I feel honored that I would be compared with such a courageous woman, though I still have a hard time seeing myself as someone so selfless. Unlike Erin, I wasn't confident or strong and the hate messages were tearing at my soul. With each new message, I could feel the hate and the passion in the person who wrote it and it overwhelmed me. I didn't know what to do or where to turn. Since I had exposed Kathie's gang for being a part of the bombardment, the messages slowed down, but I continued to receive ten to twenty a day for months. With each new Web site I joined or service I obtained, it seemed like a new venue for the haters to bombard Raye's family and myself. The hate got to be so bad that I eventually removed Raye's family members from the forwarding service so they wouldn't have to see anymore. The intensity of the messages was like bullets. I would recover from one, and then another, and then another, and it never stopped. Hate messages were coming at me from every direction, and Raye wasn't their only target.

"I wouldn't sign this petition if my life depended on it. You are as much to blame as the bastard who killed that beautiful child.

And you still have pics of that monster on this website. You are in denial you sick bunch of bastards! Rot in hell Raye Dawn...."

"You've got to be kidding me...any DECENT mother would have PROTECTED her child. There is no way in hell that this woman did not know that her daughter was being ABUSED and for that she should ROT IN HELL!!!!!! This was not one incident of abuse (which by the way is one too many) but this is many, many instances of abuse!!!! God help you for trying to protect a MURDERER!!!!"

The following message came from someone in my county. I remember being frightened that someone within just a few miles of my own home could say something like this: "Her mother needs to burn in hell for not protecting Kelsey, not SAVED! Someone needs to break both of her mothers legs and then punch her in the stomach until she dies so she can know the pain and suffering her little girl went through that her mother didn't stop!!!"

"Murderer. That's all that is needed to be said. Even if Raye Dawn didn't land the fatal blow, she was absolutely an accessory. May she rot in jail then burn in Hell."

"Are you fucking kidding!! No matter how it looks to you blind people, Kelsey was ONLY with the [maternal family] for the last 6 weeks of her life. Pull your head out!"

"I think she should get ready to burn in hell for the things she done to this baby. I think she is the one who killed Kelsey herself and Mike Porter took the fall for her."

"YOU GUYS ARE RETARDED DO YOU NOT KNOW THAT THIS LITTLE GIRL DIED CAUSE OF THIS DUMB BROAD GO

TAKE YOUR SORRY ASSES AND YOU DIE AND SEE HOW IT FEELS!!!! assholes!"

One petition signature had "fuck you" in every field except the e-mail address where it said, "fuckyou@starfucker.com." "Star" is a favorite addition to many of the hateful messages on the Internet and resembles Ursula's, (Kathie's best friend's) name. She stated, "god knows what she did, she killed her baby and tried to use a statistic to her advantage, and blame it on the step father, she killed Kelsey, if she couldn't have her, no one else would, how you make this site and sleep at night, enjoy your judas piece of silver, that poor baby."

The hate continued. They poured into my inbox day-after-day. This message was one of the most disturbing of all. In order to get the full effect, it's presented in its original form.

Username: Burn in Hell
UserE-mail: gofuckyourselves@yahoo.com
UserTel: 555-getraped
UserState: Put a Bullet in your Brain Raye Dawn, you fucking bitch
UserCounty: You never deserved Kelsey. She deserved a much better mother.
Date: 15 Aug 2007
Time: 20:59:40
Comments:
Go fuck yourselves. If that fucking psychobitch had done ANYTHING AT ALL to protect her daughter, Kelsey would be alive today. I hope she fries. Or gets

raped in prison. Perhaps then she would finally understand everything Kelsey was put thru because she refused to stand up to her psycho hubby Mike Porter. And to top it off, instead of being adults and admitting what those 2 monsters did, you trash her dad's family. Her dad defended this country, what the fuck did Raye Dawn do besides abuse children and get knocked up? Oh drugs, that's right. She was the druggie, not Kelsey's dad. I hope she fries.

In an effort to alleviate my stress from the ongoing hate, I found a way to cope in what I like to term, "video therapy." My "therapy sessions" resulted in the creation of close to eighty videos. At times when I felt frustrated, angry, or I had the often-overwhelming feeling of helplessness, I made a video. By the time I was finished writing, editing, and uploading my video, the frustration would subside. I had done something constructive with the excess energy that still makes my heart flick today when I read the messages. There were times when I was so frustrated that one video didn't do the trick and I had to make two, but the video therapy helped me through the pressure that was continually mounting.

# 35 "Kathie, I forgive you."

"When you hold resentment toward another, you are bound to that person or condition by an emotional link that is stronger than steel. Forgiveness is the only way to dissolve that link and get free." ~ Catherine Ponder

It was two months after Raye's conviction for enabling child abuse when she appeared before the trial judge for her formal sentencing. Since she was taken into custody after the verdict, she had spent her days in prayer and contemplation over what she wanted to convey to the judge. Instead of throwing herself on the mercy of the court and begging for a lighter sentence, she stood and turned to the side of the courtroom, whose occupants were mostly dressed in pink, the color of Kathie's Web site.

Raye looked directly into Kathie's eyes and stated, "Kathie, I forgive you."

Laughter was heard throughout the courthouse as Kathie, her family members, and their supporters (including Celia, one of the jurors) found Raye's act of forgiveness amusing. Interviews taken after the sentencing revealed Kathie's anger over the fact that she was forgiven. She stated to the press, "Take her away! Keep her! Let her think about what she's done."

She told one member of the media, "Now she thinks she's God."

She also expressed her delight that Raye would be going to prison for twenty-seven years.

The most shocking interview was from Celia, a member of the jury who convicted Raye and then immediately joined Kelsey's Purpose after the trial. She wore a pink shirt to the sentencing, and had an entirely new look from hairstyle to hair color to makeup. It seemed that she attended the sentencing with an expectation of the possibility of going on camera. She spoke on behalf of the paternal family to members of the media. She stated, "Maybe she'll [Raye] come out [of prison] and instead of forgiving the Briggs, she'll ask for their forgiveness."

A reporter asked of this juror, "What did it mean to the family today; the twenty-seven years?"

Celia answered, "From what I've talked to them…just gonna give them time. As long as it was more than a year, they're happy with it."

Reporters asked the juror, "Why are you here today?"

Celia answered, "I wanted to see this thing through. I was a little bit worried. I had butterflies…saying, I've got to see the final chapter and see what proceeds from here on out and from what I heard today, I'm pretty happy, but if anything does go on…if they go to Chandler, I'll be at Chandler."

Ms. Ballard asked Celia, "Tell me what you thought of her statement saying, 'I forgive you' to Kathie. Did you see or hear anything during the trial that made you believe that she was taking responsibility for her role in this?"

Celia responded, "From day one, I did not feel, did not see…saw no emotions from Raye Dawn as far as her taking her part of the blame for it. And her telling Kathie that she forgave her? Kathie is the one who tried to protect this child, not her, and it should have been the other way around. She should have been asking for forgiveness from Kathie and that right there was kind of ironic…she was secure like she was going to get to walk away, but she won't." Celia shook her head from side-to-side.

A reporter asked, "What would you like her to say?"

Celia answered, "I truly believe that she should have turned to the Briggs and said, 'You know, I'm apologize and I hope you can forgive me for what my part is as far as allowing little Kelsey to pass on and that in time that you'll come back to see me that I've changed and that we can all move forward,' but still remembering Kelsey as a part of it."

Celia then closed her eyes and smirked and then added through a smile, "It's bittersweet today."

The interview ended with her laughter that matched the laughter in the background from the Briggs family and their supporters.

The day of Raye's sentencing was a particularly emotional day for me. I had been to the county jail and I knew she was fairly safe there. However, I worried about how she would be treated in prison. I remember thinking that she would be transported back to the county jail and then on to our state prison for female inmates. Of course, some of our forum members had the inside scoop through Kathie, and they posted that she would be going to a prison in Southern Oklahoma first and she would be arriving at the prison that night. I was terrified for her, as well as her family. Thankfully, the process was swift. She was only kept in that specific prison for a day or two and then she was transferred to the all-female prison. On the day that I heard where she was transferred, I called the prison to inquire about how she was doing, as I did for my daughter on every first day of school. An elderly gentleman answered the phone and told me that she was fine. He said that a roommate had been assigned to her who was very well-respected. He also stated that she seemed to be adjusting as well as could be expected.

I hung up the phone and wiped away the tears that had fallen for Raye. I could not imagine her pain; she was now dealing with circumstances that nobody should have to endure, especially a grieving mother.

I put my worry into action and I renewed my plan to help Raye by drafting a letter to the trial judge that I intended to attach to the collected petition signatures.

November 28, 2007

Dear [Trial Judge],

I am writing to you today to appeal to you on behalf of Raye Dawn Smith. I realize the verdict has been cast, and she is now in state custody. However, I think a grave injustice has been made.

I am not related to Raye's family. I do not live in Lincoln County. And I am not a long-time friend of Raye Dawn's. I am an individual who saw the mayhem that the Briggs family has caused in what I used to be proud to call my home state of Oklahoma. As a citizen of Oklahoma I feel it's time to stand up and do the right thing for the sake of an innocent mother who was denied counseling and has not been allowed to grieve the death of her child. I have seen all the evidence the jurors saw. I have read some of the testimony from the trial, and I have spent countless hours pouring over police reports. I know you're not interested in my opinion, but I believe this is a case of accidental death. I believe Mike Porter was trying to save Kelsey and injured her with his sloppy version of CPR and he teamed up with the Briggs to turn on Raye Dawn. The Briggs are out for revenge, fame, and money, and that's it. How long will we sit by and watch the injustice carry out? Mike Porter already sealed his fate with his plea, but Raye Dawn has continued to proclaim her innocence; an innocence that hundreds of people around the world believe in as well.

I know you are a man of reason, so I am enclosing hundreds of signatures on a petition for a new trial for Raye Dawn. I beg you to read these petition signatures with an open mind and let your heart guide you in your decision.

Raye Dawn deserves to have a fair trial. A fair trial will never be heard for her in the State of Oklahoma. You know that. The Briggs do not play by the rules. They violated the gag order that was in place before Raye's trial. They are still spreading their lies. When will they be silenced? When will the State of Oklahoma and Lincoln County take back control of justice?

Respectfully yours, Truth Seeker

This letter was never delivered and neither were the petition signatures. I began to work closely with Raye's family members in doing what was best for Raye's defense. It was determined at the time that any direct contact with the judge while Raye's attorney worked toward an evidentiary hearing or a new trial could be seen as possible tainting. Since we strived to play by the rules, the petition signatures instead became words of support for Raye. I shared each positive message with her family members, which were in turn passed on to Raye.

At the time that I drafted the letter, it's clear that my perception of Mike Porter's culpability was a bit skewed. Shortly after Raye's sentencing, I was given documentation that was used in Raye's appeal so that I could upload it onto the Web site. One of the documents was a statement from Mike Porter's daughter's school counselor. In the statement, she described how Mike Porter's eight-year-old daughter had told her that Mike Porter had been mean to Kelsey when nobody was looking. According to the counselor, Mike Porter's daughter had seen her father "spank Kelsey until her bottom was real red" and "bang Kelsey's head against a brick wall until Kelsey threw up." The idea that a man could do those things to a child was beyond disturbing to me. After reading the statement, I knew that Mike Porter was a monster. For months, I had been going back and forth due to the lack of evidence I had seen against him to prove without a doubt, that he had purposely murdered Kelsey. Also, I had been inundated with arguments from Kathie's gang. Evidence that later came to light of the child pornography and other disgusting videos, pictures, and instant message conver-sations that were found on Mike Porter's computers further solidified my belief that he is undoubtedly a monster. Somewhere, deep down inside, it seemed that Kathie agreed. She called him a "monster" on her Web site and stated that she believed him to be guilty of the original charges against him—sexual assault and murder. However, she could not let her good sense get in the way of her hate for Raye. She posted on her Web site shortly after Raye's conviction, "I am no longer obsessed with Raye Dawn, she's in prison." She followed this post with her thoughts about Kelsey's sexual assault, stating, "That doesn't mean that Raye Dawn wasn't using an object and doing it herself." With this level of blind hatred toward Raye, there was no way I could abandon my mission to expose the truth.

Raye has told me on numerous occasions that Kathie Briggs does not work because Raye Dawn is her job. I was beginning to see what she meant by those poignant words.

In response to my efforts to help Raye, a "new member" posted the following on Kathie's Web site. "I agree, Mike Porter maned up and has taken his prison term like a man, [Raye's prisoner number] well as cried, moaned and well just look at this The Conspiracy Against Raye Dawn [A video link was posted]"

Ursula responded, "I read on another site where Raye Dawn is actually housed now on death row for her protection. Does anyone know if this is true? They say she hardly comes out of her cell or socializes with anyone anymore? This allegedly comes from someone who's been to the prison to visit someone and was told that by the inmate they were visiting. I'd like to know if that's true? Anyone else heard this?"

Kathie replied, "I have heard from more than one source that Raye Dawn is in protective custody and is housed on death row. The women's prison is a very short distance from Meeker and many people either know a prisoner or someone that works there. Stories about Raye Dawn circulate frequently in our small town. She too has the option of being housed out of state for her protection."

Being housed out of state would not protect Raye. Kelsey's Purpose members have posted her address on numerous occasions and she has received hate mail and dead flowers since her wrongful imprisonment.

Of course, the reports of her being housed on death row were false. Raye quickly moved up in the prison system and is in the least-secure area. She has also finished a program in which she learned how to counsel and mentor. She now spends her days mentoring other prisoners. How could somebody on death row earn trust from the guards and become a mentor? As usual, certain people will say anything that paints Raye in a bad light.

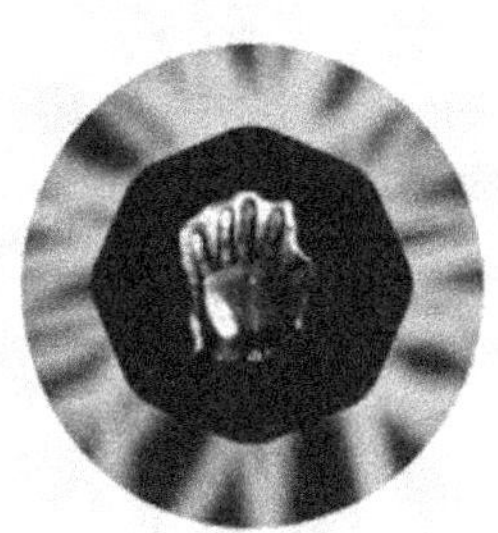

# 36 Oklahoma State Bureau of Investigation

"Terrorism is in good part an effect of government propaganda; it serves to deflect attention from governmental abuse toward a mostly imagined, highly dangerous outside enemy" ~ Mark Poster

In the case against Raye, Kelsey's paternal family members have mentioned hindsight on multiple occasions. They've stated that with hindsight they realize they "should have done more to save Kelsey." With hindsight, everything becomes clearer. All of our victories and mistakes are easily seen with hindsight. Odd behavioral patterns in people once trusted are suddenly visible when that person's true character is exposed. In fact, this was an issue brought up at Raye's trial. I'm sure that everyone who knew Kelsey would like to go back and change things, but it seems the only ones involved in the tragedy that are allowed to use hindsight are Kathie and her family. In their eyes, everyone is to blame except for them, even though, according to witnesses, their mistakes would also make them accountable for not protecting Kelsey.

In December of 2007, Kelsey's Purpose closed for the first time in the history of its existence and loyal supporters jumped ship after I posted the e-mails between the Briggs and Mike Porter on the Free Kelsey's Mom Web site. After reopening her forum after closing for a couple of weeks once the e-mails between the Briggs and Mike Porter were exposed, instead of posting the e-mails as Wilma promised they would do, Kathie, with the help of Lance's girlfriend, transcribed Raye's confidential Oklahoma State Bureau of Investigation interviews. These were classified interviews that never should have been in her possession. She then committed a misdemeanor crime and posted the "transcripts" on her Web site and called them "official" in a desperate attempt to deflect the attention from the damaging e-mails and back onto the one Kathie obviously hated most, Raye. Along with the few long-time supporters who hadn't abandoned ship, as well as the new supporters who didn't understand the significance of Kathie's betrayal of Kelsey in her correspondence with Mike Porter, posts were soon added to Kathie's forum that included several negative opinions about what Kathie claimed Raye had stated in her interviews. In these posts, Kathie's supporters pointed out all of the "red flags" that Raye had missed as she described Mike Porter's actions that had struck her as odd while she revisited everything that she could remember happening since Mike Porter entered Kelsey's life. These discoveries came to light while contemplating Mike Porter's actions after the first interview, when she had been told that her daughter was murdered and had not died from a seizure.

What struck me as odd was the fact that none of the people commenting took into consideration that the interviews on which they were basing their opinion of Raye were mere interpretations made by Kathie and Lance's girlfriend. There was nothing "official" about what they had transcribed and posted.

One thing that was never pointed out to those who trusted the validity of the interviews was the fact that Raye used hindsight in her second interview with the OSBI. In an effort to figure out exactly what happened to Kelsey, she reported the things that now seemed suspicious in Mike Porter's actions. With the loss of her beautiful, beloved daughter, and the realization that she never really knew her husband, memories took on new meanings. Once, they were of a man who was a good father and who would do anything to help her raise her child. Now, in the darkest depths of her imagination, she didn't want to see the memories in a new light or envision what the stranger in her bed had done to her child. She revisited her memories honestly and openly and reported what she knew to the officials in an effort to solve the murder of her child.

Upon reflection, she very naively discussed every detail of their lives with no holds barred and her honest and open admissions were eventually used against her. In a normal case where everyone follows the law and works together for the greater good, as the DA described it, her "full cooperation" would have helped to put the perpetrator behind bars and ensure he was listed on a sex offender registry. However, in this case, when the desired outcome is something other than justice for a dead child and the one “fully cooperating” is the ex-mother-in-law’s main target, Raye didn’t stand a chance. In hindsight, the release of the interviews was also a deflection of their latest scheme in which they would soon reveal my identity, breaking multiple laws in the process.

# 37 Rally for Hope

"Many of the great achievements of the world were accomplished by tired and discouraged men who kept on working." ~ Author Unknown

In March of 2008, Kathie Briggs posted my name, picture, and home address on Kelsey's Purpose. Her Web site had grown to 20,000 members and her members were told, "Go get her." Shortly after the order, we discovered bullet holes in our truck, and then someone keyed it. My sense of security was ripped away during three days of Kathie and her hounds shredding my life and making fun of my professional abilities. They posted all of my personal and professional information—including my resume as well as posts that I had made on a Yahoo writer's group—onto a Web site that was supposed to be dedicated to fighting child abuse.

The fact that a group that was supposed to fight abuse spent so much time abusing people never made sense to me.

If you are the type of person who cares about people and wants to stop abuse, then *why abuse?* This question haunted my thoughts while I researched Kelsey's Purpose and the true intentions of the group. *How can abusers fight abuse?* It made no sense to me.

Before Kathie and her group shared my information, I had searched for and found a replacement for myself. One of the moderators that I loved and trusted took over the leading role in the fight for Raye and I stepped into the shadows. I was sick of the abuse and afraid for my safety as well as the safety of my family. I took out a life insurance policy and alerted all of my family members to the danger that I had found myself in so if anything happened to me, they would know where to look for suspects. However, every time I have tried to walk away and refocus on what I need to do for myself and my family, "they" drag me back into the fight. Their actions directly contradict what they claim they desire. If they wanted me to quit supporting Raye, all they had to do was leave me alone. I would have walked away a long time ago. It's not something I'm proud to admit, but it's the truth. Once I realized the lengths to which these people were willing to go in their mission against Raye, I wanted nothing more to do with them. I wanted no part in their game. From the moment I was bombarded with hate mail, it took everything I had to stay and fight. My sympathy for Raye and her family kept me going, but once Raye had other supporters who were willing to "go to bat" for her, I felt my purpose had been served. I had done my part. However, as the character, "Brad," learned in the movie, *Malibu's Most Wanted*, the only way out is "in a box." Kathie's own supporters have learned this lesson. I have heard about and read several messages from Kathie and her family members and supporters to former Kelsey's Purpose members whose eyes were opened to what they were sucked into, and who decided to no longer support Kathie; they were bombarded with hate mail and threats just for talking to me. *Why?*

Although we were all beaten down and weary, the members of Raye's support group moved forward. I had found a replacement that started planning a rally against wrongful convictions and she lined up guest speakers and got the plans underway. In the meantime, Raye wrote a letter to the state lawmakers that we delivered to them in May of 2008, along with information that had not yet been made public about the case. I e-mailed Raye's family and we discussed the time and place we would meet to pass out the literature. To our surprise, when we arrived, a camera crew from Ms. Follett's news station was waiting for us.

As we approached the stairs to the State Capitol building, we thought perhaps there was something else going on at the Capitol building that day and we didn't think much about their presence. However, they stopped us on our way into the building and then followed us around for at least an hour asking for a copy of Raye's letter, which we refused to give to them. Within two hours, and before any of us even made it home, the letter was posted on Kelsey's Purpose and Kathie and her hounds were ripping it apart. It was also on the news that evening with Ms. Follett displaying her disgust with the letter, and the report included quotes from Kathie and the district attorney. It was unbelievable!

Every lawmaker received the following letter with their packet:

"Dear Lawmakers: Kelsey Smith-Briggs was sexually assaulted and murdered at the age of two years and nine months. According to the Ryan Luke Law, her records should have been released after her death, but they've been suppressed and kept hidden. Why?

Attached are just a few of the supervised visitation notes taken by DHS in May and June of 2005, just before Kelsey's death. As you can see, Kelsey showed no fear of her mother, but the same can't be said for her paternal grandparents. Could this be why her records have been suppressed?

As lawmakers, you have the power to ensure your laws are followed and obeyed. Release Kelsey's records and allow the public that has judged her mother, Raye Dawn, so harshly to see what really happened to precious Kelsey.

Thank you for your consideration. Friends and family of Kelsey and Raye Dawn"

Raye's letter was also attached and is presented as follows:

My name is Raye Dawn Smith and my daughter was Kelsey Shelton Smith-Briggs, the beautiful two year old little girl that was killed by her step-father on October 11, 2005 in Meeker, Oklahoma. I have been wrongfully convicted of enabling child abuse, because the District Attorney Richard Smothermon has made the statement that I "should have known." Not that I knew anything, but I "should have known." So many things went wrong in my case and they continue to go wrong to this day. I am trying to reach out to anyone who will listen to me and read the information available on my web-site www.freekelseysmom.com.

So many lies, stories, and half truths have been told, but very little has been told about what kind of a child Kelsey was and no one has ever heard of the wonderful relationship Kelsey and myself had. Just because Richard Smothermon, Patty High (special prosecutor), Kathie Briggs (Kelsey's paternal grandmother), Mike Porter (step-father), and/or the media say something doesn't make it true. This is who Kelsey and I were...

Kelsey was born December 28, 2002 at 10:00p.m., nineteen inches long, seven pounds, with a head full of black hair, and olive skin. She was always a happy baby and we were together all the time. She sucked her thumb until one day she broke herself when she decided she didn't need that comfort anymore. She did everything early, from sleeping all through the night, to crawling, to walking, to talking. She was a very busy baby, but a very good baby. Did I mention well mannered and very independent? She would tell you "God bless you" if you sneezed. If she was trying to get past someone and it was a tight squeeze she would say, "Cuse (Excuse) me" and if anyone tried to help her do something she would say, "No, I do it." Everything Kelsey did was an event to me. I would call my mom and my grandma almost everyday at their places of work just to tell them something Kelsey did or said throughout the day. We would watch movies together, dance together, go shopping together, sleep together, and some days until noon, put puzzles together, color together, and we even made a cake together. In 2005 we made a strawberry shortcake together with strawberry icing and sprinkles. I helped her with the icing, but she had a big time shaking the sprinkles all over the cake. I can still see the look on her face smiling from ear to ear, clapping her hands when I clapped with her and told her, "Good job!" October 10, 2005, the day before my entire life turned upside down, Kelsey and I were sitting in the truck waiting on our new furniture at Mathis Brothers. Kelsey was in the back seat in her car seat and she began counting 1, 2, 3,...and when she got to ten she kept going 11, 12, 13, 14, and then stopped. I had never heard her count that high before, and when I turned around and looked at her in amazement, she just smiled as big as ever with a look on her face as if thinking, "You didn't know I could do that, did you?" She could always make me smile and made me proud everyday.

When my mom had Kelsey in her care all of May and part of June, 2005, she made a statement my mom says she will never forget. My mom and Kelsey were taking the trash down through the pasture to the dump when Kelsey reached down to the radio knob, turned it on, and said, "I haffa (have to) hear good music." Laughing, my mom asked her, "What do you know about good music? You're momma has spoiled you rotten." Kelsey just smiled at her, knowing she had made a funny. Although Kelsey was only two and a half years old, I think back on her short life, and we did a lot together. From hanging out watching movies, her favorite being Shrek, to going through a cave in Branson, Missouri, to going down the water slides together at White Water, and eating crawfish and crablegs. The memories make me smile and laugh everyday, but some days are a lot harder than others. Even though the memories are great, we were ripped of many years to come. I think about the things we were able to do, but not without thinking about the things we will never be able to do. I will never see her tie her own shoe; ride a bicycle with or without training wheels; go to her first day of kindergarten; graduate from the eighth grade; go on her first date. I will never get to teach her to drive a car, teach her to put makeup on, take her shopping for her prom dress and her wedding dress...I will never see my baby grow up.

April 11, 2008 my son turned two and my daughter has now been gone for two years and six months, and to this day there is not a day that goes by that I don't talk about her or think about her. It will be this way for the rest of my life. I watch mothers here at the prison on visitation day play and laugh with their daughters, and hug and kiss them hello and goodbye, and I think of how I would give up anything this world has to offer to do all of those things with Kelsey one more time. I pray to God all of those mothers know how lucky they are and that they never take one day for granted. In court and out of court lies have been twisted and stories have been stretched, but one thing they can't twist or take away are the memories, because those are mine and they can't take away the truth of who we were.

I was silent for almost two years, because I was advised by my attorney not to make any statement, and besides that, a gag order was in place. Trying to follow the rules and the law, it doesn't take a genius to see where it got me. Kathie Briggs, Kelsey's paternal grandmother, had a website up with in about a week of Kelsey's death, stating that it was Kelsey's purpose to be abused and murdered to bring awareness about child abuse in the state of Oklahoma. She passed out stickers with www.kelseyspurpose.org slapped across them, a bash board in my name was put on the web. Harassing phone calls with a baby crying in the background were made to my grandma, Mildred Fowler. A harassing phone call was made to the church DURING Kelsey's funeral at the Meeker Assembly of God Church. A friend of my mom received phone calls threatening to ruin his real estate business, and his entire neighborhood in Northwest Oklahoma City received a horrible letter in their mailboxes stating that a child abuser, child molester, and a child murderer was living in the neighborhood. Kelsey's Purpose Signs were put at the entry of our neighborhood with Channel Four's, Cherokee Ballard there, as it was aired on the evening news. All of this was handed over to the District Attorney, Richard Smothermon, but not one thing was ever done about it. Protests took place in front of the District Attorney's office with signs stating, "No Deals for Raye Dawn." A petition was even done in order to keep my son away from me when he was born. My son is absolutely no business of Kathie Briggs. There was even a petition to bring charges against me, even though I was working with the District Attorney's office to the fullest extent. There were no protests or petitions about Mike Porter receiving a deal, or about keeping my son away from him – the person whom murdered and sexually assaulted her granddaughter on October 11, 2005. In fact the Briggs family agreed to the plea bargain of murder and sexual assault being dropped, and to him pleading to "Enabling Child Abuse." District Attorney, Richard Smothermon, exhumed my baby's body to look for sexual assault, and then he turned around and dropped it! Do you have any idea what I went through when I was told they were going to do that? Let me tell you, it almost killed me knowing they were going to disturb my daughter's resting place, and it will bother me for the rest of my life, even more because now I know they did it for NO reason.

A person may wonder why the Briggs family would be so easy on this sick and twisted person, and never speak a negative word about him. I wondered too, but since my trial I have learned the reason why. Seventy nine days after Kelsey's death, Kathie Briggs and her daughters, [Rita] and [Wilma], began corresponding with Mike Porter through e-mails, discussing the entire case and conspiring together as to how they could get me put into prison. Of course this was a violation of Mike Porter's bond, and from the information we were given in court, Richard Smothermon knew of this and also about the Briggs and Porter meeting. Why was Porter not rearrested for his violation? Not only did Kathie Briggs talk to Mike Porter, but she talked to a few witnesses, as is evident in the e-mails between the two and that was a violation of the gag order that was in place. Now I know where some of the lies that were told in court came from.

I testified at Porter's preliminary hearing, not wanting a plea deal in return, because that's not what it was about. That morning before I took the stand, with my attorney by my side, I told Richard Smothermon, "I want you to know that I'm not doing this for you. I'm not doing this for me. I'm doing this for Kelsey." He nodded and said, "I know, or we wouldn't be talking." I said, "Well, I just wanted to make sure you knew that." Everything I've done in this case from January 2005, up until now has been for Kelsey. I just wanted to do what I knew was right. I have even been told that the reason I'm in prison is because I did do the right things. That just doesn't make sense to me, I was raised to tell the truth, and if you didn't do anything wrong, you don't claim that you did. I was offered five years incarceration and five years probation and of course, I refused, but then the day before my trial was over, I was offered a blind plea of spanking Kelsey on the diaper with a hairbrush. I stated, "No, I didn't do it. I won't take it." I never hurt my baby and I didn't sit back and allow someone else to hurt her. How is the district attorney, Richard Smothermon, going to tell me that I "should have known?" They wanted to drop the entire case on September 8, 2005. The district attorney's office, Department of Human Services (DHS), Community Home Based Services (CHBS), and C.A.S.A. were all there throughout the entire process, and they didn't know anything either.

During those last nine and a half to ten-months of Kelsey's life, I did everything that was asked of me and more. If my attorney told me to do something, I did it. If DHS told me to do something, I would. If the judge told me to do something, I did. If anyone of them told me to do something, I would and I did. When I asked DHS to tell me what all I needed to do to have my daughter returned to me by June, they told me that I wouldn't be able to get it done by then. As much as that upset me, I didn't focus on that, and told them to just tell me what I needed to do and let me worry about that. I just knew I wanted my daughter back, as soon as possible. And to everyone's amazement, I accomplished every little thing within about four months. I took a parenting class, a six-week domestic violence class, an anger management class, a domestic violence inventory (D.V.I.) test, and when I completed all of that, they had me take several more evaluations. They were all normal or above. I received certificates for all of this and a letter of recommendation from my counselors, stating I had completed all my classes and there was no need to be further counseled.

During all of this my daughter, Kelsey, was being shifted here, there, and everywhere. It was extremely hard on her and I could see that. One night in March, 2005, after she got out of her bath, I noticed her hair had fallen out in the back. Being upset, as any mother would be, I rushed her across the street to my grandma, Mildred Fowler, had her look at Kelsey and take a picture of the bald spot and was asking her what would cause this. Of course she didn't know, but the next morning I called DHS, my attorney's office, and got her an appointment with Dr. Kelli Koons. They did tests on her, but I have yet to know exactly what caused that, other than probably stress. The doctor told me that Kelsey's hair had indeed fallen out, because the hair follicles were not raised, as they would be if she had pulled her hair out. A few days later I mentioned this to Kathie Briggs, and she told me Kelsey was pulling her hair out, and I knew that was not the case, because not only had the doctor told me that, but I had NEVER seen Kelsey pull out anyone's hair, let alone her own. At one visit, Mrs. Briggs sent a cabbage patch doll with Kelsey and said she got the doll for her so she could pull the doll's hair out instead of her own. Flabbergasted, I told her that whether she was pulling her hair out or it was just falling out, there was a problem somewhere and we weren't going to just cover it up. Neither DHS nor the district attorney's office ever acted as if her hair failing out was a big deal. Why?

On April 14, 2005 Kelsey sprained her ankle while on a trip to the zoo with her aunt and cousins. They came and picked me up and we took Kelsey to the doctor where she/he told us it was indeed sprained. The doctor told us to have her to continue to walk on it as tolerated and then rest it. That Monday I married Mike Porter, and I have a picture proving she was standing and walking that day. She was limping, but she was walking. That day at five o'clock, my older sister and I took Kelsey to meet Mrs. Briggs, and four days later when I picked Kelsey up, she was NOT walking at all, she was crawling. When I asked what was wrong with my baby...why she was crawling, Kathie Briggs told me that earlier that week she took four steps and fell and didn't want to walk anymore. Why didn't she take her to the doctor??? She took Kelsey when she thought her nose was broken, which it was not, but she didn't take her because she QUIT WALKING??? I didn't take her to the doctor, because I had already taken her. Since I was told that Kathie Briggs made the statement that she didn't care what the doctor said, she was NOT going to make Kelsey walk on her foot, so I thought her foot had gotten stiff and sore from not walking on it. Never in my wildest nightmares did I ever think that my baby had two broken legs. But come Monday I took her to DHS and then to the doctor and that's when I found out my baby had not one, but two broken legs. I remember crying and screaming out to my mom, "Mom, what's going on?!" So you see it is a fact that Kelsey was NOT with me when her legs were broken, but I "should have known?" I was only doing what everyone was telling me to do. In May, 2005, I accompanied my mom and Kelsey, me being in a separate car, to Children's Hospital to have Kelsey tested for Brittle Bone Disease. Worried something was medically wrong with her, this was just one more step I wanted to take to see what was going on with my daughter. Later that summer, DHS and I were informed that the results came back "inconclusive". I wanted to have her tested further, but DHS said they would not be paying for a second test, because the insurance wouldn't pay for it, so my family and I was going to pay for it ourselves. I was informed that the Briggs family was extremely upset about having her further tested, and they were NOT going to help with the funds. Why would they be upset about having her further tested to make sure she didn't have a serious disease? That didn't, and still doesn't, make any sense to me. So you see, I still don't know if she even had Brittle Bone Disease, because the test didn't rule it out. I was going above and beyond even what the state was willing to do. But I "should have known?"

On one instance Kelsey had a bruise on her nose and I showed it to Kathie Briggs, telling her and her daughter…what had happened. They told me that they didn't even see it, because they were sick of all of this and they were sure I was too. Not believing my ears I called my mom to tell her what they had just told me. Later I learned that Kathie Briggs immediately ran home and called DHS. It is impossible to work with a liar!

The days Kelsey and I would meet at the DHS office she would sometimes ask me very difficult questions. On one occasion when I was leaving she asked me, "Mommy, I go with you?" I would tell her through tears, "No, baby you can't go with me." Looking so sad and confused she asked, "Mommy, what happened?" How do you tell a two-year old what happened when you as an adult don't even know? In June after court, the day she came home, I was holding her as we walked up to the door and she said something I will NEVER forget. She hugged my neck and said, "Mommy, I so proud you, we're home." Do you have any idea how that made me feel? Out of all the people involved, Kelsey, my two-year old, told me she was proud of her mommy. I pray and hope every night that Kelsey knows how much I fought for her, day in and day out, and that I'm still fighting for her.

That summer I enrolled Kelsey into a play therapy group for her to receive counseling, because like I told DHS, if someone hurt her, I wanted to know what they did, who it was, and then that person and me were going to have a talk. I received her acceptance papers in the mail the day she died when I was on my round trip to pick up her stepsister. The most Kelsey ever went without seeing or talking to a DHS worker, CHBS worker, CASA worker, and/or a doctor was seven days, and they were in and out of our home day in and day out from June to October 11, 2005. Out of one hundred and twenty two days, they were in our home thirty-five of those. I would let Kelsey talk to them when they would call, because who better for them to talk to other than Kelsey herself? At one point and time I asked DHS for a round table discussion with everyone involved, and I have yet to see that happen. Why? DHS has done it with my son. Why wasn't I allowed that for Kelsey's well being? During the summer of 2005, Kathie Briggs refused to go to the DHS office to visit with her granddaughter, because she didn't want any more bad things said about her. I'm sorry, but that is just ridiculous. I have been called everything under the sun, but if I could see my daughter again, I really don't care and still don't. From January, 2005, to September 8, 2005, we had what felt like a million court dates, and on September 8 NO ONE from the paternal side, not even their attorney, even bothered to show up to fight for their visitation rights, but guess what, Kelsey's mommy was still there fighting for her baby. The district attorney's office and Kelsey's attorney were asking the judge for the entire case to be dropped, because everything was going so good, but because of the Ryan Luke Law they couldn't do that. Kelsey was there that day and they all saw her, so if anything with her was out of the ordinary, I'm sure they would've taken action. Obviously, she was doing great. I still remember what I dressed her in that day.

To this day I have never claimed I was a perfect person or a perfect mother, but I NEVER hurt Kelsey or allowed anyone to hurt my baby. Kelsey was my pride and joy, and to me the world revolved around her and still does. It hurts so bad to see on the television and/or in the newspaper that anytime there is a story done about DHS my baby's name is right in the middle of it. She was a human, a child, a grandchild, a cousin, a niece, a soon to be big sister, NOT a poster child for DHS. I think back and read about all the things I did to get her back, and it kills me that I lost her anyway. I could sit here all day and tell you what I did for her when in all actuality no one seems to care. Kelsey lost her life for NO reason, I lost my daughter for NO reason, and even though I worked with the state before her death, day in and day out, I still not only lost her, but for the time being I've lost my son. And for what, because I "should have known?"

I've been asked a million times if Kelsey could talk and the answer is, "Yes, she could talk up a storm as if she was half grown." Then I've been asked, "Did she ever say anything?" Yes, she said some things, such as: "I don't like [April]!" (Kelsey's stepmom), and, "I don't want go see Kafie (Kathie)!"...and talking one day about Mike Porter, she said, "Daddy not mean to me." I have witnesses to these statements, CHBS worker being one. Believe me, I realize what Mike Porter did to my precious baby on October

11, 2005, but those are the kind of things she told me, so how was I supposed to know? I agree people are allowed their own opinion, but sent to prison on an opinion? That's absurd! The district attorney, Richard Smothermon, stated publicly that I "should have known", but he told former Judge Craig Key in private that he KNEW I was INNOCENT, but because of the other family he had to charge me with something. My son is growing up without me because Richard Smothermon didn't have guts enough to stand up and be an authority figure over the Briggs family.

Now this man, Richard Smothermon, is wanting out of office to become a workman's compensation judge. He still has two years to serve in office. How loyal is he to the community and district he has promised to serve? Plus, he doesn't even live in the district where he serves as district attorney. He lives in Edmond. State officials have been informed of this on several occasions, but nothing has been done. Why? A lady running a tag office had to shut her place of business down, because she didn't live in the same county as her tag office, but there is nothing done about a district attorney doing the exact same thing? Richard Smothermon has made the statement that the "Kelsey Case" has done him in. If he had done the right thing in the first place, what he KNEW was the right thing, he wouldn't be in this predicament. Richard Smothermon told my attorney, Steve Huddleston, that he "Didn't have a problem with my mom having my son and me being supervised by my mom," but of course DHS didn't allow it, because they were already getting call-ins on my son, and I didn't even have him. Now does that sound like a district attorney who really, truly believes a mother enabled child abuse?

Speaking of my mom. To this day she has yet to be questioned by the OSBI and/or the district attorney's office. Why? She was the first one on the scene on October 11, 2005 and she had interaction with Kelsey and myself almost everyday for the two and a half years of Kelsey's life. I've wondered if it was because not questioning my mom made it easier for Richard Smothermon to prosecute me if he never heard the truth.

I am pleading with you to do the right thing and support me in this case. My daughter's memory and my son's life, as well as my own, is counting on it. I want the DHS files and the OSBI interviews made public; the Ryan Luke Law demands it. I have written to a couple of representatives and senators to ask for this, but as of this moment, I have received no response. What's the point of putting a law into effect if no one is going to use it for what it was put into law to do? So many wrongs need to be made right and it is long over do. I've always felt this way and I always will. I am asking you to please check more into the facts of this case and help my family and me. My family as well as myself, would be more than happy to speak with you. Please, I am asking you and your colleagues to please find it in your hearts to fix the part of the tragedy that can still be fixed. I pray this letter finds you well, and I appreciate you taking the time to hear me out. The truth is out there, someone just has to take the time to listen to it, read about it, and then act upon it. Please do the RIGHT THING. Sincerely, Raye Dawn Smith

Raye stated in her letter that she had remained silent for two years because of gag orders, and the fact that she was following the law. She now wanted to have her voice heard, but not only was nobody listening, every word she said would be judged and ripped to shreds by a gang of bullies.

A week or two after delivering the packet to lawmakers, Gayla (Raye's mom) and I returned to the Capitol building alone and we passed out flyers for the upcoming rally. It had been obvious to us on our first trip there that Kathie had made friends in the offices of some of the lawmakers. Among the warm welcomes, we also received dirty looks and cold stares.

After passing out all of the flyers in record time (since we just went door-to-door and placed the flyers on desks without saying much of anything to anyone), we were stopped by three security guards on the bottom floor who were there to arrest us. Apparently, "complaints" had been lodged by lawmakers' assistants. We were led into the security room and, after a few minutes and their realization that we posed no threat we were released with a warning. Inquiries have been made since that day and we're told that people pass things out at the Capitol building all the time and nobody ever complains. We were targeted for a reason.

On the day of the rally, I made the last minute decision that I would attend. I didn't know if it would be wise since Ursula had threatened to be there and had made multiple public threats about bringing the press and getting "in my face." Other than a few drive-by's from Lance with the local police following closely behind him, the rally was a success. We had Raye supporters visit from several different states and I got to know those who had found a place in their hearts for Raye and her family. They are, to this day, like angels to me with hearts that are pure and full of compassion. I don't know where I would be without them.

The rally ended with a candlelight vigil in a field near the prison. I had called the prison warden and asked for permission to bring a small group onto the premises to pray. She denied my request. Gayla scoped out a neighbor who said we could use his property to say our prayers. We weren't there for five minutes before a swarm of prison guards arrived in their vehicles and threatened to arrest us. It seemed everything we did was ending in possible arrests, although our intentions were pure.

Everything we had gone through seemed worthwhile when Raye's great-uncle took my hand in his and told me, "I pray to God every day that he will let me hang on until Raye comes home." His words bring tears to my eyes even now and my heart went out to him as I vowed to hang in there and do what I could to help see that his prayers were answered.

# 38 Freedom March

"Freedom is never voluntarily given by the oppressor; it must be demanded by the oppressed."
~ Martin Luther King, Jr.

In March of 2009 a new and wonderfully compassionate Raye supporter had written on my Facebook wall, "There has to be something that we can do to help Raye." The plea was familiar; it was the same thing I had said in the beginning, but I was beaten down and I had run out of ideas. At the time, I was becoming aware that Raye wasn't the only innocent person in prison. This was a tough conclusion for me because I believed that everyone incarcerated belonged there. I also supported the death penalty. The idea of ridding the earth of people who posed nothing good for society was acceptable to me. However, since my eyes were beginning to open to wrongful convictions, my views were quickly changing and I started an online group entitled "40 to

Freedom" that discussed wrongful conviction cases. I was open to the possibility of other wrongful convictions, but I didn't know of any cases that I personally felt justified the term "wrongfully-convicted."

Once the online support group gained members, a few cases that were brought to my attention touched my heart; I started making videos for the family members and I purchased and maintained Web sites, just as I had done for Raye. Since all of these things were happening and the new Raye supporter wanted to come up with something big, I thought that everyone marching on their respective State Capitols on the same day at the same time would undoubtedly get attention. The new owner of Raye's support forum she called "Raye of Hope," came up with the name "Freedom March." In less than three months, we threw it together and it was a success! We had families of those who have been wrongfully convicted find our cause, and people raised their voices against wrongful convictions in sixteen states. It was amazing!

In Oklahoma, we had several special guests. Dennis Fritz was among them. He had been wrongfully convicted of murder and had spent eleven years in an Oklahoma prison. His case was the subject of a John Grisham novel. He had spoken at our first rally and was a dedicated supporter of Raye and her family. Also, family members of three other local wrongful-conviction cases joined us, as well as a young lady who is a strong Raye supporter and a resident of London. She came all the way to Oklahoma to participate in and speak at our march. It was exciting! Not only was our march successful, but after spending a week with this young lady, we took her into our hearts and she is now like a daughter to me. Through all of the trials and tribulations I've faced, the bonds that I've made with giving and compassionate people like her have made it worth while.

Other bonds were made as well. The Freedom March served as a network for family members of the wrongfully-convicted. As one of our founders put it, "It doesn't matter if the evidence supports the conviction. Arguing evidence in a public forum gets us nowhere. The fact that the family is suffering and is fighting for their loved one is what matters. Showing support for family and loved ones of the incarcerated is sometimes all that's needed."

On the day of our first march, despite efforts to get media attention, only one news channel was interested and ran a story on our activities. Due to the fact that we carried signs for all of the wrongfully-convicted cases in which family members had joined forces with us nationwide, the media focused on the signs that did not involve Raye. Even though Raye's family members spoke, they didn't interview them and only covered our guest speakers who were involved in other high-profile cases. It was good coverage for the other cases, but a real disappointment for Raye's family. It seemed that the media had their story and, because our efforts threatened to change the story, they chose to avoid it altogether.

# 39 Putting a "Price Tag on" Kelsey

"What is a cynic? A man who knows the price of everything and the value of nothing." ~ Oscar Wilde

In the spring of 2009, Raye received a letter from Lance's attorney regarding the $15 million lawsuit Lance had filed against the state in connection with Kelsey's death. The letter asked that she not appear in court to make any claim to the $625,000 settlement that Lance had agreed to accept in lieu of the $15 million.

Raye called me about the letter and she was in great distress. "How can they put a price tag on my baby?!" she screamed into the phone. I had no answer. The only conclusion I could draw was that the evidence did not support the lawsuit and the state offered a settlement so Lance took it.

Raye read the letter to me and what I gleaned from the language was that the attorneys were acknowledging her as Kelsey's mother, which meant she was eligible for half of the settlement, and Kathie's alleged plan to put Raye in prison so that her entitlement would be erased was in jeopardy. I encouraged Raye to send the letter to her attorney and seek his advice. My initial response was that she should go for it, and she had already decided to do just that.

She told me, "I don't want this money to go up his arm or up his nose."

After a few moments, she regained her composure and told me that if she were to get the money, she would donate it to St. Jude Children's Research Hospital in her father's memory, and in Kelsey's memory to the local infant crisis center that had been on the news frequently discussing how they were in need of funding. She wanted to help save babies and children who were sick, in honor of Kelsey and her father. These were her plans from the moment she discovered she could be entitled to half of the settlement. Rumors, of course, began circulating that she wanted the money for herself. The media took these rumors and ran with them in a vicious attack against Raye's intentions for the money. The rumors were false. Raye wanted to honor her daughter, not collect "blood money," and her family supported her plans.

Shortly after Raye received the letter, Gayla saw a newscast in which volunteers were being requested to help the infant crisis center with car seat checks. The day the organization needed help just happened to be Gayla's day off from one of her many jobs so she spent a few hours volunteering. She felt it was a sign from God that Raye would be awarded half of the settlement and those who were struggling to save children would benefit. I was hopeful, as well.

The media frenzy surrounding the settlement included a petition that was created by a woman in Canada who has brutally attacked me online. Although I have never even had a conversation with her, her comments are vicious and biting. Her petition was covered by Ms. Follett on a newscast and added to her news channel's Web site, which is our local Fox station. Someone took the liberty of signing my name to the petition and, when Kathie was asked about the petition in her deposition she stated, "It was inappropriate" and that she asked to have it removed. She also denied knowing the woman who created it. She said, "She's just some woman online." This random woman took part in creating a hate group on Facebook against Raye, which myself and supporters were able to have removed. She then created another group that was to target both Raye and myself. She quickly gained over 400 members that were misled with lies; one was featured in her group's introduction. Note that the warden to whom she refers is, actually, a female. She stated:

"The Warden at Mabel Basset Correction Center in Oklahoma, has been contacted and he assure's us that it is not Raye Dawn on Facebook or Twitter or Myspace.... He was not happy to find out that someone was impersonating his inmate, and promised to have the matter investigated further, as it is a CRIME TO IMPERSONATE SOMEONE YOU ARE NOT AND IT IS PUNISHABLE BY LAW...( THEY ARE NOW ONTO YOU JODY MICHELLE ROBERTS ORTIZ, AND IT'S ONLY MATTER OF TIME BEFORE WE ALL WATCH YOU GO DOWN FOR YOUR CRIMES. I WONDER IF ALL YOUR FIGHTING FOR RAYE DAWN'S FREEDOM WAS WORTH YOU LOOSING YOURS, WHO KNOW'S MAYBE THE TWO OF YOU CAN SHARE A PRISON CELL TOGETHER...YOU BOTH DESERVE EACH OTHER! ) I would just like to remind everyone, that we can not leave death threats to Raye Dawn in our wall posts or our discussion board Topic's, post's or reply's... You are allowed to say that you think Raye Dawn should have recieved the death penalty and the same with Mike Porter, but you are not allowed to legally threaten to do it...We all need to rally and protest and stand united and be the voice for an abused child... We need Stricter Sentences for Monster's like this... And they should not be allowed to use facebook's social networking site, to try to gain supporter's so she can get granted an appeal... This is Morally wrong... Facebook know's it, Raye Dawn knows it, and so do her supporters...They lie to everyone and then say the Briggs are liars... I have read through weeks of DHS reports, Police interigation Reports, OCYI Reports, I have even viewed Kelsey's Autopsy Report and it made me literally sick to my stomach...I have gone to the Free Kelsey's Mom site, and viewed what they have posted on it, and I found out that they have only posted half of the reports, and there are some to that have been altered from the originals...Raye Dawn is strongly supported by the editor of Craig Key's book ... Which he is the Judge that returned Kelsey back to Raye Dawn and Mike Porter in June of 2005... He wrote this book with hopes that he would get re-elected as a Judge, and to line his own pockets off the earnings of the book... He did not get reelected....And the book failed miserably... It was a total flop, that some would only say was worthy of toilet paper! We had a group about getting Raye Dawn off facebook, and facebook decided to let her stay and shut our group down...Read what she is guilty of below, and you give us your opinion...."[43]

Like the other hate group, this group was soon closed, but has since been replaced with yet another group that targets Raye and me. It's a never-ending battle and the media only add to it. Ms. Ballard and Ms. Follett also host a group on Facebook that is continually flooded with vile, mean-spirited comments. It seems they allow bashing because drama

[43] See Appendix B – Exhibit 17

is attractive to some people and it sells books, t-shirts, and hats that are said to be a "fashionable way to spread the word about who killed Kelsey." Raye doesn't stand a chance against people with such poor taste in judging what's appropriate. The hate that is being generated from this group is immense and Raye isn't their only target. My name is commonly mentioned within every one of their groups as an example of "evil." Their form of logic makes no sense because they know nothing about me, except the stories my bullies have told.

During the media frenzy regarding the settlement, Kathie lobbied for an emergency law to be enacted so that Raye wouldn't be entitled to claim any of the settlement. She contacted lawmakers and her plea to them was featured on the nightly news. My computer skills had improved by this point. I went from someone who could barely put together a Web site and who knew nothing about images to someone who could create PDF documents out of Web pages, screen shot statements to keep for evidence, and record videos from television and the Internet. This is one occasion where my newly acquired skills came in handy. I recorded the interview and paused the screen where it briefly displayed Kathie's letter written on July 8, 2009 to her State Representative and then it was forwarded to Ms. Follett. I transcribed the letter and sent it to Raye's family members and her attorney. It said, "I am looking for someone willing to write a new law or (adjust?) one already on the books. As you may know we will be going to court yet again in Kelsey's case. Raye Dawn has filed a claim to receive half the wrongful death suit received by the state. This is not something a family should have to face after all we have been through. She is in prison in connection with her child's death and now she wants to gain financially. It makes no sense to me. This could open the door for other inmates to claim or file wrongful death suits. It could also be a motive for a parent to sit back and allow a child to be killed. That may sound like a far stretch, but it is possible. Currently the law as I understand it states you cannot gain financially if you are convicted of murder or manslaughter. It should state you can not gain financially if you are convicted of a crime in connection with the death. Please let me know if you are interested. I will be doing a story tonight on Fox on this subject. (then it looks like a smiley face) Thanks, Kathie"

On the Internet, Ursula is still pushing for murder charges against Raye. *Could this letter give us insight into their current campaign and into the charges that I and others feel that they sought all along?*

In preparation for the settlement hearing that was scheduled for January of 2010, depositions were taken of key witnesses including Mike Porter, Kathie, and Lance. Raye was also deposed.

Despite arguments from Raye's attorneys that Lance not be allowed to attend Raye's deposition, he positioned himself across from Raye and mocked her. Raye's attorney posed the question, "Do you find something funny about the abuse and death of your daughter?"

During that same timeframe, Mike Porter was also deposed. Raye's attorney traveled to the Missouri prison where Mike Porter is housed "for his protection." The attorney didn't recognize Mike Porter when he was first brought into the room, and neither did I when I watched the video that was made that day. His formerly heavy frame, clean-shaven face, and round cheeks were now replaced by a thin face and a goatee. His current looks were a far cry from the clean-cut man I first saw on the news.

Through every question, he stared coldly into the camera and answered, "I respectfully decline to answer that question." No question asked of him caused him to shake his calm demeanor, not even when Raye's attorney asked if he had ever sexually abused his own daughter. However, he did attempt to cover smirks when asked about deceiving Raye. Conversely, while there was little reaction from Mike Porter, Lance's attorney, who also attended the deposition, had plenty to say. To the question of sexual abuse and his own daughter and many other questions asked of Mike Porter, Lance's attorney's voice took on a high-pitched tone and he screamed, "Are you kidding me with that question? You're badgering this witness!"

When the deposition first began, Mike Porter informed Raye's attorney that he would not answer any question. He claimed that his attorney had placed a call to Lance's attorney and informed him that no questions would be answered. At the time of his claim, there was no denial from Lance's attorney. However, once the judge was called because Mike Porter was not cooperating, and Raye's attorney informed the judge that Lance's attorney had been notified that Mike Porter was not going to cooperate but Raye's attorney's office was not informed, Lance's attorney denied that he ever received such a call. Mike Porter shook his head and denied he had made that statement as well, even though it was recorded. Lance's attorney left before the deposition ended with the parting words of, "I'm leaving with the understanding that you're going to continue to answer every question as you have been doing." He repeated this to Mike Porter several times and then shook Mike Porter's hand on the way out the door.

In the weeks before the depositions, I actually joined Kathie's Web site and spent hours searching for evidence that would assist Raye's attorney in deposing Kathie. The deposition was a slow process with every misstatement from Kathie argued with her own words to prove her statements were false. Immediately after her deposition, an un-moderated public forum (Kathie's supporters' new "bash board") sprung to life with posts about how people didn't realize how much I had helped Raye's attorney. *How did they know what I was e-mailing to her? Have they tampered with my e-mails as well as Raye's sister's account?* Ursula shared information that I helped the attorneys and she knew that it was shared with a female associate attorney and not Raye's main attorney, who is a man. *How did they know who I e-mailed?* The hate against me grew to a loud roar. I was being quiet and they were mad because they knew what I was doing behind the scenes. They seemed to act above the law and I was in their way. They began working day and night to ensure everyone hates me as much as they do.

Although I had quit Raye's family after bullet holes were discovered in my truck and my home was burglarized, the paperwork I started in January of that year so that I could occupy the "friend" position on Raye's short list of allowed visitors came through just after I quit. I was no longer saying anything publicly in support of Raye, but I had made a promise to her that I would help her tell her story. The appellate court judges had received her appeal in January and by May she was restless and wanted something to keep her mind busy. I thought it was the perfect time to get back to work on her book. The plan was for me to visit and ask questions, then come home and work on the chapters and mail them to her as we progressed, and to also e-mail them to certain family members, including her sister whose e-mail account, we later discovered was being tampered.

The first time I went to see Raye in prison was a bad day for me. I didn't know what to expect and I imagined the fear and sadness that Raye and her family members had experienced when seeing the prison for the first time. On the drive there, I called a dear friend of mine and she helped to keep me calm. My emotions took over, and the closer I got to the prison, the stronger the feelings became; I was almost in a state of hysteria by the time I reached the parking lot. My biggest fear was entering the prison in that panicked state and Raye seeing me and that my reaction would be upsetting to her. I just couldn't do it!

As I approached the prison, the exterior alone was quite intimidating. When I pulled into the parking lot and parked, a gentleman approached my window and asked if I had any change for a dollar bill. I hung up the phone with my friend and searched my truck for change, which took a few minutes. I don't know if it was divine intervention, but he was a young man and appeared to not have much in the way of spare money. Finding money for him to use to purchase whomever he was there to visit some snacks took my mind off my fear and my fast-beating pulse began to slow down. The throbbing in my ears also subsided.

I took my truck key off the key ring and grabbed my Ziploc bag full of quarters and my identification, and I concentrated on remembering my tag number as I followed the young gentleman up the steep, concrete steps that led to the main gate. The man pushed the buzzer on the gate and yelled "Visitor!" and the large steel gate squealed on its tracks and opened. My legs felt weak, but I moved forward, following his lead, and I stood with him between two gates that led into the building. I looked to both sides and saw a chain link fence with razor wire on top and rolls of razor wire in front of them that were taller than me.

After the gate behind us closed, the gate in front of us opened and we followed the path into the foyer where an armed guard waited at a desk with a sign-in sheet and a list of names and another armed guard stood by the metal detector and frisked visitors who had been approved to go inside the visitation area.

Although I was told I had been added to the list, my name wasn't there. I was turned away and relief washed over me as I made my way through the large gates and past the razor wire. I was going home and more relieved than disappointed. I told myself that the hard part was over because on my next visit, I would have already made it into the building and I knew what to expect. There would be no surprises.

The following week when I returned, my name had been added to the list and I was allowed to go inside and see Raye. She looked well. She had made some good friends and people were treating her nicely because she was a model prisoner. The guards were all very polite and helpful and I left the visit feeling even more relieved.

The hardest part of the visits was sitting across the table from Gayla, Raye's mother, and Mildred, Raye's grandmother. The pain was evident in their eyes and my heart broke for them. They shouldn't have to drive to a prison week-after-week to visit Raye. She should be home.

With each visit, I grew more at ease. Gayla and Mildred would try to keep the mood light and we talked about a variety of topics, not just Raye's book. After a few weeks, I had enough information from Raye to get a feel for who she was and what her book should include. It was a different environment than I was accustomed to working in, so it took more hours of work than usual. I would go in each week with questions, but since I could not take notes, I forgot a lot of what we discussed before I arrived back home. Also, most of the content of our previous discussions that took place while she was in the county jail were about Raye's and Lance's relationship before Kelsey was born, so we hadn't gotten very far. I recall one statement she made to me about the first time Lance had hit her. She told me that it was her fault. When I posed the question again after two years had lapsed and Raye had grown in her faith, she said she realized that it was not her fault; a man should never hit a woman. When she stated her new opinion, tears filled my eyes because I knew she was no longer a victim of Lance's abuse; she was now a survivor. With Raye's permission, I now present the first chapter of her book:

As I walked down highway 62 past the Rainbow, a tall, dark figure came into view. From a distance, I could make out the confident stance of my father, but he was gone. I knew it couldn't be him. "Daddy?" I questioned as my pace quickened and my heart raced. "Daddy?" I whispered, in awe of my vivid imagination.

The Assembly of God Church loomed in the shadows behind my father. He seemed larger than life and I wanted nothing more at that moment than to reach out and touch him. I moved swiftly through the parking lot and seemed to float in the air without hearing the familiar crackling sound of loose gravel crushing beneath my feet. I stopped in front of my rock, my father, the first man in my life I had trusted to protect me. Fear gripped my heart and I let out a small cry as I struggled with wanting to touch him and being afraid that when my hand met his body it would find only an illusion.

"It's gonna be okay, kid," he said in his familiar, reassuring voice. He reached for me with both arms and hugged me close. I could feel his warm touch, his strength. It was not at all what I feared it would be. His arms were strong like before the cancer ravaged his body. He smelled of the outdoors; that smell of sweat and steel that always made me feel safe and loved. "It's gonna be okay, kid." he repeated. My daddy had never lied to me, but I couldn't help but question if it really would be.

With a tear running down my cheek I looked into his hazel/brown eyes and asked, "Are you sure?" "Yes" he reassured me, and a heavy weight lifted off my chest as I trusted him.

Sitting in the county jail was the last place I thought I would be today. How could the jury not see that I was innocent? How could they believe the lies of those who were bent on destroying me? My child was gone and the man who stepped in after my father died, the man who was supposed to be my rock violated my trust and took my daughter's life.

I loved him and thought he was a man of honor, integrity, and that he would be a good father to Kelsey as he had been to his two children. So why am I here? I don't understand.

A cold chill ripped through my body and I wanted to do nothing but curl up in my daddy's arms. The jail was cold and sterile like a hospital, but with a slight smell of body odor and constant screams and cries of its captives.

My head felt fuzzy as I tried to sort out the events of the last few months. I just didn't understand.

As I sat in the large room surrounded by cells, the coldness became overwhelming. "I'm cold. Can I have a blanket?" I asked a lady jailer. "I don't give a shit about your comfort." she spit back at me.

"It's gonna be okay." The man sitting next to me said.

I thought *you have no idea what has happened.* But the kind words reminded me of my dream. "Are you sure?" I asked, searching for any reassurance I could find. "Yes" he answered. I knew it would be okay.

Going through the intake process was the first time I felt violated. I cried throughout the finger printing process and getting my pictures taken. But when I had to strip in front of a strange woman and allow her to check me from one end to the other that was the point that I realized my life wouldn't belong to me for as long as it took to get people to see the truth.

As I put on the orange jumpsuit, pink socks, and what my mom calls "Jesus sandals," I cried and kept telling myself, *this isn't right. It's not right.*

After I was processed, I was finally able to make a phone call. "I want to call my mom." I told the jailers. "You have to call collect." They told me. "But no one is home!" I cried. "I have to call a cell phone." Finally, I was taken into the nurse's office to use the phone and I dialed my mom's cell phone number. When she answered we both cried. I told her, "I don't understand." She said, "I don't either." I said, "I'm ready to go be with Kelsey." She didn't respond. She knew what I meant. I felt it was time for me to go and be with my child. I wasn't suicidal, but I didn't want to live any longer.

During my first few days in jail I refused to eat anything. I didn't feel I had a reason to live any longer since I had been separated from my son and Kelsey was gone. What did I have left to hang on to?

After writing the first chapter, something inside told me to take a break. Comments were being made on the Internet such as "I'd love to read Raye's book" and I had a bad feeling but I didn't know what it was. Also, the hate on the Internet against me was getting worse and, with my resolution to not retaliate in the haters' childish manner, I was left with few options to use to combat them. Looking back, it's a true blessing that I stopped working with Raye when I did. The first chapter has been read by Kathie and her supporters due to their admitted crime of tampering with Raye's sister's e-mail account. They read the first chapter before Raye's attorney did. This could have jeopardized Raye's appeal, due to the fact that I was merely writing what I remembered Raye telling me, and my recollection is not always accurate. Although complaints have been made to the police and the FBI, those who are hacking into e-mail accounts with the sole purpose of spying on Raye and her defense have yet to be charged.

# 40 The Bully is Revealed

"Those who think the information brought out at a criminal trial is the truth, the whole truth, and nothing but the truth are fools." ~ F. Lee Bailey

Distance creates clarity and I tried to figure out why the bullies were somewhat quiet and then started their attacks on me with brute force in the summer of 2009. I was already struggling with trying to find peace in my life after being bombarded with hate for so long, but when the attacks reached their peak, I shut down and became almost non-functional. With the recent discoveries of e-mail tampering into Janet's (Raye's sister) e-mail account, the fact that they knew I was helping Raye's attorney prepare for depositions just before it happened, and statements on a public forum where they stated that I went to extreme lengths to help Raye, it's crystal clear. The main bully had been denying her identity for years, but, suddenly, she knew she was caught.

Ursula admitted it was she all along, yet she called me a liar for denying my identity.

Through e-mail tampering, which is against the law, Ursula and her friends posted the thoughts and opinions of Raye's attorney as well as information about what I was sending to Raye's attorney to help with her defense. They had a hijacked viewing of the day-to-day steps that were being made in Raye's defense, which is in violation of Raye's right to defend herself. Private e-mails I addressed to Raye's family members were copied, screen shots were made, and they were posted on a blog that was created immediately after I created my blog that is nothing but harassment for Raye's family and me. In their eyes, they have done nothing wrong, but crimes such as e-mail tampering, perjury, stalking, harassment, and cyberstalking should be punishable by law.

On January 9, 2008, I received this e-mail from Raye's sister: "I got booted and couldn't get back on. My computer has been doing this lately. Kathie probably has got a hold of it!!" It seems that, subconsciously, she already knew what was happening.

**THE HEARING**

The hearing to decide the distribution of the lawsuit settlement took place in January of 2010. Throughout the hearing, I took intensive notes and made sure that the quotes were accurate and verbatim. Like Ms. Follett's notes from Raye's trial, they were not perfect. I didn't capture every word because I have forgotten shorthand and arthritis makes writing by hand something painful. When I began posting my notes to my blog, I was called a liar and, soon, members of the left side of the courtroom, none of whom took a single page of notes, suddenly posted their version of the hearing with notes that contradicted my own. Just like with Raye's Web site, they claim everything is altered or a lie, but my notes accurately portrayed what took place that day. *How do you prove your integrity when vicious people work to destroy everything you do with claims of foul?*

Raye testified at the hearing. Since it was a Federal Courtroom, she wasn't allowed to wear "street clothes" or to be unchained. For her protection due to ongoing threats from Kelsey's paternal family and their supporters, the two prison guards who had transported her to the hearing sat directly behind her throughout the day and a US Marshall sat within reach of her at all times, even when she was on the stand. The Marshall was seen admonishing Lance on more than one occasion because he was trying to intimidate Raye.

Raye took the stand in her grey prison scrubs and with both of her ankles shackled—a constant reminder of the binds that have been placed on her due to public scorn. She relayed the events that happened on the day of Kelsey's death. Her emotions were raw and there wasn't a dry eye on the side of the courtroom where I sat. However, smirks and giggles could be seen and heard from the paternal family's side, as well as from Ms. Follett, who sat a couple of rows behind me. Raye poured her heart out and described her relationship with her daughter and the last time she saw her alive, and Kelsey's paternal family laughed. I didn't understand how they could be so cold and unfeeling. The judge watched Raye intently and I was hopeful that he had seen past all of the dramatics that had been played out earlier in the day, when Lance's family member described him as a "broken man" who was suicidal and had no joy in his life. They also denied any claims of Lance doing drugs or being an alcoholic, even though these are aspects of his character that had been publicly admitted. Their description was a far cry from the man that Raye's attorney had described just months before who sat across from Raye and held up his fingers for "two" and "seven" as he laughed at the number of years Raye would be in prison while she was questioned about abuse allegations and her daughter's death.

As Raye's testimony progressed, I noted that she described events just as she had in Mike Porter's preliminary hearing that took place just months before Lance reportedly asked the district attorney to give him a plea for a lesser charge. My tears smeared the pages and my shoulders shook as I joined everyone around me in sorrow over the unthinkable loss of Kelsey. I stopped writing and listened to Raye's heartfelt testimony.

In order to properly portray what happened that day, I present a portion of Raye's testimony from Mike Porter's preliminary hearing that took place on August 23, 2006--the same testimony she gave in the January 2010 hearing. The district attorney, who charged Raye, asked the questions as follows:

Q –You had a child by the name of Kelsey; correct? A – Correct.

Q – What was her date of birth? A – 12/28/02

Q – When did you marry Mike Porter? A – April 18, 2005.

Q – I want to draw your attention, ma'am, if I could, to [the date of Kelsey's death]. Do you recall that date? A – Yes, I do.

Q –Do you recall the afternoon hours of that date, approximately noon on? A – Yes, I do.

Q –Could you tell this Court approximately from noon on what happened in your day? Where were you? A – …the CHBS worker, showed up about noon.

Q – Where were you physically? A – We were at the house…

Q – Is that within the confines of [your] County? A – Yes, it is. And [the CHBS worker] showed up for our normal visitation. She came every week, once a week.

Q – Could you tell the Court who [she] is and what she's doing? A – She is a CHBS worker. And she just comes in and checks on Kelsey and the house and everything once a week.

Q – And at this point in time, there was active involvement in yours and Kelsey's life with the Department of Human Services; correct? A – Yes.

Q – Was [the CHBS worker] a part of that? A – Yes, she was.

Q – Approximately what time did she get there? A – She got there about 12:00.

Q – How long did she stay? A – She stayed for about an hour. To be exact, an hour and 16 minutes.

Q – How do you know that to be exact? A – When she was leaving, I happened to look at the house phone and it was 1:16 when me and Kelsey were walking her out.

Q – What did you and Kelsey do after [the CHBS worker] left the residence? A – She began to play with a turtle that we had seen outside.

Q – When you say "she," you mean Kelsey? A – Uh-huh. And we put it up on the white deck, and she played with it. I told her to try and feed it, and she didn't want to feed it, because she said there was a – she thought there was a snake in there. So I tried to explain to her that it was just a turtle. And so I left her and let her – I left her on the deck and left the door open. I went in there to get us something to drink, came back out there, and she had gotten some leaves off of the bushes and she was throwing them at him. And then I went back into the kitchen and she came back in there. And I said, "What's the matter?" And she said, "Mommy, I had an accident."

Q – What did you do? A – I just took her black sweats off of her and took her panties off of her and put them in the dirty clothes, and then I asked her what she wanted to eat.

Q – What was she wearing after you took her sweats and her underwear off? What was Kelsey wearing? A – She was wearing a black biker-run T-shirt.

Q – Anything else? A – No.

Q – Did you ever put another diaper onto her? A – No.

Q – What was she wearing at that time? Diaper? Underwear? What was she wearing? A – She wore Pull-Ups and panties.

Q – Approximately what time in the afternoon was this, if you recall? A – It was probably about – in between 1:30 and 2:00.

Q – What did you-all do next? A – We looked for her something to eat, because I told her she had to eat. And she told me she didn't want to eat. I said, "You have to eat something." And she told me, "No." So I told her she had to go to time out. I said, "because you have to eat." So she went to time out to her room; I went to the bathroom. And I came back and I could hear little footsteps coming down the stairs, and she told me – she said, "Mommy, I want some berries."

Q – What did you take that to mean? A – I said, "Berries?" I said, "You mean raisins?" And she said, "Uh-huh."

Q – Okay. A – And then she came down the stairs most of the way and then she stopped and then leaned towards me and I caught her and then we both laughed. And then I went in there and got her the little box of raisins.

Q – Okay. A – And then I told her, I said, "Mommy is tired." I said, "I'm going to go lay down." And she said, "I lay by you." And I said, "Yeah."

Q – Do you know approximately what time this was? A – It was close to two o'clock, because when we got in there to lay down, Montel Williams' show was already on.

Q – What time does that come on? A – Two o'clock.

Q – On what station? A – Forty-three.

Q – Where was Mike Porter during this day? A – He was at work.

Q – Do you remember what time he had left for work that day? A – I believe it was about 7:30 or so.

Q – Had you had any contact with Mike Porter throughout this day up until two o'clock? A – Yes, I had.

Q – And describe for the Court what that contact was. A – When I went to go wake Kelsey up that morning, I went upstairs and she was still asleep in her bed. And I noticed a towel was under her head.

Q – Okay. A – And so I went down – back downstairs and called Mike Porter. And I said, "Did you put a towel under [Kelsey's] head?" And he said, "No." And I said, "Well, she must have put it there."

Q – Was there any other contact or discussion between you and the defendant that day? A – Yes. Before me and Kelsey went to sleep, I had called him and told him that we were laying down to take a nap.

Q – Any other discussions about the day with him at that time? A – No.

Q – After you laid down about two o'clock, what do you next remember?

A – We laid down and she was taking the raisins out of the box and was eating them and she would close it after she got out each time. And we had a discussion about – I told her, I said, "Kelsey," I said, "close that box." And she said, "Mommy, I have to get some." And I said, "Well, get some." And we laid there for a minute and then she said, "Mommy, I love you so much." And I said, "I love you too, Kelsey."

Q – What happened next? A – She went to sleep.

Q - When she went to sleep, can you recall how she was laying on the bed? Well, first of all, let me backtrack. What room were you in? A – We were in my bedroom.

Q – And is that located – the house ... east of Meeker on Highway 62; correct? A – Correct.

Q – And it's set back on a hill? A – (The witness nodded her head.)

Q – Is it a two-story or one-story? A – It was two-story.

Q – And the master bedroom, where is that located? A – It's located downstairs.

Q – Okay. And is that the bedroom that you went to sleep in? A – Yes.

Q – That you went to lay down in? A – Yes.

Q – When Kelsey went to sleep, what was she wearing? A – She was wearing her black biker T-shirt that went to her knees.

Q – Anything else? A – No.

Q – Is there a reason you didn't put another diaper or other pants or panties on her? A – No. Just after I took her pants and her panties off, we just started looking for something to snack on and then just went to lay down.

Q – When she went to sleep, how was she laying? A – On her back.

Q – What happened next that you can recall? A – I remember – I don't remember if Mike Porter woke me up or if I just woke up, and he was standing at the edge of the bed.

Q – So is it fair to say, then, you also napped? A – Yes.

Q – So when you say "Mike Porter," you mean the defendant? A – Yes, sir.

Q – What happened when he arrived at the house? A – Then when I woke up, he was standing at the edge of the bed. And I said, "I'm not going to" – I said, "I'm not going to take her."

Q – What did you mean by "I'm not going to take her," and who did you mean? A – I mean Kelsey, because she had just fallen asleep.

Q – When you say "I'm not going to take her," where were you going? A – I was going to pick up [Mike Porter's] daughter at school in [another town].

Q – And your decision to pick her up, whose decision was that on this day? A – It was his. He had told me earlier at some point.

Q – Do you recall when he had told you? A – No. It was either that morning or the night before that we had discussed it.

Q – Where was [Mike Porter's daughter] in school? How far or how long would it take you or anyone to get from your house to [the school]? A – About 20, 25 minutes.

Q – And you had to pick her up and drive her, or someone from the family had to pick her up and drive her every morning; correct? A – Correct.

Q – And pick her up after school? A – Correct.

Q – Was that normally done by you or normally done by Mike Porter? A – It was done by both of us.

Q – Was there any set schedule to it or just random? A – No. Just random.

Q – So this was not the first time you had gone to pick [Mike Porter's daughter] up from school? A – Correct.

Q – So you made the decision at that time not to take Kelsey with you; correct? A – Correct.

Q – What happened then? A – So then I slip out of bed, and I stand there and watch her for a second.

Q – Why? A – Because usually when I would get up, she would wake up most of the time.

Q – And had she woken up at this point, what would you have done with her? A – I would have taken her with me.

Q – Why? A – Because I would – if she was awake, I would always take her with me.

Q – But at this point, she was not awake? A – Right.

Q – Was she sleeping? A – Yes.

Q – Was she breathing? A – Yes.

Q – Everything appeared normal to you about her? A – Yes.

Q – What happened next? A – Then I told Mike Porter I wanted to show him the turtle that Kelsey was playing with. He follows me outside. And I look around for a second for it, and I didn't find it. So I get in the truck and I leave. And then as I'm backing up, I stop, I roll down the window, and I said, "Take care of my baby."

Q – What happened next? What did you do? A – Then he nodded his head and rolled his eyes.

Q – Okay. A – And then I leave and then I go pick [Mike Porter's daughter] up.

Q – Okay. A – I come back.

Q – Do you recall what time you came back to the house, approximately? A – It was probably – it had to have been about 3:30 or 3:40.

Q – From your time you left the house, was there any other person present at the house when you left other than Kelsey and the defendant? A – No.

Q – When you arrived back at the house, what did you see? A – I see the First Responder and the ambulance.

Q – What did you do? A – All I remember was I turned in the driveway. And then the next thing I remember, I jump out of the truck and I see them hand Kelsey from one person to the other.

Q – When you say "from one person to the other," do you recall who these people were that – A – It was the ambulance and First Responders. I'm not sure who handed her to who.

Q – Fair enough. What did you do? A – I started screaming and asking what was wrong with my baby. And I was trying to get into the ambulance, and they wouldn't let me in.

Q – What happened next? A – And I kept screaming and telling them if she just hears my voice she'll be okay.

Q – At this point, Raye Dawn, had you had any – did you have any indication what had happened? A – No.

Q – What happened next? A – Then I wait and they're working on her. And I keep asking my mom, "Mom, what happened? What happened?" And all she said was – she just kept shaking her head. And then she said, "I guess she had a seizure."

Q – But at this point had any medical personnel apprised you of what was going on? A – No.

Q – What happened next? A – Then we stayed there for a while, and I also yelled and screamed that they need to get an ambulance – a helicopter in there. I said, "She needs to get taken to Children's." And then they said they had to get her to the nearest hospital as soon as possible.

Q – And did they do that? A – Yes.

Q – And where did they take her? A – They took her to [a nearby] Hospital.

Q – Now, when they transported her, where did you go? A – I rode in the passenger seat of the ambulance.

Q – The ambulance that Kelsey was in? A – Yes.

Q – Had you – from the time you got back to the house to the time you got into the ambulance, did you ever have any discussions with Mike Porter about what had happened or what was happening with Kelsey? A – No.

Q – What happened when you got to the hospital? A – They take Kelsey from the ambulance into the hospital, and we all stand outside and we wait. And then the next thing that I really remember is I heard a thud, and I look over and Mike Porter is laying on the ground.

Q – Is this outside in the parking lot? A – Yes.

Q – Were you ever apprised by any medical personnel about Kelsey? A – They –

[Mike Porter's attorney]: Objection: Hearsay.

The Court: If you'll wait, ma'am. Your objection is hearsay. [DA]?

[DA]: Not offered for the truth of the matter; offered to tell about what her reactions to it were.

The Court: It will be received for that purpose. You may answer the question.

A – Can you repeat the question? Q – Were you ever told by medical personnel at that time what was going on with Kelsey or what was wrong? A – They had just – one woman came out and told me that they were still working on her, but it wasn't looking good.

Q – Were you later apprised at any point that she had not lived? A – They told me later. I believe it was in one of the hallways.

Q – What did they say? A – I believe she said, "I'm sorry, but there's nothing we can do."

Q – Did you have an opportunity at the hospital, Raye Dawn, to discuss with Mike Porter what had happened? A – I didn't.

Q – When, if ever, did you ever have an opportunity to talk to the defendant about what had happened from the time you left the house to pick [Mike Porter's daughter] up until the hospital? A – Did you say when did I have the chance? Q – Yes, ma'am. A – The only chance I really had was whenever we left the hospital and went back to the house.

Q – When you left the hospital and went back, who did you ride with? A – I rode with Mike Porter.

Q – What was the tenor of that discussion? What was discussed in the car? A – I asked him – I said, "When did she get a Pull-Up on?"

Q – When did you notice – or did you notice that she – she being Kelsey – had a Pull-Up on? A – I noticed whenever I got out of the pickup that as they were handing her from one person to the other that had had one on.

Q – So you asked the defendant when she got a Pull-Up on? A – Yes.

Q – What was his response? A – He said, "I put it on her when I was waiting on the ambulance."

Q – Did you ask him why he did that? A – Yes.

Q – What was his response? A – He said that that's all he needed was for all them people to be coming up there and her not have any pants on. And I said, "I would have told them."

Q – Did he ever give you any explanation during that ride, or subsequently after that, for what had happened to Kelsey? A – No. He just said that she had a seizure.

Q – What did he tell you happened after you left the house? A – I'm sorry? Say that again.

Q – Did Mike Porter ever tell you what he said had happened after you left the house to go pick [Mike Porter's daughter] up? A – He just said that she – he walked in and she was having a seizure.

Q – Did he expound on that or give you much detail on that or is that all he told you? A – No. That was pretty much all he told me.

Q – You now know subsequently that [Kelsey's] had an autopsy to determine cause of death; correct? A – Yes, sir.

Q – When were you first made aware that that was a possibility, that the autopsy was a possibility? A – I learned that night at the hospital.

Q – Did you have any discussions or were you asked to permit the autopsy to be done? A – I believe so.

Q – Do you recall signing some paperwork to permit it? A – Yes.

Q – And you're the one that signed that; correct? A – Yes.

Q – Did you want an autopsy done, ma'am? A – Yes.

Q – For what reason? A – I wanted to know what was wrong with her.

Q – Did you ever have any discussions at the hospital with the defendant in regards to whether or not an autopsy should be done? A – Yes. At some point – I don't remember if it was before I had held her for the hour and a half or if it was after, but…

Q – Can I stop you there for just a second? A – Yes.

Q – When you say you held her, when was that? A – After she had died.

Q – Did the hospital allow you to hold her for a while? A – Yeah.

Q – I'm sorry. Go on. What was the discussion between you and the defendant? A – He asked me, he said, "They're not going to cut her open, are they?" And I said, "I have to know what was wrong with her."

Q – Okay. Raye Dawn, from the time you left – when you left the house to go pick [Mike Porter's daughter] up, was Kelsey alive? A – Yes, she was.

Q – Was Kelsey breathing? A – Yes, she was.

Q – Was there anything unusual about her that you noticed about her condition? A – No.

Q – When you left the house that day to go pick [Mike Porter's daughter] up, to your knowledge, had anyone abused her, hurt her, sexually abused her, or anything? A – No.

Q – At what point did Mike Porter become actively involved in yours and your children's life? Do you recall? A – It was pretty soon.

Q – Can you give us an estimate of when? A – It was before January.

Q – Prior to Mike Porter being involved in your life, had there ever been any DHS involvement or any injuries to Kelsey that you can recall? A – No.

Q – And, subsequently, there were several injuries and much DHS involvement; correct? A – Correct.

Q – Including a broken clavicle, bruising, and some broken legs; correct? A – Yes.

Q – Did all of that happen after Mike Porter was involved in your life? A – Yes, sir.

Q – And that would have been approximately January of 2005? A – Yes, sir.

DA: Nothing further, Judge.

After the hearing, Raye's attorney submitted the evidence that he did not present in court in an effort to spare the families from the added heartache. Although the judge stated that he would read through whatever was submitted after the hearing, it was apparent that he did not. He submitted his answer less than twenty-four hours after receiving the brief and the verdict was not good: Lance would get the entire settlement.

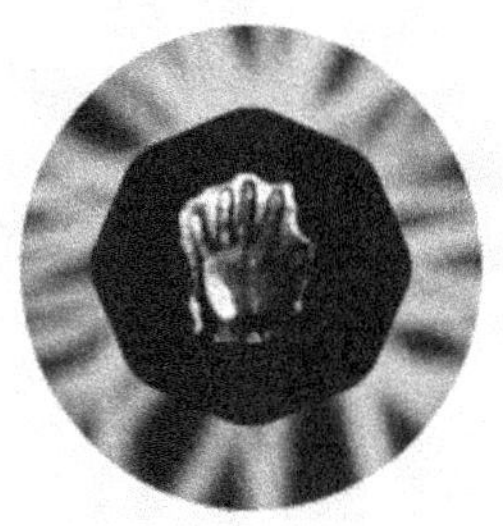

# 41 Stalker Blog and Book

"Only when we are no longer afraid do we begin to live."
~ Dorothy Thompson

My journey in helping Raye has been fraught with twists and turns, valleys and mountain tops. I've experienced emotional swings which had not entered into my previously-quiet existence. I was a committed work-a-holic writer and business owner who was fulfilled by being a mom and a wife. Not in a million years could I have imagined the stark difference becoming personally involved in this drama would make in my life in a matter of just a few months. In February of 2007, I had been clueless about anything having to do with Raye or Kelsey. On the single occasion I'd heard their names, I immediately dismissed them from my mind because I didn't have time to get involved in anything that didn't serve to help with the pending adoption or to better the lives of my family and the children in Mexico. Just one year later, the compassion I felt for a grieving family in need had put me in the line of fire of a gang of bullies on a mission and there was no escape.

My identity was discovered in March of 2008 and the claim was that it was revealed through "subpoenas," though several inquiries have turned up no existence of a single subpoena. At the time my identity was discovered, posts were made on Kelsey's Purpose as well as on other "bash boards" with not only my name, but my home address, business Web site address, picture, and the order, "go get her." Soon after these posts were made, bullet holes were discovered in my truck and then it was keyed. A few months later, my home was burglarized but nothing was taken. I started getting hang-up phone calls at the same time, and I have just recently started getting them again. *Coincidence?* Perhaps…

I was advised by Ursula, Kathie's best friend, that if Raye's Web site was removed, "all of this would go away." Otherwise, my name and reputation would be destroyed on the Internet and in the media…this is a threat they have attempted to carry out with a vengeance. The reasoning was presented that they could do more damage to me by destroying my business than by suing me. Her threat is as follows: "…From what I have been able to find out, you have nothing to compensate them if they do sue you. But...a couple of investigative stories published in the news will have such a lasting impact. Everytime someone 'searches' your name when looking for a writer, editor, or voice over...well guess what? It will pull up a link to the newstories too. Personally, I think that would do you greater monetary harm than sueing you. Legit people won't want to hire an editor or writer with so much negativity and controversy publicly displayed by that person who has continually trashed and disrespected the memory of a murdered, innocent child by posting the evil lies all over the web like you have done about Kelsey's paternal family. Did you forget that the Briggs really do have connections? Do you doubt that the reporter that you all trashed as being a drunk maybe wouldn't jump at the opportunity to do a story on the revealing of truthseekers identity with all the facts that have been twisted and altered by that person? and with the connection to Judge Key? ...You know something to put some thought into...you have stated on FKM that you aren't perfect...how much would someone find out on you to be splasing all over the internet if they decided to take the time to dig into YOUR past? You started this battle, you can end it. You started the websites, you can end them and all of this can go away."

Over the next two years, I struggled with emotionally shutting down; it was hard to handle such harsh assaults on my person and reputation, not to mention the suggested threats to me physically and my family, which also accompanied the experience. I quit Raye's family more than once, and I began to fear for my life with no help from authorities due to a lack of laws in Oklahoma that protect stalking victims.

Over the years, it seems that those who have threatened and harassed myself and others have continually projected their own actions onto me. I am now called vile names with evil descriptions and accused of multiple crimes of which I can only maintain my innocence. *How do you defend yourself from a non-event?*

In December of 2009, the bullies recruited someone who stated that she was going to contact all of my clients and tell them that I'm the devil. To show her support for the bullies, she threatened to add to the destruction of my business. "The devil..." *Who even thinks of something like that?*

Following are examples of some of the statements that were posted to me or about me at that time by a group of people that I have never met nor held a conversation with...to clarify, I have never met a single person who posts these comments about me. (I did not respond to any of the comments made, though it appears I had from the way their statements were phrased):

"I can be someones best friend or worst enemy...it all depends on how I am treated...I have access to amazing amount of information and ways to get it...you play in my life or that of my friends and I will play in yours..."

"Jody is the devil...My brother is looking into her online dealings...soon we will have answers and more evidence for my attorneys"

"If I ever find out who your stalker is, if you even have one...remind me to buy them dinner for making your life hell"

"You think your life is hell now..wait until you piss off the wrong person...A simple posting will be the least of your worries..."

"I'm done with you Jody Ortiz...You want to keep playing this game...Go ahead...You will have a miserable life...Your an evil woman and you know it...You're an empty woman. I'm sick of you and your boring...I may have wasted the last 2 weeks of my life on you and I wish I could get them back...I will not waste anymore time on you...your a pity....."

"I would feel sorry for you if you weren't so damn pathetic...Enjoy your sorry excuse of an existence..."

"Quit your sh*t Jody...Im not gonna hold your hand and make you feel all warm and fuzzy simply because your a coward piece of crap...You stalked and prey on peoples lives, like you did with Gayla...You two biotches deserve each other...I'm sick and tired of you crying like your the god damn victim..You brought this on yourself...Quit playing like you have no idea whats going on...You wanna play games...Now we are going to play games...Let's see how you like your own bullsh*t played back on you...Good luck finding where I or someone else post about you...Good luck with that..."

"Jody is a b!tch that takes pleasure in destroying lives...I take back my promise...I won't sink to her level...But when someone else does...I will celebrate and smile and laugh at Jody's misery..."

"This wench really thinks she is so smart...NOT... I would love to sit in a courtroom with Jody, to prove that all her lies are just that LIES..."

"I believe the facts in this case... Nothing More, Nothing Less.... You wanna believe your garbage and lies that is your problem... One you will live with for the rest of your sorry ass life... As for us being accused of breaking and entering into your home, shooting at your truck, and or keying your truck, well from where I live, that would be very hard to do... So maybe we aren't the only ones you have pissed off...I would check your enemy score card again...Oh and one more thing....The virus you gave the Organization that I am affilated with now has traced the virus back to where it came from... It is now in the our Legal Departments hands..... So you have not just messed with us as you call us, Kathie Groupies... You have now messed with an Organization, and one that has Lawyers who can have you tied up in civil litigation for the next 10 years.... So lets see, criminal activity, stalking, defamating ones character, posting on a public blog that people are who they are not...... NEED I SAY ANYMORE... On that note, a very wise lady once told me to never argue with idiots as they will only beat you with experience, and I tend to live my life these days to those words.....So this is the last post that I will address to any of Raye Dawn's Supporters....You [another Raye supporter] seem to come on here like a highschool girl with a score to settle... And a fight to cause... So here is one for you, if you want to fight so much, Stick your head up your ass and fight for air.... Cause your a waste of it just like Raye Dawn......"

That was it! I could take no more. The fear that had taken hold of my life since early 2008 was replaced by anger. I became sick of hiding from the bullies. I was no coward. I started writing this book and I started a blog. I was tired of being their victim. I was mad as hell and I was going to take back my life. My daughter and I watched the movie *Julie & Julia* and I was inspired. It was based on a true story of a woman who cooked and blogged her way through Julia Child's cookbook. In 365 days, she made over 500 recipes. I thought to myself, *I wonder how many days of blogging it will take to make the bullies go away?*

This all began because I was trying to find out the truth about a horrible crime and about the guilt or innocence of a young mother whom I researched while editing a book. I was an inquiring professional and somehow I had gotten pulled into a vast vacuum of insanity. ENOUGH!

On December 14, 2009 I posted a video I had just taken of a man in a truck who was parked outside my home watching me and I stated, "Hello world! I started this blog to document my daily struggles with ending the hate on the Internet. Let's see how many days it takes me to finally be heard. Day one: I'm shocked at how people can read something and take it as fact and then jump on the hate parade. Why do people think that toying with lives and picking apart details about people they know nothing about is fun? What is missing in their lives that they spend hours every day harassing and stalking people? Why won't the Web sites that allow the hate do anything about it? Last week I arrived home to find a truck parked across the street from my driveway. I questioned some men working next door, and the truck did not belong to them. As I walked back to my driveway, I could see the shadow of someone sitting in the truck, watching me. Was he taking pictures? Was it a scare tactic? Was he stalking me? Or was it someone casing the area for a future burglary? Daily, thoughts such as these go through my mind. Every engine noise, every stranger becomes someone suspicious. Two years ago I would have walked up to the truck and asked if the person needed help. Two years ago my gate was always open to visitors. Today, my gate is shut and locked with a variety of no trespassing signs greeting each possible visitor. Today, my life has changed."

My new blog was quickly found by my bullies and they started four of their own in answer to mine. Each day, I post on my blog, and they find something to harass me about on their respective blogs. Videos have been made about me; poems have been written; and a screenplay was said to be created about a paranoid writer who, of course, is murdered in the end. The torture is a game for them and one that, to this day, they are still playing.

Recently, Kelsey's paternal step-grandmother (Lance's now ex-wife's mother) began to question what she had been told about some of the facts in the case. In response, she and her daughter were viciously attacked.

She "friended" me on Facebook and soon received the following message from Lance, an echo of an ongoing warning for us all who dare speak the truth and question the facts in this case:

"I can't believe how fake you have been and you would stoop to the level of the Smiths. I don't think you wana open that can of worms. You are truly a dissapointment and acting no better than Gayla. Honestly, nobody cares about your opinion and you need to keep them to yourself. You and your entire family have never TRULY cared about Kelsey. Go on with your life and **keep your mouth Shut.**"[44]

[44] Emphasis by book author

# 42 Raye's Supporters

"Compassion is sometimes the fatal capacity for feeling what it is like to live inside somebody else's skin. It is the knowledge that there can never really be any peace and joy for me until there is peace and joy finally for you too."
~ Frederick Buechner

Raye's story would have never been told had it not been for the loving, selfless people who stepped up and lent their support. You know my story, now I present some of their stories:

**Hod from Texas: (***My replacement on the forum)*

I first heard about this case in August of 2007. I was sent a video message on myspace.com. I remember watching the video and thinking "how beautiful" Kelsey was. At the end of the video there was a website (Kelsey's Purpose) so I went there because I wanted to learn more. This was just about a month or so after Raye's trial, but before her sentencing and there was so much trash talk on this site that I originally thought was about helping children. I read a few of the posts. They were talking about how they couldn't believe that the "other" family had actually posted pictures of Mike Porter on their site.

Well naturally, I wanted to see what this monster looked like – so I headed on over to their site... I checked out the pictures they were talking about and read some of the posts. I admit that most of them were just supporters of Raye and family that seemed like they were just trying to sort out this whole mess and make sense of it. After sifting through both sites going back and forth – I originally felt that this mother didn't receive a fair trial. I wasn't quite ready to say that she was "innocent" – but it was quite obvious to an outsider that what we all think of and consider to be "fair and just" didn't happen in this trial – not by a long shot.

I then started communicating on a regular basis with friends and family through e-mail and phone conversations. I have always been amazed at how much of an open book they are. If I have a question, they answer it. If they don't know, they find it. Once I asked Gayla about the title to the car the Raye's sister owned (the one they described in the trial-but it was actually sold long before this witness ever remembered seeing it) – so Gayla got the information from the state on the sale. Then there was a time that I read through the trial notes and I noticed that in Raye's other sister's testimony she stated that on the day of their wedding they went to buy the rings – and I thought "Humm, how could that witness have seen a ring if there wasn't one?" So I ask about a receipt, and again Gayla goes digging and finds the receipt (and yes it was dated April 18, 2005) – what I'm getting at is that the family is open and tries to provide you with anything you want in an effort to get to the truth, they want the truth too!

I have been affected by the hate that is involved in being a "Raye" supporter. I have been publically ridiculed for my opinion on websites, blogs, & forums. My husband's business was even attacked at one point and all of business information posted stating something to the effect of "don't use this business because they support child killers"..that's not exact...although I'm sure that "Clay" could find, copy, and paste the exact post in two shakes of a lamb's tail...I've had to change my e-mail information, and I feel that I constantly have to watch my Facebook Account for those who might bash me and my family for who we support. I have been ridiculed and chastised for discussing my daughter's rape. I felt it was relevant because I was at home, I knew the neighbor, I always had a creepy vibe and "watched him" – but still she was lured, groomed, and then raped by him. I was just trying to make the correlation that sometimes as mothers we think that we know every single thing about our children but that is a false sense of security – because we don't. My daughter held on to her secret of being raped by the neighbor from the time she was 13 until she was 16. I was actually chastised and when my daughter tried to get involved she was chastised as well. I was told that we shouldn't be talking about it! I remember having a "forum" conversation about the fact that my daughter speaks openly and publically about her rape and that it is therapy for her, the people she speaks to and myself not to mention all of the counselors have encouraged it. But this group of women who are supposed to be child advocates – chose to chastise a child for standing up – what the hell?

The core of that group just has too much to hide. They act as if we all have some strategy, as if we are all sitting around a huge table having meetings about what and how we are going to make our next move – when all we are doing is supporting an innocent woman who has been open and honest about every aspect of her life from her childhood, to drinking, to drugs, and more. I just don't see this same honesty and openness coming from the Kathie side of this.

No, Kathie didn't kill or abuse Kelsey. No, Lance didn't abuse or kill Kelsey. I don't think they had a thing to do with it... but... I'm sure that shuffling Kelsey around like a deck of cards didn't make it obvious "where and when" she was being injured. To this day, no one can pinpoint where and when certain injuries occurred. Even the prosecutor's own witness was confused on the stand and he is supposed to be an "expert witness." I still don't understand how these charges were made to "stick." When you think of enabling abuse, you think of the mother who stood by and watched her child be drowned and beaten like the story of Baby Grace. You think of mothers who leave their children in the care of known drug dealers, wife abusers, or those who are always involved in domestic violence. You don't expect a woman to be arrested and convicted for leaving her child with her husband who had no criminal history, no mental or violent history, who appeared to be an all-around upstanding citizen with children of his own.

I am affected. My children are affected. This case has changed my life and altered how I feel about leaving my youngest child (now 9) with anyone. He goes with me everywhere now. No spending the night at his cousins, no spending the night at his grandma and grandpa's. I don't want my child hurt or worse and I certainly don't want to be put in prison for what I SHOULD HAVE KNOWN!!!

**Kylie from Australia**:

I was sent a video from an innocent friend who had forwarded it via Facebook from another innocent friend down the typical, e-mail chain line. The video depicted Raye as a monster and Mike Porter as a monster also. However, I found it EXTREMELY odd that the video was more so directed at Raye than the murderer. It didn't make any plausible sense to me whatsoever. I had never heard about this case prior to being sent this video.

The photo of Kelsey and her mother in that video showed a mother who dearly loved her child and a child who adored her mother. I immediately doubted the video in its entirety. From there I launched my own search on the web to ascertain the truth. The reason that I was so interested in Raye and her story was because my son was quite young when his father's parents attempted every trick in the book to have him taken from me via the Family Court in Australia; abuse, neglect, lie after lie, etc, etc. He was even abducted on three separate occasions by this family and it took police efforts to have him returned to me. Thankfully, the Court saw through all their lies and I have not heard from that family since.

The father of my son was a drug abuser and dead beat that didn't care about his own child and would break into my home even after we separated, steal money, trash my belongings, and assault me because as he put it "I deserved it." He served jail time for the continuous attacks. Lance, after my research, reminded me so much of my son's father with his abuse and lack of absence in his child's own life. I then and there had no doubt that there was more to this case. Therefore my initial reaction to the story sent to me about Raye was that I believed it to be absolutely ludicrous. There were too many discrepancies, simple as that. And I had already lived that life myself, I was much wiser in the ways of the world and how families repeat the same process of hate time and time again, regardless of where you live on this earth.

I only learned about the other side when I met friends on Facebook who had befriended Raye's profile as I had out of genuine concern for her well-being. Some of the abuse was absolutely unbelievable. Here we are supporting this woman, and here are a bunch of strangers spewing vendettas and hate and intimidating threats. From my own experience Kathie's Web site appears to have the mere purpose of training up cyberbullies, nothing more. 'Feed The Stranger Lies, Let The Hate Breed.' That would be a more appropriate slogan for that site.

I have seen with the hate that there is no room for constructive arguments. Those bullies are not interested in conversing and discussing a topic at a mature, adult level. Instead their remarks are hateful, spineless and hurtful, and that is putting it nicely. They have all simply been brainwashed with the limited information they have ingested and refused to read anymore.

The hate has affected me to the mere point of anger and frustration that individuals believe the media and their portrayal of an innocent woman as a monster. A photo of a child being taken with a so called 'reputable' journalists for the paternal family and stating, "Here is one our biggest fans" as the caption under the photo. How do you justify a child as a fan when another child has died to merely endorse this image, what does that young child actually know? How can you justify lies as credible news? It makes you sick to the stomach when adults can influence children and the media can do it to the masses.

I have been attacked via the web, I have been sent abusive e-mails stating things such as “Found you, watch your back bitch” “Are you scared now? You should be? I know where you live” “She killed that kid, you should be ashamed of yourself, you’re dead” “You are just like her, you sick freak.” I also note that e-mail accounts have been corrupted and simple words of support have been laid to bare on the web for others to devour and change them to their own accord. I have also attempted to converse on a mature level with people from the other side only to have my words misconstrued and made fun of with detrimental abuse.

What do you say about a wave of constant haters that have not ONCE completely reviewed the facts? What can you say other than shake your head and wonder why there is so much hate for Raye who attempted to do everything right for her lovely, angelic daughter and yet a pedophile and murderer is not given a second thought in this hateful campaign? How does that work? It doesn’t. I didn’t realize witch hunts still existed in modern times, I guess I was wrong. I pity the sheep that follow the misguided flock, I really do. I believe that if there were a truthful media outlet out there that would show the world the truth then things would change rapidly for Raye for the better and hopefully Mike Porter would be convicted of murder and as a pedophile. (If only a media outlet like that existed – no ratings for the truth - but time for a super amount for B.S. though.) I intend to stand behind that woman until she is free. That is my strongest and sincerest belief that Raye is innocent and deserves freedom.

**Christine from the UK**:

The case was brought to my attention by a member of my family posting it on a social networking site. She posted a video and I watched it. My initial reaction was "how could anyone do such a thing to such a beautiful child". Me being me decided to look further and watched video after video on YouTube, delving deeper and deeper with each one. I soon realised that what I had seen in the beginning was only the tip of the iceberg and that there was much more to this story than I first thought.

As I delved deeper, I found all the court papers and autopsy reports and gradually formed the opinion that the paternal family had so much hate for Raye that they were willing to go to any lengths to hurt her so, therefore, there was definitely a lot more to this story. I couldn't believe that the 'family' were able to e-mail the person who was alleged to be responsible for little Kelsey's death. I don't know where else that would have been tolerated so to that end it seemed that anything would go to make sure they had Raye put in prison. The length of time, however, was unbelievable. I really found it hard to accept that no-one seemed to see what the paternal family was doing and that everything they did then and do now is one huge cover-up. At least that's what it looks like from where I am sitting.

I encountered some opposition on one of the sites on the social networking site from one particular person. I don't even think this person knows either family but because I disagreed with her she called me various names. One of the words began with C and she also called me a hag. I deleted them soon after. Other than that I have tried not to get into arguments with anyone because I think it is counter-productive.

My thoughts about the hate - I just don't know why they hate her so much. She loved that little girl. A mother who dresses her child beautifully and goes to great lengths to make her look pretty and to take so many lovely pictures of her couldn't possibly have changed virtually overnight. Those are the things that I did with my only little girl and I adored her. All the things she was asked to do by the Authorities and the medical people, she did so on the face of it, it seems that they couldn't stand the thought of Raye divorcing Lance.

My current belief is that Raye should get a retrial as the one she had was so full of holes but I don't think it should be in Oklahoma. Where? I don't know. I just don't think she had any idea what was going on at all as I think she was so ground down by everything that was going on around her all the time with the paternal family she was very vulnerable.

This case has dominated my thoughts for months now. Perhaps because I have a daughter the same age as Raye and two granddaughters 2 and 4. Luckily their situation is not the same but "there by the grace of God go any of us". I wish Raye well in the future and hope her family can get some peace.

**Wendy from Idaho** (*Charity to me*):

I came upon this case on a memorial Web site. I was reading the bio/description and truly found it quite confusing. So I was compelled to search for more information. This led me to Raye's website. I checked every single piece of information I could find - this included any website including those set up by the paternal family, et al. I came to my own conclusion, believing that Raye is not only wrongfully convicted, but has received an excessive prison sentence and was in fact railroaded into prison to satisfy the vindictiveness and anger of her ex in-laws and their family. Everything about this case reeks of injustice. Not only to Kelsey, but all parties involved. I was completely surprised that this could happen in America. That the media played a significant role was interesting to me. It has redefined my perception of the criminal justice system in America. I have great empathy for the maternal family and the lack of concern of all parties involved in their blatant disregard of the feelings of this family.

I have attempted on several occasions to create a dialogue/discussion with the paternal family's supporters based on factual information. Instead of dialogue, I am attacked, harassed, name called - it is behind my back, in front of face. They have composed blogs about me, told me I will "go to hell," told me I am "unGodly," criticized my very core beliefs and values, called into play my relationships with others that they have no knowledge of, threatened me repeatedly, threatened to sue me...it is endless. What I think is interesting is that I am simply expressing the facts as I know them. I have tried repeatedly to use restraint. I have attempted to try to see things from their perspective. Nothing seems to work. They remind me of a pack of insecure wolves - no self-esteem. They achieve comrade and hierarchy in maintaining a relationship with the "ring leader" Kathie and this relationship provides them with validation and a feeling that they are part of a "family" out to save the world from Raye. It is so disturbing to me that I think one could actually write a dissertation on it and study the effect this "pack" mentality has on simple rational and logical decision-making. There is disregard for any feelings I may have. They have no sense of empathy or humanity - only as it relates to fulfilling an agenda set forth by their leader, Kathie. I have never even heard some of the offensive language they have used against me from anywhere or anyone else in my life. It has been a huge eye opener and has affected my ability to trust anyone on the internet anymore. As time has passed, I engage less and less because I see it has no value except to rile the hornet's nest and allow them to accumulate more nasty stuff to use to say that I am in fact a bad person. They justify everything they do!

I think these people suffer from some sort of inability to be rational. Their sense of humanity is askew. In fact, most that I have engaged with have serious drug addiction or mental health issues and actually identify with the characters in this case. There seems to be transference in many ways - people advocating for Kathie have been abused or have abused their own children, and operate on anger and resentment and become the victim--thinking they are in fact Kelsey and speak for her and her family. It is as though they believe they are in fact a *part of this family*. It is bizarre to say the least. In getting any sort of attention, their insecurities are fed on some level and they feel more and more powerful to act in any way they believe. Haphazardly - much like Kathie. It is an illogical and uneducated approach and my guess is that most of them lack a formal education. I find them distasteful and their Carte Blanche is to create pain, distribute tales and lies, hurt Raye and her entire family and any one is fair game - no matter who they are, who chooses to advocate for her. They have no democracy. It is a dictatorship led by Kathie and fueled and fed by the likes of the central hateful characters of her posse with no conscious. All under a thin veil of advocating for poor wee Kelsey - this beautiful child they call their own.

**Holly from Tennessee**:

I came across this story in August of 2008 when someone sent me a link to a video on Facebook. Seeing the beautiful picture of the little girl that was with the link I had to go and check it out. As soon as I watched the first minute of the video I knew something bad had happened to this beautiful little angel named Kelsey after about 3 minutes into the video I could tell just by the way the video was set up she had been abused and died as a result of abuse. When I had finished the video I was so upset and crying I almost had to leave work (work is where I was when I watched it) that was on a Friday. I went home and could not get beautiful little Kelsey out of my mind. I was filled with so much anger towards her mother Raye, her stepfather Mike Porter and the judge and had so much sympathy for her paternal grandmother Kathie and her father Lance and could not believe this was so I thought at the time let to happen. As hard as I tried I could not stop thinking about her. I told everyone about this awful video I had seen and every time I would talk about Kelsey I would start to cry. I thought to myself there has got to be more to this story. I have got to see how this happened. So this is how my research into this story began. I Googled everything in reference to her and quickly learned I was completely wrong about my first reaction to Kelsey's mother Raye, because I just kept thinking how could this mother have let this happen?

I learned that Kathie and Lance are not the grandmother and father they have everyone to believe. As a matter of fact, the only thing that was true was Mike Porter was a monster who killed little Kelsey and he had everyone, I mean everyone, fooled. I learned that Raye actually loved Kelsey very much and did everything she could to protect her. Raye was so busy having to defend herself against Kathie and her false accusations about Raye and trying to keep Kelsey out of dhs custody because of Kathie that Mike Porter slipped in completely undetected and abused and killed

Kelsey...now Raye sits in prison wrongfully convicted for another person's crime.

In January of 2009 I decided I had to go to Oklahoma. I had spoken to Jody Ortiz who set the trip up and made arrangements for us to stay with Raye's cousin. I could not believe how they were so open to welcome complete strangers into their home, considering all they had been through. While I was there, I felt as if I were part of the family. Everyone was so loving and caring. Everyone was so close. All you could feel was love. With my research and my visit, it was confirmed Raye did not belong in prison and I would do what I could to support her. I also met several other members of her family, including Raye's mother, and my heart broke for them as they would fight to get Raye out of prison.

While I was in Oklahoma, I attended a hearing. The paternal family and a few of their supporters were there and Kathie looked even more evil in person. During testimony Kathie never shed one tear. Lance taunted Raye. I could not believe what I was seeing from that side. Everyone seemed so cold. When Raye testified, she could recall every detail in reference to Kelsey. She cried a lot and everyone on the maternal side was crying, including me and my friend who made the trip with me.

I support Raye. She needs to be free so she can talk about her tragic story and help other women and their children. I believe Kathie did not really care to hear the truth about Kelsey. I believe Kathie wanted Raye in prison so badly she was willing to go to any lengths to do that and I know Kathie is enjoying the fame and financial gain she is receiving due to Kelsey's tragic death. Raye told Kathie she forgave her. I just wonder if little Kelsey will too.

**Marsha from Missouri**:

I heard about the case from Raye's sister. She is married to my brother.

The night Kelsey died I was at my mother's and my brother called and told us Kelsey had passed away. Initially, everyone thought it was seizures. We knew that Kelsey was having some medical issues and that Raye was taking her to the doctor all the time to see what was going on. Therefore, when we received the news that Kelsey was gone; we were devastated. In the weeks ahead my brother would give us updates. We were not surprised to hear that Mike Porter was being investigated for Kelsey's death because of the way he was acting at the hospital the night Kelsey died. Mike Porter was the most emotional and was faint like with the news of Kelsey's death.

Further, at no point did I ever believe that Raye abused Kelsey or knew about the abuse. The Raye I know was taking her child to the doctor 18 times in a 4/month period to see what was going on with her. And something else I would like to point out - A child Kelsey's age has some vocabulary skills, however, not enough to express to her mother that she was being abused by Mike Porter.

I heard about the other side from my brother and sister-in-law. I have never been personally attacked by them, but I see what hate can do to innocent individuals. Raye is in prison because of hate. The mass media has no regard for the 'real truth'. The media has blatantly turned a deaf ear to the truth while pointing a finger at Raye because 'she should have known'. What about the doctors that initially diagnosed Kelsey with seizures? Shouldn't they have known? What about DHS; they talked to and saw Kelsey everyday. Shouldn't they have known?

This has saddened our family because we love my sister-in-law; therefore, we hurt for her as she grieves the loss of her precious niece, Kelsey and the incarceration of her baby sister Raye.

Constant hate shifts blame. Therefore, if hate continues to live, grow and fester then no one will look at the 'real truth' or the real killer or real abuser(s). The ones spewing the hate wants no attention drawn to them because they are afraid of what may come out...therefore, constant hate shifts blame.

**Laura from the UK**:

I first heard about the case via a YouTube video, I came across it accidently. The video was entitled 'The True Kelsey Story (original),' the video really touched me and I couldn't stop watching it. I couldn't understand how a mother could sit and watch while her child was being abused, as the video led you to believe this is what happened. I watched more videos and began to come across photo's of Kelsey with a woman, in the photo's Kelsey was always beaming away, so was the woman. I soon discovered that the woman in the photo with Kelsey was in fact her mother. Alarm bells started to ring in my head. I'd been led to believe that Kelsey's mother was neglectful, someone who didn't care about their child but only themselves, but here were photos of a mother and daughter as happy as can be, the love really did shine through and I didn't see a mother who would sit by and let her child be killed. I saw a mother more proud of her baby than anyone could be, a mother deeply in love with her child.

I started to look further, I came across videos by FreeKelseysmom, they told a different story and unlike the first video I had viewed, these videos had reference to official documents. I also visited the FreeKelseysmom website where I could read the official documents for myself. I then joined the forum, and it was here that I discovered the level of hate that there was for people who were speaking up for the truth. I was also shocked to find out how influential the media was on the case. I'm from the UK and over here things are done slightly differently. Our news reporters report from an unbiased view point, they tell a story and that's it. They don't add their opinion on the case to the report.

I've never come across such hate as I have in the last few years, not only for Raye, but for her family as a whole, for Jody Ortiz, and for anyone who dare speak the truth, (including myself). I've seen people directly threatened, belittled, called names, abused, you name it. I myself have been threatened a number of times, at one time I was told 3 lawyers were coming after me (of course lies), but this is done to anyone who speaks up, they are threatened, so they will keep their mouths shut. I've always believed it's important to stand up for what you believe. I think you can have a fair debate with someone, but fair doesn't mean anything to some people... a number of women decided to have an argument with me over my Degree. According to them I couldn't possibly have the Degree I said I did, and they also stated (even though they've never met me) that I wasn't competent enough to do my job as a nanny... why is this relevant to anything? Why is what I do relevant to Raye and Kelsey? It's not, but this is another tact they do, put down someone's life to make them go into hiding. I'm often called a liar and a coward. When I ask them to prove the lies I've told, they cannot, and I'm no coward. But nothing I've faced can compare to what my friend Jody Ortiz has faced. She has lived in fear because of the hate. She's had her home broken into, her car keyed, and numerous threats on the internet, all because she stands up for Raye and reveals the liars for what they are. The way I look at it is for years people have been trying to silence Jody, now if she was a liar as many claim she is, surely they'd let her run with what she had to say, then come back and show her lies...but they can't do that, because Jody doesn't tell lies, and that's the point, people want to silence her because she speaks the truth.

As for the Hate I don't think there is anything anyone can do about it. For some it seems that is all they are all about. There are people out there who have online blogs, and all they do on them is talk about others. I've refused to communicate with one such woman, she spends her time attacking anyone who supports Raye, immediately they are liars, and this is what she does? I'm doing this to help Raye, I want people to see the truth out there, as many of us do, we have a purpose. But I can't see the purpose of those attacking us for our beliefs, I don't get it, and I don't think I ever will.

**Emily from Pennsylvania**:

I first learned of Kelsey in September of 2009. A friend has posted a video of her story to my Facebook page. It was the video most commonly viewed. It was heartbreaking. After crying for what seemed like forever, I became very angry at who could do this to such a perfect child.

After all the years of working with children, for some reason, this story stuck with me. I started doing some research and found more than I ever bargained for. I spent weeks reading website, blogs, official documents, and talking to anyone I could connect with about Kelsey's story. I realized that the circulated video that has been watched by millions does not portray the true story and is not based on fact. I came to believe that while Kelsey's story is tragic, her mother, Raye, is innocent.

It did not take long for me to realize that most people do not agree with my opinion. My opinion is based on fact and research and was not formed lightly or quickly. What I did not realize is that putting my opinion in a public place (such as Topix or Facebook) would open me up to harassment, bullying, threats, intimidation and false allegations. All of these activities have taken place over the internet, in cyber world. Many of these people hide behind screen names and say things I can't believe they would ever say to me in person. None of them know me or anything about my life. Instead of engaging in any sort of adult dialogue, they would send me e-mails calling me names and insulting my intelligence. I suppose compared to others, I have had it easy. Before I had even spoken with people involved in this story, I read the words of these cyberbullies. They were vicious and vile. There were not seeking justice for a little girl rather going after anyone who dared speak out in defense of Raye. They went after Kelsey's maternal family, friends, supporters, saying whatever they wanted, and with a vengeance. There were no limits and no boundaries. With this type of behavior, no one is held accountable for their actions. They can say whatever they want about whomever they want and damn the consequences. As an adult, I accept responsibility for my actions and words. This is a lesson these folks could learn from.

**Lysa**:

In late September, 2007, I had a MySpace account and my cousin's wife had sent a bulletin about child abuse and "Clay's" video for Kelsey was at the bottom. I watched it and fell madly in love with this sweet little angel. It broke my heart to see that she was abused and killed. At first, I believed that the paternal family was trying to help get justice for Kelsey and that Raye was an evil and cruel woman. I then joined the Kathie forum and talked to Kathie a few times. The times I did talk to her, she told me very brief versions of different events but couldn't get her dates straight, though I didn't realize that at the time as I didn't know the maternal family's side of the story.

However, soon, I found out that she'd e-mailed Mike Porter and met with him. When I saw the e-mails, I read them and was sickened that this woman I'd thought so highly of (and thought was genuinely out to protect children) was such a cold and vile woman. I then went to the Free Kelsey's Mom site and read up on the maternal family's side of the story. I was truly impressed. Not only did they tell detailed versions of incidents that occurred during Kelsey's last nine months, but they had correct dates and none of their stories had holes in them, unlike Kathie's. So, I told Kathie I no longer wanted to be in a forum that supports sick people like her. I couldn't believe she was able to keep people so brainwashed for so long. Since then, every time there's something new that comes out, it's almost always in Raye's favor and just proves to me that she was unfairly treated and definitely wrongfully convicted.

I've been lucky enough to not have been bothered by anyone in the paternal family or anyone who follows them. It breaks my heart that they threaten and destroy (or attempt to destroy) other's lives just because they want the truth out whereas the paternal family wants nothing but lies out simply because they hate Raye. What really upset me is when I realized that the only reason Kathie wanted Raye in prison is because Lance had a lawsuit against DHS that would get him $15 million and Raye would've been entitled to half of it. Being a money hungry type of person that Kathie is, she didn't want Raye to have any of it. In my opinion, that'd be the perfect motive for someone to be put in prison. I firmly believe no one in the paternal family ever cared about or loved Kelsey. Kelsey had to have felt that too, since she cried whenever she had to visit with them and was so miserable when Kathie had custody of her. I truly hope that Raye gets a new trial and is released. She deserves nothing less; especially after all she's been through.

**Gayla's cousin (Someone posing as Gayla's cousin on the Internet):**

On May 5, 2008, the following message was posted on a public forum using Gayla's cousin's name:

"This mother could not help her daughter because she was too stuck on herself. She was a horrible mother to Kelsey. She wanted a man to support her so badly so she wouldn't have to work. She manipulated him to buy her own mothers home in her name when she didn't even have a job and had never held down a job that paid more than miniumum wage. She is a conniving manipulating B! It's too bad that she didn't get life in prison. That's what she deserves. She doesn't deserve to EVER get out of prison. What's more, her mother and grandmother have NOT sold their houses to finance Raye Dawn's attorney. They are asking for the public to support their daughter/granddaughter. Her grandmother has even bought another house with the money that people have donated. Don't be fooled by these manipulating women. They are just out for your money and always have been. Meeker ran two of them out of town, just one more to go."

In response, Gayla's cousin had this to say, "It's shocking, frustrating and a horrible violation of my privacy for anyone to use my name to defile my own family! I have the deepest respect for my aunt (Raye's grandmother) one of the finest, Christian salt-of-the-earth women I've ever known and who also happens to make the best fried potatoes and pinto beans I can remember, not to mention her signature pineapple cream pie and mile high meringue. And my closest cousin, Raye's mother and I grew up together swapping late night secrets, spending our days making forts in the hay barn and exploring together on their dairy farm near our home town. I was a 'town' girl and learned a lot about life on their farm. Gayla, Raye's mom, looked out for me all through junior high and school and has remained a loyal friend all these years. Since I moved away at a young age, I didn't get to know her children as well as I would have liked, but she kept me posted about her daughter Raye's accomplishments, a darling, beautiful and talented girl--truly the apple of her daddy's eye. I was always so impressed with Gayla's commitment to motherhood-always doing her best for all her kids, even her stepchildren and later for her grandchildren. I'm so thankful to have the family and the upbringing I had. It has served me well through some tough times in my life. While Raye made the mistakes of marrying two lousy husbands and living in a state that takes particular pleasure in punitive action toward women, she never deserved to serve a day incarcerated in prison. This is a travesty from day one. God bless us all...until justice is truly served."

**Raye's family (*Written by another one of Gayla's cousins and my dear friend, Sherri*)**:

The words that come to most of us (the family) are fear, anger, confusion, sadness, dishonesty, deception, disillusioned, disabled, disappointment, disheartened...

The events of the past six years from the time of the first allegations of child abuse were made toward Raye about Kelsey have been life changing for most in our family. Some have never been in a court room; others couldn't even imagine the thought of the Department of Human Services being involved with the family. Child abuse or really any abuse of any sort had never happened in this family like it has been presented the past six years. Many know us, who we are, where we come from and how we live. The thought that came rushing in our minds was "How can this be happening?"

Our grandparents grew up here and made a home for the family. Most of the maternal side of Raye's family stayed in this area, most of the paternal side of Raye's family reside either in Kathie's small town or nearby. We became part of our schools and community. We participated in the parades and elections. We attended church and sang in the choir. We volunteered when needed. We had jobs and businesses in the community. Many have served in our Country's military. The people of our small town knew and still know who we are and what kind of family this is. Kelsey was a part of this family. How can such allegations and torment happen against us? It is something that none of us understand because we can't even comprehend or believe that people can really be like that to smear our reputation and create an abused situation for Kelsey. None of us could ever create a 'blog' on the world wide internet and bash a 99 year old great grandmother or a 74 year old aunt of someone's family. Innocently we walked into an unknown world of hate and deception as they used Kelsey as the pawn--something that this family has prided themselves to not ever encounter. Honesty, hard-working, and God-loving are how we were nurtured from previous generations and how we nurture our future generations. One thing that this whole ordeal has created in this family is a sense of fear and a loss of trust in others. Once, we were very naive about those around us and trusted the good we saw in people, accepting people for where they are and move forward. We can't do that anymore thanks to those who have exploited Kelsey's memory and story with lies and false allegations against Raye and her family. We trust no one. We lock our car doors when we go in at our town's post office and Dollar General Store. We scan the parking lot when we go to the grocery store to see how many 'pink stickers' are on the cars. We look down the waiting line at the check out to see if we recognize anyone with a pink Kathie t-shirt on. We don't go to parades like we use to. We are quiet and stay to ourselves. We don't linger in town because we might be blamed as stalking or following someone. We can't go to community events without the police following us because someone told them we may be a threat to the event. Why? Why do we feel like we are being watched or someone always looking for us? It's because of the fear that we have never faced before. A fear that we don't know how to fight or cure. No matter what we do, say or how we approach this, it is always turned and hurts Kelsey's memory and Raye with her case. We feel that if we just keep quiet, then 'they' won't have anything to use against Raye and help protect Kelsey from being the poster child for child abuse. It hasn't worked. The hate campaign that has been created for Raye over the last five years has only grown. She is in prison for 27 years with no parole! What more do they want from her or her family? Blogs, Facebook pages, books, fliers, events, rallies, posters, stickers, signs, t-shirts all spread the hate for Raye and the family with the untrue stories and not what really happened to Kelsey. We take it personally when it's one of our own. We support Kelsey and will do anything to help the truth be known. Being hated from people we don't even know or have ever dealt with is a struggle to handle day after day. How do you learn to live a life while looking behind your shoulder? How do you forgive?

Through all this, our family has gained many good things, not just the bad, but truly good. We keep Kelsey's memory of who she really was close to our hearts. God has blessed our family with the gift of friends and good people that cross our paths. Our faith has grown in spite of the hate that grows. We have found our strength in God's love. We have our faith and our hope through our places of worship. We have the knowledge of what is right and good and what is wrong and evil. We have all drawn closer to our God knowing that all of this is in His hands. We do what we can and what we know is right. Keeping our integrity that God has nurtured in us all these generations, we will prevail and overcome. God promises it to his children.

The words that come to most of us (the family) are: Forgiveness, Trust in God, Hope, Love, Helping others, Understanding, Truthfulness, Joy, Prayer.....

# Conclusion

"You have your way. I have my way. As for the right way, the correct way, and the only way, it does not exist."
~ Friedrich Nietzsche

Raye is patiently waiting for an answer to her appeal. I no longer visit her at the prison. We've yet to get back to work on her book due to concerns with an ongoing issue of disappearance of letters and e-mail tampering.

Gayla is still being accused of various crimes, including murder and conspiracy to murder, though no investigations of these alleged crimes have ever taken place, except on the "bash boards," and no charges have ever been filed.

For more information and updates on the case, go to www.FreeKelseysmom.com.

# Epilogue

**"If" by Rudyard Kipling**

If you can keep your head when all about you
Are losing theirs and blaming it on you;
If you can trust yourself when all men doubt you,
But make allowance for their doubting too;
If you can wait and not be tired by waiting,
Or, being lied about, don't deal in lies,
Or, being hated, don't give way to hating,
And yet don't look too good, nor talk too wise;
If you can dream - and not make dreams your master;
If you can think - and not make thoughts your aim;
If you can meet with triumph and disaster
And treat those two imposters just the same;
If you can bear to hear the truth you've spoken
Twisted by knaves to make a trap for fools,
Or watch the things you gave your life to be broken,
And stoop and build 'em up with wornout tools;
If you can make one heap of all your winnings
And risk it on one turn of pitch-and-toss,
And lose, and start again at your beginnings
And never breathe a word about your loss;
If you can force your heart and nerve and sinew
To serve your turn long after they are gone,
And so hold on when there is nothing in you
Except the Will which says to them: "Hold on";
If you can talk with crowds and keep your virtue,
Or walk with kings - nor lose the common touch;
If neither foes nor loving friends can hurt you;
If all men count with you, but none too much;
If you can fill the unforgiving minute
With sixty seconds' worth of distance run -
Yours is the Earth and everything that's in it,
And - which is more - you'll be a Man my son!

# Appendix A

Kelsey – The two-year-old girl who was sexually assaulted and murdered in 2005

Raye – Kelsey's Mommy

Gayla – Raye's mom and maternal grandmother to Kelsey

Lance – Kelsey's biological father

Mike Porter – Kelsey's step-father who was charged with Kelsey's murder and sexual assault and then met with and conversed with Kathie and her daughters in an effort to frame Raye – He was allowed to plead to 30 years for enabling child abuse, is protected in an out-of-state prison, and will never have to register as a sex offender

Kathie – Lance's mother and ex-mother-in-law to Raye

Royce – Lance's stepfather and Kathie's husband

April – Kelsey's step-mother

Susan – April's mother

Jack – April's stepfather

Mildred – Raye's maternal grandmother and Kelsey's great-grandmother – She was repeatedly attacked and harassed by Kathie and her supporters immediately following her great-grandchild's death

Whit – The first Raye supporter who came to my rescue

Matt Byers – The police officer who has been ridiculed for his investigations of Kelsey's case due to his desire to charge Kathie with stalking Raye

Judge Craig Key – The Judge who wrote a book about the facts in Kelsey's case almost two years after her death

Wilma – Lance's older sister

Rita – Lance's sister

Ursula – Kathie's closest friend and the person who originally attempted to blackmail me and who threatened me. She has made good on her threats with an ongoing assault against me and my character

Ms. Follett – Kathie's reporter/friend who posted notes online every day of Raye's trial

Ms. Ballard – Kathie's reporter/friend who had Thanksgiving dinner with her

Celia – The juror who joined Kathie's gang immediately after Raye's trial which she treated casually as she listened to testimony wrapped in a NASCAR blanket and then spoke in an interview immediately following Raye's trial with information not presented in court

Katrina – The juror who, according to witnesses, watched television, discussed the case, and researched it online during the trial

Fog – The juror who slept throughout Raye's trial

# Appendix B

Exhibit 1- Repair order for Mike Porter's truck after August, 2005 accident:

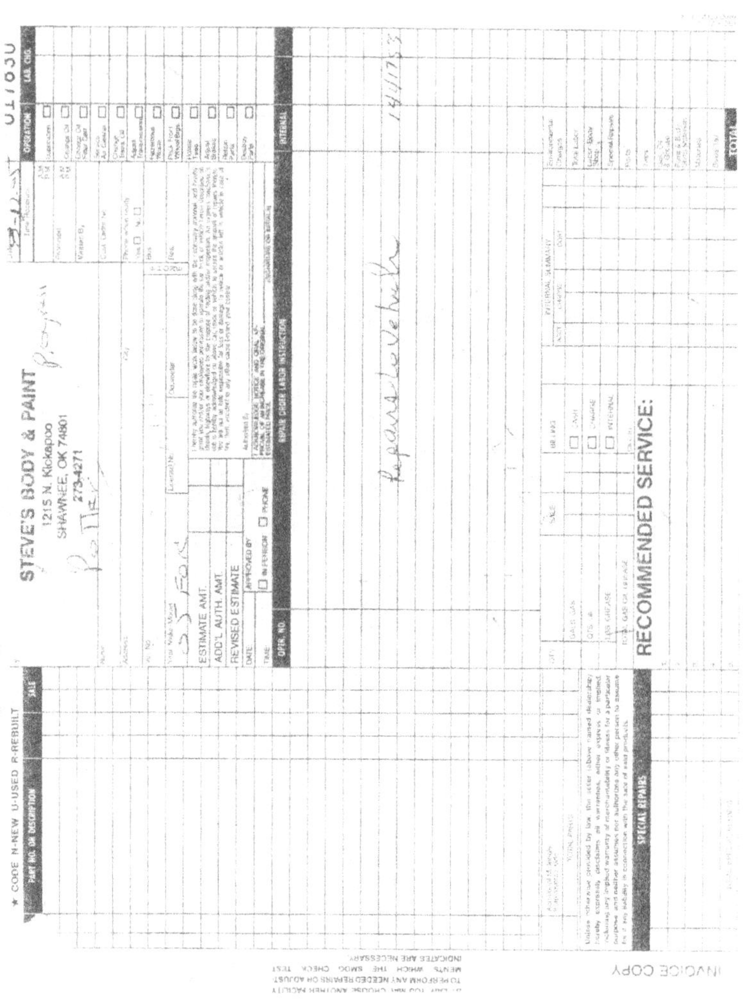

017630

STEVE'S BODY & PAINT
1215 N. Kickapoo
SHAWNEE, OK 74801
273-4271

★ CODE N-NEW U-USED R-REBUILT

PART NO. OR DESCRIPTION | SALE

OPERATION | LAB. CHG.

ESTIMATE AMT.
ADD'L AUTH. AMT.
REVISED ESTIMATE
DATE | APPROVED BY
TIME | IN PERSON | PHONE

OPER. NO. | REPAIR ORDER LABOR INSTRUCTION | INTERNAL

Repairs to vehicle

CASH
CHARGE
INTERNAL

GALS. GAS
QTS. OIL
LBS. GREASE
TOTAL GAS OIL GREASE

SPECIAL REPAIRS

RECOMMENDED SERVICE:

TOTAL

INVOICE COPY

Exhibit 2 - Mike Porter's user account on Kelsey's Purpose:

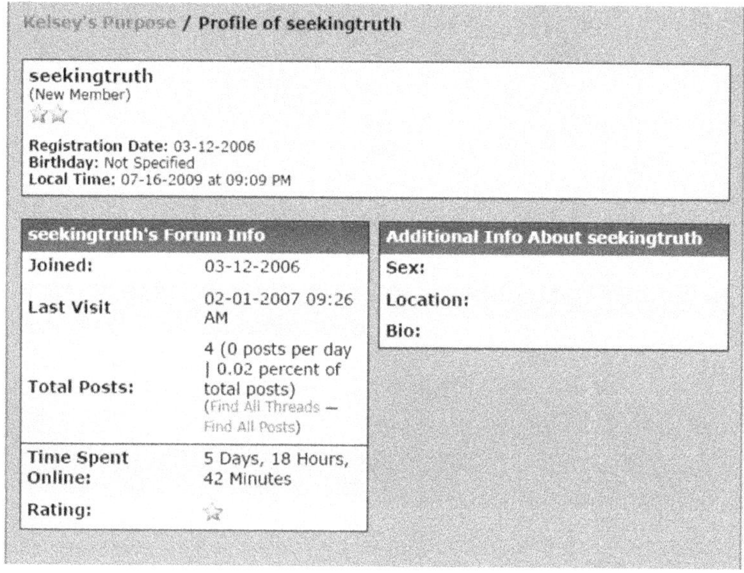

Kelsey's Purpose / **Profile of seekingtruth**

**seekingtruth**
(New Member)

**Registration Date:** 03-12-2006
**Birthday:** Not Specified
**Local Time:** 07-16-2009 at 09:09 PM

| seekingtruth's Forum Info | |
|---|---|
| Joined: | 03-12-2006 |
| Last Visit | 02-01-2007 09:26 AM |
| Total Posts: | 4 (0 posts per day \| 0.02 percent of total posts) (Find All Threads — Find All Posts) |
| Time Spent Online: | 5 Days, 18 Hours, 42 Minutes |
| Rating: | |

| Additional Info About seekingtruth |
|---|
| Sex: |
| Location: |
| Bio: |

Exhibit 3 - Kathie Briggs deposition, 2009, admits to giving up visits with Kelsey (read depositions at www.RayeDawnSmith.com):

she was convicted that your family would now receive the entire $15 million as opposed to just half?

A No.

Q Would it surprise you to know that we have witnesses that say that you did just that?

A Yes, I would.

Q Did you e-mail Debra Nguyen on September 6, 2005, and tell her that none of your family would be present at the September 8th hearing or at any more supervised visits with Kelsey?

A Yes.

Q So you did have supervised visits with Kelsey, didn't you?

A In May, not after June.

Q Why would you be writing her in September that you would not be at any more of the supervised visits, then?

A They allowed Ashley to have a couple of supervised visits at the DHS office and said I was welcome to come if I wanted to.

Q And why didn't you come?

A Because I didn't -- they were not reporting accurately what happened in those visits.

Q What were they reporting?

A They were stating -- they were not telling the positive things. They would say Kelsey would bite and hit, which she did, but they wouldn't tell what she did in the other visits.

Q So instead of seeing your granddaughter, you chose -- instead of dealing with what DHS was saying and seeing your granddaughter, you chose not to see her; is that correct?

A Not under supervised conditions.

Q How is it you are affiliated with the Concerned Citizens of the 23rd Judicial District?

A I don't know what you mean.

Q Well, are you familiar with that organization?

A No.

Q Are you familiar with the ad they published in the newspaper encouraging Smothermon to charge Raye Dawn?

A I know who those people are, but it wasn't me.

Exhibit 4 - Kelsey's Purpose pamphlet:

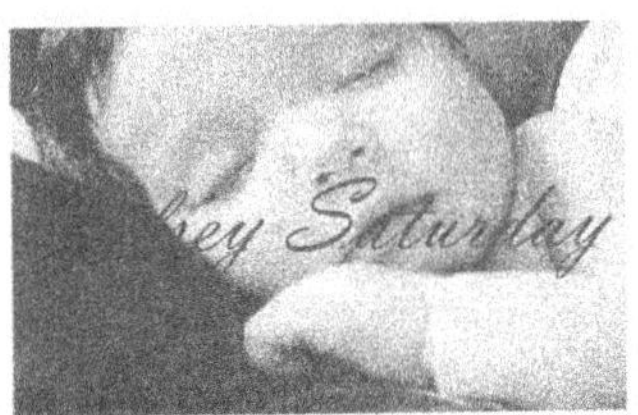

**A Nationwide Outreach Event**

**Kelsey Briggs**
**2002-2005**

Exhibit 5 - The following statement is from the State's answer to Raye's appeal about Kelsey's broken legs:

> Furthermore, unlike other injuries, the leg fractures were less directly linked to the defendant and there was no link to Michael Porter. Taking this portion of

Exhibit 6 - The following post is just one example of the political threats made toward the district attorney and others on the Kelsey's Purpose forum. Note that this threat was made at a time when Kelsey's Purpose members were picketing and protesting a plea for Raye.

**kjbriggs**

Kelsey's Grandma

Posts: 1,140
Group: Super Moderators
Joined: Nov 2005
Status: Offline
Reputation:

**Post: #19**

**RE: 2yr. old's death becomes part of judicial campaign**

I wonder if our District Attorney does not get a conviction if this will be an issue in his next election? I wonder if Logan Tucker's case will be an issue in Woodward if that case is not handled properly? I know David Prater is using cases against Wes Lane in his campaign. Using someone's past cases in a campaign is not out of the ordinary during a campaign. It brings public awareness to the candidates performance on the job. Negative campaigning is spreading flyers around town that have nothing to do with the campaign. Yes, this is what the Key supporters have been doing. Negative campaigning is having others sign their names to letters that have been written for them.

Judge Craig Key has called the paternal grandmother's of a dead child some choice names and we have the tape. Doesn't sound like the type of thing a fine Christian man would do, does it? If Sheila Kirk really wanted a nasty campaign I can assure you she has the ammunition. She may get up on November 8th and wish she had, but I really don't think so. Win, Lose, or Draw she will be proud of what she has done in her efforts to bring ethics back to the courthouse.
This post was last modified: 11-04-2006 11:38 AM by kjbriggs.

KELSEY
BRIGGS
2002-
2005
WWW.KELSEYSPURPOSE.ORG
Elect
Sheila
KIRK
for Judge
Enclosure 2

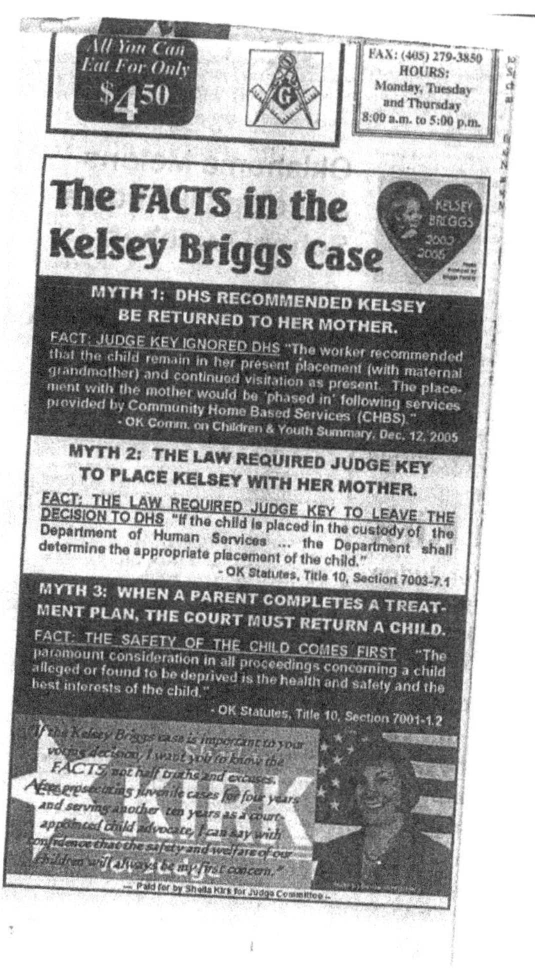

All You Can Eat For Only $4.50

FAX: (405) 279-3850
HOURS:
Monday, Tuesday and Thursday
8:00 a.m. to 5:00 p.m.

## The FACTS in the Kelsey Briggs Case

KELSEY BRIGGS 2002 2005

**MYTH 1: DHS RECOMMENDED KELSEY BE RETURNED TO HER MOTHER.**

FACT: JUDGE KEY IGNORED DHS "The worker recommended that the child remain in her present placement (with maternal grandmother) and continued visitation as present. The placement with the mother would be 'phased in' following services provided by Community Home Based Services (CHBS)."

- OK Comm. on Children & Youth Summary, Dec. 12, 2005

**MYTH 2: THE LAW REQUIRED JUDGE KEY TO PLACE KELSEY WITH HER MOTHER.**

FACT: THE LAW REQUIRED JUDGE KEY TO LEAVE THE DECISION TO DHS "If the child is placed in the custody of the Department of Human Services ... the Department shall determine the appropriate placement of the child."

- OK Statutes, Title 10, Section 7003-7.1

**MYTH 3: WHEN A PARENT COMPLETES A TREATMENT PLAN, THE COURT MUST RETURN A CHILD.**

FACT: THE SAFETY OF THE CHILD COMES FIRST "The paramount consideration in all proceedings concerning a child alleged or found to be deprived is the health and safety and the best interests of the child."

- OK Statutes, Title 10, Section 7001-1.2

"If the Kelsey Briggs case is important to your voting decision, I want you to know the FACTS, not half truths and excuses. After prosecuting juvenile cases for four years and serving another ten years as a court-appointed child advocate, I can say with confidence that the safety and welfare of our children will always be my first concern."

KIRK

— Paid for by Sheila Kirk for Judge Committee —

Children 12 & under $2[50]

Saturday, Oct. 7th

8 am til 10:00 am

he FACTS in the
elsey Briggs Case

KELSEY BRIGGS 2002-2005

MYTH 1: DHS RECOMMENDED KELSEY BE RETURNED TO HER MOTHER.

CT: JUDGE KEY IGNORED DHS "The worker recommended the child remain in her present placement (with maternal dmother) and continued visitation as present. The place- with the mother would be 'phased in' following services vided by Community Home Based Services (CHBS)."

- OK Comm. on Children & Youth Summary, Dec. 12, 2005

MYTH 2: THE LAW REQUIRED JUDGE KEY TO PLACE KELSEY WITH HER MOTHER.

CT: THE LAW REQUIRED JUDGE KEY TO LEAVE THE CISION TO DHS "If the child is placed in the custody of the artment of Human Services ... the Department shall mine the appropriate placement of the child."

- OK Statutes, Title 10, Section 7003-7.1

TH 3: WHEN A PARENT COMPLETES A TREAT-NT PLAN, THE COURT MUST RETURN A CHILD.

CT: THE SAFETY OF THE CHILD COMES FIRST "The mount consideration in all proceedings concerning a child ged or found to be deprived is the health and safety and the interests of the child."

- OK Statutes, Title 10, Section 7001-1.2

Kelsey Briggs case is important to your ing decision, I want you to know the ACTS, not half truths and excuses. prosecuting juvenile cases for four years serving another ten years as a court- inted child advocate, I can say with ence that the safety and welfare of our ren will always be my first concern."

LCN photo by Kim

Carmen Miller gets a tattoo from Deseree Currid during Satu Chandler Chamber of Commerce Downtown Getdown celebr The Chamber hosted an art contest and the winners from the class were: first place, Garrison Melson, Davenport; second Abigail Miles, Carney; and third place, Dakota Foster, Carney. ners in the Chandler Junior High/High School art contest were place, Michelle Waldman, $50, second place, Barry Parks, $30, place, Chaiz Diaz, $20, and honorable mention, Paig Stegmar Austin Webb.

Meeker News

## Kelsey Briggs walk to be held Sund

The first annual Kelsey Briggs Walk Against Child Abuse will be held at the Shawnee Airport Sunday October 8th at 2:00. Prevent Child Abuse Oklahoma will be sponsoring this event. The walk is open to the public and there is no entry fee. You can pre-register or get more information at kelseybriggswalk@yahoo.com or call Teri Sigman at 405-279-2746. T-shirts can still be ordered the day of the walk. In case of heavy r walk will be post poned until be 15th.

Kelsey's case has brought spread attention for abused ch in Oklahoma. Kelsey died afte months of documented abu October 11, 2005 in Meeker stepfather and mother have been charged in connection wi death.

On October 11th, membe Kelsey's Purpose will rem Kelsey by driving with their lights on. For more on Kelsey's go to www.kelseyspurpose.org

*Nearly Me*
MASTECTOMY PRODUCTS
*Fitting in the privacy of your home.*
*We accept Medicare assignments.*
RICHARD'S DRUG
324 E. Main • Shawnee
(405) 273-7810

ur Featured
election for
ctober:

Exhibit 7 -

**kjbriggs**
Kelsey's Grandma

Posts: 1,107
Group: Super Moderators
Joined: Nov 2005
Status: Away
Reputation:

**RE: "Walk for Justice" March 11th** **Post: #3**

Okay, brilliant is not a word ever used to describe anything I have ever done before. That might get a chuckle out of my family.

I want everyone to know that it will not be necessary to cross streets during this walk if you have children with you. There is enough parking area for us without putting the children in danger of cars.

I really hope as many as possible will be there. We heard another rumor today that a deal could be made for the mother. This is not justice for Kelsey if that happens. It sends a very bad message for all who witness abuse and do nothing. Once they know they will be held accountable maybe they will put their children above the perpetrator. I urge all of you to call the Attorney General and any other elected official with your outrage at this possibility. Our DA has already stated on camera his case against Mike Porter is strong and he does not need Raye Dawn. Therefore; he does not need to make a deal with someone who did not protect her child for nine months of

Exhibit 8 (Read visitation notes at www.FreeKelseysMom.com – click case and then timelines) -

**Visitation Date:** 07/06/2005 **Visitation Type:** Step-Parent

**Court Ordered:** No

**Location:**
CWS - DHS - office - visitation room, 2020 East First Street, Chandler, Oklahoma 74834

**Comments:**
Mrs. Briggs came in to the office alone. Worker asked where Mrs. Kathy Briggs was and she told worker that she would not come to the office because DHS told in court what a bad person she was and she did not want anybody to state any more bad things about her. When Kelsey came for her visit she was sleeping and Mrs. Briggs was informed that this is Kelsey's nap time and she will have to roll with the flow of the nap time as parents do. Mrs. Briggs said she would hold her and did so the whole hour while Kelsey slept. Mrs. Briggs sat down with her on the sofa and worker sat with them. Mrs. Briggs started crying and worker asked her what was the matter and Mrs. Briggs said "she has no one and this is the only person she can have in the form of her husband who is overseas". Mrs. Briggs talked with worker about the ISP and visitation perhaps at the Pottawatomie County office with secondary worker. Mrs. Briggs said what ever is comfortable for Kelsey but she would like to have it closer to her work and home

**Who was Present:**

**Supervised By Txt:**
Yolanda Hunter, CWS II

**Supervision Type:** **Status Category:** Completed

Exhibit 9 - Deposition of Kathie Briggs – 2009

Q Okay. How many reports did you make to DHS concerning Kelsey?

A I don't -- most of the reports that were made, I think I made one, maybe two. I think most of them were made by Ashley.

Q Okay. Did DHS ever tell you to stop calling?

A Yes.

Exhibit 10 -

RICHARD L. SMOTHERMON
DISTRICT ATTORNEY, DISTRICT 23
STATE OF OKLAHOMA

February 23, 2007

Enclosed is a copy of the gag order issued on the 15th day of February, 2007 in the Raye Dawn Smith case. As an endorsed witness the State of Oklahoma was ordered to give you a copy.

If you should have any questions, please contact me at 405-275-6873.

Thank you,

Lorie Ball
Victim Witness Coordinator
District Attorney's Office

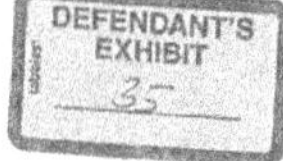


331 N. Broadway, Carnegie Building • Shawnee, OK 74801 • Phone: 405-275-6800 Fax: 405-275-3575

*Twenty-Third Judicial District Court*

*Pottawatomie and Lincoln Counties*

POTTAWATOMIE COUNTY COURTHOUSE
325 N. BROADWAY
SHAWNEE, OKLAHOMA 74801

| | |
|---|---|
| DISTRICT JUDGE | 405-275-1296 |
| ASSOCIATE DISTRICT JUDGE | 405-273-4308 |
| SPECIAL DISTRICT JUDGE | 405-273-0971 |
| COURT CLERK | 405-273-3624 |

May 18, 2006

Richard Smothermon
District Attorney

Paul Sutton

Steve Huddleston

Gentlemen:

Repeated violations of the gag order entered in the case of State vs. Michael Porter have occurred. The latest violations have occurred after strong warnings to both Mr. Smothermon and Mr. Sutton. This situation is not acceptable.

Therefore all three of you are ordered to appear in Lincoln County Courtroom #2 on Friday, May 26th at 10:30 a.m. I will have inquiries to make of all you as officers of the court. Further orders, including the possibility of sanctions, may result.

If you have any questions, please call me at (405)273-0971 (Shawnee) or (405)258-0408 (Chandler).

Sincerely,

Dawson R. Engle

Dawson R. Engle
Special District Judge

DEFENDANT'S EXHIBIT 36

Exhibit 11 -

| Date | Custody | Alleged Incident/Injury | Kelsey's Condition |
|---|---|---|---|
| April 14, 2005 | Miste Smith | Kelsey sprains right ankle at zoo after falling off platform flip flop shoes. | Limping on right leg |
| April 14, 2005 (overnight) | Kathie Briggs | | |
| April 15, 2005 | Raye Dawn Smith, Miste Smith | | Limping on right leg |
| April 16, 2005 | Raye Dawn Smith, Miste Smith | | Can't get her to sit down; she wanted to jump on the trampoline. |
| April 17, 2005 | Raye Dawn Smith | | |
| April 18, 2005 (until 5:00) | Raye Dawn Smith | | Standing on courthouse steps day of Raye Dawn's wedding to Mike Porter. Still limping on right foot. |
| April 18-21, 2005 | Kathie Briggs | | Takes four steps and refuses to walk. She crawls. |
| April 21, 2005 (after 4:00) - April 25, 2005 | Raye Dawn Smith | | Kelsey is not walking. |
| April 25, 2005 | Raye Dawn Smith | Diagnosed with bilateral tibia fractures. | |

Exhibit 12 –

Q Were you physically abusive to Raye Dawn during the marriage?
A I hit her one time.
Q When did you hit her?
A I'm not sure on the exact date.
Q Okay. Where did you hit her?
A I slapped her in her face.
Q Why?
A Because she was embarrassing us.
MR. WHITE: She's asking about during the marriage.
THE WITNESS: Yes, sir.
MR. WHITE: All right.
Q (BY MS. TEBOW) Where was this at? Do you recall?
A The Illinois River.
Q Okay. And you believe you guys were married when you were at the Illinois River?
A No, I believe it was before our marriage.
MR. BURCH: Listen to her question and

think about it.

THE WITNESS: Can we take a break?

(A short break is taken.)

Q (BY MS. TEBOW) Okay. Mr. Briggs, we were talking about the Illinois River trip before we took a break. Do you recall when that took place?

A Shortly before me and Raye Dawn got married.

Q Was it during the summer of '03? I'm sorry. That wouldn't be right. Summer of 2000?

A I believe so.

Q And you said that you had slapped her across the face; is that right?

A Yes.

Q Did it leave a hand print?

A No.

Q Was there ever a time that you bloodied her nose?

A Yes.

Q When did that happen?

A At the river.

Q Was that the same incident, or did that transpire later?

RAYMOND LANCE BRIGGS - 08/27/09

66

Q That caused her nose to bleed?

A Yes.

| First Name | Last Name | MI | Soc. Sec. No. | Birth Date | Race |
|---|---|---|---|---|---|
| Raymond | Briggs | L | | | White |

| Address | City | State | Zip | Phone No. | Sex |
|---|---|---|---|---|---|
| | Meeker | OK | 74855 | | Male |

NARRATIVE

=========

On above time and date, I Officer Roland was dispatched to 527 South Dawson in reference to a domestic. Lincoln County Sheriffs Office advised me that the reporting party was Raye Don Briggs ( DOB. ). I arrived at approximately 1955 hours. I was the first officer to arrive. Shortly after, two Oklahoma Highway Patrolman ( Jerry Treadwell and James Watson ) arrived. Upon my arrival Raye Don approached me and told me what was going on. She stated that she and her husband ( Ramond Lance Briggs DOB. ) got into an arguement over her not super sizing his value meal from McDonalds. She said that she was getting ready to go out with some friends and he got really mad and took her clothes, and keys away from her. She then stated that he pushed her up against the wall with his forearm at her throat. She said after he pushed her around and yelled at her, she then started walking northbound on Highway 18 to use the pay phone to call for help. While she was walking her grandmother picked her up and took her to use the phone, then took her back to the residence to wait on an officer to arrive. She stated that between the time she had left and the time she arrived back at the residence Ramond had gotten into his truck and was driving North bound on Highway 18. I, Officer Roland did observe visible injuries to Raye Don Briggs on her neck and collar bone area that were consistent with the type of assault she stated had occured. At this point Jerry Treadwell asked her if she wanted to press charges and she stated " yes ". The two officers drove around the Town of Meeker to see if they could locate him. Approximately five minutes later James Watson contacted me on the radio and said that he had found Mr. Briggs at the laundry mat in Meeker and needed me to come up there to talk to him. I left a voluntary statement for Raye D. Briggs to fill out and told her that myself or one of the other officers would be back to get more information from her. She said that she would stay at the residence until we came back. I then got into my patrol car and headed to the laundry mat to meet with the other officers. Upon arrival I noticed that the officers had already had Mr. Briggs in handcuffs and in the front seat of one of the patrol cars. Officer Treadwell advised me that he had already informed Mr. Briggs of his miranda rights and told him that he was under arrest for domestic assault and battery. Officer Treadwell then took Mr. Briggs out of his car and put him into my car. Officer Treadwell told me that he would go back to the residence and take a voluntary statement and get all the information from Mrs. Briggs, and when he was done he would meet me at the Lincoln County Sheriffs Office. I then told Lincoln County that I was enroute to their facility with Mr. Briggs. I arrived at Lincoln County Sheriffs Office at approximately 2043 hours. Shortly after my arrival Officer Treadwell arrived with Mrs. Briggs voluntary statement and other information.

I then started going through the process of getting Mr. Briggs booked into the jail. I issued him citation # 004422. I charged him with domestic assault and battery. End of report.

Exhibit 13 –

Q Can you explain to me why you would have your military uniform on in a photograph at

Young Reporting Services * (405) 236-8426

RAYMOND LANCE BRIGGS - 08/27/09

149

Kelsey's grave site in December?
A Because that was Veteran's Day.
Q In December?
A In December?
Q Uh-huh.
A No.
Q And I can show you the photo.
A I believe it was -- yes, I can say. It was because a wreath was given for fallen soldiers, and one was given to my daughter, and I went out there in my soldier's uniform to give it to her.
Q Was this a ceremony, or did you just go out there by yourself and do it?
A There was no ceremony.
Q All right. And then who took the photograph?
A I believe it was my mother.

Exhibit 14 –

[Rita]

Administrator

Posts: 175

Group: Administrators

Joined: Nov 2005

Status: Offline

Reputation:

Post: #106

RE: Comments on OSBI interviews.

During Mike Porter's interview, he kept grabbing his heart and acting like he was having chest pains and he acted like he was going to vomit a time or two and was very dramatic. I have never seen such a drama queen. His body language was screaming guilt. He was beyond nervous and then toward the end he says he wants an attorney and he wants to see his wife. Watching the tape is so different from reading it. I truly feel that this man is responsible for the death of Kelsey. [Rita] Kelsey's Aunt Rees

Exhibit 15 –

On 11-9-02 at approximately 2035 hours I Sgt. Leabo was stationary at Main and Fowler. I observed a vehicle west bound on Main at a high rate of speed. I activated my radar and it indicated that the vehicle was traveling at 38 MPH in a 30 MPH zone. I pulled my patrol car out behind the vehicle and activated my emergency lights. The vehicle stopped at approximately 1 ½ mile west of town on Hwy 62. I called the dispatcher and informed him of the stop and my location. I exited my patrol car and approached the driver and informed the driver why I had stopped him. I then asked him for his driver's license and insurance verification. The driver was identified as Raymond Briggs, DL# [redacted] by his Oklahoma driver's license. I then returned to my patrol car and ask the dispatcher to check the status of Briggs's DL by number. The dispatcher informed me that Briggs's license was valid Officer Combs Meeker #5 then notified me that we had a warrant on Briggs that had not been [pl]ace on the warrant list. Officer Combs then informed me that he was at the Meeker Police [De]partment and that there was a warrant on Briggs. I then exited my vehicle and approached Briggs. I asked Briggs to step out of his vehicle and I informed him that Meeker had a warrant for his arrest and he was being placed under arrest for that warrant. I then placed him in double locked handcuffs and secured him in my patrol car. I then called the dispatcher and asked him to send the next wrecker to my location. I then completed an impoundment record on Briggs's vehicle and waited for the wrecker. Russell's Wrecker arrived and impounded the vehicle. I then transported Briggs to Meeker Police Department and pick up a copy of the warrant. I then transported Briggs's to Lincoln County Jail booked and jailed him for the Municipal Warrant # 02-341,342,343,344. Briggs's while in route to Lincoln County Jail made many verbal threats towards my family and me.
End of Report

Exhibit 16 –

Weekafer September 6, 2006 Shawnee News Star Meeker Paper

# Justice demanded from District Attorney

To the editor,

This letter stems from news of the recent developments in the pending criminal cases involving the mother and stepfather of Kelsey Smith-Briggs.

After watching coverage of Michael Porter's preliminary hearing held on August 23, we were very disturbed by the news that Raye Dawn Smith, Kelseys' mother, is currently in plea negotiations with the District Attorney. This news is even more shocking given Mr. Smothermon's past public statements concerning the possibility of a plea negotiation between his office and Kelsey's mother. In that press conference, Smothermon spoke of society's demand that parents be held accountable when they do not uphold their moral responsibility to protect their children. He said that Raye Dawn Porter knew or should have known her daughter was being abused.

Smothermon also stated that he had no intention of offering Raye Dawn any kind of plea bargain, and that he had enough evidence to convict the stepfather without her testimony. His emphatic statements to the media make the recent development all the more surprising.

We would like to know why it seems that people who "ONLY" fail to protect or enable their children to be abused are not considered to be as culpable as the actual abuser? Why would Mr. Smothermon even consider any kind of plea negotiation for this woman after stating on TV he did not need her testimony? What would the reasoning behind it be? Why would he even consider using her testimony?

Her testimony is not credible. Of course she has to point the finger at Mike Porter. It seems Mr.Smothermon has made a deal with the devil.

Another recent child abuse case comes to mind, that of a very young child named Akaysha McGee. The mother and mother's boyfriend were both charged in the beating of this child, arrested and each subsequently jailed on a $250,000 bond. The mother in that case was able to give a time line for each individual bruise, and in exchange for her testimony she received a plea deal of two years from Mr. Smothermon.

Two years for a mother that stood by and watched as her child was savagely beaten. This leads us to wonder how light the punishment for the mother in Kelsey's case will be? We would be hard pressed to believe that she will ever admit any actual wrongdoing such as witnessing any abuse.

Why is Mr. Smothermon sending a message that it is not acceptable to beat children but it is acceptable to stand by and watch or not protect your child? More importantly, why are the citizens of the 23rd Judicial District allowing our District Attorney to send this message?

We would encourage all of you to take the time to let your feelings be known in regards to people being slapped on the wrist for allowing their children to be beaten andkilled.

Mr. Smothermon, we demand justice.

Liana Rowe, Oklahoma City, Ok
Lori Watson, Tulsa, Ok
Lorri Justice, Little Rock, AR
Tina Moore, Broken Arrow, Ok
Jamie O'Dell, Tulsa, Ok
Julie Barto, Norman, Ok
Louella Ryan, Harrah, Ok
Daphne Spencer, Meeker, Ok
Beverly McKinney, Ninnekah, Ok
Frances Ferguson, Warr Acres, Ok
Barbara Troyer, Oklahoma City, Ok

*(Note: This letter was e-mailed along with complete addresses and phone numbers of each name listed)*

This letter stems from news of the recent developments in the pending criminal cases involving the mother and stepfather of Kelsey Smith-Briggs.. After watching coverage of the stepfather's preliminary hearing held on August 23rd, we were very disturbed by the news that Kelsey's mother is currently in plea negotiations with the District Attorney. This news is even more shocking given Mr. Smothermon's past public statements concerning the possibility of a plea negotiation between his office and Kelsey's mother. In that press conference, Smothermon spoke of society's demand that parents be held accountable when they do not uphold their moral responsibility to protect their children. He said that Kelsey's mother knew or should have known her daughter was being abused. His emphatic statements to the media make the recent development all the more surprising.

We would like to know why it seems that people who "ONLY" fail to protect or enable their children to be abused are not considered to be as culpable as the actual abuser? Why would Mr. Smothermon even consider any kind of plea negotiation for this woman! What would the reasoning behind it be? Why would he even consider using her testimony?

Another recent child abuse case comes to mind, that of another very young child. The mother and mother's boyfriend were both charged in the beating of this child, arrested and each subsequently jailed on a $250,000 bond. The mother in that case was able to give a timeline for each individual bruise, and in exchange for her testimony she received a plea deal of two years from Mr. Smothermon. Two years for a mother that stood by and watched as her child was savagely beaten. This leads us to wonder how light the punishment for the mother in Kelsey's case will be? Why is Mr. Smothermon sending a message that it is not acceptable to beat children but it but it is acceptable to stand by and watch or not protect your child? More importantly, why are the citizens of the 23rd Judicial District allowing our District Attorney to send this message? We would encourage all of you to take the time to let your feelings be

...ent all the more surprising.

We would like to know why it seems that people who "ONLY" fail to protect or enable their children to be abused are not considered to be as culpable as the actual abuser? Why would Mr. Smothermon even consider any kind of plea negotiation for this woman! What would the reasoning behind it be? Why would he even consider using her testimony?

Another recent child abuse case comes to mind, that of another very young child. The mother and mother's boyfriend were both charged in the beating of this child, arrested and each subsequently jailed on a $250,000 bond. The mother in that case was able to give a timeline for each individual bruise, and in exchange for her testimony she received a plea deal of two years from Mr. Smothermon. Two years for a mother that stood by and watched as her child was savagely beaten. This leads us to wonder how light the punishment for the mother in Kelsey's case will be? Why is Mr. Smothermon sending a message that it is not acceptable to beat children but it but it is acceptable to stand by and watch or not protect your child? More importantly, why are the citizens of the 23rd Judicial District allowing our District Attorney to send this message? We would encourage all of you to take the time to let your feelings be known. MR. SMOTHERMON, WE DEMAND JUSTICE.

Please contact Mr. Smothermon at the following address, which is his office:
331 N. Broadway Ave
Shawnee, Ok 74801
(405) 275-6800

Paid for by Concerned citizens of the 23rd Judicial District, Daphne Spencer, Spokesperson

Exhibit 17 –

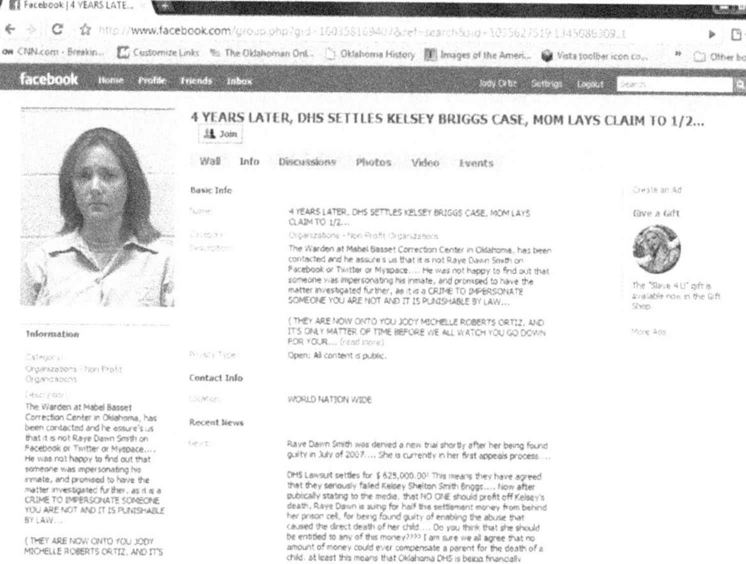


Below are two posts from the 30 pages about me that were posted on Kelsey's Purpose. (Notice the pictures of Kelsey used as avatars.)

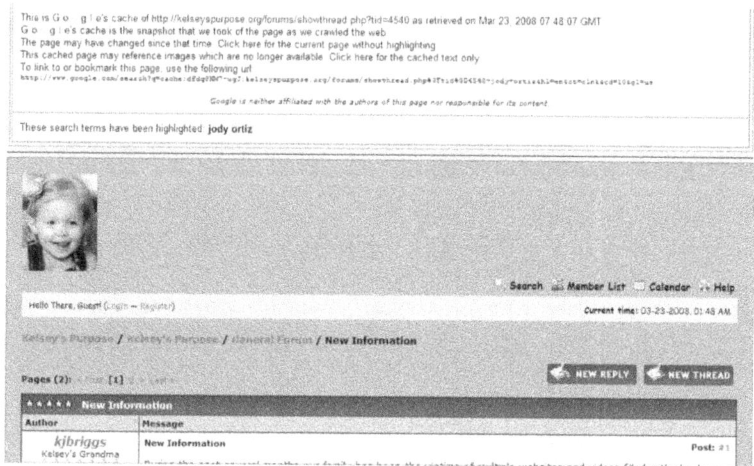

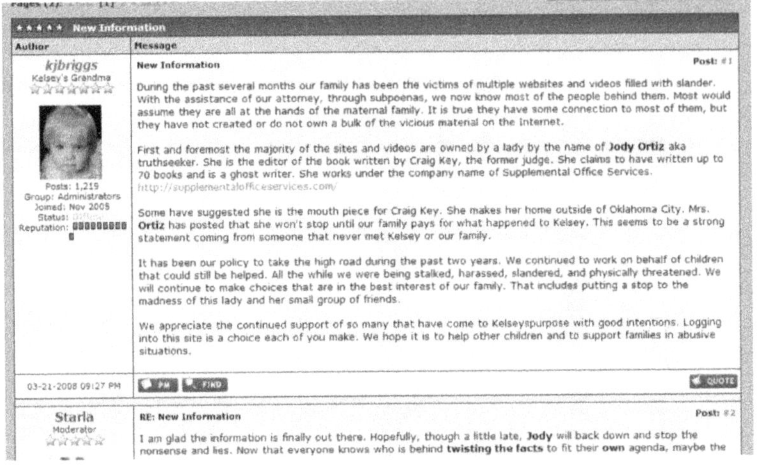

**New Information**

| Author | Message |
|---|---|
| kjbriggs<br>Kelsey's Grandma<br>Posts: 1,219<br>Group: Administrators<br>Joined: Nov 2005<br>Status:<br>Reputation: | **New Information** Post: #1<br><br>During the past several months our family has been the victims of multiple websites and videos filled with slander. With the assistance of our attorney, through subpoenas, we now know most of the people behind them. Most would assume they are all at the hands of the maternal family. It is true they have some connection to most of them, but they have not created or do not own a bulk of the vicious material on the Internet.<br><br>First and foremost the majority of the sites and videos are owned by a lady by the name of **Jody Ortiz** aka truthseeker. She is the editor of the book written by Craig Key, the former judge. She claims to have written up to 70 books and is a ghost writer. She works under the company name of Supplemental Office Services.<br>http://supplementalofficeservices.com/<br><br>Some have suggested she is the mouth piece for Craig Key. She makes her home outside of Oklahoma City. Mrs. **Ortiz** has posted that she won't stop until our family pays for what happened to Kelsey. This seems to be a strong statement coming from someone that never met Kelsey or our family.<br><br>It has been our policy to take the high road during the past two years. We continued to work on behalf of children that could still be helped. All the while we were being stalked, harassed, slandered, and physically threatened. We will continue to make choices that are in the best interest of our family. That includes putting a stop to the madness of this lady and her small group of friends.<br><br>We appreciate the continued support of so many that have come to Kelseyspurpose with good intentions. Logging into this site is a choice each of you make. We hope it is to help other children and to support families in abusive situations. |
| 03-21-2008 09:27 PM | PM FIND QUOTE |
| Starla<br>Moderator | **RE: New Information** Post: #2<br><br>I am glad the information is finally out there. Hopefully, though a little late, **Jody** will back down and stop the nonsense and lies. Now that everyone knows who is behind **twisting the facts** to fit their **own** agenda, maybe the |

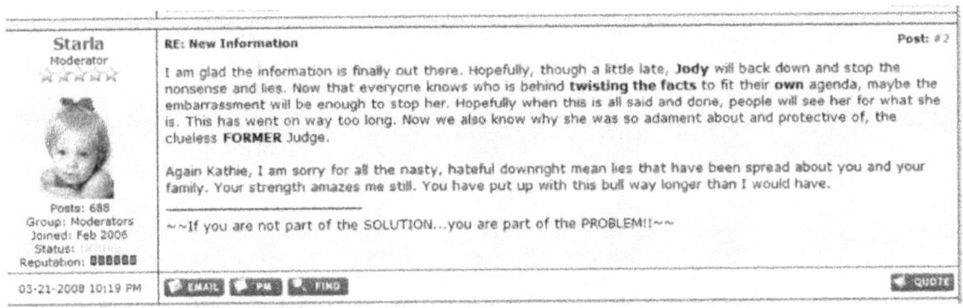

| | |
|---|---|
| Starla<br>Moderator<br>Posts: 688<br>Group: Moderators<br>Joined: Feb 2006<br>Status:<br>Reputation: | **RE: New Information** Post: #2<br><br>I am glad the information is finally out there. Hopefully, though a little late, **Jody** will back down and stop the nonsense and lies. Now that everyone knows who is behind **twisting the facts** to fit their **own** agenda, maybe the embarrassment will be enough to stop her. Hopefully when this is all said and done, people will see her for what she is. This has went on way too long. Now we also know why she was so adament about and protective of, the clueless **FORMER** Judge.<br><br>Again Kathie, I am sorry for all the nasty, hateful downright mean lies that have been spread about you and your family. Your strength amazes me still. You have put up with this bull way longer than I would have.<br><br>~~If you are not part of the SOLUTION...you are part of the PROBLEM!!~~ |
| 03-21-2008 10:19 PM | EMAIL PM FIND QUOTE |

Below are posts from blogs about me where Kathie's supporters state that the district attorney that charged Raye got a subpoena to identify me and then he reportedly turned my information over to Kathie Briggs, according to Kathie and her supporters.

> encouraged. Also, as I was told, Richard Smothermon issued a subpeona to identify who owned the http://www.richardsmothermon.com/ site when it was just in the beginning stages. The subpeona showed, according to what I was told, that SHE owned that site, along with the freekelseysmom site and others. If I remember correctly there were 13 sites altogether she owned at that time.

(Smothermon). He found out about it and had the website subpoenaed to find out who owned it. It was Jody.

The following post is from a Facebook page that is administrated by Ms. Follett and Ms. Ballard. This is just a sample of the language that can be found on that page any day of the week. (Notice that Kelsey's picture is used as an avatar.)

and you....you are a pathetic, STUPID,selfish, obviously blind, sorry excuse for a mother! You make me sick...I wouldnt want to ask her anything....she would just play stupid and lie!! I just wonder what went though both of thier heads when they did it????? Did they actually think they were going to get away with it and live happily ever after without Kelsey?????? Did you ever think of the consequences????? Karma....its a bitch!!!! I also would like to know if either of them think it is going to be pretty when they get out??? So many know thier names....they are going to be HATED...it wont be pretty I can tell you that. Has anyone thought about ??? Imagine that poor kids life when he gets older and gets told the truth, both your parents are jail birds, they abused and murder your 1/2 sister when she was just a baby, your dad gave up all rights to you, you have another 1/2 brother and sister you will never meet. That poor kid is going to loose it when hes older. Best thing for him is to have no contact with the evil mother, be adopted, and NEVER be told. That is the only way that kid will ever have a NORMAL life!!!! I wonder if Raye/Porter even realized what they did to him!!!! That is 2 kids that they ruin thier lives. Lock them both up and throw away the friggin key!!!! I cant stand looking at either of them.....I want to vomit!!! Geez...Porter has a way with making people do that. All but dumb Raye... she cant see anything before her eys...or so she claims. Why dont you just bang your head against the walls and try to knock some sense into yourself. You classless POS!!!

about an hour ago · Report

Inbox > Message Detail Print P

**Subject:** Lance Briggs sent you a message on Facebook...
**From:** Facebook <notification+ze66ldze@facebookmail.com> (Add as Preferred Sender)
**Date:** Thu, May 13, 2010 1:58 am
**To:** Raye Dawn Smith <truthseeker@thetruthaboutkelsey.com>

facebook

Lance sent you a message.

Lance Briggs

**Lance Briggs** May 13, 2010 at 7:58am

Subject: I Really Want To Be Your Friend

Please except me so you can tell me all about your jail cell and all the new friends you have made. Is your big bed comfortable, is the food first class, how is the view from in there? I have so many more questions to ask, let's be friends and catch up stranger. Well I'm sure you won't except me so you better get use to being in there bitch cuz your gona be in there for a long long long time! :D

Watch for the upcoming book, *"Bash Board Bullies"* that exposes all of the hate campaign, including posts from this group such as the following:

Actually, he does look pretty damn hot.
Saturday, June 10th 2006 @ 12:01 AM

Posted by Anonymous:

Oh wouldn't this be funn?!?! Mike Porter is found innocent but Raye Dawn is found guilty and goes to prison for a very, very, very long time. She becomes, ugly, haggard, and a girlfriend. Mike goes to the Briggs' to express his sympathy and regrets. He gets close to one of the Briggs daughters. They get married and raise Blaine. The rage and bitterness becomes more than Gayle and Mildred can stand. They get arrested for plotting to murder Kathie. They are convicted and sentenced to the same penetentiary as Raye Dawn!!!!!
Saturday, June 10th 2006 @ 12:06 AM

Posted by Anonymous:

I guess that's how you get everyone to be quiet, say Porter is hot haha Porter's hot, Porter's hot
Saturday, June 10th 2006 @ 12:07 AM

Posted by Anonymous:

Wow 12:06 - you put a lot of thought into that lol
Saturday, June 10th 2006 @ 12:08 AM

Posted by Anonymous:

I had to think of something during all the damn car seat posts.
Saturday, June 10th 2006 @ 12:09 AM

Posted by Anonymous:

You had to say car seat again didn't you
Saturday, June 10th 2006 @ 12:11 AM

Posted by Anonymous:

I'M SORRY I'M SORRY I'M SORRY

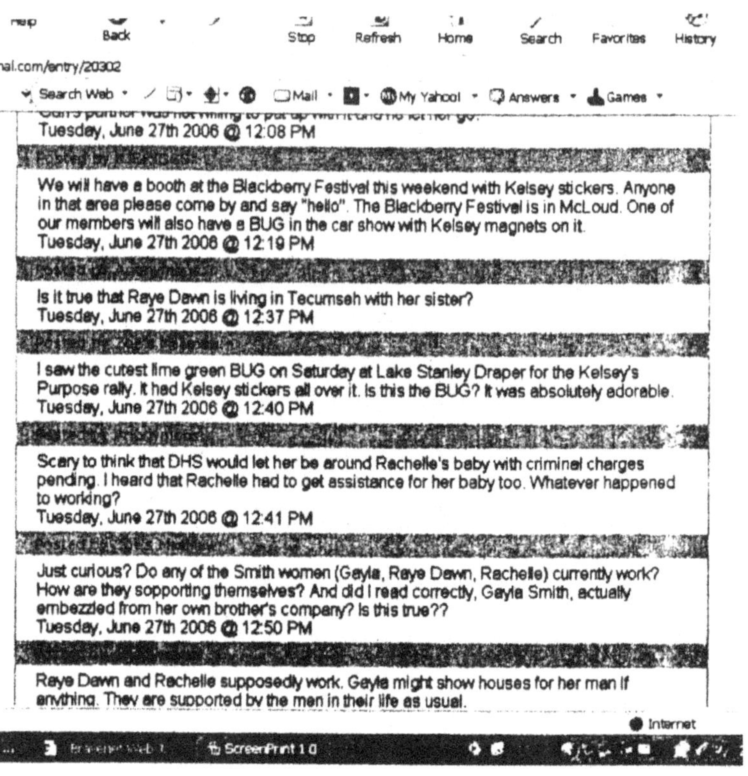

Tuesday, June 27th 2006 @ 12:08 PM

We will have a booth at the Blackberry Festival this weekend with Kelsey stickers. Anyone in that area please come by and say "hello". The Blackberry Festival is in McLoud. One of our members will also have a BUG in the car show with Kelsey magnets on it.
Tuesday, June 27th 2006 @ 12:19 PM

Is it true that Raye Dawn is living in Tecumseh with her sister?
Tuesday, June 27th 2006 @ 12:37 PM

I saw the cutest lime green BUG on Saturday at Lake Stanley Draper for the Kelsey's Purpose rally. It had Kelsey stickers all over it. Is this the BUG? It was absolutely adorable.
Tuesday, June 27th 2006 @ 12:40 PM

Scary to think that DHS would let her be around Rachelle's baby with criminal charges pending. I heard that Rachelle had to get assistance for her baby too. Whatever happened to working?
Tuesday, June 27th 2006 @ 12:41 PM

Just curious? Do any of the Smith women (Gayla, Raye Dawn, Rachelle) currently work? How are they sopporting themselves? And did I read correctly, Gayla Smith, actually embezzled from her own brother's company? Is this true??
Tuesday, June 27th 2006 @ 12:50 PM

Raye Dawn and Rachelle supposedly work. Gayla might show houses for her man if anything. They are supported by the men in their life as usual.

Where have I been? EBay?? What kind of things would anyone want to purchase from that family? Plus, I believe court costs, legal fees and attorney fees can be quite costly.
Tuesday, June 27th 2006 @ 1:33 PM

What are they selling Raedawgs scratch and sniff panites? Or Mildew Fowlers scratch and sniff dentures? I know Gala is making some money showing Prick Jame's homes. On her knee's.
Tuesday, June 27th 2006 @ 1:44 PM

WHAT!!!! The Smith's never paid for Kelsey's funeral??? You have got to be kidding me!!! My blood is just boiling! Now let me get this straight. They have money for cigarettes and alcohol. They have money to pay thugs to beat people up. They have money to run all over town harrassing people about displaying Kelsey stickers. They had money for bond for Raye Dawn. Yet, they could or would not pay for Kelsey's funeral services???
Tuesday, June 27th 2006 @ 1:44 PM

How evil and demonic do you have to be to hack a murdered childs web site? Just ask Judge Key! The red faced brat.
Tuesday, June 27th 2006 @ 1:48 PM

I heard they used the victims compensation fund to pay for her funeral. I guess they could do that since that was before the mother was criminally charged.
Tuesday, June 27th 2006 @ 1:59 PM

Why do you think Gayla should be charged?
I think that she may also be guilty, but I was just wondering what your view is.
Friday, June 9th 2006 @ 4:38 PM

Everyone in Meeker thinks that Gayla and Mildred both should be charged.
Friday, June 9th 2006 @ 4:39 PM

From what Gayla has told people and on the tv, she seems like the type that would lie for her own daughter just to protect her children from anyone else and in the meantime, she didn't protect Kelsey. If she truly was there and saw Kelsey often, she should have seen all the signs of abuse and by now changing her story and saying that she saw how Mike was jealous, etc., she is just as guilty as Raye Dawn.
Friday, June 9th 2006 @ 4:43 PM

Posted by Anonymous

I agree that Gayla seems like quite the B*tch in this situation.
Friday, June 9th 2006 @ 5:09 PM

I think it's a run for the money on who's the most responsible of that family, they are all non caring human feces.
Friday, June 9th 2006 @ 5:11 PM

does anyone know who's got the baby now? Does Gayla have it yet? Poor child, if she does. Surely Mike wouldn't allow that.
Friday, June 9th 2006 @ 5:13 PM

Mildred didn't "knowingly" harm Kelsey. That's the key word. She didn't know what she was doing. That's right...that's the ticket, she didn't even know that she didn't have a seizure at the funeral.
Saturday, February 4th 2006 @ 12:31 AM

Posted by Anonymous

Mildred is common knowledge around Meeker and especially around Lewis Mfg.
She used to be a fine upstanding woman.
Saturday, February 4th 2006 @ 12:32 AM

Mad - Mildred would be left out of it if she would just come out and tell the damn truth. If she would come out and say "I am just supporting my daughter and granddaughter. I do not know what went on in that house. I know Kelsey was abused and I do not know who did it. I know it was not Lance or Kathie. I will support my family and that is all. I will not lie for them, or withhold information for them. I will tell everything that I know, even if it makes my daughter or granddaugher look bad. Yes, Raye Dawn is an alcoholic and yes I tried my best to cover it up. Yes she has slept around and treated people like shit generally. No she was not a good mother most of the time. But I do not believe she killed Kelsey so I wil support her." IF MILDRED SAID THAT THEN I WOULD SAY "EVERYBODY LEAVE HER ALONE AND BASH RAYE DAWN AND GAYLA". BUT SHE WIL NOT DO THAT SO SHE DESERVES WHAT SHE GETS. SHE HAS DONE JUST AS MUCH TO COVER SHIT UP AS ANYONE.
Saturday, February 4th 2006 @ 12:33 AM

I think you are wrong. This site is for people who failed Kelsey. Mildred

You are right 2:25, Gayla is really messed up. She still keeps secrets from her mother so she can missuse her. They like to keep Mildred in the dark.
Tuesday, February 14th 2006 @ 2:31 PM

Posted by Anonymous:

Poor poor Mildred. They better hold a press confrence for her. She needs peoples sympathy for her getting left out in the dark.
Tuesday, February 14th 2006 @ 2:40 PM

Posted by Anonymous:

How could Gayla see poor Kelsey abused and not do or say something. Poor little Kelsey Did you ever think maybe Gayla was rough with Kelsey too? It is possible. I think of that baby every day and cry alot. I know all of you do too! Thanks for trying to get justice for Kelsey. I wish I could do more.
Tuesday, February 14th 2006 @ 2:42 PM

Posted by Tired of Waiting for Justice:

So true. Mildred has ALWAYS been in the dark pertaining to what the Smiths are doing. She IS a good woman, but she has been misguided by all this and stands by someone, or some people that she should not stand by and she SHOULD know better. But you've got to remember, she IS 74 years old and I'm sure that her mind is starting to fail her. I just hope she doesn't think that her darling Gayla will take care of her when she needs it.
Tuesday, February 14th 2006 @ 2:44 PM

Posted by Anonymous:

anon - 2:42. If you are in Oklahoma you can do more. Do you check Kelsey's purpose for upcoming rallies and events?
Tuesday, February 14th 2006 @ 2:44 PM

Posted by Anonymous:

I am sure that Gayla will take care of her - the same way she took care of her "beloved"

**Bibliography**

"Child Abuse Pages – Kelsey Briggs." *ANGELIZD's Place*. July 18, 2010.
<http://www.angelizdsplace.com/child30.htm>.

Clay, Nolan. "Witness to Describe Kelsey's Treatment." *NewsOK.com*. July 18, 2010.
<http://www.newsok.com/article/3075428>.

Fuhrman, Mark. *The Murder Business: How the Media Turns Crime into Entertainment and Subverts Justice*. Washington, D.C.: Regnery Publishing, Inc., 2009. Pp. 8-9, 66, 88.

Jon, Barry. '"Oklahoma Prosecutor Smothermon Pushes False Charges? The Murder and Exploitation of Kelsey Smith-Briggs" *US Observer*. July 18, 2010.
<http://www.usobserver.com/archive/june-07/Kelsey-smith-briggs.htm>.

Jon, Barry and Ron Lee. "Sentenced for Another's Crime: Jury Convicts Mother Despite Evidence." *US Observer. July 18, 2009.* < http://www.usobserver.com/archive/july-*07/raye-dawn-verdict.htm>.*

Key, Craig. *A Deadly Game of Tug of War: The Kelsey Smith-Briggs Story*. Garden City, NY: Morgan James Publishing, 2007. Pp. 60, 86.

Morava, Kim. "Kelsey's Father Gets Deferred Sentence for Domestic Violence." *Shawnee News-Star*. May 24, 2010.
<http://news-star.com/stories/011307/new_46279.shtml>. (online article has since been removed from website.)

---

[i] http://www.angelizdsplace.com/child30.htm

## About the Author

Jody Ortiz is a wife and a mother who currently works as a freelance writer. She has written for various fields including: financial, insurance, mortgage, construction, religion, inspiration, how-to, memoir, education, and academic. Her resume includes ghost writing over 70 books (she's lost count); several have been published in the business genre, and she has ghost written a four-hundred page novel.

Jody's experience has opened doors to clients from all over the world including: Hong Kong, Switzerland, Australia, U.K., Wales, Turkey, Canada, Mexico, South America, Israel, South Africa, and so on.

In her spare time, she has volunteered as a Girl Scout leader, delivered meals for Meals on Wheels, and volunteered with St. Vincent de Paul where she delivered food to those in need and developed a database to keep track of donations.

Jody's recent exposure to wrongful convictions has led to her position on the board of Raye of Hope, an Oklahoma based organization that gives a voice to those who claim to be wrongfully convicted. Jody is also on the Board of Directors for Survivors in Action, a nationwide non-profit advocacy group that supports victims of crimes including domestic violence, identity theft, elder abuse, cyberstalking, stalking, child abuse, rape, and sexual assault.

Although Jody was paralyzed for over two years from the overwhelming amount of hate she receives on a daily basis from her attackers, through her strong faith and encouragement from her family as well as her loving supporters and friends, Jody learned to face her fear and her harassers head-on. She is now reclaiming her life through telling her story of survival to the world and is working to change laws in the process to assist other victims of stalking and cyberbullying.

Contact Jody at jo@jodyortiz.com to schedule speaking engagements and book signings.

www.ingramcontent.com/pod-product-compliance
Lightning Source LLC
Chambersburg PA
CBHW022041020426
42335CB00012B/493
*9781962490030*